The Which? Guide to an Active Retirement

Acknowledgements

Editor: Jane Vass, a freelance financial researcher with direct experience of work in the financial services industry. For nearly ten years she worked in the Which? Money Group, latterly as its head.

Researcher: Helen Stevens

Contributors *(earlier editions):* Jonquil Lowe; also Anthony Bailey, Jane Bell, Amanda Bristow, Dr Steve Carroll, Philip Cullum, Sharon Dee, Lindsey Etchell, Ben Gurney, Amanda Jarvis, Liam McCormack, Avril Rodway, Tess Sullivan, Roger Taylor, Sue Todd, Virginia Wallis, Cat Weakley, Kim Winter

The Which? Guide to an Active Retirement

Edited by Jane Vass

 CONSUMERS' ASSOCIATION

Which? Books are commissioned and researched by
Consumers' Association and published by
Which? Ltd, 2 Marylebone Road, London NW1 4DF
Email address: *books@which.net*

Distributed by The Penguin Group:
Penguin Books Ltd, 27 Wrights Lane, London W8 5TZ

First edition September 1993
Reprinted September 1994
Second edition May 1995
Third edition May 1997
Reprinted July 1999
Fourth edition January 2000

Copyright © 1993, 1994, 1995, 1997, 1999, 2000 Which? Ltd

British Library Cataloguing in Publication Data
A catalogue record for this book is available from the British Library

ISBN 0 85202 809 1

For a full list of *Which?* books, please write to Which? Books, Castlemead, Gascoyne Way,
Hertford X, SG14 1LH or access our website at *www.which.net*

Cover and text design by Kysen Creative Consultants

Typeset by Saxon Graphics Ltd, Derby
Printed and bound in England by Clays Ltd, St Ives plc

Contents

★ An asterisk next to the name of an organisation in the text indicates that their address and/or contact details can be found in this section

Introduction

As we enter the new millennium, we must confront the fact that our 'third age' – the age of healthy retirement – could last longer than the second age, over 30 years. We think carefully about what we should do with our working lives but put very little planning into our retirement years, which could be just as important and even more rewarding.

In almost any retirement scenario, working or not working, finance will be a key issue. You need an adequate income to support whatever lifestyle you choose. Find out your financial situation before embarking on retirement by:

- completing form BR19 from the local Benefits Agency to find out how much state pension you can expect
- using the free tracing service of the Pension Schemes Registry to track down any pension schemes with which you have lost touch
- writing to your pension providers for a benefit statement and for information on the options open to you
- thinking about moving your personal pension plan to a safer fund to safeguard your money if you are close to retirement
- making up any financial shortfall in your annual income by making last-minute investments.

Since 1997 the government has introduced a flood of new legislation. The new 'stakeholder pensions' to replace personal pensions, the Second State Pension, Individual Savings Accounts (ISAs), and changes to widows' benefits and disability rights are just some of the recent developments that those facing retirement may have to consider. *The Which? Guide to an Active Retirement* covers all the financial planning necessary for retirement, taking into account all the recent legislation.

But work itself need not end with retirement. Government research in 1999 confirmed that many older people remain active, getting a great deal of satisfaction from work – both paid and unpaid – after the official retirement date. If you want to keep working, this fully updated edition of the *Guide* includes details for older people on how to find work, your rights at work, the tax implications of continuing to work, and even, for those so inclined, how to start a business.

The *Guide* also takes a fresh look at day-to-day living in retirement, covering housing, transport and leisure. Ill-health is not an inevitable companion to ageing and the book's 'Good Health Guide' gives practical details on how to deal with common problems and on how to make the most of the health services, both private and public.

If you still find yourself with questions, the address section, which provides contact addresses, telephone numbers, web sites and email addresses for all organisations named in this book, should take you to more specialised sources of advice.

Part 1

Planning ahead

Chapter 1

Building a firm foundation

If you are already attempting to reconcile the demands made on your purse and energies by a family, a mortgage and a job, then planning for retirement may be low down the list of your priorities. However, although there are some last-minute things you can do to ensure an active and happy retirement, it is easier if you can start to think and plan some years in advance.

When to start planning

The days are gone when you could be reasonably sure of your retirement date long before the event. There has been a general trend in the UK towards people stopping work (voluntarily or involuntarily) at earlier ages. For example, employers which provide good pension schemes might offer employees early retirement at 55 or even earlier in an attempt to slim down the workforce.

Retiring from your main job will not, of course, necessarily mean the end of working altogether, and if you are self-employed or working in a more flexible and individual field, you may never 'retire' at all.

As a result of the trend towards early retirement, only about three out of four men aged 55 to 59 and one in two men aged 60 to 64 are now working (or job hunting). In 1980, by comparison, nine out of ten 55 to 59-year-olds were working and seven out of ten 60 to 64-year-olds. The proportion of women working in their late 50s has stayed more constant, at around 50 per cent, and the number of working women aged 60 to 64 is actually rising slightly, to around three out of ten, and is projected to increase further as in future women will have to wait longer for their pensions. The state pension age for women is being moved from the age of 60 for women born before 6 April 1950 to 65 for women born after 5 March 1955 (see page 34 if born between these dates).

Whenever you eventually stop work, it can take years to build up an adequate income for your retirement. So, however far away from retirement you are, the first thing to think about is establishing a firm financial footing. The Retirement Planner starting on page 14 gives you some suggestions for what to do at each stage.

Will your pension be enough?

The state retirement pension on its own does not provide a reasonable income in retirement and, whatever the political developments, it is difficult to see how this could be reversed by the time you retire. It is forecast that by 2030 there will be 2.7 people aged 20 to 65 for every person over 65, compared to the current ratio of 3.7 to 1 now. This is not the whole story – for example, not everybody of working age is actually working – but it does show why governments of all political persuasions are cautious about extra spending on pensions. Although you may also qualify for an income from the State Earnings Related Pension Scheme (SERPS) this, too, has been cut back to be less generous for people retiring after 5 April 1999. Further changes are on their way with the replacement of SERPS by a new State Second Pension, planned to take effect some time after April 2002.

The limited level of state pension puts more onus on you to save for your retirement. The most obvious – and usually most suitable – way of doing so at the moment is either through an employer pension scheme or through your own personal pension plan, if you are self-employed or not a member of an employer scheme. Chapter 6 covers employer schemes, and Chapter 7 personal pension plans. However, the Government proposes to introduce a new type of pension, the stakeholder pension, as an alternative to personal pension plans from April 2001 (see Chapter 7).

The most an employer scheme can give you (to comply with Inland Revenue rules) is two-thirds of your final salary on retirement. Since a typical scheme will give you a percentage of your final salary for each year of membership, each year you put off joining will entail less pension at retirement – although (within limits) you can make Additional Voluntary Contributions (AVCs) to make up for lost time.

EXAMPLE

Ian joined his current employer, and its pension scheme, when he was 21. He is now 35: normal retirement age in his employer scheme is 60 for both men and women, but there is a clear trend to earlier retirement and he expects to retire at 55. That would give him 34 years of membership and since his pension scheme pays one-sixtieth of final salary for each year of membership he should get a pension of 34/60 times his final salary. Assuming his salary remains at £25,000, that would give him a pension of just over £14,000.

However, Ian's case is not entirely straightforward. He left his employer when he was 31, rejoining the company (and the pension scheme) two years later. The pension scheme took his previous years of membership into account, but the two-year break reduces his pension to 32/60 of £25,000, i.e. just over £13,000. So he is making Additional Voluntary Contributions to make up for the lost years, in order to get as near as possible to the 2/3 of final salary, which is the maximum pension allowed – £16,666.

A personal pension plan is 'money purchase' (as is the planned stakeholder pension). This means that instead of being linked to your salary your contributions are invested on your behalf, and you have your own 'pension fund' which is used to purchase you a pension on retirement. The earlier you contribute, the longer your money has to accumulate, as Table 1 shows.

Table 1: How much to invest in a personal pension plan?

| | Monthly contribution (after tax relief at 23%) needed for: | | | |
	Man aged	Contribution £	Woman aged	Contribution £
	24	39	19	50
	34	76	29	94
To get a pension	44	166	39	204
of £10,000 a year	54	449	49	558
at age:	**65**		**60**	

Source: Legal & General

Note that Table 1 assumes that your pension fund grows at a steady rate of 7 per cent a year and that the fund can be converted into a pension at an interest rate of 6 per cent a year. You might be lucky enough to choose a plan which performs very much better than this, or a company which has smaller charges. This would compensate you to some extent for investing for a shorter period. The converse is equally true: you also run the risk of picking a company whose investments plummet, or whose costs soar. But it is investment performance that has the most dramatic effect. A 12 per cent growth rate, for example, would cut the monthly contribution needed from a 34-year-old man from £76 to just £45. Investing for a longer period at least offers a chance for the inevitable peaks and troughs to be evened out over time.

Retirement planner

Life stage	What to do
Starting work	Don't assume your state pension will give you a comfortable retirement. See Chapter 3 for an explanation of state pensions. Start a pension of your own. If you can join an employer's pension scheme (Chapter 6), this is usually your best option; otherwise consider a personal pension plan or stakeholder pension (Chapter 7).
The family years	Make a will, if you have not already done so. Otherwise, your money may not go where you want it to and sorting out your affairs on your death may take longer than it need. Chapter 32 gives more information.
	Check that you have adequate protection for your family if you die, or become ill or disabled. See Chapter 8.
	You cannot usually get money from your pension until retirement date (not necessarily when you stop working). See Chapter 10 for other ways of investing for retirement which allow you to keep your options open: to support a child through college or university, say.

Approaching middle age

Now is the time to put as much as you can into your pension. If you are in an employer scheme, it must give you the option to make Additional Voluntary Contributions (AVCs) to boost your retirement benefits. If your scheme is a poor one, consider instead a 'free-standing' scheme (FSAVC), but beware of extra costs with this option. See Chapter 6.

If you have a personal pension plan, you can contribute more than the normal maximum allowed by the Inland Revenue once you are over the age of 35. You can also pay in extra if you have not contributed the maximum possible in previous years. See Chapter 7.

If you have not got any life insurance, should you buy some now before your age pushes the cost up? Chapter 8 may help you decide. If you have any existing policies, when do they mature?

You may have contracted out of the State Earnings Related Pension Scheme (SERPS). However, the way contracting out works has changed, so see Chapter 6 to check whether it is time to opt back in to SERPS.

Approaching retirement

Work out a detailed budget for your retirement, not forgetting the effects of inflation. You need to think about how your income will keep pace with inflation both until you stop work and after retirement. Chapters 3 to 5 give more guidance.

Check how much state pension you can expect. Complete form BR19 (from your local Benefits Agency – address in the phone book) and send it to the Retirement Pensions Forecast and Advice Unit at the address shown on the form. Allow several weeks for a reply.

Ask the administrators of any employer pension schemes to which you have belonged what benefits you can expect. If you have difficulty getting information from scheme managers the Occupational Pensions Advisory Service (OPAS)* may be able to help.

If you have lost touch with the administrators of a pension scheme, the Pension Schemes Registry* runs a free tracing service.

If you have a personal pension plan, ask the pension provider for a benefit statement and information on options you have. You will usually be given only an estimate of your pension, because most personal pension plans invest your money in a unit-linked fund, whose value varies in line with investment performance. To reduce the risk of your investment falling in value before retirement, consider switching to a less risky fund, such as a 'cash' or 'deposit' fund. See Chapter 7.

If your pension income isn't going to be enough, there may be last-minute steps you can take to boost it – see Chapter 6 for employer pension schemes and Chapter 7 for personal pensions. Consider a pre-retirement course – the earlier you do this, the more you are likely to benefit. See page 18.

Think about the long-term care you might need as you grow older. Chapter 9 looks at ways of paying for it.

Check that your home will suit your needs once you stop work. If you are thinking about moving to a different part of the country, consider doing so now rather than when you actually retire. See Part 5.

The Benefits Agency should write to you about four months before you reach state pension age and ask if you want to claim state retirement pension. If you do not get a letter, contact the local Benefits Agency office.

Retirement Cut your running costs. Chapter 5 covers balancing income and spending. Things you can do now to reduce your outgoings later include improving insulation in your home and replacing your car, washing machine or other such goods for models which are more economical to run.

Take time to decide what to do with any lump sum you receive on redundancy or retirement. It may be worth paying off at least some of your mortgage. Chapter 10 will help you decide.

Your tax position will almost certainly change. See Chapter 15 for how to rearrange your finances to make the most of the tax system. Once you are 65, you may get higher tax allowances.

If you are concerned about inheritance tax on your death, see Chapter 33 for the steps you can sensibly take to reduce it.

A warning against inflation

Even if inflation runs at only 2.5 per cent a year, £1,000 invested in a building society will be worth only £781 after 10 years in terms of purchasing power, and £610 after 20 years (ignoring any interest received). To look at the effect of inflation another way, Table 2 shows typical prices of some basic groceries in 1977 and 1997. Although the average annual rise in the Retail Prices Index over this period may not seem high, at 6.6 per cent a year, the practical effect was that many everyday items doubled in price within 20 years.

Table 2: Prices of selected groceries compared, 1977 and 1997

Item	1977	1997
Apples per lb	18¾p	38p–48p
Streaky bacon per lb	82p	£1.59
Bread – large loaf	28p	49p
Butter per lb	55p	£1.48
Cheddar cheese per lb	55p	£2.10
Instant coffee – 4oz	£1.09	£2.03
Milk per pint	11½p	29p
Tea – 4oz	35p	66p

When planning your retirement, inflation is a crucial factor to consider. It will have an impact on the amount of money you need to save in order to provide yourself with an adequate pension. Even low inflation is likely to be accompanied by low interest rates: if you are living off your savings, what is important is the gap between the rate at which inflation erodes your savings and the return you can get from investing them. In Chapter 3 there is an explanation of how to calculate the future effect of inflation and make provision for it financially.

Preparing yourself emotionally

Some people see retirement as a happy release; for others, the end of work seems the end of their useful life. People may have no friends outside work and may have simply no idea what to do with themselves all day. Added to this may be financial worries.

It may help to reduce stress when you do retire if you can 'wean' yourself off work gradually, by working part-time. And, although it may take some self-discipline, consider starting now some of those activities you have always looked forward to taking up in retirement, such as a hobby or sport, voluntary work or further education. A pre-retirement course is a good opportunity to air any worries about the emotional and financial implications of retirement.

EXAMPLE

About three years before he retired, Mr Duncan attended a very useful pre-retirement course at the local technical college. It lasted five days, including two half-days on finance. Among the 100 pages of handouts received was a budget sheet. Using this, Mr and Mrs Duncan kept records of their spending for the three years running up to retirement so that they could see where the money was going, and they gradually reduced their expenditure to the after-tax amount of their pensions. As a result there was no sudden reduction in their standard of living when they retired.

Pre-retirement courses

These are run by commercial companies such as insurance companies, voluntary organisations, companies which provide courses for their own employees, and local authorities (though the number of authorities able to do this has reduced significantly in past years). They can be free to the individual or cost several hundred pounds; take up a few hours a week at the local college or be combined with a week's holiday; be run by experienced lecturers with relevant · qualifications or – since they are not regulated in any way – people with none.

The Pre-Retirement Association★ publishes an invaluable guide to the course providers currently operating; the 1999 edition costs £9.50 plus £1 postage. Questions to ask both yourself and course organisers include:

- What do you want from the course? Hard factual information, or an opportunity to think more generally about retirement? Can you influence the course content?
- Who will be running the course? What qualifications do they have? Is anybody giving financial information authorised to provide independent financial advice (see Chapter 11)?
- What will be expected from you? Can you bring your partner?
- What background material will be provided?
- How many participants will there be, and what is their background likely to be?
- How much does it cost and what does this include (particularly if it is a residential course)?

Other help

Both Age Concern★ and Help the Aged★ publish a wide range of useful free leaflets, as well as providing other services for older people. They also have telephone information lines.

Chapter 2

Coping with sudden retirement

You may find yourself effectively retired, because of redundancy or ill-health, before the date you had anticipated. If so, the reason you leave work could make quite a difference to both your rights and your finances.

Early retirement

Benefits from your state retirement pension – or a personal pension plan taken out purely as a way of contracting out of the State Earnings Related Pension Scheme (SERPS: see Chapter 6) – cannot be drawn before the age of 65 for men and women born after 5 March 1955, or before the age of 60 for women born prior to 6 April 1950 (see page 34 if born between these dates).

Employer pension schemes usually allow early retirement, though the minimum age at which the Inland Revenue allows you to draw the maximum pension is normally 50. For schemes set up before 14 March 1989 the earliest age at which the maximum pension can be paid is usually 60 for men and 55 for women. In practice, employers are likely to be less generous than the Inland Revenue, though if the employer is slimming down the workforce, better terms than normal might be offered.

Always check the details on the pension statement you are given by your employer, such as when you joined the scheme, your age and any pension transferred from a previous employer. If you have concerns which you cannot clear up with your employer, the Occupational Pensions Advisory Service★ (OPAS) may be able to help.

If you have a personal pension plan, unless you are in one of the occupations listed on page 95, the earliest age at which you can draw a pension is 60 for plans started before 1 July 1988, and 50 for other plans (though you can transfer to a plan with the younger age). But drawing your personal pension early means you will probably get less than if you had contributed until the planned pension age, when your money would have had longer to grow. Some pension providers may also impose early retirement penalties.

Early retirement on health grounds

Although you cannot receive a state retirement pension early, you may get other state benefits: for example incapacity benefit, or disability living allowance if you need help with personal care and getting about. For guidance on the state benefits available if you are sick or disabled see Social Security leaflet SD1 or phone the Benefits Enquiry Line.*

Ill-health may force you to scale down your work. If you are working 16 hours or more a week and are receiving one of a range of disability-related benefits, you may be able to claim the Disabled Person's Tax Credit to top up a low income.

There are no Inland Revenue limits on the age at which you can draw an employer pension on health grounds, and the limits on amounts are relaxed. Each scheme usually sets its own conditions, which may be more rigorous than the Inland Revenue rules (though possibly more generous than those on voluntary early retirement).

If you have to retire because of ill-health, you can draw a pension from a personal plan at any age, though again the amount is likely to be smaller than it would have been had you contributed to the plan until your planned retirement date. In future. the amount of any incapacity benefit you claim may be reduced if you receive a pension of over £85 a week from an employer or personal pension.

You may also have some relevant insurance. Permanent health insurance, whether a personal purchase or a perk from your employer, will pay out an income if you are unable to work due to ill-health or disability, but usually stops at retirement age. Credit insurance covers loan payments for you if you cannot make them yourself because of sickness, accident or redundancy; but often only for one to two years.

Note that with all the options above, definitions of 'ill-health' will vary, and medical evidence may be required.

Compulsory redundancy

For job loss to be classed as redundancy, normally the position must disappear; it is not redundancy if an employer immediately takes on a direct replacement. It does not matter if the employer recruits more workers of a different type, or in some other location (unless your contract could have required you to move to there).

If your job loss is classed as redundancy you get certain rights – unless you are self-employed, on some fixed-term contracts, or in some occupations. Chief among these rights is statutory redundancy pay for anyone who has been employed continuously by the employer for at least two years. If the employer cannot pay, the state may make the payment on the employer's behalf. The legal minimum (the employer may pay more) is:

- for each complete year in which you were aged between 18 and 21, half a week's pay
- for each complete year in which you were aged between 22 and 40, one week's pay
- for each complete year in which you were aged between 41 and 64, one and a half week's pay.

The maximum number of years taken into account is 20 and the maximum payment is £6,600. However, you have no legal entitlement to redundancy pay if you are 65-plus or over the company's normal retirement age, and your entitlement is reduced after your 64th birthday. For information about how redundancy pay is taxed, see page 206.

You may also have the right to a reasonable amount of time off, with pay, to look for another job or arrange training; a right to a minimum period of notice, and, if there is a recognised trade union whose members are affected, a minimum period of consultation. See the employment legislation leaflets available from your Jobcentre (in the phone book under 'Employment Service') or phone the Redundancy Payments Helpline.*

Voluntary redundancy

You may get a better deal for volunteering; another incentive might be if you could qualify for early retirement as well. But be careful. Your employer may be entitled to offset part of your pension payment againt the redundancy payment. Although volunteering for redundancy will not lead to disqualification from receiving Jobseeker's allowance, any pay-off or pension you get may affect the amount of allowance (see below). Also, credit insurance usually covers loan payments on compulsory, but rarely voluntary, redundancy.

Making the best of redundancy

Your employer may be prepared to negotiate. As well as negotiating on pay, ask about extending perks: you may be able to continue to qualify for the company's private medical insurance scheme, or discounts on the company's products. Consider asking your employer to pay for counselling or financial advice, but check what strings are attached; in particular find out whether the adviser represents only one company or is fully independent. Chapter 11 should help.

Unfair dismissal

Your company should follow some consistent procedure before dismissing staff, and these procedures may be set out in company disciplinary or redundancy selection procedures. If these procedures are not followed, or if you believe you were unfairly dismissed or selected for redundancy, you can take your case to an independent employment tribunal, providing you have one year's continuous service with the employer. You must do so within three months of the dismissal. If you believe your employer is acting in breach of your employment rights, e.g. by making you redundant because of race or sex or for trade union reasons, there is no qualifying length of service. Applying to an employment tribunal is free and legal representation is not essential. Leaflets on how to apply to an employment tribunal are available from Jobcentres.

Jobseeker's allowance

Jobseeker's allowance replaced both unemployment benefit and the income support previously received by the unemployed, from

October 1996. In order to qualify, you must be under state pension age, and capable of and actively seeking work. You must attend a New Jobseeker Interview at your local Jobcentre, following which a Jobseeker's Agreement will be drawn up, covering conditions such as the steps you intend to take to get work. Leaflets are available from post offices, libraries and advice centres, or contact your local Jobcentre for details.

Jobseeker's allowance can be either contribution- or income-based. If you have paid enough National Insurance contributions you can get the contribution-based allowance for up to six months: for people aged 25 or over, the amount for the year from 6 April 1999 is £51.40 a week. No amount is payable for dependants. If you have not paid enough National Insurance contributions, or have already received six months of contribution-based allowance, you may get income-based benefit; the amount is the difference between the amount you or your family are assessed as needing, and your weekly net income. However, you get no income-based allowance if you have savings over £8,000, while savings between £3,000 and £8,000 reduce the amount payable. Income-based Jobseeker's allowance works very like income support, described in Chapter 5, which you may qualify for when your Jobseeker's allowance stops at state pension age.

Note that if you receive more than £50 a week (before tax) from a pension, any contribution-based Jobseeker's allowance will be reduced by the amount of pension over £50. Your allowance may also be affected if you leave your job voluntarily without good reason, or do not comply with various requirements, such as accepting job offers. Taking voluntary redundancy is not treated as leaving your job voluntarily.

Always get in touch with your Jobcentre as soon as you become unemployed, or know that you will be, even if you will not qualify for Jobseeker's allowance. This means that you should get National Insurance credits in order to protect your rights to benefits (or pensions) in future. If you are aged 60 or over you do not need to do this, as you get credits automatically.

Coping emotionally

Loss of a job is rated as one of the most stressful events that you can experience. Warning signs that you may be under more stress than is good for you include changes in eating or sleeping patterns, or an increase in smoking or alcohol intake. One of the most obvious early signs of stress to look out for in another person is an intensification of personality traits. For example: a defensive person may become suspicious, a careful person over-meticulous. To reduce stress, try to find ways of replacing the social contact and discipline of a job; perhaps by keeping to a daily routine, taking regular exercise or taking on voluntary work. It might help to talk things over with your GP.

Part 2

Your finances in retirement

Chapter 3

Planning your income

When you retire, there are four main sources of income which you may rely on:

- state pensions and state benefits
- private pensions, either from employer schemes you belonged to while working or from personal pension plans you took out
- interest and other income from investments and savings
- pay or profits from work you continue to do after retirement.

Incomes of people retired now

In the year to 5 April 1997, nearly three-quarters of all pensioners relied on state benefits for at least half of their income. Reliance on state benefits is greatest amongst older pensioners, who tend to be significantly poorer than the more recently retired. There are several reasons for this. Firstly, older pensioners are less likely to have built up a substantial pension through a private pension scheme. In 1996–97, 70 per cent of recently retired pensioners (men aged 65 to 69 and women aged 60 to 64) had a pension from an employer's scheme which, on average, provided £122 a week. Among pensioners as a whole, and taking into consideration 65 per cent had such a pension, the average was significantly lower at £91 a week.

Older pensioners are less likely to work, partly because of employers' reluctance to employ older workers and partly because health tends to deteriorate with age. In 1996–97, recently retired pensioners had average earnings of £51 a week, compared with £13 for pensioners as a whole. In addition, older pensioners are largely excluded from the earnings-related part of the state pension scheme (see page 37) which started up in 1978. And lastly, unlike state pensions, other sources of retirement income often fail to hold their value in the face of inflation, so what may have started out many years ago as a healthy income could now be worth much less.

The result is that pensioners who have retired more recently are noticeably better off than their older colleagues. In 1996–97, pensioners as a whole had an average income of £154 a week after taking into account housing costs. Recently retired pensioners averaged £222 a week – i.e. they were over £60 a week better off. The message is clear: if you want to live comfortably in retirement, you cannot afford to rely simply on the state – you will need income from other sources as well.

Average income of a retired household

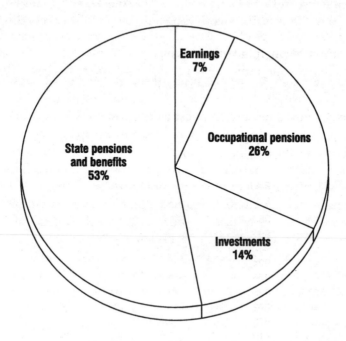

Source: *The Pensioners' Income Series 1996/7*, Department of Social Security, 1998

The effect of inflation

Inflation and retirement income

If your income does not rise as fast as the prices of the things you need or choose to buy, you will be able to afford less and less of those things as time goes on. Inflation in the UK is usually measured in terms of changes in the Retail Prices Index – this is based on a varied basket of goods and services weighted to reflect the spending patterns of the population as a whole (and so does not necessarily reflect the spending of retired people). The rate of inflation can vary enormously: back in 1975, it was running at a yearly rate of 27 per cent – in other words, prices were rising by more than a quarter over the space of just one year; but in August 1999, inflation fell to a low point of just 1.1 per cent a year.

However, even a very modest rate of inflation can have a huge impact on prices over time. Table 1 shows the impact various rates of general inflation would have on £1,000 of income over time.

Table 1 shows that if you had an income of £10,000 at the start of your retirement at the age of 60, say, its value would have fallen to just £360 by the age of 95, assuming inflation averaged 10 per cent a year. And, even if inflation averaged only two per cent a year throughout your retirement, the buying power of your £10,000 would have fallen to £5,000 – half of its original value.

Table 1: How inflation reduces your income

After this many years:	... the buying power of £1,000 of income would fall to this much, if the average yearly inflation rate was:						
	1%	2%	3%	4%	5%	7%	10%
	£	£	£	£	£	£	£
1	990	980	971	961	952	935	909
2	980	961	943	925	907	873	826
3	971	942	915	889	864	816	751
4	961	924	888	855	823	763	683
5	951	906	863	822	784	713	621
10	905	820	744	676	614	508	386
15	861	743	642	555	481	362	239
20	820	673	554	456	377	258	149
25	780	610	478	375	295	184	92
30	742	552	412	308	231	131	57
35	706	500	355	253	181	94	36

So, when you plan your retirement, it is essential that you think about what impact inflation may have over the years. Either you need pensions or other income which will increase year by year with inflation, or you need to set aside some savings or other source of funds to boost your income later in retirement. See Chapter 10 for more on investing in retirement, and Chapter 12 for working in retirement.

Inflation and retirement savings

It is not just in retirement that you need to keep an eye on inflation. It will also affect the amount you need to accumulate to provide your eventual pension. Suppose you are 55, currently earn £30,000 a year and hope that your personal pension savings will provide a retirement income of £15,000 a year, in terms of today's money. It might be estimated that you would need a pool of £150,000, in today's money, to provide that pension. But, even if inflation averages a modest yearly rate, £150,000 will be worth less by the time you come to retire. So how much will you need to have saved by then to provide yourself with the equivalent of £15,000 a year in terms of future money values?

Table 2 helps provide the answer. It shows how much money you would need in future to match the value of £1,000 today in terms of buying power, given different rates of inflation between now and retirement. For example, if inflation averaged three per cent a year over 10 years, £1,344 at that time would be worth the same as £1,000 today. This means that, in the example above, you would need a fund of 150 x £1,344 = £201,600 at the age of 65 to provide a pension of £20,160, which would have the same value as £15,000 in today's money. And, if inflation averaged 10 per cent a year instead, you would need a fund of 150 x £2,594 = £389,100.

It is important to be aware of the impact of inflation on the amounts you need to save. Many projections of the income which a pension plan will provide are given in terms of future money without being adjusted for inflation. You might be tempted to think that being a half-millionaire by the time you retire will mean being rich, but your 'riches' may not buy very much by that point.

Table 2: What you need to keep up with inflation

After this many years:	... you would need this much money to buy the same as £1,000 today, if the average yearly inflation was:						
	1% £	2% £	3% £	4% £	5% £	7% £	10% £
1	1,010	1,020	1,030	1,040	1,050	1,070	1,100
2	1,020	1,040	1,061	1,082	1,103	1,145	1,210
3	1,030	1,061	1,093	1,125	1,158	1,225	1,331
4	1,041	1,082	1,126	1,170	1,216	1,311	1,464
5	1,051	1,104	1,159	1,217	1,276	1,403	1,611
10	1,105	1,219	1,344	1,480	1,629	1,967	2,594
15	1,161	1,346	1,558	1,801	2,079	2,759	4,177
20	1,220	1,486	1,086	2,191	2,653	3,870	6,727
25	1,282	1,641	2,094	2,666	3,386	5,429	10,835
30	1,348	1,811	2,427	3,243	4,322	7,612	17,449
35	1,417	2,000	2,814	3,946	5,516	10,677	28,102
40	1,489	2,208	3,262	4,801	7,040	14,974	45,259
45	1,565	2,438	3,782	5,841	8,985	21,002	72,890
50	1,645	2,692	4,384	7,107	11,467	29,457	117,391
55	1,729	2,972	5,082	8,646	14,636	41,315	189,059
59[1]	1,799	3,217	5,720	10,115	17,790	54,156	276,801

[1] The maximum period for which pension savings can be left invested is from age 16 to age 75 – i.e. 59 years

What the state provides

It is likely that you will qualify for some pension from the state when you reach pension age. The main advantage of state pensions is that they are fully inflation-proofed, in line with the Retail Prices Index, both during the time you are building up an entitlement to them and while they are being paid out. The drawback is that state pensions are low – insufficient, on their own, to support a comfortable lifestyle and vulnerable to politically motivated change.

However, state pensions can be a useful backbone for your retirement income which you should supplement through your own additional savings. To work out how much extra pension income you will have to plan for, you will first need to know roughly how much income you can expect from the state.

There are two main state pensions: the basic pension and pension from the State Earnings Related Pension Scheme (SERPS).

The Government plans to replace SERPS with a new State Second Pension in 2002.

How much basic pension?

In the year from 6 April 1999, the full state basic pension is £66.75 a week (£3,471 a year) for a single person. A married couple get more – up to £106.70 a week (£5,548.40 a year). If both husband and wife qualify for a basic pension in their own right they can get a maximum of 2 x £66.75 = £133.50 a week (£6,942 a year) between them.

You build up your entitlement to basic pension by paying National Insurance contributions throughout your working life. If you have not paid enough contributions for a full basic pension, you may still qualify for a reduced-rate pension. But it is possible to pay too few contributions to qualify for any pension at all.

How you qualify for basic pension

In the context of state pensions, the term 'working life' is officially defined. Generally, it means the tax years between the one in which you reach the age of 16 and the last tax year before you reach state pension age.

For women born after 5 March 1955 and for all men, state pension age is 65, giving a maximum working life of 49 years. If you are a woman and you were born before 6 April 1950, your state pension age is 60 and your maximum working life is five years shorter – i.e. 44 years. Anyone born before July 1932 may have a shorter than normal working life.

Women born between 6 April 1950 and 5 March 1955 are caught in a transitional period during which women's state pension age is being progressively raised from 60 to 65. To work out your state pension age, add to age 60 one month for each tax month (or part tax month) that your birthday falls after 5 April 1950. A tax month runs from the sixth day of one month to the fifth day of the next month.

You need to have paid National Insurance contributions for about 90 per cent of the years in your working life in order to qualify for the full basic pension, while you need to have paid contributions for about a quarter of those years in order to receive any basic pension at all. In between these limits, you qualify for basic pension at a reduced rate. Table 3 gives a guide to how much basic pension you will get if you have a standard working life of 44 years or 49 years.

You generally pay National Insurance whenever you are working – either as an employee or while self-employed or in a partnership. Table 4 shows the type of contributions that you pay. Only complete tax years of contributions count – so, for example, a year in which you were self-employed and paid National Insurance for 36 weeks but travelled abroad for the remaining 16 weeks will not count towards your pension unless you choose to make voluntary payments of National Insurance for the 16 weeks.

Table 3: How much basic pension?

If you've paid National Insurance contributions for this many years . . .	You'll get this percentage of the full basic pension . . .	
	Women born after 5 March 1955 %	Women born before 6 April 1950 and all men %
9 or less	0	0
10	26	0
15	39	35
20	52	46
25	65	57
30	77	69
35	90	80
40	100[1]	91
44	100	100[2]

[1] The fulll pension for a woman with a working life of 44 years is payable if she has 39 or more years of contributions
[2] The full pension for a man or woman with a working life of 49 years is payable if they have 44 or more years of contributions

If you are not working

In some non-working situations you will qualify for National Insurance credits, which are the equivalent of contribution payments in your record for basic pension purposes. You qualify automatically for these credits if:

- you are claiming certain state benefits, such as Jobseeker's allowance, maternity allowance or incapacity benefit

- you are a man or woman with a pension age of 65 who is aged 60 or over during the tax year and unemployed (regardless of whether you have 'signed on')
- you are in full-time education during the tax years in which you reach ages 16, 17 and 18, and were born after 5 April 1957
- you take part in an approved training course during the tax year (which does not include going to university), and were born after 5 April 1957.

Table 4: Types of National Insurance contributions

Types of contribution	Description	Can it count towards your pension?
Class 1 Full-rate	Paid by employees, including company directors[1], but not people earning less than a 'lower earnings limit'	YES
Reduced-rate ('small stamp')	Paid by some married women and widows – they can choose to switch to full-rate	NO
Class 2	Paid by self-employed, but optional for people with profits below a lower limit and for some married women and widows	YES
Class 3	Voluntary – you choose to pay if you want to fill in gaps in your contribution record	YES
Class 4	Paid by self-employed on profits between lower and upper 'earnings limits'	NO

[1] Before 6 April 1975, company directors counted as self-employed

If you cannot work because you are at home caring for children or other dependants (for example, an elderly relative) you may qualify for 'home responsibilities protection' (HRP). With this, you do not get credits for National Insurance but the number of years for which you need contributions in order to qualify for a given level of pension is reduced. You can get HRP only for full tax years – for example, if you had been self-employed for 36 weeks of the tax year but at home caring for your children for the remaining 16 weeks, the year would not count towards your basic pension unless you paid voluntary contributions to cover the 16 weeks. You get HRP automatically if you are receiving child benefit; in other circumstances, you will usually need to claim it.

How much SERPS pension?

The State Earnings Related Pension Scheme (SERPS) provides pensions which are additional to the basic pension. You can build up a SERPS pension only if you are paying full-rate Class 1 National Insurance – so, if you are self-employed, unemployed or on low earnings you cannot belong to SERPS. The amount of pension you eventually get is linked to your earnings (between a lower and upper limit) during part or all of your working life, which means that the amount of SERPS pension built up varies from person to person.

Even if you are eligible for the SERPS scheme, you may be 'contracted out' of it. This means that instead of accumulating SERPS pension, you build up a pension that will be paid from an employer pension scheme (see Chapter 6) or a personal pension plan (see Chapter 7). In this case, either you and your employer will pay lower National Insurance contributions or part of your National Insurance payments will be returned by being paid into your pension scheme or plan.

The formula for calculating SERPS pension is complex – particularly as the rules were changed in 1988. But you do not need to work through complicated sums yourself because you can get a forecast of your SERPS pension from the Benefits Agency based on your contributions to date. This assumes you carry on contributing up to retirement. See page 15 for details of how to apply for this forecast.

Table 5 gives you an idea of the maximum SERPS pension you could get in terms of today's money, depending on when you will reach state pension age. Once you start to receive your SERPS pension, it is increased each year in line with price inflation.

Table 5: How much SERPS pension?

Tax year in which you reach state pension age	Maximum SERPS pension in 1999 money Weekly amount
2000–01	£107
2005–06	£100
2010–11	£94
2020–21	£92
2030–31	£90
2040–41 and after	£87

The State Second Pension

The government plans to replace SERPS with a new State Second Pension, probably in 2002. In late 1999, the scheme was still on the drawing-board, but as originally proposed, it would cover some groups of non-working individuals (e.g. carers and some people with disabilities), as well as all employees who earn more than a certain limit. The government is also considering whether it should cover self-employed people.

As with SERPS, you would qualify by paying the appropriate National Insurance contributions or by being given credits. To begin with it would also be earnings-related, although it would be skewed to give proportionately better pensions to people on lower incomes. In time, though, it is planned that the state second pension should evolve into a flat-rate pension, with transitional arrangements for people who have built up substantial earnings-related rights in SERPS and earlier versions of the scheme.

Moderate and higher earners would be strongly encouraged to contract out of the State Second Pension, building up their own second-tier pension from an employer's pension scheme, personal pension plan or stakeholder pension.

Graduated pension

There was an earlier state pension scheme related to earnings which ran from 6 April 1961 to 5 April 1975 and provides 'graduated pensions'. Unfortunately, the scheme was designed without adequate safeguards against inflation and the pensions it provides are now very small.

The scheme worked as follows: people paid different amounts of National Insurance depending on their earnings. The total paid was divided into 'units' – for men, every £7.50 paid counted as a unit while for women every £9 paid counted. In the 1999–2000 tax year, scheme pensioners receive 8.67 pence in graduated pension for every unit. This gives a maximum weekly pension of £7.45 for a man or £6.23 for a woman. Graduated pensions are increased each year in line with the Retail Prices Index.

Information about your state pensions

Through your local Benefits Agency office, you can contact the Retirement Pension Forecast and Advice Service* run by the Department of Social Security (DSS). This can provide you with information about the basic, SERPS and graduated pensions you have built up so far and a forecast of the amount of state pensions you could build up by retirement, together with advice about any steps you could take now to increase your future pension (for example, making voluntary National Insurance contributions or switching to full-rate contributions if you currently pay the reduced Class 1 rate). See page 15 for information on how to get hold of a statement and forecast.

If you have any other queries or problems relating to your state pension or National Insurance position, contact your local Benefits Agency office, preferably in writing – do not forget to put your National Insurance number on all correspondence.

There are plans to produce integrated pension statements, combining state and private pension rights, but these plans are at an early stage. The combined forecast could be provided through employers as part of an individual's annual pension statement, or through pension providers.

Chapter 4

Planning your spending

It is probable that your income in retirement will be considerably less than it is while you are working, but this will not necessarily imply a lower standard of living because your expenditure will also change. The financial impact of retiring will vary between individuals.

Work-related expenses

If you go out to work every day, you are likely to be paying out for a range of work-related items. Unless you live close enough to work to be able to walk or cycle to the office, you will probably be paying for bus or train fares, or paying for petrol and some wear-and-tear related repairs on your car. Some employers provide a company car and/or pay for a car's running costs, in which case you may not be paying out directly – but you will be paying some extra tax on the value the Inland Revenue thinks you are getting from this perk. Once you retire, you will save on the fares or car costs associated with work.

Working away from home also means that you may be paying for lunch and drinks every day. This could be costly if you are buying expensive sandwiches or restaurant meals. On the other hand, if your employer provides subsidised food and drink in a canteen or via vending machines, expenditure on refreshments may be minimal.

You may save on clothing costs once you stop work. An employer will generally provide any special uniform or protective clothing required, but many people simply need to look smart and must do this at their own expense. After retirement, you will be able to please yourself regarding dress, which may mean you can rely on cheaper, more casual clothes.

You should not overlook the 'extras' associated with work – things like drinks after work with friends, contributing to birthday and leaving presents, taking part in sweepstakes, and so on. You will save these amounts once you retire. Perhaps you currently pay for various newspapers and magazines; on retirement, you might decide to cut back on such literature. On the other hand, your workplace may give you access to newspapers or journals you want to subscribe to – at your own cost – once you retire. While you are working, you will be paying National Insurance contributions: these will cease, unless you are under state pension age and continue with some work or are under age 60 and decide to pay voluntary contributions. You may also be paying into an employer-run pension scheme: these payments will cease once you retire.

If you work from home, retiring is likely to have less impact on your spending, but you should still have a realistic look at how your costs might change – for example after retirement you might go out more, which could mean paying less for heating and lighting at home. If you are self-employed or run your own company, then stopping work will clearly reduce your spending substantially; on the other hand, you may find that items once bought through your business (which probably meant claiming tax relief on them, and possibly getting back the VAT) are available only at full cost.

Life insurance

While you are working, your employer may be providing you with free life insurance cover. Once you retire, you will have to decide whether this is still a priority. Life insurance costs more as you get older, so could constitute a hefty expense; your need for it is likely to decline when you no longer have children who are dependent on you. However, you may still need cover to protect a dependent spouse and you should also consider the position of anyone else who may be financially dependent on you, such as an ageing parent. Chapter 8 gives further information on life insurance.

You may find that spending on life insurance increases later in life, if you expect to leave a reasonable estate when you die and wish to protect dependants from inheritance tax (see Chapter 33).

House and car insurance

You may be able to cut the cost of premiums for house insurance once you retire. Some companies recognise that elderly customers pose a lower risk because they spend more time at home, which tends to deter burglars. Chapter 22 details companies which either offer a discount to, or arrange special policies for, mature policyholders.

Car insurance also usually gets cheaper as you get older, and many companies offer particularly good deals if you are over 50 or retired. This is because statistically, drivers over the age of around 50 tend to have fewer accidents than younger people. To find out about special deals, ask two or three insurance brokers to get quotes for you, and check what offers are available from 'direct insurers' (who don't deal through intermediaries like brokers).

If you have not had your own car insurance policy for some time (because you have had a company car, say), you might not qualify for a no-claims discount. Ask your employer for evidence of your claims record before giving up work: some insurers may be prepared to give you a discount on the strength of this.

Household expenses

If you have been buying your own home, by the time you retire you are likely to have paid off your mortgage or to have only a small loan outstanding. If you do still have a mortgage, see Chapter 10 for the pros and cons of using some of your retirement or redundancy money to pay it off. If you rent your home, this expense might not be affected by retirement.

If your home is usually empty every weekday while you are out at work, retirement may mean a significant change in your fuel bills. You will probably be at home a lot more and so will need to have the heating on more often, possibly at a higher temperature as a result of feeling the cold more. In the winter months, you will also be using the lights with greater frequency. Being at home more also means increased use of household appliances such as the kettle. (See Chapter 24 for more on use of fuel.)

You may be reluctant to undertake big jobs around the house as you grow older, so you should consider allowing for the possibility of paying someone else to do decorating for you, say, and to dig the garden once or twice a year.

Telephone bills

Once you are retired, you may find that phone calls you used to make from work are now made from home, or you might find that you use the phone a lot more to keep in touch with friends you used to see through work. However, calls connected with work or to contact your working partner may cease and you may prefer, once you have more time, to visit people rather than talk on the phone. So, you will need to evaluate your own particular use of the phone and how this might change after retirement.

• If you often make calls outside your local area, especially in the evenings and at weekends, you may save money by changing your telephone company (see Chapter 24).

If your use of the phone is very low, you could save money by switching to BT's 'Light User Scheme'* service. Alternatively, if you find yourself using your phone more, some telephone companies offer schemes for private customers who use the phone a lot.

Travel

Do not automatically assume that stopping work will reduce the amount of miles you travel. You may have more opportunity to go out, so your travelling could increase.

If you currently have the use of a company car you will need to consider alternative arrangements after retirement. Buying, insuring and running your own car will be a significant extra expense. If you do not expect to use a car much, you might instead consider using public transport or taxis and, perhaps, hiring a car occasionally. It is undoubtedly convenient, however, to have your own vehicle, and many cheap places to shop are accessible only by car.

If you and your partner each run your own car, you may find that after retirement you can cope perfectly well with just one. Similarly, if you currently have a large car, you could discover on retiring that you will be happy to run something a bit smaller – in both cases, you could save on fuel and insurance costs.

Public transport is often cheaper if you are older or retired. For example, British Rail operates a Senior Railcard for those over 60, which for an £18 annual fee gives you a one-third discount on most rail tickets. Similarly, many bus and coach companies offer cheaper tickets to older customers. Your local council should be able to give you details of concessionary travel schemes operating in your area. For more information see Chapter 25.

Holidays and leisure

When retired, you are likely to have a lot more leisure time, and one pleasurable way to fill this is to take more holidays. This won't necessarily imply increased spending, since you will have the freedom to take holidays at off-peak times when travel and accommodation will often be much cheaper. There are also many special deals aimed at older people.

However, on the whole, you should allow for higher spending on leisure activities after retirement than before.

Spending on your health

When you reach the state pension age, you will be entitled to free prescriptions for medicines – assuming present rules continue. Apart from that, it is sensible to allow for some increase in health-related spending during retirement. There are two aspects to health problems. The first is an increasing tendency with age to suffer problems which require some hospital treatment.

When you were working, a spell as an in-patient might have meant losing some earnings. At least, in retirement, any private pensions continue to be paid. However, if you are in hospital for more than six weeks, your state pension will be reduced. The official view is that you are being kept by the state anyway while you are in hospital, so getting your full pension as well would amount to being paid twice. However, many household expenses carry on even if you are in hospital, so the reduction in income could be a problem which you should plan ahead to alleviate. There might be extra expenses too – e.g. if your partner has to travel often to visit you in hospital or you have to pay for someone to come in and do the jobs you normally do about the house.

One solution could be to take out a hospital cash plan. These pay out a specified cash sum for each day that you are in hospital and usually in a range of certain other circumstances too: for example, if you need dental treatment or to visit a chiropracter. There are usually a lot of exclusions and conditions with hospital cash plans and the probability of having to claim under some sections can be rather remote. But for older people, who are more likely to make claims than youngsters, hospital cash plans can be reasonable value for money. An alternative is to set aside your own pool of savings, for example as part of your emergency fund, which you can draw on to cover any income shortfall or increased expenses due to a hospital stay.

You might prefer to be treated privately rather than on the NHS. This has some advantages, such as being treated rapidly and at a time of your own choosing, enjoying more private, hotel-style facilities while in hospital and having some choice about the doctors who treat you. On the downside, private treatment is costly. One way to cope with the cost is to take out private medical insurance (PMI). PMI can be prohibitively expensive for older ages and no longer qualifies for tax relief. However, many companies now provide budget schemes with limited cover. If you had PMI as a perk of your job when you were working, investigate whether you can continue to have cover at a preferential rate through the same insurer once you have retired.

The second aspect of health in older age is that you are more likely to suffer some kind of long-term disability – see Table 1. This can have all sorts of implications for your expenditure:

- You might need to adapt your home, e.g. putting in grab rails/slopes to replace steps/a stair-lift, building a downstairs shower-room or converting a downstairs room into a bedroom. You might make these changes after disability has struck or you might choose to plan ahead, making some adaptations to your home just in case mobility becomes more difficult later on. In extreme cases, you might decide to move house – e.g. to a bungalow or sheltered housing.
- You might have to pay for people to come and do jobs you once did yourself – e.g. a gardener, a cleaner, a handyman, someone to do the shopping.
- Your partner might need to pay for someone to sit with you if they want to go out.
- If you find it hard to cook, you might turn to meals on wheels or meals taken at a day centre – charges are modest.
- You might become reliant on taxis and dial-a-ride schemes when you want to go out. This would add to your costs if you had been used to walking or cycling.
- You might join a scheme to summon help in an emergency – e.g. if you have a fall or get stuck in the bath. There are usually costs in setting up the link as well as a weekly or monthly fee.

Table 1: People with long-standing illness or disability[1]

	Men		Women	
	All aged 16 and over	**65 and over**	**All aged 16 and over**	**65 and over**
Musculoskeletal system	18%	28%	21%	40%
Heart and circulatory system	10%	26%	9%	24%
Respiratory system	8%	11%	7%	8%
Eye complaints	2%	4%	2%	5%
Ear complaints	2%	4%	2%	4%
Any long-standing illness or disability	39%	62%	41%	62%

[1] 1996–97
Source: *Social Trends 1999*, TSO 1999

You might consider taking out critical illness cover (CIC), which pays out a large lump sum if you are struck down by a specified life-threatening condition, such as a heart attack, stroke or cancer. The lump sum can be used in any way and could help you to make any necessary adaptations to your home or lifestyle.

If your health problems become very severe, you might get to the stage at which you either need nursing care within your own home or you have to move into a residential or nursing home. See Chapters 9 and 31 for more about this.

EXAMPLE

Mr Davis took early retirement at 55, after working 34 years with the same company. He had no outstanding debts and his mortgage has been paid off, but he contradicts people who expect him to be in a good enough financial position now to sit back and enjoy life.

'There are, of course, some savings after retirement, in travelling costs and contributions to company pension schemes,' he says. 'But these are more than outweighed by a number of additional expenses, such as eating out more often, extra leisure activities, far more use of my private car, petrol costs, and – especially during the winter – higher heating costs of my house, which are currently approaching £1,000 a year.'

Chapter 5

Balancing your income and spending

In order to find out whether you can expect to have enough to live on in retirement, you need to combine your expected income and your likely expenditure. The Calculator in this chapter will help you to do this.

Using the Calculator

We recommend that you fill in the Calculator twice: first time around, consider your position at the start of retirement; second time, try to work out how your income and spending may square up ten years or so into retirement. This will help you to see, first, whether you are on track with your general retirement planning and, secondly, whether you need to take any extra measures to protect your position later on.

Fill in the Calculator in today's money. So, for example, if you expect to qualify for a full-rate basic pension from the state, put in the current rate (see Chapter 3) – do not try to guess what it is going to be years ahead. Similarly, express your expected spending in today's money. Think about how much you pay now for various items and try to estimate the proportionate change in those expenses after retirement, but do not try to inflate them for future price increases.

If you are married, you and your spouse should each fill in the relevant column in the 'Income' section and work out your after-tax income separately (see Chapter 15 on married couple's allowance). You can then add both your after-tax incomes together and complete the rest of the Calculator as a couple.

After-tax income

The Calculator uses 1999-2000 tax allowances and rates. First, it asks you about sources of taxable income. Second, it guides you through a rough estimate of the tax you might pay on your income. Finally, you are asked to add on any tax-free income you expect to receive. Note that, for the sake of simplicity, the Calculator assumes that you and your spouse will not be higher-rate taxpayers after you retire.

Your expenses

The Calculator asks you to estimate your spending under various categories, inputting yearly totals. If a category does not apply to you, leave it blank. In some cases, you are asked to fill in amounts to cover major expenditure such as replacing your car or making home improvements, which you might save up for. If you would pay for these out of capital that you have accumulated, leave the entry blank, but bear in mind that if your capital was producing investment income, this would fall after you had spent the capital.

The Calculator asks you about your loan repayments. Do not include credit card repayments here if you have already included credit card expenses under other headings – for example, if you usually buy petrol using your credit card, enter the amount under petrol, not loan repayments. If you anticipate taking out a loan to buy furniture or a car, say, enter either loan repayment costs or the item's total amount in the relevant section, but do not complete both categories.

Income versus spending

When you have filled in all the figures for income and spending, subtract total spending from total income. If the resulting number is positive, you are on course for a financially secure retirement. If the answer is negative, your income – on current plans – will not be enough to support the lifestyle that you want. See page 51 onwards for steps to remedy the situation.

The Retirement Calculator

		At the start of retirement		Ten years into retirement
	Your income	*husband*	*wife*	
A	State basic pension (full rate is £3,471 for the 1999–2000 tax year) – see page 34			
B	Other state pensions and/or taxable state benefits – see Chapter 3			
C	Pension(s) from employer pension scheme(s) – see Chapter 6			
D	Pension(s) from personal pension plans – see Chapter 7			
E	Taxable income from investments – enter gross (i.e. before-tax) amounts – see Chapter 10			
F	Earnings/profit from a job or self-employment – see Chapter 12			
G	Other taxable income			
H	Taxable income – add A + B + C + D +E +F + G			
	Your income tax bill			
I	Personal tax allowance – see Chapter 15			
J	Blind person's allowance (£1,380 if you qualify)			
K	Any tax-allowable deductions you pay before deducting tax relief – see Chapter 15			
L	Add I + J + K			
M	Deduct L from H			
N	If M is £1,500 or less, take 10% of M. If M is more than £1,500, write in £150			
P	Take M and deduct £1,500 plus any investment income recieved with a tax credit (see p.234)			
Q	If P is 0 or less, leave Q and R blank. Otherwise multiply savings income within P by 20%			
R	Multiply all other income within P by 23%			
S	Add N + Q + R			
T	If applicable, from S deduct the married couple's (or any related) allowance restricted to 10 per cent – see Chapter 15			
U	Tax on your income. If T is 0 or less, U = 0. If T is greater than 0, U = T			
V	After-tax income – subtract U from H			
W	Any tax-free income (e.g. £100 winter fuel payments for state pensioners, proceeds from long-term life insurance) – see Chapter 15			

	At the start of retirement *single person/couple*	Ten years into retirement

Your retirement income

X Total income in retirement – add V + W
for both partners _____ _____

Your expenses: living at home

a Food shopping and household basics _____ _____
b Buying and repairing household equipment
c Newspapers/magazines/books _____ _____
d TV licence/videos/music _____ _____
e Dog/cat/other pet _____ _____
f Clothes/shoes/cosmetics/hairdressing _____ _____

Your expenses: living it up

g Sports and hobbies: materials/lessons/other _____ _____
h Dining out/theatre/cinema/concerts/exhibitions _____ _____
i Holidays/holiday home/second home _____ _____
j Other indulgences (e.g. smoking, drinking) _____ _____

Your expenses: transport

k Costs of owning a car: tax/insurance/servicing/
repairs/breakdown insurance _____ _____
l Renting a car: rental charge/insurance _____ _____
m Costs of running car: petrol/diesel/oil _____ _____
n Train fares/bus fares/coach fares _____ _____
o Other travel costs _____ _____

Your expenses: home related

p Mortgage/rent _____ _____
q Repairs/service charge/decoration/furnishing _____ _____
r Buildings and contents insurance _____ _____
s Council tax/water rates _____ _____
t Gas/electricity/oil/solid fuel _____ _____
u Home help/window cleaner/other paid help _____ _____
v Gardening
w Telephone _____ _____

Your expenses: health-related

x Dentist _____ _____
y Optician
z Hospital cash plan/private medical insurance _____ _____
aa Long-term care insurance _____ _____
bb Other health-related expenses _____ _____

		At the start of retirement	Ten years into retirement
		single person/couple	

Your expenses: caring for others

cc	Spending on children/grandchildren	_____	_____
dd	Financial help for elderly relatives	_____	_____
ee	Christmas/birthday/other presents	_____	_____
ff	Gifts to charity/church collections	_____	_____
gg	Protection-type life insurance – see Chapter 8	_____	_____
hh	Other caring expenses	_____	_____

Your expenses: saving and borrowing

ii	Saving to replace car/household equipment	_____	_____
jj	Saving to finance home improvements	_____	_____
kk	Saving to cover higher health spending later on	_____	_____
ll	Other reguular saving	_____	_____
mm	Loan repayments (other than mortgage)	_____	_____

Your expenses: other

nn	Postage/stationery/other	_____	_____
Y	Total expenses: add up all expenses a–nn	_____	_____

Balancing income and spending

Z	Subtract Y from X and enter at Z. If Z is 0 or greater, you should have enough to live on during retirement. If Z is a minus figure, you will not have enough. Look at ways of increasing your income – see below	_____	_____

Not enough income?

One way to cope with a shortfall of income in retirement would, of course, be to economise on your spending, but really this is not ideal. First, consider ways in which you could boost your income.

Your state pension

If you expect to have more than enough income at the start of your retirement but you are worried that you will be short of money later on, you could consider putting off the start of your state pension in order to earn extra pension later.

At present, your state pension starts to be paid when you reach the age of 60 if you are a woman or 65 if you are a man. But, under current rules, you can defer your pension for up to five years in order to earn extra pension. If your retirement is many years off, you will have the option to defer your pension for up to ten years in exchange for a higher amount. There is more information on page 163.

Building up your own pension

If you are still some way from retirement, you have time to build up a pension income. Chapters 6 and 7 describe how you can save tax-efficiently for retirement through an employer pension scheme, stakeholder pension or personal pension. Certainly, if you are not yet saving in this way, you should start as soon as possible. If you are already contributing through an employer scheme, have you thought about boosting this form of saving by making Additional Voluntary Contributions (AVCs)? See pages 77–9.

Other forms of saving

Even if you have time enough to build up a pension, you might be put off saving this way, perhaps because you generally cannot get your money back before retirement. In this case, you could consider other forms of saving, such as through an individual savings account (ISA). Chapter 10 looks at suitable alternative investments.

If you are close to retirement, you may already have savings – or be about to receive a cash lump sum from a pension scheme or plan – which you could invest to provide you with extra income during retirement, either straight away or later on. Once again, Chapter 10 can guide you to appropriate investments.

Carrying on working

Retiring from your normal work does not mean you have to give up work altogether. State pensions and pensions from a pension plan or former employer scheme can all be paid to you even if you are still working. See Chapter 12 for advice on working during retirement.

You would be unwise to rely on the possibility of working to supplement an otherwise insufficient retirement income. If you run into health problems, you might be unable to carry on working; you might have to give up work to care for your husband or wife or parent, perhaps; and, if the economy is in recession, there may be no demand for your labour.

However, the government is attempting to encourage disabled people back into employment through a 'New Deal' employment programme for the disabled (contact your Jobcentre) and Disabled Person's Tax Credit. Despite its name, the tax credit is effectively a means-tested state benefit, but it is administered by the Inland Revenue, and if you are an employee it is usually paid by being added to your pay packet. You can claim if you work at least 16 hours a week, you are receiving one of a range of disability-related benefits, and you are on a low income. If you have capital of more than £16,000 (excluding your home) you will not be eligible for the tax credit. For more information contact the Tax Credit Helpline.*

Income from your home

If you own your own home it is likely to be one of your most valuable assets, but money tied up in your home cannot help you pay the bills. If your home is large for your needs once you retire, you might consider moving somewhere smaller, thereby releasing some capital which you could invest to provide an income. But think very carefully before taking this course of action: the change from working to retiring can be very stressful and moving to unfamiliar surroundings may make the adjustment even more difficult. See Chapter 20 for points to consider before moving home in retirement.

One way to generate income from your home would be to take in a lodger. As long as you find a suitable person, this could also have the advantage of providing you with some help around the house with heavy jobs and some companionship. Under the Inland Revenue 'Rent-a-Room' scheme, you can earn up to £4,250 a year in 1999–2000 by letting out a room in your home (and providing associated services such as food and laundry) without having to pay any tax on the income. For more information see Chapter 18.

Equity release

When you reach your 70s, it could be worth considering an equity release scheme. These come in a number of forms.

In the safest and simplest type of scheme, a home income plan, you take out a fixed-interest mortgage for up to, say, 75 per cent of the value of your home. The proceeds of the mortgage are used to buy you an annuity, which will give you a regular fixed income for life. Interest on the mortgage and basic-rate tax on the annuity are deducted from the income you receive (see Chapter 18 for more on the tax implications). The mortgage does not need to be repaid during your lifetime: it is usually repaid out of the sale of the property on death.

You should avoid the following variations:

- Schemes with varying mortgage interest rates – when interest rates are high much of your annuity income will be eaten up by mortgage repayments.
- 'Roll-up' plans that allow you to add the mortgage interest to your loan rather than paying it every month. The size of your loan will increase at an alarming rate, and you may be asked to pay off the interest once it rises above a certain level – if you cannot pay, you may be forced to sell your home.
- The use of mortgage proceeds to buy investment bonds rather than an annuity. These bonds can go down and up in value. If the investment return is too small to pay both the interest and your income, then some of the capital invested in the bond may be used – so the remaining money will have to work even harder to make up this loss and still pay an income.

Unfortunately, home income plans now offer rather small incomes – not helped by the abolition of mortgage-interest tax relief on new schemes (see page 208). You will usually get a higher income from a 'home reversion' scheme. In this case, you sell all or part of your house, retaining the right to live there as a tenant for the rest of your life. You can then use the cash from the sale to buy an annuity. Reversion schemes are worth considering, since they provide a higher income than home income plans and do not have to be used to buy an annuity; with most, however, you do not benefit from any subsequent increase in value of the part of your home you sold.

Another possibility is to set up your own scheme. Several building societies and some banks will provide an interest-only mortgage while leaving you to invest the cash released (though the warnings above on variable interest rates apply).

If you want to raise capital from your home specifically to pay for repairs, improvements or adaptations, the Home Improvement Trust* may be able to help. The Trust is a not-for-profit company that exists to help older people arrange loans to pay for repairs, improvements or adaptations.

Equity release can provide a useful boost to your income, but if you are considering this it is essential to get the scheme vetted by your solicitor. A number of different types of scheme have been launched recently, including a roll-up interest scheme with a guarantee of no negative equity, and 'shared appreciation' mortgages where instead of paying interest you give up a percentage of any increase in your property's value. The different types of scheme all have different pros and cons. Age Concern★ publishes various useful factsheets, including *Raising income or capital from your home*. Aspects to consider are:

- What might happen if you want to move house – you may be able to transfer your scheme, providing your new home is acceptable to the lender.
- What might happen if you want to sell up altogether, e.g. to move to a nursing home.
- The amount of scope for increasing your income. Most home income plans provide fixed income, but you may be able to borrow more to boost your income later.
- The effect on any state benefits. Means-tested benefits such as income support will be reduced or lost altogether.

Help if your income is very low

If you are on a very low income, you may be eligible for social security payments from the state which aim to meet your basic living expenses, such as food, clothing, footwear, fuel and accommodation. Most of these benefits are not paid out automatically – you must claim them. The main benefit is income support; it is estimated that around one million eligible claimants aged 60 or over fail to apply for this. Sometimes, this is because the amount of benefit involved seems too low to bother about. But, in other cases, people are put off claiming because of the benefit system or because they perceive that there is a stigma attached to claiming.

What counts as a low income?

How low does your income have to be before you qualify for this help? There is no single answer to this. The main benefit you might be eligible for is income support. The government lays down minimum levels of income (called the 'applicable amount') which people in different circumstances are deemed to need and, if your income comes to less than the amount deemed applicable to you, you may be entitled to enough income support to bring you up to that amount. Note that if your only income is the state basic pension, it is likely that you will be eligible for some income support to top it up.

The applicable amount of income support will be made up of several elements:

- · **The personal allowance** For the 1999–2000 tax year, this is £51.40 a week for a single person (over the age of 24) and £80.65 a week for a couple (if one or both are over 18).
- **Personal allowance for a child** Extra amounts ranging from £20.20 to £30.95 in 1999–2000 are payable for each child dependent on you – the amount varies according to the age of the child.
- **Premium payments** On top of the personal allowance(s), you may get a premium payment which reflects the extra income a person in various circumstances is deemed to need. If you qualify for more than one premium payment, you usually get just the highest one but, in some circumstances, you may be eligible for more than one premium payment. Premiums which are particularly relevant to retired people are shown in Table 1.
- **Housing costs** Extra amounts may be payable to meet accommodation costs – e.g. mortgage interest payments (but usually only after a delay of nine months) and some service charges – which will not be met through 'housing benefit' (see page 60).

The allowances and premiums are usually increased each April in line with the change in the Retail Prices Index over the year to the previous September.

The sum of allowances, premium payments and housing costs makes up the 'applicable amount'; whether you receive the full amount, a reduced amount or nothing at all depends on your income and capital.

You should note that in April 1999 income support rates for pensioners increased by an additional amount so that some people who previously were not entitled to benefit could qualify. The government has been referring to the new higher rates of income support as a 'minimum income guarantee'.

Table 1: Some income support premiums, 1999–2000

Premium	Description	Amount in 1999–2000
Pensioner premium	For pensioners aged 60 to 74	Single £23.60 Couple £35.95
Enhanced pensioner premium	For pensioners aged 75 to 79	Single £25.90 Couple £39.20
Higher pensioner premium	For pensioners aged 80 or more, or pensioners aged 60 or more and disabled	Single £30.85 Couple £44.65
Severe disability premium	For severely disabled people. This can be paid in addition to the higher pensioner premium	Single £39.75 Couple[1] £79.50
Carer premium	For people looking after someone who is disabled. This can be paid in addition to any other premium	£13.95

[1] Paid at the single person rate of £39.75 if only one member of the couple qualifies

EXAMPLE

Rose is a fit 82-year-old and lives alone. She has virtually no savings and qualifies for a reduced state basic pension of just £18.31 a week. She qualifies for housing benefit (see page 60) to cover the rent for her council bungalow and is eligible for income support. The amount of income support she can get is calculated as follows:

Applicable amount:	
Personal allowance	£51.40
Higher pensioner premium	£30.85
Total	£82.25
less Rose's income	£18.31
Income support payable	£63.94

The income limits

Income, for the purpose of calculating your entitlement to income support, is defined as money coming in from all sources: for example, your state pension(s), pension from a previous employer, pension from a personal pension plan, and any earnings from a job or business you run. Income does not include payments in kind, such as meals, or the repayment of expenses incurred while doing your job.

Some types of income are partially or fully ignored. For example, if you take in a lodger or sub-let part of your home, some of the money you receive is ignored. If, at the time you retire, you are still owed some pay by your employer, it will be ignored. If you work part-time, the first £5 of your earnings (£10 for a couple) will usually be disregarded.

Any income you receive from savings or investments is also ignored, but instead you are deemed to receive a certain notional income from your capital (see below). If interest you amass is re-invested it is deemed to increase the amount of your capital.

The capital limits

Your capital, for income support purposes, includes cash, bank and building society accounts, shares, unit trusts and any other investment you have. It does not usually include the value of your home if you own it, provided you are living there. Your personal possessions, such as your furniture, car and so on, usually do not count as capital, and the surrender value of life insurance policies is generally ignored. If you run your own business, your business assets are not counted as part of your capital for as long as the business is trading.

If your capital comes to £3,000 or less, it is ignored and will not affect your entitlement to income support – the limit applies to your joint capital, if you are a couple. If your capital amounts to more than £8,000, you will not be eligible for income support at all – once again, this limit applies to your joint capital if you are a couple. If you have more than £3,000 of capital but less than £8,000, you will be deemed to be receiving a set amount of income, as shown in Table 2 – this is called 'tariff income'. Your tariff income will therefore reduce the amount of income support to which you are entitled.

If you deliberately reduce your capital – by giving assets away to your family, say – in order to become entitled to income support or to increase your entitlement, you will be treated as if you still have the capital. If, however, you have to run down your capital to meet your living expenses, once it falls below £8,000 you will be able to claim income support.

Table 2: Income you're deemed to receive from your capital

Capital held by you, or by you and your partner	Assumed weekly income
£3,000.01 to £3,250	£ 1
£3,250.01 to £3,500	£ 2
£3,500.01 to £3,750	£ 3
£3,750.01 to £4,000	£ 4
£4,000.01 to £4,250	£ 5
£4,250.01 to £4,500	£ 6
£4,500.01 to £4,750	£ 7
£4,750.01 to £5,000	£ 8
£5,000.01 to £5,250	£ 9
£5,250.01 to £5,500	£10
£5,500.01 to £5,750	£11
£5,750.01 to £6,000	£12
£6,000.01 to £6,250	£13
£6,250.01 to £6,500	£14
£6,500.01 to £6,750	£15
£6,750.01 to £7,000	£16
£7,000.01 to £7,250	£17
£7,250.01 to £7,500	£18
£7,500.01 to £7,750	£19
£7,750.01 to £8,000	£20
over £8,000	You are not eligible for income support

Source: Benefits Agency leaflet IS20 *Income support guide*

If you move to a home

Before 1 April 1993, the cost of accommodation and meals in a residential or nursing home, up to a maximum limit, could be met through income support and the normal rules about applicable amounts did not apply. This continues to be the case for people who were already in this position before April 1993. For people on low incomes who move into homes from 1 April 1993 onwards, responsibility rests with the relevant local authority instead of the Department of Social Security (DSS). For more information see Chapter 9.

If you go into hospital

If you have to go into hospital as an in-patient, your income support is unchanged for the first six weeks (though if you qualify for the severe disability premium, this may stop after four weeks). After that, it is reduced.

If you are a single person, after six weeks you will get a much lower hospital personal allowance instead of the normal personal allowance and premium(s). This is set at either 25 per cent or 20 per cent of the basic state retirement pension rate and is supposed to help you meet continuing household costs, such as water rates and standing charges for fuel, phone, and so on. The higher rate of 25 per cent is paid from your seventh week in hospital to week 52. If you are in hospital for more than a year, the allowance falls to the lower 20 per cent rate or less if the hospital manages your money for you or a doctor certifies that you are unable to use the allowance.

If you are a couple and only one of you goes into hospital, there is generally no change to your income support for the first six weeks. After that and up to week 52, your normal applicable amount less the lower hospital personal allowance applies. After 52 weeks, you and your husband or wife are each assessed separately for income support.

If you are a couple and you both have to go into hospital, there is no change to your income support for the first six weeks. From the seventh week to week 52, you get twice the higher hospital personal allowance, and after 52 weeks you are each assessed separately for income support.

Any housing costs normally met through income support continue to be met while you are in hospital for as long as you are responsible for them. But, if you are in hospital for more than a year or it becomes clear that you will be, the housing cost payments will usually stop. If your husband or wife or someone else continues to live in the home, they may be eligible to claim housing costs through their income support instead.

Other state benefits

If you are on a low income, you may be eligible for housing benefit to help you meet accommodation costs, such as rent. This is paid by your local authority. You may also qualify for Council Tax Benefit (contact your local authority).

If you get a state retirement pension or any other state benefit, you will automatically receive a winter fuel allowance of £100 for each pensioner household. Also, from autumn 2000, you get a free TV licence once you are 75 or over. You may claim help with exceptional expenses, such as funeral costs, from the social fund. The social fund is also able to make interest-free loans to help you spread the cost of paying for an expensive one-off purchase, such as a washing machine. And if you need money urgently to meet your living costs or to buy some essential item, you may be able to get an interest-free crisis loan from the social fund. To find out about social fund payments and loans, contact your local Benefits Agency – look in the phone book.

If you qualify for income support, you will also be eligible for help with the cost of National Health Service (NHS) services. You will get:

- free prescriptions (these will be free anyway if you have reached state pension age)
- free dental treatment
- free eye tests and money-off vouchers for glasses if you need them
- free NHS wigs and fabric supports (for example, to support your abdomen or spine)
- help with travel costs to and from hospital for NHS treatment.

How to claim income support

You will need to fill in a detailed claim form which you can get by writing to, or calling in at, your local Benefits Agency or by filling in the coupon in leaflet IS1 *Income support*, which is available from Benefits Agency offices and many post offices. If you are not happy with the decision made in your case, you can ask for it to be reviewed or you can appeal (see Table 3 for useful leaflets to guide you through these procedures).

Payment is weekly, either direct into your bank or building society account or by orders that you cash at the post office. If you already get a state retirement pension paid by order, you may get an order book which combines both benefits.

Table 3: Useful leaflets if you are on a low income

Number	Name of leaflet
RM1	Retirement
RM2	Approaching Retirement?
RM3	Retired
IS1	Income support
IS8	Home-owners – help with housing costs
IS20	Income support guide
IS50	Income support – help if you live in a residential care home or nursing home
CTB1	Help with the council tax
RR1	Help with your rent: housing benefit
RR2	Guide to housing benefit and council tax benefit
CWP1	Extra help with heating costs when it's very cold
SB16	Guide to the social fund
N19	Going into hospital?
N192	Earning extra pension by cancelling your retirement
N1246	How to appeal
N1260	Guide to reviews and appeals
HC11	Help with NHS costs
D11	NHS dental treatment
G11	NHS sight tests and vouchers for glasses
H112	NHS hospital travel costs
P11	NHS prescriptions
WF11	NHS wigs and fabric supports
D49	What to do after a death
SSCC1	Care in the community: income support and other benefits

Table 3 lists leaflets which may be useful if you are on a low income. You can obtain them from the local Benefits Agency office. Alternatively, many post offices, libraries and advice centres have these leaflets.

Borrowing

Clearly, borrowing to meet a permanent shortfall in income compared with expenses is not a sound policy and you should avoid this. But, if you need to buy a large item, it may make sense to spread the cost over a period of time by using credit or taking out a loan.

Some shops and sales outlets offer 0 per cent finance – often available, for example, when you buy a car or electrical goods. Check for any hidden charges, though in general this type of credit is a good deal if you would have bought the car or electrical appliance anyway.

Be wary of shop or store cards which operate like credit or charge cards – the interest rates on these are often extremely high. Normal credit card charges can also be high if you generally have an outstanding balance, but if you use them for borrowing over a short period they can be cost-effective and very convenient. If you pay off your credit card balance every month, the cost will be small – or even nothing at all if it is a card which does not levy an annual fee – and, used in this way, credit cards can be a relatively safe and convenient way of buying costly items.

Avoid going overdrawn on your bank account without notifying your bank first – this can work out very costly as you will usually have to pay interest on the overdraft, charges for all your account transactions over a given period and extra fees for letters from your bank notifying you that you are overdrawn. If you can arrange an overdraft in advance this may be a reasonably priced way of borrowing, but your bank may try to persuade you to take out a personal loan instead – if so, check the cost carefully and compare with other forms of borrowing available.

In general, avoid loans secured on your home – they will generally be cheap compared with unsecured loans but, if you do not keep up the payments, you could lose your home. Also be wary of fixed-term loans for longer than you really need: lenders are entitled to charge early repayment penalties.

If your borrowing gets out of hand, do not be tempted to take out further loans to pay off creditors who are getting angry or threatening legal action. Get help at once – your local Citizens Advice Bureau (see phone book) can assist you, and some local authorities run debt advice agencies. National Debtline* may also help. Contact organisations to which you owe money and offer to pay back the borrowing or outstanding bills at a steady rate which you can manage. *The Which? Guide to Money* from Which? Books* also gives sound advice for balancing your budget in later life.

Chapter 6

Pension from an employer scheme

If you work as an employee, it is quite likely that your employer runs a pension scheme which you can join. If not, consider instead taking out a personal pension plan or one of the new stakeholder pension schemes, when these are introduced in 2001.

You do not have to join your employer pension scheme, but usually it will be a good way of saving for retirement because, once you join, your employer must pay in money on your behalf – you may also be required to contribute – and employer pension schemes qualify for special tax treatment:

- You and your employer get tax relief on the contributions you pay.
- The invested contributions build up tax-free.
- You can take part of the proceeds at retirement as a tax-free lump sum. (The rest must be taken as pension, which is taxable.)

Employer pension schemes generally provide a range of benefits other than just a retirement pension – for example, life insurance and a pension for your dependants if you die – see Chapter 8. If these other benefits are useful for you, an employer scheme is likely to be more attractive than a personal pension plan, because in the latter case you would have to pay in extra or take a lower pension at retirement in order to have these benefits included.

How much pension will you get?

This depends partly on what type of scheme is offered by your employer. There are two main types of scheme: final pay schemes and money purchase schemes.

Final pay schemes

This type of scheme is also called a 'final salary scheme' and is the most widely used type of 'defined benefit scheme'. They are not the most common type of employer scheme but more people are covered by them than by any other type, because large companies tend to offer final pay schemes.

With a final pay scheme, your retirement pension is worked out according to a formula based on your pay at or near retirement and the number of years for which you have been a member of the pension scheme. For example, you might get a pension of one-sixtieth of 'final pay' for each year. Pensions based on one-eightieth of final pay per year are also common.

'Final pay' will be defined in the rules of the scheme. 'Pay' may mean just your basic pay or it might also include bonuses, overtime, the value of some fringe benefits, and so on. 'Final' could mean your pay on some specified date, your average pay over the last three years, the average of your best three years' pay out of the last ten before retirement, or some other definition.

EXAMPLE 1

Alan retired from a dairy company, part of a larger commercial group, after 34 years in the pension scheme. The scheme paid a pension at retirement of one-sixtieth of final pay for each year. 'Final pay' meant the average of the best three years' pay out of the last ten, which worked out at £16,000 for Alan. His pension was calculated as follows:

$\frac{1}{60} \times £16,000 \times 34 = £9,067$ a year.

The great advantage of final pay schemes is that you have a good idea in advance of roughly how much pension you will get at retirement in terms of today's money. Moreover, you know that if your earnings rise then your expected pension will increase too, so your expected pension keeps broadly in line with inflation up to the time when you retire.

Money purchase schemes

These are also called 'defined contribution schemes'. Since many smaller companies, sometimes with only a few employees, run this

type of scheme – in addition to some large employers – money purchase schemes are very common. Note that some employers may
choose to convert their existing money purchase pension schemes
into stakeholder pension schemes, described in Chapter 7. There
was also a proposal, in late 1999, that employers should be able to
choose to have their defined contribution schemes governed by the
tax rules for stakeholder pensions, even if they do not qualify as
stakeholder pensions, rather than by the existing rules for employer
pension schemes described in this chapter.

With a money purchase scheme, your employer – and you too, if
it is a contributory scheme – pay in contributions which are usually
a set percentage of your pay. The contributions are invested to build
up a fund, which is used at retirement to buy a pension. How much
pension you get depends on 'annuity rates' at the time you retire.
The 'annuity rate' is the rate at which insurance companies (or
friendly societies) are willing to convert the lump sum which makes
up your fund into a regular income for life.

So, the amount of pension you get from a money purchase
scheme depends on four things:

- how much is invested
- how long the money is left invested
- how well the invested money grows
- annuity rates at the time you retire.

If annuity rates are low at the time you retire, you may find yourself with a smaller pension than you had expected. A useful available option, if the rules of your scheme allow it, is to put off buying
an annuity and instead draw an income direct from the pension
fund when you first retire.

Drawbacks of a money purchase scheme include the fact that
you cannot accurately estimate how much pension you will get at
retirement – either in terms of today's money or in terms of future
money values. In addition, although your contributions will generally increase in line with your pay, there are many other unpredictable elements, so that there is no link between the pension you
are building up and inflation up to the time you retire.

EXAMPLE 2

Sheila recently started work for a small engineering company with 25 employees. The company runs a money purchase pension scheme. To build up a retirement pension for Sheila, the firm pays into the scheme contributions equal to 10 per cent of Sheila's salary, and Sheila is required to contribute a further five per cent of her pay. This year, Sheila will earn £14,000, so a total of [10% × £14,000] + [5% × £14,000] = £2,100 will be paid into the scheme on her account.

The contributions which are paid in year by year are left to grow. If the £2,100 paid in this year grew by, say, one per cent more than inflation a year until Sheila's retirement in 15 years' time, the fund would have grown to £2,438 in terms of today's money. If the annuity rate then were, say, 7 per cent, the £2,438 could be used to buy a pension of £170 a year.

Assuming the growth and annuity rates did not change, each subsequent year's contributions would buy less than £170 pension because they would not have been invested for as long.

Other types of employer scheme

Some employer pension schemes combine both final pay and money purchase elements – for example, you might get a retirement pension which was the best of a pension worked out according to a final pay formula and the pension which could be bought with the fund built up by investing contributions. These combination schemes are often referred to as 'hybrid schemes'.

Final pay schemes are not the only sort of defined benefit scheme. Other less common variations include:

- **Average pay schemes** These are similar to final pay schemes except that the pension formula is based on the average of your pay throughout the whole time you belonged to the scheme, not just pay at or near retirement.
- **Revalued average earnings schemes** With these, your pension is based on pay during the whole time you belonged to the scheme, but each year's earnings are increased in line with inflation up until retirement. Such schemes can offer very good pensions, especially if your earnings peaked in mid-career rather than near retirement.

- **Salary grade schemes** You earn a set amount of pension for each year that your pay falls within a given band on the salary grid. The higher your earnings band, the more pension you 'earn'.
- **Flat rate schemes** With these, you get a fixed amount of pension for each year that you are in the scheme.

Group personal pension schemes

Increasingly, employers are turning to group personal pension schemes. Your employer arranges for a pension provider to offer personal pension plans to you and your fellow employees. The plans might have special terms – for example, lower than usual charges, more flexibility to alter contributions or additional benefits. But a group personal pension scheme (GPPS) is not an employer's scheme in the true sense. Your employer does not have to make any contributions to the personal plans and they are governed by the rules set out in Chapter 7, not the rules set out here.

EXAMPLE 3

Ralph earns £31,000 a year and belongs to a group personal pension scheme promoted at work. Ralph contributes 3 per cent of his earnings to the scheme and his employer adds a further 5 per cent. He has been in the group personal pension shcme for two years so far and expects to carry on with the plan until he retires in 15 years' time at the age of 65. By then, his pension fund is projected to have grown to £103,000 which, at present annuity rates, would mean a pension of about £8,500 a year. But that is in terms of future money; if inflation averaged, say, 3 per cent a year, the pension would be worth about £5,400 in current money. That's less than Ralph has worked out he needs.

Pension increases

Pensions built up from 6 April 1997 onwards must be increased in line with inflation up to a maximum of five per cent a year once they start to be paid. This applies to the whole pension, regardless of whether the scheme is contracted-out or not (see page 72). Schemes can choose to pay more (provided they do not breach Inland Revenue limits – see page 70).

For pensions built up before April 1997, the picture is more complex. Contracted-out pensions had to be increased by a specified amount (see page 72), but there was no legal requirement for other pensions to be increased at all. In practice, most schemes did make increases which could be:

- **Guaranteed** Public sector schemes – e.g. those covering civil servants, teachers and the police – guarantee to increase pensions in line with price inflation without any limit. Such open-ended promises are rare in the private sector, but guarantees of a rise in inflation up to a maximum of three per cent, say, were common prior to April 1997.
- **Discretionary** The scheme reviews the position, usually annually, and announces whatever increase seems appropriate and can be afforded. The whole increase might be discretionary, or a discretionary element might top up a low guaranteed increase.

Tax-free lump sum at retirement

One of the great advantages of employer pension schemes (and personal pension plans – see Chapter 7) over other types of retirement saving is that you can take part of the retirement proceeds in the form of a tax-free lump sum. With some schemes – particularly those covering people who work in the public sector, such as local authority employees and health service staff – you will receive the tax-free cash automatically. With other schemes, you can choose either to simply take a pension from the scheme or to swap part of the pension for a tax-free cash sum.

The rate at which pension is converted into lump sum by the employer scheme will depend on the rules of the scheme. For example, your pension might be reduced by £1 for every £12 you take in cash. As a rough guide, if you are entitled to the maximum pension of two-thirds of your final salary, and you opt to take the maximum lump sum of 1½ times your final salary, your pension will be reduced to about half your final salary.

Lump sum or not?

If you have the choice of taking the lump sum, what should you do? The conversion of pension to lump sum is usually based on the life expectancy of an average man or woman. So, if your health is poorer than average, you will probably be better off taking the largest lump sum that you can.

It used to be the case that even if your health was average or good you would do better by taking the lump sum and investing it in a purchased life annuity. Annuities you buy yourself provide a partially tax-free income (see Chapter 10), unlike a pension, which is taxed in full. If you have a money-purchase scheme, it is often still worth taking the cash. However, if you are in a final-salary scheme the argument is less clear cut nowadays.

If your pension scheme makes generous discretionary – i.e. not guaranteed – increases to pensions you should think carefully before deciding to swap pension for tax-free cash. The conversion rate will not usually take into account benefits which are not guaranteed, so you would be giving up the probability of pension increases without receiving any compensation for this.

Note that, in most schemes, while taking a lump sum reduces your own retirement pension, it will not reduce the amount of any widow's, widower's or dependants' pension which would be payable if you died.

Limits on your pension and lump sum

Because pension schemes benefit from special tax advantages, the Inland Revenue places limits on the benefits which you can have from a pension scheme. Due to a series of changes to the laws concerning pensions, there are three different tax regimes which could apply to an employer pension that you have built up. The three regimes are shown in Table 1. In addition to the limits shown, under any of the three regimes pensions can be increased each year, once they start to be paid, as long as they do not exceed the maximum possible pension increased in line with changes in the Retail Prices Index.

The Inland Revenue limits are set in relation to final pay, but this does not mean that they apply only to final pay schemes. In

Table 1: Inland Revenue limits on your pension and lump sum

Tax regime [1]	Limit on pension [2] at retirement [3]	Limit on tax-free lump sum at retirement [3]
Post-1989 regime Applies to: **(a)** a scheme set up on or after 14 March 1989; or **(b)** a scheme set up before 14 March 1989 but you joined on or after 1 June 1989; or **(c)** a scheme set up before 14 March 1989 which you joined on or after 17 March 1987 but before 1 June 1989, if you elect to be treated under the post-1989 regime	Two-thirds of final pay up to a maximum of £60,400 [4]	One-and-a-half times final pay up to a maximum of £135,900 [4]
1987–9 regime Applies to a scheme set up before 14 March 1989 which you joined on or after 17 March 1987 and before 1 June 1989 (unless you have opted to be treated under the post-1989 regime – see above)	Two-thirds of final pay	One-and-a-half times final pay up to a maximum of £150,000
Pre-1987 regime Applies to a scheme you joined before 17 March 1987	Two-thirds of final pay	One-and-a-half times final pay

[1] As well as the three categories of scheme listed here, it is possible for you to have joined a scheme after 1987 or 1989 but for the pre-1987 or 1987–89 regime rules to apply. This might be the case where, say, your employer's business had been restructured or party to a merger.

[2] This is the limit which applies if all your own benefits from the scheme are taken as pension. If part is taken as a lump sum (or certain other benefits), the maximum you can take as pension is reduced to less than the amount shown here.

[3] Under the 1987–89 regime and pre-1987 regime, these maximum limits apply at the normal retirement age for the scheme. Under the post-1989 regime, the limits apply at any age within the range 50 to 75.

[4] This is the limit proposed for the 1999–2000 tax year. The limit is based on an 'earnings cap' – a ceiling on the amount of final pay which can be used in the calculation. The earnings cap is usually increased each year in line with the Retail Prices Index.

fact, the limits apply to most employer pension schemes – even money purchase schemes. (However, the limits do not apply to group personal pension schemes which are instead covered by the rules in Chapter 7.) The rules set out here put an upper limit on the pension and lump sum which an employer scheme may provide but, in practice, most schemes provide less than the maximum benefits permitted.

Contracted-out pensions

Chapter 3 described the State Earnings Related Pension Scheme (SERPS). You may be 'contracted out' of SERPS through your employer pension scheme. This means that both you and your employer pay lower National Insurance contributions; you give up your right to build up SERPS pension for as long as you are contracted out and instead build up a pension in the employer scheme. Precisely what this means for your pension income overall depends on when, and the way in which, you are contracted out. (If you have belonged to more than one scheme and/or had a personal pension plan, you may have been contracted out on different bases at different times.)

Final pay schemes

If you were contracted out on a final pay basis before 6 April 1997, you could not lose out compared with what you would have had from SERPS because the state basically underwrote your pension. It worked like this: your employer's scheme had to pay you a defined pension at retirement called the Guaranteed Minimum Pension (GMP) and, once it started to be paid, the scheme had to increase the GMP by inflation up to three per cent a year. But, each year throughout retirement, the Department of Social Security (DSS) would calculate the full SERPS pension you would have had if you had never been contracted out, including the full index-linking which applies to state pensions (see page 37). From this, the DSS would deduct your GMP (including the three per cent increases). Whatever was left would constitute your remaining SERPS pension. So your SERPS pension plus GMP(s) would always total the full SERPS pension which you would have had without any contracting out.

For contracted-out pensions built up from 6 April 1997 onwards, the link with SERPS has been abolished. Instead, your employer's scheme must provide a package of benefits which, for at least nine out of ten scheme members, is at least as good as the benefits from a 'reference scheme'. The reference scheme benefits are fairly generous and most employees are likely to get a higher contracted-out pension than the SERPS pension given up – but there is no guarantee of this. In particular, you could lose out if inflation is high after you have retired, because the scheme does not have to increase your pension by any more than five per cent a year and the state no longer tops up the increases.

Money purchase schemes

If your employer scheme is contracted out on a money purchase basis, it is not committed to paying you a set amount of pension at retirement. Instead, it is committed to investing a given amount on your behalf. The amount is the savings which you and your employer make by paying lower National Insurance contributions – called the National Insurance rebate – plus tax relief on your part of the savings. It is your employer that agrees to invest this sum – he may or may not require you to contribute towards the scheme.

With this form of contracting out, you may be better or worse off than if you had not contracted out. This is because the amount of pension which the invested National Insurance rebate eventually provides depends – like any money purchase pension – on how well the investment grows and on annuity rates at the time the pension starts to be paid.

After retirement, the scheme increases the pension which results from the invested rebates by up to three per cent a year (or the rate of inflation if less) for pensions built up before 6 April 1997. The DSS, through your SERPS pension, at least partially tops this up if inflation runs at more than three per cent a year. For pensions built up from 6 April 1997 onwards, the scheme must increase the pension in line with inflation up to a maximum of five per cent a year, but the DSS no longer tops up the scheme increases.

Personal pension schemes

If your employer scheme is not contracted out, you can be a member of it and still contract out independently. You can do this by taking out a personal pension plan which is designed solely for contracting out. For details, see Chapter 7.

Should you contract out?

If your employer scheme is contracted out on a final pay basis, you will be automatically contracted out. Under the pre-April 1997 system it did not matter that this was the case since you could not lose by being contracted out in this way. Under the current system, the position is not so clear-cut, but you are unlikely to lose out.

If your employer scheme is contracted out on a money purchase basis, you cannot tell in advance whether this will be to your benefit or to your disadvantage. It depends on how your invested rebates grow and annuity rates at retirement. ('Unisex' annuity rates – i.e. the same for men and women – have to be used in the case of contracted-out pensions, even though women tend to live longer than men.) Until April 1997, the National Insurance savings (generally referred to as 'rebates') for contracting out were the same for everyone, regardless of age and sex. This meant that contracting out was likely to be a better deal for younger people (whose rebates would be invested for longer) and for men (whose rebates were invested for longer and who gave up less SERPS pension overall because they retired later). From April 1997 onwards, the rebates are age-related, making contracting out attractive even at older ages.

However, to contain costs the government has capped the rebates, so that from around your mid-fifties (if male) or mid-forties (if female) you might still be better off staying in SERPS. The difference between men and women remains because, although women's retirement age will in future be the same as men's, women currently in their mid-forties and older will still retire earlier than men of the same age.

What you pay

Some pension schemes are 'non-contributory' in which case you pay nothing at all – your employer foots the whole bill for the scheme. However, most schemes are 'contributory' and you will usually pay in a set proportion of your before-tax earnings – four or five per cent, say. Any contributions you pay qualify for tax relief at your highest rate.

EXAMPLE 4

Janet pays 3.5 per cent of her pay into her firm's pension scheme. In the 1999–2000 tax year, she earns £13,000, which means that she pays 3.5% x £13,000 = £455 into the scheme. However, the cost to her is less than £455 because the contributions are deducted from her pay before income tax is worked out. This means that she gets tax relief on the full amount at her highest tax rate of 23 per cent. This gives her tax relief of 23% × £455 = £104.65, making the true cost of the contributions to Janet just 77% x £455 = £350.35.

The Inland Revenue limits the amount which you can pay into an employer pension scheme in any one year to 15 per cent of your pensionable earnings. In addition, if you are covered by the post-1989 regime, there is also a cash limit which is related to earnings: for 1999–2000, only pensionable earnings up to £90,600 can be taken into account. This gives an overall maximum level on contributions of 15% × £90,600 = £13,590. The limit is usually increased each year in line with changes in the Retail Prices Index.

When is your pension paid?

The rules of your pension scheme will set a 'normal retirement age'. In the past, this was often the same as the state pension age – in other words, currently 60 for women and 65 for men. But, since the early 1990s, in order to comply with European legislation, many schemes have moved to an equal pension age – most commonly 65 – which applies to both men and women.

Inland Revenue rules prevent the maximum pension and other benefits being paid at very early ages. For schemes covered by the pre-1987 regime or 1987–89 regime, the earliest age at which the maximum pension can be paid is usually 60 for men and 55 for women. For post-1989 regime schemes, the lowest age for the maximum pension is 50 for both men and women. The Inland Revenue allows earlier ages than these for people working in certain types of job – for example, divers or professional footballers.

Special rules also apply if you have to retire early because of ill-health, which allow a scheme to pay out higher than normal pensions. These may be based on the number of years you would have worked if you could have carried on until normal retirement age.

Except in the case of ill-health, you should expect a lower pension if you decide to retire early. In a final pay scheme this will reflect the fact that you have fewer years' membership of the scheme and, possibly, that your final pay may be lower than if you had stayed right up until retirement. In a money purchase pension scheme, the lower pension reflects the fact that you will have paid in contributions for fewer years, the invested contributions will not have had as long to grow and your fund will have to buy a pension expected to last for longer.

If you carry on working after the normal retirement age for your scheme, what happens to your pension will depend on the rules of your scheme. You may be able to carry on making contributions and building up further pension. Often, however, you will simply get what are called 'actuarial increases'. This means that your pension is calculated at your normal retirement age and is then increased each year reflecting the expectation that, when it does start to be paid, the pension will be paid out over a shorter-than-normal period.

If you leave a scheme early

Once you have belonged to an employer pension scheme for two years, it is required to provide you with a pension which will be paid at retirement – this is called a 'preserved pension' or, sometimes, a 'deferred pension'. You can either leave these pension rights with the scheme or transfer them to another employer scheme, to a personal pension plan or to a special plan designed for this purpose, called a 'section 32 plan' or 'buy-out bond'.

If the only rights you have built up are those to a contracted-out pension, the scheme might 'buy you back' into the state (SERPS) scheme, in which case you will have no more claim on the employer scheme but will get SERPS pension from the state instead.

If you have belonged to a pension scheme for less than two years, the scheme does not have to promise you a pension and, instead, you can be offered the return of the contributions you have paid to date together with reasonable interest less tax deducted at a special rate. You cannot receive any contributions paid on your behalf by your employer.

Boosting your pension

If you are concerned that your retirement income may not be high enough to meet your needs, you may be able to increase it by building up extra pension in your employer scheme. Provided your total contributions towards the scheme remain within the 15 per cent limit set by the Inland Revenue (and the cash limit if the post-1989 regime applies to you), you can pay in extra amounts called 'Additional Voluntary Contributions' (AVCs). These qualify for tax relief in just the same way as other pension contributions.

AVCs are used to buy extra pension, pension increases, or widow's pension perhaps, either direct from the employer scheme or to top up the benefits from the employer scheme. However, AVCs which you started to make on or after 17 March 1987 cannot be used to provide or increase a tax-free lump sum. At present, you have to take the benefits from an AVC scheme at the same time as benefits from the main scheme. But the government has announced that in future you may be allowed to take AVC benefits earlier, provided you have reached at least age 50.

The extra contributions can either be paid into an AVC scheme run by your employer or paid into your own 'free-standing AVC' (FSAVC) scheme. All employer schemes must offer some kind of AVC facility. How it works will vary from scheme to scheme. For example, in a final pay scheme, your AVCs might buy extra years of membership, thus boosting your pension and other benefits, which are calculated according to a formula based on the number of years you have been in the scheme. But often the AVC scheme works on a straightforward money purchase basis – the AVCs are invested to provide a fund which, at retirement, is converted into pension and/or other benefits at the going rates which then apply.

FSAVC schemes always work on a money purchase basis. They are similar to personal pension plans (see Chapter 7) except that the fund which builds up must be used to buy benefits which, when added to your benefits from your employer scheme, do not come to more than the maximum amounts allowed under the Inland Revenue rules. The government has announced that, in future, you may be allowed to convert a personal pension plan which you have built up into an FSAVC scheme.

In theory, the main advantage of an FSAVC scheme over an AVC scheme run by your employer is that, with an FSAVC scheme, you have added flexibility and the freedom to choose how your contributions are invested. Traditionally, employer AVC schemes have tended to take a cautious approach to investment in order to keep down the risks but, with an FSAVC scheme, you can choose a much higher degree of risk and potential reward, if you want to.

However, the downsides of FSAVCs can be considerable – higher charges, and the reluctance of employers to make contributions to an FSAVC, even if they make contributions to an in-house AVC scheme. These downsides outweigh the possible advantages in most cases, and there have been concerns about the mis-selling of FSAVCs to people who would have been better-off with AVCs.

An FSAVC scheme can also be used for contracting out of SERPS (see page 72) but quirks in the rules mean that you will usually do better to contract out via a personal pension plan rather than an FSAVC scheme.

EXAMPLE 5

Mrs Black started an FSAVC scheme four years before taking early retirement from her job as a college lecturer. By retirement, she had built up a fund within her FSAVC scheme of around £6,500. A year before she retired, the insurance company with which she invested had estimated that her FSAVC scheme could be used to provide extra pension of around £641 a year. However, by the time she retired, a pension of only £366 a year was offered. The insurance company explained that annuity rates had fallen. The reduced income also reflected the fact that the pension had to be paid at an early start date and thus was expected to be paid out for longer overall. Although the small print for the FSAVC did warn that the pension would be subject to current annuity rates, Mrs Black felt that the warnings were not clear enough. She was locked into a pension which was much lower than her expectations, which made a nonsense of her retirement planning.

Since the Inland Revenue maximum limits on the benefits you can have from a pension scheme are set in terms of your final pay, while FSAVC and some AVC schemes work on a money purchase basis, it is not easy in advance to know whether or not using the proceeds of your AVC or FSAVC scheme will take you over the limits. In the past, going over the limits could mean that your AVCs were wasted but, for AVCs started since 27 July 1989, any 'excess' contributions can be repaid to you at retirement after deduction of tax at a special rate. However, for the vast majority of people, there is plenty of scope to add to the benefits from the employer scheme without going over the Inland Revenue limits.

·How safe is your pension?

In the Robert Maxwell affair, nearly £450 million was stolen from the pension funds of companies (such as Mirror Group Newspapers) in the Maxwell empire, shaking the complacent view which most people had held about the safety of company pension schemes. Yet, although this affair captured the newspaper headlines, employer pension schemes in general have not been prone to the scandals which have been so prevalent in other areas of the financial services industry. It is impossible to guarantee absolute safety from fraud, but employer pension schemes generally have a good record. The risk to you of retiring with an inadequate income if you do not make pension savings far outweighs the risk that you will lose your money if you put it into an employer pension scheme.

However, it was clear that the piecemeal and complex legislation surrounding employers' schemes was not adequate. An enquiry was set up which ultimately led to the Pensions Act 1995. This introduced a regime which aims to make employers' pension schemes more secure. The main measures are:

- **The Occupational Pensions Regulatory Authority*** **(OPRA)** This regulator has tough powers to investigate pension schemes. However, rather than proactively checking on schemes, OPRA is largely reactive, responding to reports of potential fraud and suspicious activity.
- **Whistle blowing** The experts involved in an employer scheme will be under a duty to report to OPRA if they suspect that something might be amiss with the scheme.
- **More effective trustees** Trustees – the people responsible for looking after the pension fund and ensuring it is used according to the scheme rules – have new responsibilities and face hefty fines if they don't match up to the job. Trustees must agree an investment policy and must ensure that proper experts are appointed to advise on and help run the scheme. They must

keep track of the employer's contributions to the scheme and take action if money is not paid in according to schedule. Although there is no legal requirement for training, OPRA expects trustees to be properly trained for this demanding role.

- **Member-nominated trustees** Although trustees are meant to act in the interests of all the scheme beneficiaries and not represent any one group, the Maxwell affair highlighted the dangers where an employer dominates the trustee role. So, at least a third of the scheme trustees must be nominated by the members. However, the employer can opt out of this requirement if the members agree. Also, the employer can veto the appointment of a trustee who is not a member of the scheme – which could prevent members nominating, say, a trade union official.

- **Minimum Funding Requirement** Pension funds must be checked periodically to ensure that the assets are sufficient to pay the future benefits as they fall due on the retirement or death of members. Schemes also have to show that the pension fund could pay everyone the accumulated rights due to them if the scheme went bust today.

- **Compensation fund** This will pay out if your employer goes bust and the shortfall in the scheme has arisen from fraud, theft or some other dishonesty. There are limits on the amount paid out, and no payment may be made at all in some cases, so some members will still lose out.

Pension rights and divorce

Even in these days of liberation, many women still rely largely on their husbands to save for retirement. This reflects traditional attitudes to gender roles; in the past, it was often expected that on marriage women would give up any career and concentrate on family responsibilities. Women might return to work later but often this would be to lower paid, possibly part-time jobs, which offered little or no prospect of adequate pension saving. Meanwhile, men have been traditionally cast as the breadwinners and are more likely to have spent their working lives in steady employment, often building up pension rights through membership of an employer pension scheme.

This traditional arrangement can work very well for a couple in a stable relationship, but a third of all marriages in the UK now end in divorce. Apart from the family home, pension rights are likely to be the most valuable asset a couple own. Although the rights may have been built up by the man, it will frequently be the case that they should be viewed as a joint asset. For over 25 years, pension and legal professionals have been trying to sort out how pension rights should be treated on divorce in order to be fair to both the husband and wife.

In practice, until June 1996, pensions were often left out of the divorce settlement altogether, especially if the couple made their own financial arrangement. Where the court was involved, pension rights were not normally considered unless the spouse without a pension (typically, the wife) was aged at least 45. If pension rights were taken into account, the usual solution was to award the wife a greater share of other assets – such as the family home – to compensate for the loss of expected retirement income. But this was a poor solution if there were few other assets to share out.

Since June 1996, the Pensions Act 1995 has required courts to take account of pension rights as a matter of course and gives the courts power to order that part of a pension be 'earmarked' and paid out to the ex-spouse once the pension-holder starts to draw the pension. This is a step in the right direction, but not ideal, because the ex-wife can't draw her pension before the ex-husband (a particular problem if the woman is older than the man); the ex-husband is likely to stop contributing to the pension scheme or plan once part has been earmarked (which, particularly in a final pay scheme, will reduce the expected pension); and pension schemes have the onerous task of keeping track of ex-spouses.

A better solution was proposed in legislation before Parliament in late 1999. This introduces the option of pension sharing on divorce and will allow pension rights to be treated like other assets, and transferred in part or whole from one spouse to the other as part of a financial settlement. However, pension sharing will not be compulsory – it will still be possible to offset pension rights against other assets or to use the existing earmarking arrangements.

When you reach retirement

No later than three months before you reach the normal retirement age for your job, or before the date on which you decide to retire, you should get in touch with the administrators of your pension scheme to find out how much pension you can expect and what options you have. See pages 15–16 for how to do this.

If you would like to maintain contact with other retired members, see whether there is a pensioners' association attached to the scheme. Associations can serve a variety of purposes – e.g. social, providing advice or even financial support and lobbying on issues important to pensioners. If your scheme does not have a pensioners' association, consider setting one up – your employer may be persuaded to provide administrative help, premises for meetings, and so on.

Chapter 7

Personal pension plans and stakeholder pensions

If you are self-employed or an employee whose employer does not offer a pension scheme, you will need to make your own arrangement about saving for retirement. The best way of doing this was to take out a personal pension plan, but from April 2001 you will have a further choice with a stakeholder pension (see overleaf).

Even if your employer does run a pension scheme, personal pension plans are open to you if you have chosen not to join your employer scheme. Personal plans can also be used to contract out of SERPS (see pages 73–4) if you belong to an employer scheme which is not itself contracted out.

You can invest in a personal pension plan provided you are 16 or more and no older than 75. Like employer pension schemes, personal pension plans benefit from tax advantages, which make them a better route for retirement saving than most other forms of investment. These tax advantages are:

- what you pay in qualifies for tax relief
- your invested money builds up tax-free
- you can take part of the proceeds as a tax-free lump sum (the rest is taken as pension, which is taxable).

Unlike employer schemes, personal plans do not automatically give you a package of benefits. If you want life insurance or a widow's or widower's pension to be payable in the event of your death, you will have to pay extra for these. And, when you want to start taking your pension, you will have to decide whether you want regular pension increases and, if so, your starting pension will be a lot lower than if you had opted for a flat pension.

A further disadvantage of personal pension plans is that a sizeable part of your personal pension fund – around one-fifth on average – may go in charges. With an employer scheme, charges tend to be lower and are often paid directly by the employer rather than from the pension fund. However, there will be a maximum charge on stakeholder pensions, and some personal plans are dropping their charges to compete.

Stakeholder pensions

At the time of writing, in late 1999, legislation was going through Parliament to allow the introduction of a new type of 'stakeholder' pension from April 2001. Many of the details had not yet been settled, so if you are considering investing in your own pension plan be sure to check the current position before you buy.

Stakeholder pensions will work on a money purchase basis, like personal pension plans, and will have the same tax benefits. However, unlike personal pensions, they will be set up either as trusts or (under current proposals) will be run by an authorised stakeholder manager. Another key difference is that stakeholder pensions will have to meet minimum standards. In particular, there will be a limit on the charges the scheme managers can make, and they must allow transfers to and from other pension schemes without additional charges.

Who can join?

Stakeholder schemes will be open to employees and the self-employed. You will also be able to contribute if you are not actually working, using money from savings, for example. Where an employer has employees who are not eligible to join its pension scheme but who earn more than a set amount (£66 a week in 1999–2000 or its equivalent), the employer must adopt a stakeholder scheme into which it will pay employees' contributions. However, some existing employers' pension schemes may themselves convert into stakeholder schemes. Stakeholder schemes may also be set up for groups such as members of trade unions, people working in a particular industry, or people in a particular geographical area.

How much can you contribute?

The government has proposed that the same contribution rules should apply to both personal pension plans and stakeholder pensions. You will be able to have any number of schemes as long as the overall contribution limit is not exceeded. You will be able to put in up to £3,600 each tax year, however much or little you earn, or even if you have no earnings at all. If you want to put in more, you can do so, provided you are earning and your contributions do not exceed a set percentage of your earnings (the percentages are the same as those described for personal pension plans in Table 3 on page 91). If you then stop earning, you can still contribute more than £3,600 for up to five years.

Stakeholder, personal pension, or employer's scheme?

Employers' schemes will continue to have an advantage because the employer must contribute a substantial part of the cost of the pension, but it is yet to be seen what impact the new schemes will have on the availability of employers' schemes. Stakeholder schemes are intended to be better value than personal pension plans, but if you are already contributing regularly to a personal pension plan there may be hefty charges if you want to transfer it to a stakeholder pension. Some personal pension plans now offer a low-charge switch but until the shape of the market becomes clearer, you may want to keep your options open, for example by choosing a single premium personal pension plan (see page 90).

Personal pension plans

All personal pension plans (and the new stakeholder schemes) work on a money purchase basis. This means that you cannot have any clear idea in advance of how much pension you will get when you do retire. It depends on four factors:

- how much you pay into your plan
- how long you invest for
- how well the fund of invested money grows
- how much pension you can buy with your fund (dependent on future annuity rates at the time you want to start your pension).

The younger you are when you pay into your plan, the longer your contributions will be invested and thus the larger your fund is likely to be. Similarly, if you intend to retire early, your contributions will not have so long to be invested, so you will either have to settle for a lower pension or be prepared to invest more in your plan. You can choose how your fund is invested (see page 97), which will be an important factor influencing how your fund grows.

Converting your pension fund into an annuity dictates your pension income for your whole retirement. Traditionally, you have to buy an annuity at the time you want your pension to start. This means that if annuity rates are low, you either have to put up with a low lifetime pension or put off your retirement in the hope that annuity rates will rise.

However, for personal pension plans set up on or after 1 May 1995, you can put off drawing your pension as late as age 75, if you want to and the plan rules allow it, while drawing an income direct from your pension fund. The amount of income you can withdraw is linked to what an annuity would have provided at the then going rate, and there are periodic checks to make sure that your pension fund is not being used up too fast. The maximum income is what an annuity for a single person would provide (see Table 1) as set out in tables produced by the government; the minimum is 35 per cent of the maximum.

The advantages of doing this are, first, that you can avoid the low annuity trap and yet still retire when you want to and, secondly, your fund is left invested and can carry on growing. In addition, since you take the tax-free lump sum at the time you start to withdraw an income, this is a way of releasing a substantial cash sum – if you don't really need the pension yet, you can take the minimum income allowed.

But there are drawbacks, too. If you invest your fund primarily for growth, you also risk it falling in value – a risk most people cannot afford to take near retirement. If you invest more cautiously – e.g. in deposits and government stocks – your fund may grow too slowly to support the income withdrawals you would like. So these flexible annuity plans may not be suitable for everyone.

Choices on retirement

You do not have to accept the annuity rate offered by the company with whom you have built up your pension plan. You usually have an 'open market option', which gives you the right to shop around for the best available annuity rates. It makes sense to use this option, since some companies specialise in annuities and offer very competitive rates whereas other companies do not.

How much pension you get will also depend on what choices you make at retirement:

- The earlier you retire, the lower your pension will be because it will have to be paid out for longer. (Women also get less pension than a man of the same age for the same reason – i.e. they are expected to live longer on average.)
- Your starting pension will be higher if it is paid at a flat rate which does not change over the years. But, if you choose a flat-rate pension, you must realise that inflation during your retirement will reduce the buying power of the pension (see Chapter 3), so that what seemed a generous amount at the start of retirement may be a scanty income 20 years later.
- If you are married, you may want to have a pension which will continue to be paid to your wife or husband if you die first – choosing this option will also reduce your starting pension.
- Another common option is to receive a guarantee that your pension will be paid for at least five years, even if you die within that time – this ensures that there is a pension (or cash equivalent) available for a time for your husband or wife or heirs.

Table 1 shows, for a fund of £10,000, examples of how much pension you could have got in September 1999 if you had taken up various options. Although not shown in this Table, you can also combine options, choosing, for example, a pension paid for the life of both you and your spouse and increasing by five per cent a year.

Table 1: Typical starting income from different types of annuity

Type of annuity	Income in the first year for each £10,000 invested for		
	A man aged 65	A woman aged 60	Joint annuity for man aged 65 and woman aged 60 (no reduction on first death)
Level annuity, no guarantees	£871	£679	£623
Level annuity with 5-year guarantee	£858	£676	£623
Increasing by 5% a year, no guarantee	£550	£367	£321

Rates at 17 September 1999
Source: *Moneyfacts Fax Services*

There are no Inland Revenue limits on the amount of pension you can take out of a personal pension plan, only on what you can put in.

Tax-free lump sum at retirement

You can take part of the proceeds from your plan as a tax-free lump sum instead of as pension. This is often worth doing because, even if your greatest need is for income, you can use the lump sum to buy an annuity. Annuities you choose to buy are taxed differently from the 'compulsory purchase' annuity that your pension fund buys to provide you with a pension. The pension you give up would have been taxable, but the income from an annuity you choose to buy is only partly taxable. The income from an annuity you buy is deemed to be made up of two elements: pure income, which is taxable; and return of part of your capital with each payment – this element is tax-free. So the after-tax income from an annuity you buy with your tax-free lump sum should be greater than the after-tax pension which you give up.

Inland Revenue rules limit the amount of tax-free cash you can take from your plan. The limits have changed from time to time but, broadly, if you first took out your plan before 1 July 1988 (called a retirement annuity contract), the maximum lump sum is three times the remaining pension. If you took out your plan on or after 1 July 1988 (called a personal pension plan), the maximum tax-free cash is one-quarter of your pension fund. This limit of one-quarter also applies to stakeholder pensions. If you have a retirement annuity contract, you can switch to a personal pension plan at any time, in which case the personal plan limit will apply. If you exercise your 'open market option' (see page 86) when you come to take your pension, a retirement annuity contract will automatically be converted to a personal pension plan.

Contracted-out pensions

Provided you are eligible for SERPS (see page 37), you can use a personal pension plan (or stakeholder pension when available) to contract out. You can do this even if you already belong to an employer pension scheme, as long as you are not already contracted out through the employer scheme.

If you are contracted out using a personal pension plan, you give up your right to build up SERPS pension during the period you are contracted out. However, you do not pay lower National Insurance contributions (as you would if you contracted out through an employer scheme – see page 72). Instead, you and your employer both pay contributions at the full rate but part of them, called the 'National Insurance rebate', is paid back in the form of contributions to your pension plan. Tax relief at the basic rate on your part of the National Insurance rebate is also paid into the plan. Until 5 April 1997, the rebate was the same whatever your age or sex (except that, for a time, people aged 30 or over qualified for a bonus). From 6 April 1997 onwards, the rebates are age-related. Table 2 gives some examples of the amount which the government will pay into your plan for 1999–2000.

The rebate and tax relief paid into your plan are left to grow and the resulting fund is used at retirement (on or after the state pension age) to provide you with a pension. How much pension you get depends on how well the investment grows and annuity rates at the time you retire (note that the same annuity rate applies to both men and women). In other words, you are contracted out on a money purchase basis (see pages 65–7), so you could end up with more or less pension from your personal plan than the SERPS pension which you gave up.

Table 2: What the government pays towards your contracted-out personal plan in 1999–2000[1]

Yearly earnings	Amount paid into the scheme if you are aged:					
	25	30	35	40	45	50
	Size of rebate					
	(4.3%)	(4.5%)	(4.8%)	(5.5%)	(7.1%)	(9.0%)
Under £3,432[2]	£ 0	£ 0	£ 0	£ 0	£ 0	£ 0
£ 5,000	£ 75	£ 78	£ 83	£ 94	£119	£149
£10,000	£314	£327	£347	£393	£498	£623
£15,000	£553	£576	£611	£692	£877	£1,097
£20,000	£792	£825	£875	£991	£1,256	£1,571
£26,000 or more [3]	£1,079	£1,124	£1,192	£1,350	£1,711	£2,139

[1] Including tax relief and rounded to the nearest £
[2] The lower earnings limit for 1999–2000
[3] The upper earnings limit for 1999–2000

Should you contract out?

Before rebates became age-related, contracting out looked more attractive the younger you were, because the rebates paid into a young person's plan had longer to grow into a sizeable pension fund. Contracting out has also been more attractive for men than for women, in the past, because women's state pension age has been earlier than men's, reducing the length of time for which rebates were left invested and increasing the period over which the pension had to be paid. However, the position has changed.

From April 1997, rebates are age-related. If they continued to increase right through to pension age, contracting out would look attractive whatever your age. But, to contain costs, the government has capped the rebates from age 46 onwards. Above that age, contracting out starts to look less attractive. For women born after 5 March 1955, the state pension age is the same as for men, i.e. 65. Therefore only women in their mid-40s and older have an earlier pension age.

Combining the age and sex factors suggests that contracting out of SERPS ceases to be attractive for men from their mid-50s onwards, say, and for women from their mid-40s onwards. But, if you are already contracted out through a personal pension plan, you may be better off staying contracted out rather than stopping your plan, because of the impact of charges (see page 100).

Contracting out will also look more attractive the greater your optimism about investment growth.

What you pay

You can take out a plan to which you make regular payments – for example, £50 a month or £500 a year might be the minimum regular contribution – or a plan which requires just a single lump sum – £500 or £1,000 might be the minimum in this case. Some plans are very flexible, allowing you to make additional payments as and when you choose.

There are few Inland Revenue limits on the benefits which you can take from a personal pension plan. But, as you might expect, given the tax advantages of personal plans, the Inland Revenue does put bounds on the amount you can pay into a plan. The limits currently vary according to your age and whether you have a retirement annuity contract (the type of personal pension available before 1 July 1988) or a personal pension plan.

It is proposed that, from April 2001, the same limits would apply to both personal pension plans and stakeholder pensions, i.e. contributions up to £3,600 each tax year would be allowed irrespective of your earnings, but above £3,600 the limits shown in Table 3 would apply.

· Until April 2001, however, the maximum contribution is set as a percentage of your 'net relevant earnings'. If you are self-employed, this means your profits for tax purposes; if you are an employee, this means your total before-tax pay including the value of most taxable fringe benefits (such as a company car). Table 3 shows the contribution limits which apply to personal pension plans. Only net relevant earnings up to £90,600 a year can be taken into account in 1999–2000, which puts an overall cash limit on the amount of contributions you can make. This 'earnings cap' is generally increased each year in line with changes in the Retail Prices Index.

Table 4 shows the limits which apply to retirement annuity contracts. These are set only in terms of a percentage of earnings – there is no overall cash limit. If you have both a retirement annuity contract and a personal pension plan, the relevant limits apply to each plan respectively, but your total contributions to both plans must not exceed the personal pension plan limits.

National Insurance rebates and the tax relief on them (see 'Contracted-out pensions' on pages 88–9) do not count towards your contribution limit. If you are an employee, your employer can pay contributions into your personal plan. This is a fairly rare practice with individual plans, but some employers have arranged so-called 'group personal plans' (see page 68) as an alternative to an

Table 3: Yearly contribution limits for a personal pension plan

Your age at the start of the tax year (6 April)	Contribution limit as a percentage of net relevant earnings	Overall cash limit on contributions for 1999–2000
Up to 35	17.5%	£14,700
36 to 45	20%	£16,800
46 to 50	25%	£21,000
51 to 55	30%	£25,200
56 to 60	35%	£29,400
60 to 74	40%	£33,600
75 and over	You can no longer contribute	

Table 4: Yearly contribution limits for a retirement annuity contract[1]

Your age at the start of the tax year (6 April)	Contribution limit as a percentage of net relevant earnings
Up to 50	17.5%
51 to 55	20%
56 to 60	22.5%
61 to 74	27.5%
75 and over	You can no longer contribute

[1] Personal pension plans taken out before 1 July 1988.

employer pension scheme, and, in the latter case, the employer will sometimes contribute. Any employer's contributions will count towards the limit on overall contributions.

How you pay

Currently, if you are self-employed, you make 'gross' payments to your personal pension plan – in other words, before deducting any tax relief. You then claim tax relief at your highest rate by writing to your tax office or through your tax return.

If you are an employee and you have a retirement annuity contract, you will make gross payments and will have to claim tax relief at your highest rate in the same way as a self-employed person. The tax relief due may then be given through the Pay-As-You-Earn system. If you are an employee and you have a personal pension plan, you make payments after deducting tax relief at the basic rate. You get this relief even if you pay little or no tax. If you are a basic-rate taxpayer, you have had the full relief due. If you are a higher-rate taxpayer, tax relief at the higher rate is payable and you will have to claim this either by writing to your tax office or via your tax return.

From April 2001, it is proposed that contributions to retirement annuity contracts, personal pension plans and stakeholder pensions will all be made after deducting basic-rate tax relief (any higher-rate tax relief will be claimed through your tax return or your PAYE code).

The carry-back rule

Until April 2001, when this rule is likely to be abolished, you can ask for pension contributions that you make in this tax year to be treated as if they had been paid in the previous tax year (and, if you had no net relevant earnings last year, then you can carry back the contribution two years). You must have enough unused tax relief in the earlier year to cover the contribution, and you will get tax relief on your contributions at the earlier year's tax rates.

The carry-back rule can be a particularly useful device if you run your own business, since you might not know until after the end of the tax year how much you want to contribute. Under the new tax system of self-assessment, which affects the self-employed and other people who receive a tax return, income tax due for 1999–2000 is payable in two interim instalments on 31 January 2000 and 31 July 2000 with a final instalment (or rebate) on 31 January 2001. Tax relief on contributions carried back to 1999–2000 will usually be treated as advance payments of the instalments. No relief will be given until your tax return for 1999–2000 has been sent in to your tax office. At that stage, your final instalment for the year can be worked out. In the first instance, tax relief on contributions is normally set against the final instalment due on 31 January 2001. If

---

EXAMPLE

Janet is self-employed as a freelance journalist. Her accounting year ends on 31 March each year and there is a few months' delay before her accounts are made up. In June 2000, Janet has her accounts ready and knows that she made enough profit in 1999–2000 to allow her to make a pension contribution of £8,000. She pays the contribution in June 2000, and fills in the relevant box of her tax return for it to be carried back to 1999–2000. Janet has already paid her first interim instalment of tax for 1999–2000 on 31 January 2000 which was set at £3,000. Her second instalment of £3,000 is due on 31 July 2000 and her tax return reveals that a final payment of £50 will be due on 31 January 2001. The final and second interim instalments are reduced by the amount of tax relief due on the pension contribution (which amounts to 23% × £8,000 = £1,840 since Janet pays basic-rate tax on at least £8,000 of her income for 1999–2000). This means that her final instalment becomes nil (£50 – £50), leaving £1,840 – £50 = £1,790 tax relief to set against the July instalment. The July instalment therefore becomes £3,000 – £1,790 = £1,210.

Janet's total tax bill for 1999–2000 is therefore £4,210. But her 2000–2001 instalments are based on the original £6,050 tax bill before any reduction due to carrying back pension contributions.

---

relief comes to more than the final instalment, the remainder is set against any yet-to-be-paid interim instalment(s). If the tax relief due comes to more than all the unpaid instalments for the year, you will receive a tax rebate.

When is the pension paid?

You do not have to retire from work in order to start taking a pension from a personal plan. However, the Inland Revenue does restrict you taking your pension at too early an age.

With a retirement annuity contract, the earliest age at which Inland Revenue rules let you start to take your pension is normally 60. If you have to give up your normal work because of ill-health, then it may be paid at an earlier age. Also, earlier pension ages apply to some types of job – see Table 5. However, in practice, you can always switch to a personal pension plan, in which case lower minimum pension ages apply.

The 'special pension' ages of 50 and 55 in Table 5 do not apply to personal pension plans since under their rules these ages can be chosen by anyone. With personal plans, the youngest age at which you can start to take the pension is 50, though, once again, you may be able to take the pension even earlier if you have to retire from your usual work because of ill-health.

With all kinds of plans, including stakeholder pensions, you must start to take your pension by the time you reach age 75.

Within the Inland Revenue limits, plan providers will set their own rules about the pension ages applicable to their plans. With some plans, you will be required to say at the outset when you expect to take your pension – though you may be able to change your mind subsequently without penalty. Many plans are completely flexible and leave you to decide on any pension age (within plan limits) at the time you want to start taking the pension.

You can have more than one plan at a time, so it can be a good idea to have several plans from which you can start to take a pension at different ages. This can help you ease gently out of work – perhaps cutting down to part-time employment before eventually retiring altogether. It can also help you to plan for extra income required later in retirement (see Chapter 4).

Table 5: Jobs with early retirement ages

Age	Occupation	Age	Occupation
35	Athletes	50	Croupiers
	Badminton players		Martial arts instructors
	Boxers		Money broker dealers
	Cyclists		Newscasters
	Dancers		Offshore riggers
	Footballers		Royal Navy Reservists
	Models		Rugby League referees
	National Hunt jockeys		Territorial Army members
	Rugby League players		
	Squash players	55	Air pilots
	Table tennis players		Brass instrumentalists
	Tennis players		Distant water trawlermen
	Wrestlers		Fishermen (part-time)
			In-shore fishermen
40	Cricketers, golfers		Money broker dealer
	Motor cycle riders		directors
	Motor racing drivers		Nurses, midwives etc.
	Speedway riders		National Health Service
	Trapeze artists		psychiatrists
	Divers		Part-time firemen
			Singers
45	Flat-racing jockeys		
	Non-commissioned Royal		
	Marine Reservists		

If you stop a plan early

You should be wary of ceasing to pay into a regular premium plan soon after taking it out. Charges made by plan providers tend to be heaviest in the early years of a plan and you could find that, if you stop the plan then, it has a very low value or even no value at all, in which case your contributions will have been wasted. Even when your plan does have some value, you need to check what will happen if you stop making regular payments – with some plans, charges carry on being deducted and erode the value of your plan.

If you stop a plan and it does have some value, you can leave it invested with the plan provider or, if you prefer, you can transfer it to another personal plan or to an employer scheme, provided the plan or scheme agrees to accept the transfer. There may be charges for making the transfer and you may lose bonuses payable only to people who keep the plan with the original plan provider, so check carefully before making any decision.

Boosting your pension

As you get older, you are likely to develop a clearer idea of whether your expected retirement income is likely to be sufficient. If it looks on the low side, one way to try to boost it is by investing more in your personal pension plan. As Tables 3 and 4 on pages 91–92 show, the amount that you can save through these plans increases as you get older, so there is scope for boosting your contributions.

There is another way in which you can increase the amount you save and still qualify for tax relief on your contributions: by using the carry-forward rules. However, the government proposes to abolish the carry-forward rules from April 2001 when the (rather more flexible) rules of stakeholder pensions will be introduced instead (see pages 84–5).

The carry-forward rules

If you have unused contribution relief from any of the previous six tax years, you can carry forward this relief to cover a contribution made in the current tax year. You must use up the current year's limit first and you must always carry forward the earliest year's unused relief first. You get tax relief at the current year's tax rates.

You can combine the carry-forward and carry-back rules (see pages 92–4), so if you are asking for a contribution paid in 2000–2001 to be treated as if it had been paid in 1999–2000, you can also (if necessary) set the contribution against unused contribution limits from as far back as 1993–1994.

Note that, while your contribution limits are worked out in relation to your earnings, you do not actually have to make pension savings out of your earnings in order to qualify for tax relief. Provided you have the necessary unused contribution limit and the total you contribute does not exceed the whole of your relevant earnings for the year in which contributions are paid (or being treated as paid), the actual money invested can be from some other source such as your capital, an inheritance or a redundancy payment.

How your money is invested

When you take out a personal pension plan, you choose how you want your money to be invested. There are two main types of investment – on a with-profits basis or on a unit-linked basis.

With-profits basis

Traditionally, with a with-profits plan, the amount of your investment would never fall but would grow at a steady pace as bonuses (called 'reversionary bonuses') were regularly added. Once added, a bonus could not be taken away and, although the bonus rate could change, plan providers would try to maintain a stable bonus rate – though recent years have seen many companies cutting their bonus rates. In addition, when you came to take your pension, an extra bonus (called a 'terminal bonus') would be added to the plan. The size of the bonuses reflected the general profitability of the plan provider, which in turn would reflect the performance of the company's investments, expenses faced by the company, the proportion of profits paid out to any shareholders, and so on.

These days, it is very hard to find a personal pension plan that works on a traditional with-profits basis. Instead, most plan providers offer 'unitised with-profits policies'. With these, your contributions buy units in a with-profits fund. At regular intervals, either the value of the units is increased or bonus units are added (the equivalent of the traditional reversionary bonuses) and, when you come to take a pension, a terminal bonus is added to your units. The bonuses largely reflect the investment experience of the plan provider; instead of expenses entering into the bonus calculation, distinct charges are set against the plan. In many ways, unitised with-profits plans are similar to the traditional policies, but a major difference is that plan providers retain the right to revalue the cash-in value of units – downwards as well as upwards – if investment experience suggests that this is warranted. Thus, unitised with-profits plans are not as secure for investors as the traditional plans were.

Plan providers have switched to unitised with-profits policies for two main reasons. Firstly, some companies had in the past paid out too much in bonuses on traditional policies. The situation could not continue indefinitely and, rather than cut bonuses on existing policies, the companies preferred to start from scratch with a new type of policy. The second reason is that unitised policies do have some advantages for investors: an investment can be easily switched from a unit-linked fund (see below) to a unitised with-profits fund, and charges made on a unitised plan can be expressed much more clearly than expenses influencing a traditional plan.

Despite the departure from the traditional with-profits basis, unitised with-profits plans still offer a reasonably steady, medium-risk investment. They may be worth considering if you are fairly close (within ten years, say) to retirement, or if you are a person who feels happiest avoiding higher risk investments.

Unit-linked basis

If your retirement is ten or more years' distant, say, you should consider investing on a unit-linked basis. This means that your contributions buy units in a notional investment fund. The price of your units rises and falls with the value of the underlying investments. Because the price of the units can fall, unit-linked plans are generally more risky than with-profits plans. On the other hand, since the price is linked directly to stock market investments, you expect the value of your investment to beat inflation over the long term.

You can choose to link into different types of investment fund. 'General' and 'balanced' funds tend to represent the lowest risk, being spread across a range of different investments or concentrating on very stable, solid 'blue chip' shares. For the prospect of higher returns – but inevitably linked to higher risk of loss – you can choose more specialist funds, such as those investing in, say, Japanese stocks, small companies or special situations. You can usually invest in more than one fund at a time (subject to any minimum investment limits) and switch either your investment so far and/or your future contributions between different funds.

Cash or deposit funds

As you near retirement, you may want to lock into gains which you have made with a unit-linked or unitised with-profits plan. You can do this by switching to a cash or deposit fund. This works rather like a bank deposit account in that the amount of your investment cannot fall and interest payments are added to it at intervals. The interest rate is usually linked to money market rates available on very large deposits (so it is higher than rates paid by high-street banks or building societies) and it can vary.

The return on cash or deposit funds is unlikely to keep pace with inflation over the long-term, so this form of investment is not suitable if you are a long way off retirement.

Finding out about personal plans

Personal pension plans are run mainly by insurance companies. They can also be operated by friendly societies, banks, building societies and unit trust companies. Many banks and building societies offer pension plans but usually these will be operated either by a subsidiary which is an insurance company or operated by a separate insurance company with whom the bank or building society has a commercial arrangement.

Choosing a plan is a complex task. There are several hundred plans available and you need to decide which seems to offer you the best deal in terms of how you invest, the charges it levies – see Table 6 for a summary of charges you may come across – the options available, and so on. Ultimately, the most important factor determining the size of your pension will be how well the plan provider invests your money. Unfortunately, there is no way of picking the investment winners in advance. It may be a good idea to stick to companies which have performed *consistently* in the past; equally, you would be wise to avoid companies which have buoyed up past returns by dipping into their capital reserves.

It is also wise to avoid plans making high charges, unless they offer you some other clear advantage. Research by *Which?* magazine found that the charges on the lowest-charging plans reduced your ultimate pension by 13 per cent but those on the highest-charging plans reduced your pension by 35 per cent. Therefore, it is essential to shop around before you decide on a particular plan.

You can also get information about plans direct from the plan providers and *Which?* magazine, and specialist magazines such as *Money Management* (available in larger newsagents) also run surveys of pension plans summarising their main features. But the best course is to seek advice from an independent financial adviser – see Chapter 11.

Table 6: Charges often levied from unitised or unit-linked pension plans

Name of charge	Description
Administration charge/policy fee	Either a one-off or yearly charge deducted from your contributions before the remainder is used to buy units
Bid-offer spread	The difference between the higher offer price at which you buy units and the lower bid price at which you can sell. Typically 5 per cent plus up to 1 per cent rounding
Management charge	Yearly charge set against the investment fund to cover cost of managing the underlying investments. Typically 1 per cent or 1.5 per cent of the value of the fund
Unit allocation	A given percentage of each contribution which is used to buy units. The percentage may be lower in the earlier years of the plan, and may be lower if you pay regular premiums monthly rather than yearly. Don't be misled by allocations over 100 per cent – it sounds as if you're being credited with more money than you paid in but this isn't the case. It may mean 100 per cent of the contribution less administration charge or you may be getting a refund of part of the management charge
Capital units	You may be allocated 'special units' especially in the first year or two of the plan. They usually suffer a much higher management charge (for example 3 per cent or 5 per cent of the fund). This higher charge usually continues throughout the life of the plan
Surrender charges	You're likely to be credited with only part of the value of your plan if you stop paying into it, or transfer it, in the early years. In the first few years, your plan may not have any value at all
Switching charge	If you switch your investment from one unit-linked fund to another, the first one or two switches a year may be free. Thereafter, you're likely to face a charge

How safe is your pension?

It is illegal for an investment business – which covers investment advice and most pension activities – to carry on without being authorised. In the past, various self-regulating organisations have been responsible for authorising investment businesses, but under new legislation due to be passed in 2000, this duty will pass to the Financial Services Authority★ (which has already largely taken over from the existing self-regulating organisations). To qualify for authorisation, businesses must be judged as 'fit and proper', solvent, and conduct their business in a proper manner (see Chapter 11 for more information).

If you lose money through the fraud or negligence of an investment business, and you cannot recover it from the business because it has gone bust, you can claim compensation from the Investors' Compensation Scheme★ (ICS). The maximum payout per claim from the ICS is £48,000, which may be a good deal less than the pension fund you have built up. For more details about the protection given by the Financial Services Authority, see Chapter 11.

Pension rights and divorce

As discussed in Chapter 6, a court considering a divorce settlement may be required to take into account any pension rights built up by the husband or wife. This includes pension rights within a personal pension plan. If your divorce is to be settled without the judgement of a court, you should consider getting advice about the value of pension rights and how they should be apportioned between you and your spouse.

When you reach retirement

About three months before you intend to start taking a pension from a personal pension plan, you should contact the plan provider for information about the options you have and an estimate of the pension and other benefits you can expect. See page 16 for what to do if you have problems tracing a plan provider. Bear in mind that, with most plans, you have an open market option, so get quotes from other companies as well to see who offers the best deal. If annuity rates are particularly low, consider whether you should put off taking your pension for a while until rates recover. If your current plan does not offer this option, you can switch to one which does.

Chapter 8

Financial support for the family

As well as providing you with a retirement pension, the various types of pension scheme and plan can also provide financial support for your family in the event of your death.

What the state provides

The state offers support for widows – summarised in the flowchart on pages 104–5 – but currently no special support for widowers. If, despite this, your widow or widower is left with an inadequate income (from all sources), she or he might qualify for income support from the state.

Current help for widows

In 1999–2000 the help a widow can get from the state depends on the record of National Insurance contributions which her husband built up over his working life up to the time of death. She could be eligible for some or all of the following benefits:

- **Widow's payment** A tax-free lump sum paid at a single rate of £1,000.
- **Widowed mother's allowance** A regular income available to widows caring for dependent children.
- **Widow's pension** A regular income available to widows aged 45 or more who have no dependent children.

Both widowed mother's allowance and widow's pension are taxable if all your income together is high enough for you to have to pay income tax. Both benefits are payable unless you remarry.

In the 1999–2000 tax year, the full rate of widowed mother's allowance is £66.75 a week, plus £11.35 (tax-free) for each dependent child. On top of this, a widow can receive any SERPS pension her husband built up. If her husband had an insufficient record of National Insurance contributions, the widowed mother's allowance will be reduced according to rules similar to those applying to the state basic retirement pension (see page 34).

· If you are a widow with no dependent children and are under the age of 45 you are not eligible for any special help from the state. However, if you are 45 or over at the time you are widowed, or if you are 45 or more when your youngest child ceases to be dependent on you, you will qualify for the widow's pension. This is paid at different rates according to your age at the time of your husband's death – see Table 1. Once the rate has been set, it does not increase with age. You qualify for the full rate shown in Table 1 provided your husband built up a sufficient record of National Insurance contributions during his working life. If he did not pay enough contributions, the amount of widow's pension will be reduced. You may also be entitled to some or all of any SERPS pension which your husband built up.

When you reach state pension age, you can switch from widow's pension (or widowed mother's allowance) to the state retirement pension, which will be at least the amount you were receiving in widow's benefits. Alternatively, you can choose to carry on receiving widow's benefits for up to five years longer, but at the age of 65 you must switch to the state retirement pension. If you want to earn increased retirement pension by deferring it for up to five years (see page 163), you will have to give up the widow's benefits as well.

Table 1: Amount of full-rate widow's pension in 1999–2000

Age of widow at time of husband's death [1]	Amount of widow's pension £ per week
45	20.03
46	24.70
47	29.37
48	34.04
49	38.72
50	43.39
51	48.06
52	52.73
53	57.41
54	62.08
55 or over	66.75

[1] For women widowed before 6 April 1988, the relevant ages are five years younger, with the maximum widow's pension payable for new widows aged 50 and over

Help from the state for widows and widowers
Note that this describes the system up until April 2001, when new rules will be introduced

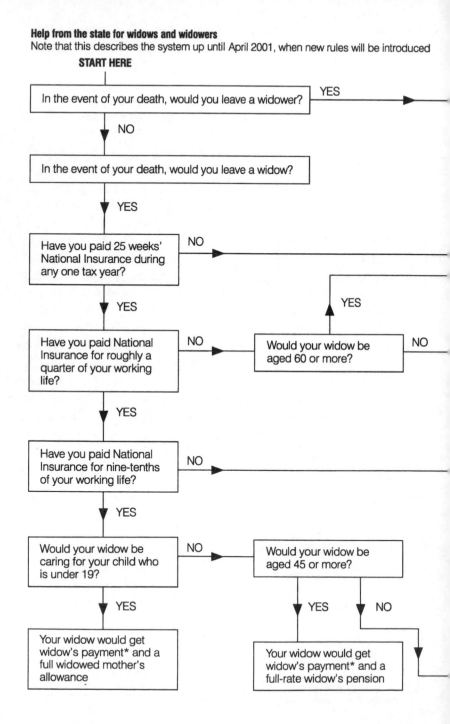

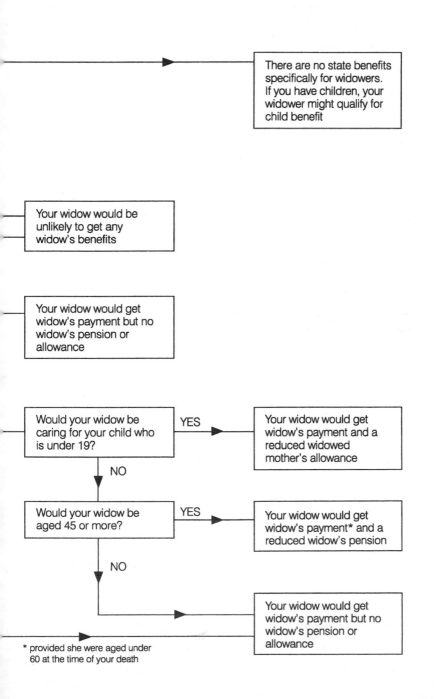

There are no state benefits specifically for widowers. If you have children, your widower might qualify for child benefit

Your widow would be unlikely to get any widow's benefits

Your widow would get widow's payment but no widow's pension or allowance

Would your widow be caring for your child who is under 19?

YES → Your widow would get widow's payment and a reduced widowed mother's allowance

NO

Would your widow be aged 45 or more?

YES → Your widow would get widow's payment* and a reduced widow's pension

NO

Your widow would get widow's payment but no widow's pension or allowance

* provided she were aged under 60 at the time of your death

Future help for widows and widowers

At the time of writing, new legislation is being passed to introduce a new set of benefits available for both widows and widowers (probably with effect from April 2001). Under the new rules, provided you have made the appropriate National Insurance contributions, your widow or widower may be eligible for:

- a tax-free lump sum of £2,000 for widows and widowers aged under 60 (or over 60 but ineligible for the state basic pension)
- widowed parent's allowance – equivalent to and with the same entitlement as the current widowed mother's allowance
- bereavement allowance – for widows and widowers over the age of 45 and without dependent children, but payable for a maximum of one year (or until retirement age or the recipient starts to co-habit with someone else)
- income-related benefits – people aged 55 or over (when the new benefits start) who are widowed within the first five years of the new system may receive income-related benefits without any job-seeking requirements, and may receive extra financial help when their bereavement allowance stops if they are then claiming means-tested benefits.

If you are already receiving widow's benefits under the current system, you will continue to get these benefits when the new system is introduced.

What employer pension schemes provide

Death before retirement

Most employer schemes offer benefits for your dependants in the event of your death. These may take several forms:

- lump sum life insurance
- a pension for your widow or widower
- a pension for children or other dependants

- possibly a refund of your contributions (but not those paid on your behalf by your employer).

Your employer may run a life insurance scheme which provides cover for all employees – even those who are not members of the pension scheme – or just for pension scheme members. Provided the life cover meets Inland Revenue rules, tax relief is given on any amount paid to provide life cover (and the cover provided does not count as a taxable benefit for income tax purposes). To meet the tax rules, the maximum lump sum payable must not exceed four times your final pay (see page 65). For people covered by the post-1989 regime (see page 72), there is also an overall cash limit on the amount of life insurance, which is £362,400 for the 1999–2000 tax year. Contributions returned can be paid out as a lump sum in addition to the life cover.

The pension scheme usually retains the right to decide who will receive the lump sum in the event of your death. This means that the lump sum does not become part of your estate, so it can be paid out rapidly without waiting for probate and does not count for inheritance tax purposes (see Chapter 33). You can nominate the person or people whom you would like to receive the lump sum and usually the scheme will respect your wishes. However, if you had failed to name someone – a young child, say – who was dependent on you, the pension scheme would probably override your nomination.

The Inland Revenue limits the amount that can be paid out in pensions to your widow or widower to two-thirds of the maximum retirement pension, under Inland Revenue rules, which you could have received if you had been able to stay on until the normal retirement age for the scheme. If you are covered by the post-1989 regime (see page 72), there is also an overall cash limit of £40,267 for the 1999–2000 tax year. The same limit applies to any one pension for a dependant. But the sum of all pensions for widow, widower and any other dependants must not come to more than the maximum pension which you could have received at normal retirement age under the Inland Revenue rules.

If you were contracted out through your employer scheme on a final pay basis for periods before 6 April 1997, the widow's pension must equal at least half the amount of the Guaranteed Minimum Pension (GMP) which you built up, provided your widow is 45 or over at the time of your death or has to look after dependent children. For widow(er)'s rights built up from 6 April 1997, the pension must generally be at least as good as that under the 'reference scheme' (see page 73) – broadly, half the retirement pension for which you would have qualified based on membership up to the time of your death.

If you were contracted out on a money purchase basis, the whole contracted-out fund which has built up must be used to provide a widow's or widower's pension.

Death after retirement

An employer pension scheme may also provide financial support for your family after retirement. Again, this may be:

- a widow's or widower's pension
- pensions for other dependants
- a guarantee that your pension will be paid for a set number of years (five years, say), even if you die within that time
- possibly, a lump sum.

No one widow's, widower's or dependant's pension can exceed two-thirds of the maximum pension you could have had under Inland Revenue rules and all widow's or widower's and dependants' pensions together must not exceed the maximum amount of pension which you could have had under Inland Revenue limits. If you were contracted out on a final pay basis before 6 April 1997, any widow's or widower's pension must equal at least half the GMP you were getting. For periods from 6 April 1997 onwards, a pension at least as good as that from the 'reference scheme' must normally be paid – broadly half the retirement pension you'd built up. Similarly, if you were contracted out on a money purchase basis, your widow or widower must receive a contracted-out pension of at least half the amount you were getting.

If there is a guarantee that your pension will be paid for five years, say, and you die within that time, the scheme usually has discretion to decide who will receive the balance of the pension – you will be asked to nominate someone and usually your wishes will be respected. The balance of the guaranteed pension may be 'rolled up' and paid out as a lump sum.

It is unusual for an employer scheme to provide you with life cover after you have retired. However, if you died so soon after retirement that you would have received less in pension than you had paid in over the years in contributions, the scheme might pay out the balance of the contributions as a lump sum. Generally this lump sum would be tax-free.

What personal pension plans provide

Death before retirement

There is no automatic package of benefits when you take out a personal pension plan (except where the plan is a contracted-out one – see below), but you can choose to pay extra for:

- a pension for your widow or widower
- a pension for children or other dependants
- a lump sum from the pension plan
- lump sum life cover from a related life insurance policy.

If you opt for your plan to include a pension for a widow or widower and/or other dependants, the only limit on the size of these pensions with a retirement annuity contract (see page 88) is the fund you have built up. With a personal pension plan, there is a restriction that the total of widow's, widower's and other dependants' pensions must not come to more than the retirement pension which you could have bought with your fund had you retired at the date of your death.

A contracted-out personal pension plan must provide a pension for your widow or widower if they are aged 45 or more at the time of your death or have to care for dependent children. The pension would be whatever amount the accumulated contracted-out fund could buy.

If you have not arranged for any widow's, widower's or other dependants' pensions to be paid from your plan, your plan will usually pay out a lump sum in the event of your death. With a retirement annuity contract, this will usually be the value of your pension fund. With a personal pension plan, the payout may be either the value of your fund or the sum of the contributions you paid in, plus reasonable interest or bonuses. You nominate whom this payment would be made to – it need not be someone who was dependent on you financially.

You can pay up to five per cent of your net relevant earnings (see page 91) as premiums to a special life insurance policy, which will pay out a lump sum in the event of your death. You get tax relief on the premiums at your highest rate, but note that the premiums you pay count towards your overall limit on contributions to personal plans (see pages 90–2). If you are concerned to save the maximum possible for retirement, you might do better to take out ordinary life insurance instead. Provided you are eligible to take out a personal pension plan (see page 83), you can take out this special insurance even if you are not making any contributions towards a personal pension. Note, however, that tax relief on such plans may be abolished on the introduction of stakeholder pensions.

Death after retirement

You will need to choose at the time you decide to start taking a pension what financial support for your family you are going to buy. The more cover you provide, the lower will be your own retirement pension. There are three options:

- a guarantee that your pension will be paid for a set period (five years, say) even if you die in the interim
- a pension for your widow or widower
- pensions for other dependants.

The maximum guarantee period allowed is ten years. You can nominate the person to receive the balance of your pension if you do die before the guarantee period is up – the recipient does not have to be someone who was financially dependent on you. The balance of the pension can be rolled up and paid out as a lump sum.

A pension for a widow, widower or other dependant may take the form of a joint annuity so that your pension would continue to be paid after your death during the lifetime of the dependant. The sum of pensions for your widow or widower and other dependants must not come to more than the pension you were receiving. If your pension plan was contracted out, it must allow for a widow's or widower's pension.

Life insurance

Employer schemes will set their own rates of pension and life cover, which may be lower then the maximum allowed by the Inland

Revenue, so you will need to check the rules for your own particular scheme. With a personal plan, you must decide what benefits you can afford to include within the scope of the plan.

If the financial support for dependants under your pension arrangements is not enough, you should consider taking out life insurance. The main types of life insurance are described below.

Term insurance

You take this out for a fixed period (the 'term') and it pays out only if you die within that time – if you survive the period, it pays out nothing. Term insurance may pay out a set amount, or the amount to be paid out may increase – as a safeguard against inflation, say. There are also decreasing term insurance policies where the sum to be paid out reduces over the term: these are useful where you want cover for an expense which is reducing – a loan which you are paying off, say, or the possibility of inheritance tax (see Chapter 33). Another variant is family income benefit insurance which, if you die within the term, pays out a regular tax-free income starting from the date of death.

Endowment policies and unit-linked savings plans

These pay out if you die within a fixed period but also if you survive to the end of the period. Since these policies pay out whether you die or not – i.e. there is an investment element – they are a lot more expensive than a term insurance policy. See Chapter 10 for more about investment-type life insurance.

Whole life insurance

This pays out whenever you die. Since the policy must pay out at some time, it builds up a capital value, which means that you may get something back if you decide to cash in the policy – i.e. it also has an investment element. Whole life insurance can be particularly useful in inheritance tax planning (see Chapter 33).

Some whole life policies are very flexible, allowing you to choose the balance of life cover and investment which they provide. If you need a high level of life cover, flexible whole life policies can work out even cheaper than term insurance in the early years. But sustaining the high level of cover requires good investment performance. If the underlying investment fund fails to grow at the target rate, you'll have either to reduce the cover or increase your premiums.

Which type of life insurance?

In general, if you need life cover at some stage during your life to provide for dependants, it is best to choose protection-only insurance – i.e. some form of term insurance – because you can usually get the cover you need relatively cheaply. However, as you get older you should look at both term and whole life insurance. If you take out a whole life policy now, you are guaranteed life cover for the rest of your life (provided you keep up the premiums), whatever your state of health. On the other hand, if you take out a term insurance policy now, you might not be able to renew it later if your health worsens.

Chapter 9

Planning for long-term care

With luck, you will enjoy robust health and independence throughout your retirement, but one person in five does need eventually to move into a residential or nursing home and, before getting to that stage, many people need varying degrees of help and care within their own home. The cost of long-term care, particularly if you need to move into a home, can be substantial. As a result, in recent years, new insurance and investment products have been launched to help you pay for long-term care.

Care in the community

Problems often arise because of deteriorating mobility – e.g. as a result of some long-term condition, such as arthritis. Many conditions associated with older age, such as senile dementia, Alzheimer's disease, Parkinson's disease, failing eyesight and so on can also cause a wide range of problems in coping with everyday tasks, such as shopping, dressing and eating.

Whereas elderly disabled people used to become long-term hospital patients, the responsibility for looking after people who can no longer cope on their own now rests largely with the appropriate local authority. The type of support and services available can vary from one authority to another, as can the level of charges made for each service. Increasingly, services are not provided directly by the local authority, but instead are bought in from private suppliers. However, your local social services department remains a first port of call for access to all types of help.

The nationwide charity, Age Concern,★ is also a valuable source of information about what is available and how to obtain help. It publishes a number of free factsheets, including *Local authority charging procedures for residential and nursing home care, Finding residential and nursing home accommodation, Financial support for people in residential and nursing homes prior to 1 April 1993, Disability and ageing: your rights to social services, Finding help at home,* and *Attendance allowance and disability living allowance.* Help the Aged★ also offers a care fees advisory service.

Care in your own home

Moving into a residential or nursing home is usually the last resort. You are likely to want to remain in your own home for as long as possible. Your husband, wife or other relatives may be able to help, but you might need support from outside the family as well. Your local social services department can organise or put you in touch with the following sources:

- **Emergency call services** You are equipped with a personal alarm and if you need emergency help – e.g. because you fall or get stuck in the bath – helpers can be with you within half an hour or so.
- **Community nurse/health visitor** For specific treatments, you should be in regular contact with your GP or hospital, but the community nurse or health visitor can help with more general health matters, such as eating well, and can help you deal with problems, such as incontinence.
- **Occupational therapy (OT) department** Devices, such as a stair lift, grab rails, raised toilet seat and so on, can be installed to help you get around the home more easily.
- **Day centre** You can spend one day a week, or sometimes more, at a day centre. Your husband or wife may be able to go with you. This gives you social contact, a hot meal and access to people who may be able to advise on specific problems. Visiting a day centre on your own may give a carer at home useful time alone either to go out on trips to the shops, bank or so on or just to have a break and recharge the batteries.
- **Home help** Someone can come into your home to do housework, gardening or shopping.
- **Care attendant** Someone can come into your home to help you with dressing, eating and so on, or just to sit with you while your regular carer is out.

- **Meals on Wheels** A hot meal can be delivered to your home each day. This is useful if you find it hard to cook for yourself and can provide useful social contact if you are on your own.
- **Community transport projects** For example, Dial-a-Ride minibus transport within a given area including help getting on and off, Shopmobility schemes that let you use wheelchairs or motorised buggies within a shopping complex, and so on.

You can make your own private arrangements with some services, such as home helps and care attendants. Your local branch of Age Concern* is also likely to have lists of people who can come into your home with a variety of services, such as hairdressing and chiropody.

Moving into a home

If, despite the help available, you find you can no longer manage at home, the time may have come to consider a nursing or residential home. This is the point at which you might face a nasty financial shock: living in such a home is extremely expensive – about £250 a week on average for a residential home, £350 a week for a nursing home – and the state will not necessarily pick up the tab.

On average, a person who moves into a home spends around three years there, which could mean a total bill of around £40,000, but it could be much more if you live in an expensive part of the country. Of course, your experience might not be average and, if you lived in a home for many years, the cost would be much greater. Paying for residential or nursing home care yourself is undoubtedly going to make a large dent in your income or, for many people, their savings and other capital.

A commission was set up to try and find an answer to the question of whether individuals or the State should pay for long-term care. This reported in 1999, but unfortunately it did not establish a consensus and at the time of writing the government has no timetable for deciding how to tackle the issue.

Help from the state

If you want your local authority to help with the cost of long-term care, you will have to undergo a means-tested assessment. The social services department will look at your needs and advise on whether these are best met through staying in your own home or moving into a residential or nursing home.

If you stay in your own home, your local authority might provide some services free but usually there will be a charge. This might be low – for example, a session at a day centre might be free but a lunch-time meal while you are there might cost a few pounds, although if you are on a low income, charges might be waived. It is up to each local authority to set its own charging policy and rates. You will normally have to pay for the services provided by private organisations.

If you are aged 65 or over and for the past six months or more have needed continual supervision or frequent help with essential daily activities such as eating, bathing, dressing and going to the toilet, you might qualify for attendance allowance. This is a tax-free state benefit which you can claim irrespective of your income and savings. In 1999–2000, attendance allowance is paid at a higher rate of £52.95 a week if you need help during both the day and the night or a lower rate of £35.40 a week if you need help only during the night or during the day. Attendance allowance stops after four weeks if you go into hospital or your local authority funds your living in a residential or nursing home.

If you are aged under 65 at the start of your disability, you might qualify for a similar benefit, disability living allowance, instead of attendance allowance.

If it is decided that your needs are best met by moving into a home, the local authority will assess what income you have available to meet the cost of living in a home. In theory, you can choose which home you want to go into. In practice, the local authority will make the assessment on the basis of a set level of fees. There is a strong commercial relationship between care homes and local authorities, with homes generally setting their fees at the level they know the local authority is willing to pay. But, if you did want to choose a more costly home, you would have to find the difference yourself.

The rules used in the means test are broadly the same as those used for income support purposes so, for example, instead of taking capital directly into account, you will be assumed to receive a set income from your capital (see page 59). However, the amount of capital you have determines whether or not you will qualify for any help with fees:

- If your capital comes to less than £10,000, your local authority will pay the residential or nursing home fees for you, assuming your income is also deemed insufficient to cover the fees yourself.
- If your capital comes to £16,000 or more, you will get no help at all paying the residential or nursing home fees. You will have to pay these yourself until your capital falls below £16,000.
- If you have capital between £10,000 and £16,000, the local authority will expect you to contribute something towards the fees. The higher your capital, the more you will have to contribute.

If you are a single person living alone, your home – valued at its market price – counts as part of your capital. Since most homes are worth a lot more than £16,000, this very often triggers the sale of your home in order to meet the fees of the residential or nursing home. If you live with your husband, wife, unmarried partner or, in some cases, certain other relatives and they are to stay in the family home, it does not count as part of your capital for the purpose of the means test. Other assets you have generally do count and may have to be sold or run down before the state will take over paying the residential or nursing home fees.

You might be tempted to give away some of your possessions – to your children, for instance – in order to run down your assets to the level at which the state will pay for care. But the means test rules allow for this. The local authority can treat you as still owning assets if it thinks that you gave them away deliberately as a way of reducing your capital. This power is very wide and the local authority can look back over years. Experts suggest that, to be safe from inclusion, any capital gifts need to have been made at least five years before the assessment is made. Age Concern★ publishes a useful free factsheet on this topic, *Transfer of assets, and paying for care in a residential or nursing home.*

In summary, the state will as a last resort foot the bill if you need to move into a home, but only if your means are already very modest or after you have run down your own capital. There are two ways of viewing this:

- as a reasonable use of your capital if disability should strike in older age (particularly bearing in mind that the majority of people have the good fortune to avoid this outcome)
- as an unacceptable erosion of capital which perhaps you had hoped to pass on to your children.

If you tend towards the latter view, you could consider long-term care insurance as a way of protecting your capital. The flowchart opposite will help you decide whether or not long-term care insurance is really appropriate for you.

Long-term care insurance

Long-term care insurance is a way of paying in advance against the possibility that you might one day need long-term care. It works as follows. In exchange for regular premiums or a lump sum single premium, the policy pays you a tax-free income if you can no longer live independently. The income can be used to provide help in your own home or to pay the fees if you move into a nursing home or (with most policies) a residential home. The higher the income you would like to receive, the higher the premiums you must pay. The maximum pay-out with many policies is £30,000 a year or £3,000 a month. Some policies allow the income to increase year-by-year.

Typically, the policy pays out if you can no longer carry out two or three 'activities of daily living' (ADLs) on your own. The particular ADLs specified under different policies vary but generally include some or all of washing, dressing, eating, going to the toilet, mobility around the home and 'transferring' (being able to get in and out of bed).

Long-term care insurance has been slow to find popularity. One reason is the high cost when balanced against the fairly high probability of not needing to claim. Many policies can be started as young as age 18 (and will cover you whenever disability strikes, not just in older age), but, generally, people are in the 40 to 60 age range before they begin to be interested in this type of insurance. Table 1 gives some examples of the premiums payable in 1999. Some companies guarantee to keep the premium unchanged for a given period – usually five years – but, otherwise, premiums can be increased without limit.

Do you need long-term care insurance?

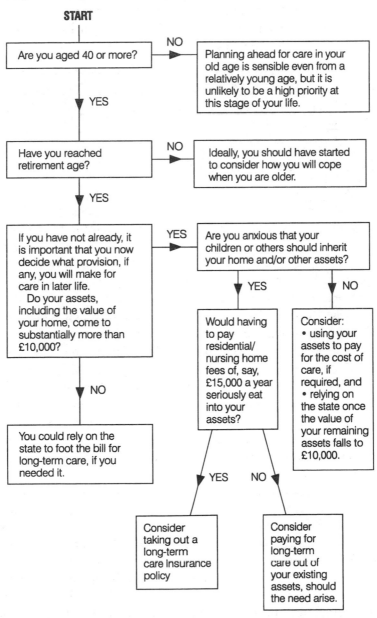

START

Are you aged 40 or more?

NO → Planning ahead for care in your old age is sensible even from a relatively young age, but it is unlikely to be a high priority at this stage of your life.

YES

Have you reached retirement age?

NO → Ideally, you should have started to consider how you will cope when you are older.

YES

If you have not already, it is important that you now decide what provision, if any, you will make for care in later life.
  Do your assets, including the value of your home, come to substantially more than £10,000?

YES → Are you anxious that your children or others should inherit your home and/or other assets?

YES ↓ Would having to pay residential/ nursing home fees of, say, £15,000 a year seriously eat into your assets?

NO ↓ Consider:
• using your assets to pay for the cost of care, if required, and
• relying on the state once the value of your remaining assets falls to £10,000.

NO ↓ You could rely on the state to foot the bill for long-term care, if you needed it.

YES → Consider taking out a long-term care Insurance policy

NO → Consider paying for long-term care out of your existing assets, should the need arise.

Table 1: What you could pay for long-term care insurance

Age when plan first started	Example monthly premiums for £1,000 a month benefit [1]	
	Men	Women
55	£33.50–£80.35	£41.10–£95.89
60	£41.90–£101.91	£51.80–£121.92
65	£54.10–£130.38	£67.10–£158.39
70	£72.80–£171.54	£91.10–£215.24
75	£94.90–£243.39	£124.60–£322.74

Source: *Money Management* May 1999

[1] Benefits vary from plan to plan – e.g. some offer level benefits, some increasing, some plans incorporate an extended waiting period. It is essential to check the detailed benefits when you choose a plan.

There are some ways to reduce the cost of long-term care insurance. Most plans are designed to pay out indefinitely once you start to need care, but a few now let you choose how long you want the policy to pay out for – usually five years. You take a gamble on whether you will end up needing care for longer than that. With all plans, there is a 'waiting period' from the time when you qualify for the benefit but before the income starts to be paid – 13 weeks is common. A few plans give the option of extending the waiting period in exchange for a reduction in premium. Finally, consider taking out insurance to cover only part of the cost of care if you have other income (e.g. from your state and private pensions) which could be used to meet the rest.

Many of these pre-funded plans work as straightforward insurance – i.e. your premiums directly pay for the cover you are getting and you get nothing back if you decide to stop the plan. However, with some providers, your premiums are invested and the premiums are paid from the investment fund. If you stop paying into the plan, the premiums continue to be paid until the investment fund is used up or, less commonly, the investment fund is paid to you as a cash sum.

If you take out a long-term care policy, make sure that the people close to you – such as family, friends or your GP – know that you have the policy, so that they can make a claim on your behalf if you are not able to do it yourself.

Choosing the right long-term care policy

Policies vary greatly from one provider to another, so carefully check and weigh up what is on offer. In particular:

- if the policy pays out, are the benefits payable for your whole life or just for a specified number of years?
- are benefits paid at a flat rate year after year or do they increase?
- once you need to claim, is there a waiting period before payments start and, if so, how long is it?
- do you have a choice about any of the above features? If yes, how much does each option save you in premiums?
- in what circumstances does the policy pay out? What sort of ADLs must you have difficulty with and how many?
- does the policy cover all forms of care – e.g. in your own home, in a nursing home and in a residential home?
- do you want to pay regular premiums or a single lump sum premium?
- what happens if you stop the plan? Is any part of a single premium repaid? Does the policy have a cash value? Does cover continue for a while?
- what happens if you die without ever having made a claim? Does the policy pay anything to your survivors?
- are premiums guaranteed to stay at a given level for any length of time? How often are premiums reviewed?

Alternatives to insurance

If you have not taken out insurance in advance and find that you need to go into a home, you could buy an annuity (see page 144) in order to meet the fees. You will need a substantial lump sum and often this will have to come from the sale of the family home. You could select an annuity yourself and independently pay the home fees, but a handful of companies offer 'immediate care annuities' where the annuity income is paid direct to the residential or nursing home. The advantage of this arrangement is that the insurer will usually have negotiated the level of fees that the home will charge, including future increases, and can offer you a guarantee that the annuity proceeds will always be enough to meet the fees.

If your husband, wife or someone else will be staying in the family home, you could consider an equity release scheme (see page 53) as a way of raising money to pay for care while still retaining the right for that person to remain in the home.

Chapter 10

Investments

New types of investment seem to be launched every week, to the despair of anybody trying to take a sensible view of investing money that will need to last them for the rest of their life, and probably a partner's too. But don't lose heart.

The 'newness' usually consists of combining two types of investment in an inventive way – so long as you look for what underlies the puff, and refuse to be inhibited in asking what might seem basic questions, you should be able to find your way through the marketing literature to the reality. That is why the second half of this chapter describes the building blocks of investment, grouping the main types of investment into the following categories, depending on what they do:

- secure schemes, offering variable interest (page 130)
- secure schemes, offering fixed interest (page 133)
- investments offering the chance of capital gain or loss (page 134)
- British Government stocks ('gilts') (page 140)
- long-term savings plans (page 142)
- investments designed specifically to produce income (page 143)
- index-linked investments (page 145).

In retirement, although it is important to review your investments regularly, jumping on to the latest investment bandwagon might not be for you. However the investments on offer may change, the sensible investment guidelines tend to prevail from year to year:

- Have you something put aside for emergencies in a place where you can get at it quickly?

- Do you know when you are likely to need lump sums, e.g. to replace your car, or extra income, e.g. if pension income will drop suddenly on the death of one partner?
- Have you thought about how much risk you can afford to take in search of higher growth? There are two main risks: the risk that you might lose your capital, or the risk that you might see its value steadily eroded by inflation. Unless you choose one of the few index-linked investments, you have to decide which type of risk you prefer.
- Have you spread your risk – in other words, do you have enough in different types of investments so that a downturn in one sector doesn't scupper your plans overall?
- Do you know the tax consequences of your investments, and have you minimised any adverse ones – without being obsessed by the desire to save tax?

EXAMPLE 1

Anthony retired at 56 and received an index-linked pension and a lump sum. He says: 'I found it important to be able to live comfortably with any investment I make. It is no use having one that makes you feel that you need to keep checking, although it is as well to check, say monthly, any investment subject to stock market fluctuation.'

This chapter can give guidance on these general questions; what it can't do is tell you exactly how to put all the answers together to suit your individual needs. Chapter 11 looks at getting advice, and Which? Books* also produces *Be Your Own Financial Adviser.*

Look for the real return

When comparing homes for your money, get into the habit of thinking of the return they give after tax. Income from investments is taxed in one of three ways. It may be:

- tax-free, such as National Savings Certificates
- taxable, but received before tax, such as income from a National Savings Investment Account: you have to pay any tax separately

- taxed: you get the income after tax has been deducted, for example most building society interest, and income from shares and unit trusts. Basic-rate taxpayers have no further tax to pay, but higher-rate taxpayers must pay extra tax. Non-taxpayers with bank and building society interest can reclaim the tax or register to have the income paid before tax.

If you make a capital gain on an investment, you may also be subject to capital gains tax. You can find more details, and a summary chart of how different investments are taxed, in Chapter 17.

ISAs – a tax-free wrapper

An Individual Savings Account (ISA) is a scheme that lets you save money tax-free in different types of investments, or in a combination:

Cash – the cash part of an ISA is a normal savings account. Most banks and building societies offer cash ISAs, and a National Savings cash ISA is available through post offices.
Stocks and shares – an ISA can include stocks and shares listed on recognised stock exchanges throughout the world, as well as government stocks. You can either 'self-select' your stocks and shares through a stockbroker, or invest in pooled investments, such as unit trusts, investment trusts and open-ended investment companies (OEICs; see page 135).
Life insurance – your money is invested in a savings-type life insurance policy. Few companies currently offer this option.

An ISA investing in just one of the types of investment above is called a mini-ISA; maxi-ISAs can include all three types. In any one tax year, you can take out either one maxi-ISA with one account manager or up to three mini-ISAs with a different manager for each, if you choose. From 6 April 2000, you can invest up to £5,000 in ISAs in each tax year (in 1999–2000 the overall limit is £7,000), but there are individual limits within this for each investment type:

- cash – up to £1,000 (£3,000 in 1999–2000)
- stocks and shares – up to £3,000 in a mini-ISA, £5,000 in a maxi-ISA (but £7,000 in a maxi-ISA in 1999–2000)
- life insurance – up to £1,000.

Within these limits, any interest, income or capital gains from investments held in an ISA is tax-free and need not be entered in your tax return. With stocks and shares ISAs, the ISA manager can, until 5 April 2004, claim back the tax credit deducted from dividend payments.

Once you have held your ISA for at least a year, you can transfer your money, in total or in part, to another ISA-provider without affecting the current year's contribution limits. If you want to transfer your current year's payments, you must transfer the whole amount paid in from the start of the tax year, keeping to the same investment types.

Some ISAs are 'CAT-marked'. CAT stands for Charges, Access and Terms. To earn the CAT-mark the ISA must meet minimum standards laid down by the government: charges must come to no more than a given limit; you must be allowed to invest low minimum amounts; withdrawals must be allowed after no more than seven days' notice; and you must be given decent terms and conditions.

ISA tips

- The ISA limits apply to contributions within a tax year, not totals in your account. So if you contribute the maximum but then make a withdrawal you can't top your account up in the same tax year.
- If you want to invest more than £3,000 in shares, go for a maxi-ISA.
- In addition to the normal contribution limits, you can transfer the capital (but not the interest) from a maturing TESSA into a special TESSA-only ISA – see page 132.

Repaying your mortgage – a good investment?

Before you invest any lump sum received on your retirement, think about using it to pay off part or all of your mortgage. Mortgage interest rates are usually higher than the interest you could get if you put the money in a savings account, particularly since the abolition of tax relief on mortgage interest from 6 April 2000. However, before repaying, you need to consider how much you owe; whether you are going to need ready access to the money (it could cost you a lot if you find you need to borrow again in future); and, of course, the return you could get if you invested the lump sum.

Don't forget, if you have an endowment mortgage, that you can pay off the amount you owe your lender while still keeping up the endowment policy. This is important, since the surrender value of policies cashed in early can be very low.

Investing before retirement

Even before you get to retirement there are investment decisions to make. Most people probably regard their pension scheme as their main way of investing for retirement. But you may be prepared to sacrifice some of the tax advantages a pension offers in order to avoid tying up money you might need before retirement. For example, you may want to help a child through college, or foresee the need to tide yourself through the possibility of a few years between early retirement and getting your state pension.

In this case, you can either commit yourself to regular saving, or put something away when you can spare it, say in a building society, and then transfer it into a lump sum investment. However, there are some investments, described below, which offer tax advantages (though none are as generous as pensions).

If you can tie up savings for 5 years

Invest the maximum you can in a cash ISA – tax-free savings accounts from National Savings, banks and building societies; other tax-free schemes are National Savings Certificates (see page 133) and index-linked National Savings Certificates (see page 145).

If you can tie up savings for 5 to 10 years

An investment which gives the possibility of a capital gain, e.g. one based on shares, probably offers the best chance of beating inflation, and 5 to 10 years at least gives time for your investment to recover from periods when values fall. Either lump sum or regular savings are possible. Investing via an ISA gives returns free of income and capital gains tax.

If you can tie up savings for at least 10 years

As well as investments where your capital can grow (or shrink), long-term savings plans (based on life insurance) are a disciplined way of saving. But steer clear of them unless you are sure you can keep the policy up, because there are steep penalties on early withdrawal. They offer tax advantages for higher-rate taxpayers (but see page 239). Friendly society tax-exempt savings plans are completely tax-free (see page 143).

Investing after retirement

For income later

When you first retire, your pension income may be enough for you not to need much extra income from your investments. Instead, you may want to make your savings grow as much as you can against the day when you need the capital, either to turn it into an income or to replace expensive durables such as a car. If so, you need to balance up the risk of losing your capital against the risk of having it reduced by inflation. Assuming that you have enough money to spread over several types of investment, consider putting some in one of the index-linked investments (see page 145), some in one of the secure investments (see pages 130–4), and some in one of the 'chance of a capital gain or loss' investments (see pages 134–140). Don't forget that British Government stocks (page 140) are a very versatile investment, and don't assume that lump sum investments are the only ones to consider. If there is a particularly attractive savings scheme on offer you can always set up your own 'feeder' account in a bank or building society account, and transfer the money across by standing order. Alternatively, National Savings Certificates, say, bought regularly will produce a stream of income as they start to mature in two or five years' time.

For income now

The few investments whose main purpose is to produce income are covered on pages 143–4. However, do not confine yourself to them. For the advantage of regular income, you may have to accept other risks, such as tying up your capital. When interest rates are low you will have to be particularly inventive to get a decent income. Some ideas are:

- Unit trust and investment trust companies often market 'income' funds, which invest in companies that tend to pay high dividends.

- Unit trusts also offer income schemes that will pay out a set income, although to achieve this when prices are falling they may have to cash in some of your units.
- If you can accept some risk, corporate bonds (see page 141) generally provide a higher income than bank or building society accounts.
- You can design your own income-producing portfolio by choosing types of investments which achieve a sensible balance between risk, security and growth, but then buying specific investments paying income at different times throughout the year. For example, shares pay their dividends at different times, as do British Government stocks, and the dates when building societies credit interest to accounts vary from society to society.
- Single-premium insurance bonds (see page 138) can be cashed in bit by bit.

Traps to avoid

Using up capital too fast

Nobody can tell for certain how long they (and their partner) are going to need an income. You have to take into account how much your investments will earn, how fast inflation will erode its purchasing power, and how long you are likely to live. For how inflation can affect your income, see Chapter 3.

EXAMPLE 2

When planning his investments to give a mixture of income and growth, Bob first made his own judgement on future inflation, interest rates and the likely course of the stock market. He wrote his thoughts down, to avoid the temptation of changing his mind from day to day. He then allocated a proportion of his capital to different types of scheme – e.g. 'secure' ones, and those based on stocks and shares. At that stage he did not know enough to choose a best buy from the products in each type, so he obtained written recommendations from several financial advisers. He entered their recommendations under the appropriate categories on his plan – not always easy, he said, because you have to read the small print to determine the specific type – and compared their proportions with his own. Bob eventually followed the recommendations of the adviser whose proportions were nearest his own, and who also seemed to demonstrate the most competence.

Forgetting that things may change

If one partner dies, pension income may drop sharply, forcing the surviving partner to depend more upon investments (unless life insurance will fill the gap). For what happens to jointly held investments and savings accounts, see Chapter 32 (they normally pass automatically to the survivor). The surviving partner's investment priorities are almost bound to change. They may be particularly at the mercy of inflation (for which see index-linked investments, page 145), and even though they will naturally want a secure investment, they should beware of putting too much in an investment which is secure in that its value cannot go down, such as a building society account, but which offers no prospect of capital growth. Also see 'For income now' on pages 127–8 for ideas on maximising income.

Selling at the wrong time

When a long-term investment matures, for example a pension or unit-linked life insurance policy, you might lose out badly if the stock market happens to be low at the time. Clearly, you cannot foresee this when you invest. One way to avoid this is to ask the company if you can transfer your money to a safer (probably more pedestrian) fund, a little before maturity. With a personal pension, you can defer turning your pension fund into an income (see page 86).

You can, of course, sell things like shares or unit trusts at any time. But if at all possible, avoid being forced to sell them when their value is very low, by making sure that you always have a safer investment to fall back on until prices improve.

Losing age-related allowance

If you are aged 65 or over at any point in the tax year, you get a higher tax-free personal allowance. But this extra allowance (along with married couple's allowance, if you qualify) is reduced once your 'total income' (see page 000) rises above £16,800 (in the 1999–2000 tax year). If you are in this position, consider tax-free or favourably taxed investments that will not swell your income, or investments where the return comes mainly in the form of capital gain. In particular, be very careful about making a taxable gain on a life insurance policy (e.g. by cashing in a single premium bond early). Although you may not have to pay tax on it yourself, it will be added to your 'total income' for the purpose of reducing your age allowance.

If you have problems

There is nothing you can do if you lose money by choosing, say, the wrong share. If a company goes bust, there may be a compensation scheme – details are given under each type of investment – though these have maximum limits. Most types of investment are covered by an Ombudsman scheme. For problems with a financial adviser, see Chapter 11.

The main types of investment

Secure schemes, variable interest

Building societies, banks and National Savings accounts are all 'secure' in the sense that the money you invest in pounds cannot fall – although the purchasing power of each pound will of course shrink as a result of inflation. The only way you can lose money is if the institution itself fails – virtually impossible with National Savings, highly unlikely with the major banks and building societies.

Smaller banks and building societies do get close to failure from time to time, but building societies in particular are usually taken over by their bigger brothers first. If this does not happen, there is a compensation scheme, which provides 90 per cent of the first £20,000 deposited, i.e. up to a maximum of £18,000. Since the maximum is fairly low, you might want to put smaller amounts in small institutions or steer clear of them altogether.

Unless you hold the account in an ISA (see pages 124–5) income from bank and building society accounts is usually received after deduction of tax (20 per cent for the year from 6 April 1999). Basic-rate taxpayers have no further tax to pay, but higher-rate taxpayers have to pay extra tax. Non-taxpayers can either reclaim tax or register to have their interest paid before tax (see Chapter 17). If you pay tax at a maximum of 10 per cent, you can reclaim any excess tax deducted.

Below are the main types of variable interest schemes on offer. However, note that rates vary hugely from institution to institution: you may get higher interest from one society's instant access account than from another's notice account. 'Best buy' rates are given in *Which?* magazine from time to time, and in some weekend papers.

Instant access accounts

Nowadays these tend to have 'tiered' interest rates, so that the more you save, the higher your interest. But beware of schemes which give instant access only if you pay a penalty. Some also offer banking services, such as a cheque book and guarantee/debit card, so that you can use them as a current account.

Notice accounts

If you are prepared to give, say, 30, 60 or 90 days' notice, a 'notice account' may give you higher interest than an instant access account. Most accounts allow you instant access if you pay a penalty, e.g. losing 30, 60 or 90 days' interest; others may waive the notice requirement if your savings exceed a certain amount. The minimum investment is usually at least £500, but often more.

Term accounts and bonds

In return for higher interest, these tie up your money either until a set date, or for a set term fixed at the outset, usually between six months and three years. Again, there will be a minimum investment. A variant is the escalator bond, which gives you a higher rate of interest for each year you keep the bond.

Regular savings accounts

Although these are now few and far between, they give higher interest if you are prepared to save regularly. You may be able to miss, say, one payment a year. Check any restrictions on withdrawals.

High-interest cheque accounts

Hybrid schemes offered mainly by banks, these offer slightly higher interest than a standard bank account, in return for your commitment to keep a fairly high minimum balance in the account. Banking services are usually limited (e.g. no cash card).

Postal-only accounts

Building society accounts which can only be operated by post tend to offer higher than normal rates in return for the fact that you cannot draw cash over the counter. Apart from that they are not intrinsically different from other building society accounts.

TESSAs

It has not been possible to start up a new Tax Exempt Special Savings Account (TESSA) since 6 April 1999, but if you already have one you can continue it. TESSAs offer a tax-free return, provided you stick to the following two rules:

- You must invest for five years. You can withdraw interest (but not capital) earlier, as long as it is no more than the interest already credited to your account, but if you do withdraw more, tax will be deducted before you get it.
- The most you can save is £3,000 in the first year, and up to £1,800 in each of the following four years, with an overall maximum of £9,000 in total over the five years.

When your TESSA matures, you can reinvest the capital saved so far (but not the interest), i.e. up to £9,000, in a TESSA-only ISA (see page 125). Capital transferred from a TESSA does not count towards the normal investment limits for ISAs.

National Savings Ordinary and Investment Accounts

Both accounts offer variable interest, although the Ordinary Account interest rate tends to change infrequently. The Investment Account is taxable, but pays interest in full: the minimum investment is £20 and you have to give a month's notice (or lose 30 days' interest) to withdraw your money. The first £70 interest each year from an Ordinary Account (£140 in a joint account) is tax-free, while anything above that is taxable but paid out before tax. However, the interest rate is very low – 1 per cent interest before tax (in late 1999), or, as long as the account is open at least one calendar year, 1.1 per cent for each calendar month in which the balance is £500 or more. See the address section at the end of this book for the National Savings phone number to ring for the latest interest rates.

HOW BANKS AND BUILDING SOCIETIES QUOTE INTEREST RATES

- **Gross rate** – the annual flat rate before taking into account how often interest is paid and before deduction of any tax.
- **Net rate** – the annual flat rate after deduction of basic-rate tax.
- **Gross AER** – or 'annual effective rate': a true rate of return taking into account how often interest is added to the account. The more often this is, the better: for example, an account paying five per cent will return £5 for every £100 if interest is added once a year, £5.06 if added twice.
- **Net AER** – the net rate compounded, and what basic-rate taxpayers will earn over a full year.

Secure schemes, fixed interest

Knowing exactly how much interest you will get is useful for budgeting. But you take on another risk: if interest rates generally rise after you have put your money in a fixed-interest scheme, you will lose out. You also usually have to commit yourself to saving for a fixed length of time. However, a fixed-interest scheme protects you against the risk of falling interest rates.

Building societies often offer fixed-interest deals, usually in the form of term accounts and bonds. However, National Savings is the main provider of fixed-interest schemes. For the phone number to ring for the latest National Savings interest rates, see the address section at the back of the guide. Also see page 143 for fixed-rate National Savings Pensioners Bonds.

National Savings Certificates

These are sold in 'issues', each having a different interest rate, and only one being available at any time. They are tax-free: you buy them in units of £100 and the maximum you can invest is £10,000. Interest is added to the value of your certificate over the period of its life (which is either two or five years at the outset). The amount of interest added increases as time goes by, giving you an added incentive to hang on to your certificates: you get no interest if you cash in during the first year. After two or five years the interest rate drops to a lower and variable rate of interest. Index-linked certificates are also available – see page 145.

National Savings Capital Bonds

The return on these five-year bonds is taxable: they are an oddity in that you have to pay tax on the interest earned year by year, even though you will not receive the interest until the bond is repaid. You have to invest at least £100. You get no interest on withdrawals during the first year, but the interest rate then rises year by year.

National Savings Fixed Rate Savings

Unlike other National Savings products, these bonds pay interest after deduction of tax. Non-taxpayers can reclaim this tax, higher-rate taxpayers must pay more. You must invest at least £500. You can choose how long you want to invest for – six months, one year, 18 months or three years. You can withdraw your money early without notice, but this will cost you 90 days' interest. The longer the investment period, the higher the interest paid, and extra interest is also available for savings above £20,000 and £50,000. The interest can be paid out monthly or annually, or added to your bond.

Chance of gain or loss

Investments based on United Kingdom or international stocks and shares or property are not 'safe'. Investment managers and unit trusts, and the marketing of investments are regulated by the Financial Services Authority*, and there is a limited investors' compensation scheme – see Chapter 11. But this won't compensate you against the normal risks of investing, i.e. that the value of your investment could slump. On the other hand you could, if you are lucky, outstrip both inflation and the return available on more secure homes for your money. For this reason, once you have found a secure home for your emergency fund and money you really cannot afford to lose, it is sensible to invest at least some of your money this way.

You can reduce the risk. One way is to invest in corporate bonds, which are effectively fixed-interest loans to companies in the form of stocks which are bought and sold on stock markets. Bondholders have priority over shareholders if the company goes bust. Another way of reducing risk is to invest your money over several years, leaving time for the ups and downs in your investment's value to even out. You can then choose a time to cash in when the values are high.

Probably the most useful way of reducing risk is to spread your money over several different companies in different fields. But stockbrokers' minimum commissions make this uneconomic unless you have at least £10,000, preferably much more. Unit trusts, investment trusts and single-premium insurance bonds are ways of pooling your money with other investors and getting professionals to manage your money for you, with minimum investments of a few hundred pounds upwards. Many unit and investment trusts also have regular savings schemes, with minimum investments of, say, £20 to £50 a month.

Unit trusts
Your money buys units in a fund, which then buys shares and other investments. The price of the units (and the value of your holding) fluctuates in line with the value of those investments.

Investment trusts
These are simply companies which specialise in investing in other companies' shares, as well as government stocks and property throughout the world. However, the value of their own shares is affected by supply and demand. For example, many trusts' shares sell at a price below the value of the assets held by the trust (or, as the jargon has it, at a discount to the 'net asset value'). But some trusts' shares, particularly popular ones such as 'split capital' trusts (see overleaf for a translation), may sell for more – at a 'premium'. The value is also affected by the fact that an investment trust, unlike a unit trust, can borrow to buy things, which increases the tendency of a trust to rise and fall in value: this is known as 'gearing'.

OEICs
Open-Ended Investment Companies (OEICs) are a cross between unit trusts and investment trusts. They are quoted companies like investment trusts, but as with unit trusts the price of the shares moves in relation to the actual value of the fund. Some unit trusts have converted into OEICs.

Single-premium insurance bonds
These are lump-sum investments in life insurance funds, which work rather like unit trusts (but are taxed very differently – see page 138).

Different types of fund

Companies managing unit and investment trusts, OEICs and single-premium bonds usually allow you to invest in a range of funds. These can be very specialist and therefore risky (e.g. 'recovery' or 'emerging markets') or pretty general and in theory, at least, less risky (e.g. 'UK General' or 'growth and income'). As well as funds investing in different areas of the world and different types of industry, you can buy:

- **Property funds** These have not been very attractive over recent years, but are often the only practical way for small investors to invest in commercial property.

- **International funds** These are a convenient and relatively cheap way to invest abroad, though changes in exchange rates can have a dramatic effect on your return.

- **'Gilt' and fixed interest funds** These invest in British Government stocks (known as gilts) and corporate bonds.

- **Money market funds** These invest in things like bank deposits, benefiting from the higher rates available for very large investors.

- **'Managed' funds** These invest in a mixture of things such as shares, property and fixed-interest investments. You can buy into 'cautious' or 'balanced' funds.

- **'Index' or 'tracker' funds** aim to reduce risks by investing in, or tracking the performance of, shares which make up a specific stock market index, such as FT-SE 100.

- **'Ethical' funds** invest in stocks and shares which meet various ethical criteria: for example, 'green' funds concentrate on environmentally friendly projects, while other ethical funds might avoid arms or tobacco manufacturers.

- **Split capital investment trusts** These offer different types of shares which give different types of return. For example, there are income shares and capital shares: people with income shares get all the income from a fund, those with capital shares all the capital. Both will receive more income or capital growth than they otherwise would, but at the cost of giving up any capital growth or income respectively.

Tax, and how to save it

Some of the return from investing in shares, investment trusts, OEICs and unit trusts comes in the form of income, and some as capital gains. Any capital gains are taxable, but only if your taxable capital gains come to more than an annual tax-free slice (£7,100 in the 1999–2000 tax year).

The income is paid out after a 'tax credit' has been deducted. The tax credit is currently 10 per cent, but basic-rate taxpayers will have no further tax to pay. Higher-rate taxpayers will have to pay 32.5 per cent tax, minus the 10 per cent already deducted. Anybody who is a non-taxpayer cannot reclaim the tax credit.

However, there are various schemes which allow tax-free investment in shares. Individual Savings Accounts (ISAs) are a tax-free wrapper for most forms of investment in stocks and shares, as well as other forms of investment (see pages 124–5 for more details). New Personal Equity Plans (PEPs) are no longer available, but you can continue to keep any PEPs you already hold. In spite of the tax relief they offer, the Enterprise Investment Scheme and Venture Capital Trusts are intrinsically risky, because of the sort of company they invest in, so are probably only worth considering for higher-rate taxpayers.

Personal Equity Plans (PEPs)

Since 6 April 1999, PEPs have been replaced by ISAs. However, you can keep any PEPs taken out before that date and switch your money from one PEP manager to another. The return from investing in shares, corporate bonds, unit or investment trusts via a PEP is free of capital gains tax and income tax, within these limits:

- Your money must be invested in United Kingdom or certain European Community shares, or in certain types of corporate bond.
- Instead of investing directly, you can invest all or part of your money either in 'qualifying' unit or investment trusts. These have up to 50 per cent of their assets in United Kingdom or some European Community shares or corporate bonds. However, you can invest part of your money in non-qualifying trusts.
- You must invest via a 'plan manager', who takes care of all the administration.

In addition to general PEPs, you might have one or more single-company PEPs. These must be invested in the ordinary shares of just one UK or EU company (investment trust companies are excluded).

Enterprise Investment Scheme (EIS)

This gives you tax benefits for new investment in the shares of some types of unquoted company. You get tax relief of up to 20 per cent on the amount you invest, and income tax or capital gains tax relief (you choose which) against losses made on the shares. Gains are tax-free, provided you hold the shares for at least five years, and if you are reinvesting money which arose from disposing of an asset on which capital gains tax would be due, you can defer the tax. The minimum investment in any one company is £500 (unless you subscribe through an approved investment fund) and the maximum overall EIS investment is £150,000 each year.

Venture Capital Trusts (VCTs)

You can invest in a spread of unquoted companies through VCTs. VCTs are companies, rather like investment trusts, which are quoted on the Stock Exchange. You get tax relief at 20 per cent on up to £100,000 in any tax year, provided you hold the shares for at least five years. The proceeds are free of both income tax and capital gains tax, and if you are reinvesting money which arose from disposing of an asset on which capital gains tax would be due, you can defer that tax.

Single-premium insurance bonds

These are technically insurance policies, so you pay no capital gains tax or basic-rate income tax on them yourself – this is paid by the insurance fund. Higher-rate taxpayers may have to pay higher-rate income tax on any gain, but you can take an income of up to five per cent of your original investment and put off any tax until you finally cash in the bond.

How to buy

You can buy shares and investment trusts through stockbrokers or banks (the Association of Private Client Investment Managers and

Stockbrokers★ has a free guide to private client stockbrokers).
Commission rates vary widely, but usually range between 1 and
1.65 per cent for deals of up to, say, £7,000, with minimum commissions of anywhere between £10 and £40. You also pay 0.5 per
cent stamp duty on purchases (not sales). Note that these are execution-only rates, where the broker simply arranges the deal – if
you want advice it will usually cost you more. The broker may also
make additional fixed charges, such as a 'settlement charge' of, say,
£2, and, with some brokers, charges may be higher if you want to
continue to have a share certificate in these days of paperless share
trading. Note that if you have access to the Internet, you will find an
increasing number of on-line share trading and information sites.
The APCIMS★ web site is a good place to start.

You can buy investment trust regular savings schemes direct
from the company, commission-free: contact the Association of
Investment Trust Companies★ for companies offering such
schemes.

You will find the unit trust and life insurance funds available,
their prices, and fund managers' addresses, in the *Financial Times*;
other papers also give some information. Instead of stockbrokers'
commission, you will pay some or all of the following charges –
your investment must grow to cover at least the charges before you
will make any money:

- Annual management charges, typically 1 or 1.5 per cent, but can
  be more, particularly if initial charges are low.
- The 'bid-offer spread': as with shares, you get a lower ('bid')
  price if you sell than if you buy ('offer' price). The spread
  incorporates the manager's initial charge, which is typically 5
  per cent but can be as low as one per cent or even zero, or as
  high as 6.5 per cent. The spread is usually one or two per cent
  more than the initial charge. Increasingly, however, funds are
  moving to a system of 'single pricing', with the same price for
  buyers and sellers. In due course, they will all be required to
  change to the new system.
- On some funds, an exit charge if you sell within a set period of
  buying (in which case there may be a low initial charge, or none
  at all).

'BROKER BONDS'

Many independent financial advisers pick and choose from the funds available to make up their own funds. They aim to choose investments which suit their own clientele and, by shopping around, to improve the return. However, some funds have high charges but mediocre or even poor performance.

British Government stocks

The government puts issues of stocks up for sale as a way of financing the public sector. Often known as 'gilts', there are all sorts of different ones on the market, maturing from one to 40 years away. Depending on which one you choose, they can be useful either for people who are happy to take a risk or for those who are not; non-taxpayers and higher-rate taxpayers; income; or growth. Also see page 145 for the index-linked variety.

Most have a set redemption date, when the government promises to pay out a fixed amount, in multiples of £100 (the 'nominal value'). So if you keep them till then you will know exactly what you will get back, though, of course, their purchasing power will have been eroded by inflation. In the meantime, most gilts also pay out a fixed income – the 'coupon' – twice a year. Keeping gilts until maturity is the low-risk route.

Happy to take some risk? You can buy and sell gilts before maturity on the stock market, where their price will depend on supply and demand. Sometimes the price will be above the amount you will get on maturity, sometimes less: it depends on things like how the fixed interest rate compares with interest rates in general and how long it is until maturity.

Gilts are free of capital gains tax, so are worth considering for people who are liable to pay this tax. High-coupon gilts are good for people who need income, or for people who pay little or no tax: higher-rate taxpayers who do not need income can buy low-coupon gilts, which pay very little interest.

How to buy gilts
New issues can be bought through advertisements in newspapers. Existing issues can be bought through stockbrokers or banks, in

which case you will have commission to pay (probably a bit less than for shares).

Alternatively, you can buy gilts by post through the Bank of England Brokerage Service*. This is relatively cheap – it costs 0.7 per cent on the first £5,000 with a minimum of £12.50 for purchases (no minimum for sales). No tax is deducted from the income before you get it, but you can choose to have 20 per cent tax deducted before payment, if you prefer.

Corporate bonds

Companies may decide to raise money by issuing corporate bonds rather than shares. Corporate bonds are simply fixed-interest loans. They work rather like gilts in having a 'nominal' value and in being traded on the stock exchange, but they usually carry a rather higher interest rate than gilts because of the risk that the company could default on the loan. There are other similar ways of investing in companies, such as through debentures (which carry a lower risk and a lower return than corporate bonds as they are secured on company assets), and convertible loan stock (fixed-interest bonds with the right to convert into shares on pre-set conditions).

You can buy corporate bonds through stockbrokers and financial advisers, and you can also include some in an ISA. Interest is paid with 20 per cent tax deducted, but higher-rate taxpayers pay more and non-taxpayers can reclaim tax. Proceeds of 'qualifying' bonds are free of capital gains tax.

Permanent Interest-Bearing Shares (PIBS)

These are fixed-interest loans to building societies. They work rather like gilts in that they can be bought or sold on the stock market for more (or less) than their face value, but unlike most gilts they have no set repayment date. Gains are free of capital gains tax and income is paid out twice-yearly, after deduction of some tax. The hitch is that although you are investing in a building society, PIBS-holders come last in the line of debtors if the society does fold, and they are not covered by any compensation scheme. You can buy them through stockbrokers, or there are a few specialist investment funds which aim to reduce the risk by investing in a range of societies' PIBS. However, with the conversion of many building societies into banks, very few PIBs are available now.

Long-term savings plans

You can use many of the investments above for regular saving, provided you can meet the minimum investment. For saving over ten years, investment-type life insurance and friendly society policies are good for discipline. But if you fail to keep them up you can lose out badly: for example, if you cash in during the first couple of years you could get little or nothing back, and even after that, returns can be poor on early withdrawals.

The financial soundness of insurance companies and the marketing of their products are regulated by the Financial Services Authority* (see Chapter 11). If your company goes under, the Policyholders Protection Board protects at least 90 per cent of any (reasonable) sum guaranteed by your policy.

All types of policy must have some life insurance built in, in order to qualify for various tax advantages. How much depends on the policy – an endowment policy is mainly for investment and there are also unit-linked savings plans; both types have little insurance, while a 'flexible cover plan' allows you to vary how much is invested and how much buys insurance. However, on the whole, keeping your investments separate from your insurance avoids tying up your money for 10 years.

With-profits policies

These add annual bonuses to the amount you are insured for: the amount depends on how well the company's investments perform. Once given, annual bonuses cannot be taken away, but there is usually an additional 'terminal' bonus on maturity or death. The annual bonus system tends to smooth out the peaks and troughs in your investment. When returns are high, the company may not pay them all out as bonuses, but use them to keep up bonuses in leaner periods. However, terminal bonuses have become more important over the years and can now make up as much as 50 per cent of your total payout – so if your policy matures in a bad year, you can lose out.

Unit-linked policies

These allocate your money to units in funds of things like shares or property. All gains (or losses), minus charges and tax, are paid out, so your policy can rise or fall in value. 'Unitised' with-profits policies, or 'with-profits' funds offered by unit-linked policies, are a mix: see pages 97–8 for how they work.

Tax

There are tax advantages, but only for higher-rate taxpayers. The return from an insurance policy is free of tax in your hands (unless it is cashed in early, in which case some higher-rate tax may be payable), because the insurance fund pays any capital gains tax or basic-rate income tax due.

Friendly Society policies work like other life insurance policies, except for 'tax-exempt' schemes, which are completely free of tax. However, the maximum investment for tax-exempt schemes is low, at £25 a month or £270 a year; and the tax advantage could be outweighed by high charges.

Income-producers

Many of the types of investment above can be used to give income – see pages 127–8 for some ideas. But there are some specialist investments. Note that minimum investments have to be fairly high (i.e. thousands, rather than hundreds, of pounds) in order to pay out a worthwhile monthly income.

Building Society Monthly Income Accounts

These normally have variable interest rates, so are affected when rates fall. Before buying, check how easy it is for you to get your money out.

National Savings Income Bonds

Income bonds also pay variable interest monthly, and you have to give three months' notice (or lose 90 days' interest) to get your money back. The minimum initial investment is £2,000. However, they are convenient for non-taxpayers since although the income is taxable it is paid out before tax. Buy them through post offices, or see under National Savings in the address section.

National Savings Pensioners Bonds

You have to be at least 60 to buy these. The minimum investment is £500, the maximum £50,000 and they pay monthly interest which is guaranteed for a fixed term of either two or five years. You do not have to give notice to get your money back at the end of the term, but for withdrawals before then you have to give 60 days' notice, during which no interest is earned. Immediate withdrawal is possible with the loss of 90 days' interest. Like most other National Savings schemes, the interest is taxable but paid out before tax. Leaflets are available in post offices, or see the address section at the back of the book for the National Savings phone number.

Guaranteed income bonds

Insurance companies sell lump-sum investments which give fixed interest, providing you invest for a fixed period (usually four or five years, but it can vary between one and ten years). As with all fixed-interest investments, the risk here is that you buy at a time when interest rates are low. They are usually variants of single-premium insurance bonds (see page 135), so check how the tax rules may affect you before you buy. Also see page 213. The Saturday edition of the *Financial Times* lists companies currently offering the highest rates.

Annuities

Also sold by insurance companies, annuities give an income, usually for the rest of your life. The amount depends on your age, sex, whether it is a joint annuity (you can arrange for it to continue either until the first death, or until both have died) and whether the income is fixed or increasing. However, you cannot get your money back again. This makes them a gamble: if you live longer than the company expects, you will do well, but the converse is equally true. You can, however, pay extra for a guarantee that income will continue for a set number of years. Because the rate you get depends on interest rates generally at the time you buy, you could end up stuck with a very poor income if rates later rise.

The income is usually paid out after deduction of some tax (though non-taxpayers can arrange with the company to have it paid gross) but only part of your monthly income is taxable – the rest counts as a return of your capital. Annuity rates vary considerably between companies, so shop around. An independent financial adviser (see Chapter 11) may help, or see *Money Management* magazine.*

Index-linked investments

There are only two types of investment that are linked to the Retail Prices Index: National Savings Certificates and British Government stocks (gilts). But all sorts of schemes are marketed which guarantee to increase your investment in line with a stock market index – for example, 'tracker' funds. These are often good-value ways of buying into the stock market, but check exactly what you are buying. In the past some 'guaranteed equity bonds' have guaranteed that your capital is index-linked, but ignored the income which most stock market investments also pay out.

Index-linked National Savings Certificates
Like other National Savings Certificates (see page 133), these are two-year or five-year tax-free investments for a minimum of £100 and maximum of £10,000. If you cash one in within a year, you get back only the money you invested. But after a year its value is increased in line with the change in the Retail Prices Index (RPI) since you bought it. If you hold your certificate for the full term, you get interest on top of inflation. When the term is up, you can keep your money where it is and your investment will continue to be index-linked, and may also get a tax-free bonus, depending on what issue of certificates you hold. If the RPI falls, the value of your certificate falls too, though you still get the interest, and it is guaranteed that when you cash it in you will get back at least what you invested (plus the interest).

Index-linked British Government stocks
These work like other gilts (see page 140) but when the life of the gilt comes to an end the person then owning it will be paid the nominal value of the gilt increased in line with inflation over its lifetime. All the stocks pay out a small income, also guaranteed to increase each year in line with inflation. However, whether or not your investment keeps pace with inflation depends entirely on the price at which you buy (or sell) the gilt and whether or not you hold it until redemption.

Chapter 11

Getting financial advice

At best, a financial adviser can steer your money into investments which are exactly right for your needs – in the process lifting a lot of work and worry from your shoulders. But at worst, an adviser can (and a few do) disappear with your money. Other pitfalls are less drastic, but also damaging to your pocket, for example ending up with an investment which suits the adviser – because it pays a high commission, say – but does not suit you.

So do you really need an adviser?

With such concerns in mind, you may think it is better to do it yourself. In any case it is worth finding out something about the different ways of saving and investing, whether or not you end up using an adviser. But there will be times when you feel you need help, or at least the chance to talk over your ideas with someone else.

The past 10 years have seen an improvement in the protection available to investors, with the implementation of the Financial Services Act 1986. This is due to be replaced by new legislation, the Financial Services and Markets Bill, some time in 2000. This will streamline the current system, setting up one single regulator, the Financial Services Authority (FSA)*, in place of a range of existing self-regulating organisations and government departments. The legislation will retain much of the existing regulatory powers, but it will also extend the regulator's scope in some respects: for example, the FSA has a duty to improve public understanding of the financial system, and is developing a range of useful free booklets. The emphasis nowadays is very much on prevention, rather than cure, based on the principle that you are your own best protection.

Where to get advice

Accountants

All qualified accountants cover personal tax, and often some aspects of investment, during their training, and many will be able to introduce you to specialists, but some firms employ specialist financial advisers (not necessarily trained accountants themselves) or have subsidiary companies which are authorised under the FSA. So, while accountants can be a good source of advice on general financial strategy and tax-planning, and may sometimes manage portfolios of investments, it is important to check exactly what they are authorised to offer and what expertise they have.

Accountants usually charge a fee for their advice, which varies greatly depending on the firm. If they introduce you to an independent financial adviser they may get a cut of the adviser's commission. They may also get commission if you buy life insurance, pensions or unit trusts through them, but if they are qualified as either 'Chartered' or 'Certified' accountants, they must tell you how much the commission is. In practice, many will set the commission against their fees.

Actuaries

Actuaries are expert at calculating probabilities and future values from statistical and other data – for example, how much an insurance company will have to charge in order to cover what it expects to have to pay out in many years' time. They are often employed by pension and insurance companies, but there are also firms of 'consulting' actuaries who can give independent financial advice. Their specialisation and independence makes them probably the best source of help with a complex pension problem, but they do not come cheap. Expect to pay several hundred pounds for their advice (see page 149 for a source of free help with employer pension schemes, through your Citizens Advice Bureau).

Banks

Most high-street banks can sell you their 'own-brand' insurance, savings schemes, investments and mortgages, or (through subsidiary companies) give you independent investment advice, manage your investments for you, write wills and act as executors, or offer tax-planning or share-dealing services. For this reason before going ahead it is important to check whether staff are acting as independent advisers or just as representatives for their own-brand products; as a general rule, virtually all banks sell their own products through their branches and other products and services through centralised departments or subsidiaries. If bank staff are acting as independent financial advisers, they cannot recommend the bank's own products unless they can show that they are 'better than the best' available elsewhere.

A bank is only as good as its parts, and before using one you should also see what a specialist can offer. The charge for advice will generally be in line with what a specialist would charge – e.g. if selling insurance, they will get commission, but if dealing in shares for you, they will make charges similar to a stockbroker's.

PORTFOLIO MANAGEMENT

This just means managing a lump sum or 'portfolio' of investments for you, in order to meet your aims in investing. The two basic sorts of service are:

- **Discretionary management** – you give them discretion to make decisions on your behalf.
- **Advisory management** – they make recommendations but leave the final decision to you.

The minimum portfolio you can get professionally managed could be anything from £10,000 to £100,000, sometimes more. For small amounts, you will usually be channelled into a portfolio of unit trusts. Fees for portfolio management vary: they can be a yearly one per cent of the value of your portfolio, say, a flat annual fee or a slice of the profits, or a mixture of methods.

Building societies

All building societies will offer advice on their own savings schemes and mortgages. They also earn large amounts of commission through selling insurance and some types of investment. However, most can sell life insurance from only one company, and general insurance from a restricted number. Few now offer independent advice, although some others do so through subsidiary companies.

See page 131 for how to get information on building society rates. You could try asking financial advisers whether they subscribe to any of the services which publish building society rates, but there is little incentive for commission-based financial advisers to give advice on building society accounts, which pay little if any commission.

Citizens Advice Bureaux (CABx) and charities

There is a CAB in most towns, and some areas have specialist money advice centres, but they are often very busy. They tend to concentrate on social security, debt and income tax problems, but are also a useful source of leaflets and can direct you to other organisations. If you have a pension problem, your CAB can also direct you to a local pensions expert from the network of volunteers run by the Occupational Pensions Advisory Service.*

Age Concern* and Help the Aged* both run general insurance services, selling house, car, travel and pet insurance policies (but not specifically advice). However, both charities are providing their services through tie-ups with commercial ventures, so you should not suspend your critical faculties when dealing with them.

Independent Financial Advisers (IFAs)

This has become the catch-all name for anybody authorised under the Financial Services Act as an independent investment adviser, but they do vary in what they are authorised to offer. Some are not much more than life insurance and pension sales people, paid by commission, while others offer a wide range of investment services, including portfolio management and employing specialists in areas like tax and pensions. Increasingly, they may offer you the option of paying them a fee rather than working on commission (if a fee is charged, they should either pass on any commission to you, or re-invest it in whatever you buy, or set it against the fee). You should be told the amount of any commission.

The range of their services depends partly on what they are permitted to offer by their regulator – only some firms are allowed to hold and manage your money, for example, while others act as middlemen only. Special expertise is also needed in particularly technical areas, e.g. transfers of pensions from one scheme to another. So it is important to check that they really have the appropriate experience and qualifications to offer the service you need.

To get a free list of three IFAs in your area, ring IFA Promotion,* or, if you would prefer to pay a fee in order to reduce the possibility of the advice being affected by commission, *Money Management* magazine* can produce a list of advisers who charge a fee. Note, though, that advisers have to apply to get on these lists, so the lists are not exhaustive and are no guide to the quality of the advice available from the advisers.

Insurance brokers and advisers

Anybody can sell general insurance and use the title of insurance broker, but they must comply with an industry code of conduct run by the Association of British Insurers.* Insurance brokers specialise in general and life insurance. They are often authorised to sell and advise on investments as well, but if they do so they must be authorised by the Financial Services Authority. They will usually be paid by commission, so be aware of the risk that this might influence their advice. Their code of conduct says that you should be told the amount of commission, if you ask (and for most investments you should now be told automatically).

Insurance companies

As well as general or life insurance, these also sell pensions and often have subsidiaries offering other products, such as unit trusts, too. If you know what you want, and are happy to be offered just one company's products, then an insurance company ought to be the best source of information about its own products.

Unfortunately, many life insurance companies sell through a sales force of commission-only representatives, who vary hugely in quality and training. So make sure that what they say is backed up in the 'key features' information that they are obliged to give you.

Investment managers

In their purest form, these manage institutional funds of investments, e.g. unit trusts or pension funds. However, they will sometimes offer services, such as investment advice or portfolio management, to private investors with substantial sums to invest.

Again, they may not charge a fee if just selling you insurance or a pension for which they get commission, but they will charge for portfolio management. Services such as tax help may cost extra.

Publications

Consumers' Association* publishes several *Which?* books on financial topics and best buy rates for a range of financial products, including savings accounts, are given in *Which?* magazine every few months.

Some newspapers also publish best buy rates in their Saturday money sections. Daily papers also list a range of share price and other information, though the *Financial Times* is the most comprehensive. For very keen private investors, *Money Management** is one monthly magazine which publishes detailed surveys of particular investments, like unit trusts and pension plans. Age Concern* has some useful financial publications.

Solicitors

Like accountants, most solicitors should be able to give general financial advice, or refer you to an independent financial adviser, but some firms may employ specialists or undertake portfolio management. They also give tax advice and write wills and act as executors (but see Chapter 32). They may get commission if you buy things like insurance or pensions through them, but they can keep this commission only with your consent: they will usually set the commission against their fees.

Stockbrokers

Although stockbrokers specialise in buying and selling things like shares and British Government stocks (gilts), they may also offer unit trusts, portfolio management and general investment advice. As well as 'discretionary' services (where they take the decisions on your behalf) and 'advisory' services (where they advise, but you make the final decisions), some also offer 'execution-only' share-dealing, where they just buy and sell on your instructions. Not all deal with private clients – write to the Association of Private Client Investment Managers and Stockbrokers (APCIMS)* for a free list of those who do. Proshare* is an organisation that exists to promote share ownership and can give general information on shares.

Stockbrokers charge commission when buying and selling shares for you (see page 139), and a fee for portfolio management. Extra services such as tax help may be charged for separately.

Trade associations

Look at an adviser's letterhead to see which trade associations he or she belongs to. These exist to promote the relevant product or service, and so are definitely not independent. However, they usually offer free leaflets, information packs and sometimes lists of members. You can also ask them for a copy of any code of conduct – not a guarantee of good behaviour, but a useful thing to wave at your adviser if you think you are not getting the treatment you deserve. If there is no independent system for handling complaints, they will sometimes mediate – though with varying degrees of vigour.

Financial Services Authority protection

Authorisation

Anyone who carries on an investment business without being 'authorised' to do so (and who is not in an 'exempt' category) will be committing a criminal offence, and any contracts you have with them can be made void. In future, businesses must be authorised by the Financial Services Authority (FSA)★, but the FSA is still in the process of taking over the functions of existing regulators, so you may still come across the following names:

- **PIA** – Personal Investment Authority – covered independent financial advisers, insurance companies and their sales forces, unit trust managers and friendly societies.
- **IMRO** – Investment Management Regulatory Organisation – predominantly institutional investment managers, e.g. pension fund managers, unit trust managers and some banks.
- **SFA** – Securities and Futures Authority – covered stockbrokers, dealers in international stocks and bonds and money market investments, and advisers, managers and dealers in futures and options.

You can find out whether or not a firm is authorised by contacting the FSA★ Public Enquiries Office. The FSA also publishes various free booklets.

Independence

Advisers selling life insurance and unit trusts must fall within only one of two categories. One category must give completely independent advice on all the products of that type on the market. Advisers in the other category must act only as representatives, selling and advising on just one company's or group's products. Representatives can be individuals, who may be self-employed, or separate companies, often known as 'appointed representatives', which might themselves employ several representatives. Both categories have to tell you how much commission they get, if any, before you buy.

Standards of conduct

Once authorised, investment firms which fail to abide by the rules can be disciplined or, at worst, have their authorisation removed. Be aware that your come-back against the adviser, should something go wrong, will also be limited if you ask him or her to work on an 'execution-only' basis (i.e. following your instructions without giving advice). Beware of signing forms agreeing to be treated as an 'execution-only' client without being fully aware of the consequences.

The main points of the rules governing the conduct of businesses dealing with private individuals are:

- Investment businesses have to take into account your best interests when dealing with you.
- In most cases an adviser has to know the customer, i.e. be fully aware of your personal and financial situation.
- Independent advisers must take into account the range of products on the market and your particular needs, and must not sell you a particular product if they are aware of another one which would meet your needs better. Company representatives have the same responsibilities in respect of the range of products and services provided by the company to which they are tied. In either case, if nothing they can offer suits your needs, they must tell you so.
- Advisers must give you a 'terms of business letter' making their status clear, i.e. whether they are independent or tied, their obligations to you and whether they are paid commission or charge a fee. Independent advisers must give additional information about the services they offer, for example whether they are allowed to handle your money.

- If the adviser is to provide regular services for you, such as managing a portfolio of investments, written client agreements are required instead of terms of business letters. These agreements give details of the services being provided and their cost, set out your investment objectives and the responsibilities of your adviser, and warn of the risks of certain investments.

- You should get all the information you need about specific products you are buying. In the case of life insurance, pension policies, unit trusts, investment trust savings schemes, and OEICs, this information should be in a 'key features' document, given to you before you buy. This tells you how much will be deducted in charges, expressed as a 'reduction in yield' – in other words, if your investment grows by 7 per cent a year, a 1.5 per cent reduction in yield will mean you end up with 5.5 per cent – and what you will get if you cash in early. The key features should also include the cash amount of commission going to whoever is selling you the policy.

- If an adviser recommends you to take out a long-term savings plan, or to cash in an existing plan early, you should be given a written statement explaining why he or she recommended the product.

- Advertisements and illustrations of benefits have to comply with rules about comparisons, references to past performance and give risk warnings if necessary. Note that all companies must work out illustrations using standard growth rates set by regulators, but incorporating the company's own charges.

- Proper arrangements must be made for keeping your money (e.g. money awaiting investment) separate from the adviser's money.

- Investment businesses must ensure that their staff are competent to deal with you, and advisers dealing with the public must have a minimum qualification.

'Cooling-off'

Financial sales representatives are allowed to cold-call, i.e. visit or telephone you without your previous invitation, unless selling some particular investments. But if you buy life insurance, pensions or unit trusts as a result of a cold-call, during which advice was given, you get a cooling-off period. This allows you to cancel within 14 days of getting a notice telling you of your rights (or before the first payment, if later). But this does not apply to unit trusts or single-premium life insurance bonds if you received no advice (i.e. bought on an 'execution-only' basis), or bought either through an advertisement or in line with your customer agreement.

How to complain

Each of the regulators is required to have some system for dealing with complaints about the businesses they authorise. However, if you have a complaint against any investment business you should first take it up with the business itself; if you are still dissatisfied with its response, the business is obliged to tell you what to do next. For example, the PIA Ombudsman★ is currently the final adjudicator for complaints against PIA members, while the Investment Ombudsman★ handles complaints against IMRO★ members.

Even if your investment is not covered by the Financial Services Act, it may be covered by an Ombudsman scheme. See the address section at the back of the guide. In future, however, all eight existing financial ombudsmen will be amalgamated into one single scheme, the Financial Services Ombudsman. In the meantime, if you are unclear about how to take a complaint forward, and the business you have been dealing with will not help, you can contact the FSA.★

Compensation

If you find yourself in the unfortunate position of having lost money in a bankrupt or fraudulent investment company, or through the negligence of an authorised adviser, there is an Investors' Compensation Scheme★ (see page 130 for protection for bank and building society accounts). Note, however, that this will only cover you if you do business with an authorised firm – so it is important to check a firm's authorisation with the FSA.★

The scheme can pay up to £48,000 – full protection for the first £30,000 invested, then protection for 90 per cent of the next £20,000.

Getting the best from your adviser

Decide what your aims are

If you have got a clear idea of what you want from your money, it will be easier to choose an adviser to help you achieve those aims. Think about when you are likely to want the money back, what degree of risk you are willing to take, and whether you want your savings to provide you with an income or lump sum.

Contact two or three advisers

Decide what type of adviser you want, then draw up a shortlist of, say, three advisers. See page 150 for how to find independent financial advisers: otherwise, try *Yellow Pages*, or personal recommendations from friends in similar situations to you. Talk to all your shortlisted advisers before choosing: the FSA produce a leaflet with suggested questions to ask.

Avoid advisers who don't ask questions

Advisers have a duty to 'know the customer' – in other words, know enough about them to make sensible recommendations. Exactly what questions they should ask is not specified by law (and you are under no obligation to answer), but should include things like:

- your age, health and marital status
- number and ages of children and other dependants
- size and make-up of family income
- your regular financial commitments
- your tax position
- your existing savings and investment
- your home and mortgage
- your existing pension and insurance policies
- how long you want to invest for
- your reasons for investing, e.g. how important it is to you to get a high income or make a capital gain
- whether you want to be able to get your money back quickly
- what degree of risk you are prepared to take with your money.

Ask exactly what sort of advisers they are

Double-check what the advisers tell you by looking on his or her business card or the terms of business letters or client agreements, and if the adviser is a representative, check that he or she still works for the firm he or she represents. Their stationery should say who the regulator is and, if the adviser is not independent, which company he or she represents. Also find out what qualifications and experience the adviser you will be dealing with has: these might be accountancy or legal qualifications, or specialist exams including some run by the Chartered Insurance Institute* (CII), the Chartered Institute of Bankers, or the Securities Institute. Note that all advisers must have a minimum qualification. For most advisers this will be an examination run by one of the institutes above.

Check what level of compensation is available should the firm crash, and whether the adviser has professional indemnity insurance. This insurance protects the adviser, not you – it pays out if the adviser has to pay damages because of their negligence or, in some cases, fraud – but at least means that the money should be there if you make a successful claim against the adviser.

Be clear about what you want your adviser to do

Do you want advice on just one type of investment, or a range? Some advisers specialise in just one area. Do you expect your adviser to plan your investments and then leave day-to-day management up to you, or do you want them to take care of all this too?

Check the cost of advice

Ask whether the adviser will charge a fee or is paid commission. Even if you do not have to hand over any money yourself to get advice, this does not mean that the advice is 'free'. Commission is deducted from investors' funds (usually even if you buy direct from the company), so in the long run the return from your investment will be less than it might otherwise have been. An adviser may agree to 'rebate' some of the commission, either by giving you cash back or by arranging for more of your money to be invested for you. However, it goes without saying that you should not choose an adviser purely on the grounds of what rebate he or she will give you.

If the adviser charges a fee, make sure you know how much it will be, and what you will get for your money. For example, if the adviser is going to be managing your money, how often will you receive a progress report? What extras are available, and at what price – portfolio valuations, tax advice, share-dealing?

Get everything in writing

Note the time, date, person you spoke to, and content of any telephone conversations and meetings. Confirm them in writing if possible (with a copy for yourself). These notes could be vital if you have a dispute.

Avoid making cheques payable to a go-between

If you invest in something, make your cheque payable to the company providing the investment, not the adviser's firm. That way there is no temptation for fraudulent or hard-up intermediaries to divert the money to their own pockets. If a firm has got to handle your money (e.g. it is managing it for you), check that it is actually authorised to do so. The money should be held in a separate client account.

Keep an eye on your adviser

If an adviser is going to be looking after your money in the long term, ask how often the adviser will keep in touch, who will be dealing with you and what happens if they leave (the turnover of company representatives can be high), and expect regular reports on your investments.

Do not be afraid to ask questions

Beware of claims that seem too good to be true – they probably are. If an adviser does not take the time to explain, or cannot answer your questions, steer clear. Personal finance may be complicated, but need not be incomprehensible.

Investing on the Internet

The Internet is a wonderful source of information and if you are a keen investor it is an excellent way to get share price information and buy and sell shares. But proceed with caution: the Internet itself is unregulated. Find out who you are dealing with before you part with your money. In particular, find out where the firm is based, who regulates it, and which company's laws apply if things go wrong. Some Internet 'cowboys' run web sites that look similar to those of legitimate firms, using similar site addresses. If in doubt, look up the firm in the phone book and call them to double check. Don't rely on the phone number in the web site – that may be bogus too.

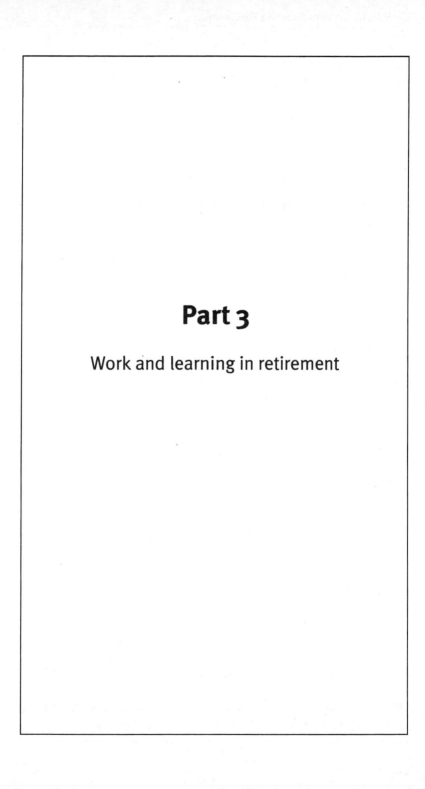

Part 3

Work and learning in retirement

Chapter 12

Deciding what to do next

You may not feel ready to leave the world of work, even after you have left your main job. Yet how realistic is it to think about carrying on working when a substantial proportion of the population remains jobless, and many employers continue to discriminate against older workers?

In practice, there are some trends which could favour older workers. First, while job losses continue in manufacturing industries, the number of employees in other industries, such as the service sector, has grown. Second, there is an increasing shift towards different patterns of work, such as part-time or casual work and self-employment. Part-time work, for example, grew by over 20 per cent between 1986 and 1996. Both these trends might be expected to suit older people.

Nor are employers' preconceptions of the suitability of older workers necessarily borne out by reality. According to the health study undertaken by the Carnegie Inquiry into the Third Age, a person's performance is governed as much by their experience and skill as by their age. Indeed, as you get older, the difference between individuals can be more pronounced than variations between age groups – so definitions of 'average' become less meaningful.

You can boost your chances of carrying on working, if that is what you want, or just enhance your leisure time, by improving your existing skills or learning new ones. The difficulty may be not so much finding a course, as deciding what direction you want to take. The government is encouraging individuals to take up opportunities for training by introducing Individual Learning Accounts during 2000. See pages 167–70 for more on lifelong learning.

Should you carry on working?

Irrespective of what other people choose to do, you have to make your own decisions about whether to carry on with your current employer, if you have the option to do so, or to look for other work. There are a number of financial factors to take into account, as well as your feelings on the subject.

National Insurance

If you carry on working, you will have to carry on paying National Insurance contributions, unless you are over state pension age (i.e. currently 60 for women, 65 for men) or your earnings are small. This applies whether you are self-employed or an employee: for more on types and amounts of National Insurance see page 36 and the leaflets on National Insurance available from any social security office (also called the Benefits Agency). If you are still working for an employer at state pension age, you should receive a certificate of exemption from the Department of Social Security to give to your employer, who will still have to pay employers' contributions for you.

The effect on your tax bill

Once you reach 65, there is an unpleasant tax trap to watch out for, which may reduce the financial attractions of carrying on working. As explained in Chapter 15, this pitfall concerns the higher age-related allowances you qualify for at that age. These higher allowances are reduced once your taxable income is above a certain level (£16,800 in the year from 6 April 1999), making the effective rate of tax on income above this level 34.5 per cent. If this applies to you, you will need to set this tax penalty against your desire to carry on working for other reasons.

The effect on your state pensions

Carrying on working will nowadays either benefit your state pension or have no effect on it, depending on what you decide to do. The 'earnings rule', under which your state retirement pension was reduced by earnings above a certain amount, was abolished in 1989.

Once you reach state retirement age, you can choose to defer drawing your state pension for up to five years. Your pension is increased by 7.5 per cent for each year you put off the pension (and proportionately for shorter periods). The maximum increase you can earn is 37.5 per cent (i.e. 5 × 7.5 per cent). The extra pension is increased in line with the Retail Prices Index once it starts to be paid.

Note that from 6 April 2010, deferring your pension becomes more attractive: for each year you delay claiming after that date, your pension will increase by roughly 10.4 per cent. You will also be able to defer your pension indefinitely, rather than for a maximum of five years.

If you decide to defer your state pension, you have to give up all your pensions from the state for that time – in other words, you cannot just give up your basic pension; you must also give up any SERPS and graduated pensions and, if you are a married man who would have received extra for your wife, or a wife who would have received a pension based on your husband's contributions, that pension has to be given up too. But once you start to take the basic pension, any increase will apply to all your state pensions as listed above.

Should you defer?

If you are a single man, it may not be such a good idea to defer your pension while current rules apply. At the age of 70, the average man can expect to live for another 11 or so years. If he gave up a full-rate basic pension for five years, he would be giving up £17,355 in total in today's prices. Once his pension started to be paid, it would be 37.5 per cent higher but it would take $13\frac{1}{3}$ years before he had received as much in extra pension as he had originally given up. Women, who at age 65 have an average life expectancy of around 18 years, and married couples, are much more likely to get a good deal out of deferring their pension. Of course, anyone who is in poor health (and thus has below average life expectancy) should also think twice before deferring a state pension in this way.

Another factor to take into account is your tax position: if your state pension would cause you to lose your higher age-related allowances (see Chapter 15), it might tip the balance in favour of deferring.

The effect on employer pensions

If you continue working for your current employer after normal retirement age, you will need to check the rules of your scheme to see whether you can continue to improve your pension – see pages 75–6 for the main options.

If you move to a different job or into self-employment, say, then like any other job-mover you will be faced with the decision of whether to leave the pension you have already built up in the employer scheme or whether to move it to a personal pension plan or a special scheme (see page 76). However, if you have built up a reasonable pension in one employer scheme, you should be cautious about moving it.

The effect on personal pensions

This is more straightforward: the more you contribute, and the longer you put off drawing your pension, the greater the pension fund that should be available to you when you eventually retire. You can contribute to a personal pension plan as long as you are under the age of 75, and as long as you continue to have 'relevant earnings' – i.e. earnings from self-employment or earnings from a job where you have chosen not to join an employer pension scheme. Older people are also allowed to contribute more than the normal maximum allowed by the Inland Revenue: see Chapter 7 for how to use these rules to your advantage.

Pensions from your new job

You may want to use your new job as a last-minute chance to boost your eventual income on retirement. But you could find your options drawing in, as your new employer's pension scheme may not accept people above a certain age. However, as long as you are under the age of 75 you will still be able to take out a personal pension plan instead.

Will you be better off?

This is not as strange a question as it may seem. As Chapter 4 makes clear, working can bring with it certain costs, the most obvious of which is the cost of getting to work (and this could take up a higher proportion of your income than before if, say, you are still working five days a week but for half-days only). Before you take the plunge, particularly if you are proposing to take a pay cut, you need to cost out your new job thoroughly.

Tax credits

The risk of losing means-tested state benefits can be a disincentive for people to move from unemployment back into work. In an attempt to tackle this the government has introduced a number of 'tax credit' schemes: effectively means-tested state benefits paid to people in work. They are administered by the Inland Revenue, and if you are taxed under PAYE (see Chapter 16) your benefit will usually be paid through your pay packet.

In October 1999 the Disabled Persons Tax Credit and the Working Families Tax Credit were launched. However, an employment credit for people aged over 50 who have been on benefit for six months or more is being piloted, and the government may extend it more widely in future. See page 53 for more on the Disabled Persons Tax Credit.

Non-financial factors

Although money is usually the main motive for carrying on working, other factors such as companionship and job satisfaction are also important. However, you will probably have to stop work, or at least scale it down, at some point, so even if you have the chance to carry on your current work after your normal retirement date, you may want to consider changing the way you work in order to build up alternative networks of friends and activities outside work.

Old employer or new job?

Even if you are happy with your current employer, you may feel that the time has come to move to, say, different hours or a different role within the company. Although some employers have schemes for seconding older staff to other roles, such as to work for charities for a few months, and others may welcome proposals for part-time working if they are trying to reduce staff numbers or change working patterns within the organisation, your employer may not agree with your proposals. You could strengthen your case by looking at your proposal from the employer's point of view and finding solutions to the objections you anticipate. For example, your bid to move to a job-share arrangement may be strengthened if you can make the bid jointly with another willing sharer. For secondments and volunteer placements, Business in the Community* offers a service matching up companies and charities (it does not deal with individuals).

Part-time or full-time?

Part-time work can provide an undeniably attractive way of weaning yourself off full-time work, and some employers are reducing the number of full-time employees in favour of part-timers – whose employment rights have been improved in recent years. However, some employment rights (such as the right to statutory redundancy pay) are lost altogether to people over state pension age. And check what benefits a prospective employer is offering; they may be less generous for part-timers than for full-time employees. See Chapter 13 for more on employees' rights.

Do be on your guard against some of the 'get-rich-quick' ads in newspapers and against those home-working schemes, often paid on a piece-work basis, where it is virtually impossible to make a reasonable income.

Employee or go it alone?

An employer may not be prepared to keep you on as a part-timer, but could still consider giving you some work as a freelance or consultant. This gives them greater flexibility but may also suit you, freeing you up to work for other people as well or giving you the chance to develop your abilities along different lines. Being self-employed also has some tax advantages, since you can set more expenses off against your tax bill. And you may see retirement or redundancy, with a lump sum in your hand, as a golden opportunity to set up on your own.

But there are potential problems. One reason that your employer may be more prepared to consider this arrangement is that you will no longer qualify for sick pay, holiday pay, and other such benefits: you will have to earn enough to pay for them and other overheads such as stationery yourself. So do not make the mistake, when working out how much to charge, of simply taking your current salary and charging it by the hour or day (unless you have some greater tactical aim in mind!).

Another potential hitch is that if various conditions are not met, the Inland Revenue may class you as employed after all – see Chapter 16.

Paid or voluntary?

If your primary reason for carrying on working is not financial – or you cannot get a paid job at the moment but want to keep your hand in – voluntary work may be the answer. However, before taking the plunge, check on the commitment you will be making and how expenses will be paid.

Try your local library, Citizens Advice Bureau or Council for Voluntary Service (in the phone book under 'volunteer') for lists of voluntary agencies in your area: local newspapers sometimes also carry advertisements. REACH★ and the Retired and Senior Volunteer Programme★ are just two of the agencies that can provide information and help to retired people wanting to take up voluntary work. The British Executive Service Overseas★ (BESO) is an agency that finds people voluntary work in developing countries.

The effect on benefits

If you are receiving Jobseeker's allowance, you normally have to be available for work for at least 40 hours a week, capable of work and actively seeking it. However, if you have been unemployed for three months or more you can study part-time, as long as you remain available for and actively seeking work, and providing your course does not prevent you from taking a job. See leaflet JSALS4 *The rules on part-time education and training* from your local Jobcentre.

If you are doing voluntary work, discuss this with the adviser at the Jobcentre when you have the New Jobseeker Interview necessary to claim Jobseeker's allowance. There is no automatic reduction in the number of hours you need to be available for work, but if offered a job you are allowed 48 hours (it is 24 hours normally) before being required to take it up.

Lifelong learning

A short course may help you decide what direction to take, even if it does not lead you back into paid employment. Local authority classes can provide a good opportunity to try out a particular subject: they sometimes offer cheaper fees for retired people. You may also qualify for a government subsidy through Individual Learning Accounts, which will be introduced during 2000. Holders of the accounts will qualify for 20 per cent discounts on the cost of eligible training courses, up to £500 a year, and greater discounts for certain key courses, e.g. computer literacy. In addition, for each one of the first one million accounts opened, the government will contribute £150, providing the holder also makes a small contribution.

Lifelong learning partnerships are being established throughout England to improve the co-ordination of local adult education. Ask at your local reference library for information about local and national training opportunities.

For more serious study, the Workers' Educational Association (WEA),★ offers a range of subjects. You do not need any qualifications to enrol and your fellow-students will be of a variety of ages and backgrounds. The study course usually lasts for 10 sessions, perhaps with field study courses on local landscapes, wildlife and history. There are also residential courses. Fees for the courses vary; enquire about reductions for retired people. Ask at the library for the address of your local branch or write to the WEA.

The Third Age Trust★ is the national representative body for the University of the Third Age (U3A) movement in the UK. The U3As are self-funded, self-managed organisations that exist to provide day-time education, and creative and leisure activities at minimal cost for men and women no longer in full-time employment. They draw upon the knowledge, experience and skills of their members to organise study and activity groups in accordance with the wishes of the membership. No qualifications are required and none are given. There are currently nearly 400 groups and over 87,000 members. Details of your nearest U3A can be obtained by sending a stamped addressed envelope to the Third Age Trust.

Distance learning

Distance learning provides a greater choice of course than may be available to you locally, but check that the course you are enrolling upon is a reputable one; you can obtain a list of accredited colleges from the Open and Distance Learning Quality Council.★

The three main providers of distance learning courses are the National Extension College★, the Open University★ and the Open College of the Arts.★ None of these bodies demands any qualifications for entry and all course material is sent via the post. You can study at your own pace and you will be given a tutor who will give you support. For details of fees and courses contact the individual bodies.

The National Extension College (NEC) offers a wide range of opportunities from GCSE and A-level courses up to degree and professional level, as well as 'starter' courses designed to ease the way for people who feel unsure of their academic skills. There are also courses for hobbies and subjects such as business skills. Fees are reduced for people on state pensions.

The Open University (OU) offers a variety of courses including BA, BSc and Masters degree courses and Diploma studies. There are also leisure courses on subjects ranging from art to computing. All new students receive a preparatory package before the course begins and there is a choice of foundation courses in the first year which help to develop learning skills. Some courses call for a week's attendance at a summer school. You should expect to pay around £3,500 over four to six years to gain a degree, but you can do individual part-time courses for as little as £200. You can pay in instalments and there is a student hardship fund. The OU has a number of regional centres which you can visit for advice; look for 'Open University' in the telephone book, or contact the Open University Central Enquiry Service.★

The Open College of the Arts★ is an educational charity which offers courses on such subjects as art and design, sculpture, textiles, music, video arts, photography and creative writing, mostly by correspondence. Completing a course may give you credits towards a degree.

Residential courses

The range of residential study courses is vast and growing all the time; the course that interests you may be held at a college, school, field study centre or country mansion in beautiful surroundings. Residential courses are a good way of combining a holiday with your study, and if you go on your own you will find plenty of single companions. The best starting point for researching such courses is

Time to Learn, a book published twice-yearly by the National Institute for Adult Continuing Education.* Another useful publication is *The Summer Academy Brochure*, available free from the Summer Academy.*

Full-time study

If you feel you want to embark on formal study for a degree, contact your local university. Some have extra-mural departments designed for people who can manage only part-time study, but you may want to be a fully paid-up, full-time student. Most universities are very welcoming to mature students, in recognition of the extra experience they can contribute. Lack of formal qualifications may not be a bar to entry.

Chapter 13

Getting a new job

While discrimination on the grounds of age undeniably exists, older people may have a lot to offer employers and canny job-hunters can turn age to their advantage. This chapter looks at how you can improve your chances, as well as your rights once you are in work.

Turning age to your advantage

Research suggests that experience and skill have as much effect on your performance as your age. Bearing this in mind, first spend some time researching the fields of employment you are interested in, thinking about what you have to offer and how this corresponds to employers' interests. But be realistic: are you prepared to change direction if necessary?

When it comes to approaching potential employers, you may need to challenge (gently!) any stereotypes of older workers on the basis of solid fact: your own individual skills and qualities. Table 1 shows typical stereotypes of younger and older workers.

For example, in your job application and at interview you may want to demonstrate, citing your previous employment, how flexible, computer-literate, or 'trainable' you could be. But, as for any job-hunter, of any age, it is essential to do this within the context of the job description: it is no good, and could even be counter-productive, to concentrate on your 20 years of management experience, say, if the job description makes it clear that the job involves working largely on your own to produce your own work. Instead, in this example, you might find it more helpful to show how your management experience has helped you organise your own time efficiently.

Table 1: How employers perceive workers

Employers think that: younger workers have:	older workers have:
Ambition	Stability
Trainability	Reliability
Flexibility	Work commitment
Health	Responsibility
Skills in using information technology	Maturity
Qualifications	Managerial skills
Mobility	

Source: Institute of Manpower Studies

Qualifications can be another false friend. With the continuous introduction of new types of educational system and training in different industries, you do not have to be very old for your qualifications to have been superseded by a new system. If so, the employer may appreciate being told what the current equivalent of your qualification is, or you might find it better to concentrate instead on relevant experience.

If you are not very computer-literate, or if your qualifications are not absolutely appropriate for the field you are interested in, you may need to consider getting some training yourself, in your own time, to demonstrate that you would be willing and able to acquire the necessary knowledge. See Chapter 12 for more on improving your skills.

Where to look

As well as the sources below, consider approaching employers 'on spec'. You can identify companies in your chosen field through directories like *UK Kompass Register*, specialist trade magazines, and local business directories. Main libraries should have these. Sources of vacancies include:

- Jobcentres (in the phone book under 'Employment Service')
- newspapers
- specialist and trade magazines; the ads will also suggest which employment agencies specialise in your field
- local radio station 'job spots'

- professional and trade associations – some provide information on vacancies
- personal contacts – as well as being effective, this is one way of breaking down employers' preconceptions
- employment agencies: check ads to see which advertise in your field of work; the Federation of Recruitment and Employment Services* publishes a yearbook of its members and their specialist services; also check publications such as *The Executive Grapevine* (ask in your library).

Where to get help

Employment agencies

Employment agencies are not allowed to charge you for placing you in a job, except for some jobs, such as acting and modelling. Instead, employers pay them – agencies may see this as an incentive to fill posts on their books, rather than putting you forward only for jobs that are exactly what you are looking for. Better agencies will interview you and give advice on the opportunities available, interviews, what salary you should expect, and how to prepare a CV. If you have any complaints about an agency, contact the Employment Agency Standards Office.*

If you are looking for paid work in the charity sector, the *Guardian* newspaper publishes voluntary sector job advertisements every other Wednesday. Alternatively, you could try writing to relevant charities 'on spec' (the local reference library should have directories of voluntary organisations), pointing out how your experience might help them.

A number of agencies provide short-term work for business executives. These include members of the Association of Temporary and Interim Executive Services* (ATIES).

Once you have booked up with an agency, keep in touch with them regularly. Make sure they check with you before circulating your CV; otherwise, it may be sent more than once to the same company, or to one where you do not want it to go. If you see ads the agency has placed for jobs you are interested in, ring up to make sure your details are put forward.

Self-marketing or career consultancies

These offer training and support in job-hunting, and may provide library facilities and secretarial services, too. Anyone can start up one of these consultancies (there are no controls), so be careful before committing yourself, especially since the fees can run into thousands. If you decide to use a consultancy, check:

- exactly what you will get for your money
- how long the company has been in existence, how many of its clients found a job, and how long it took on average
- that there are staff with both experience of the market and with counselling qualifications (the British Association for Counselling★ can tell you which consultants are members)
- the company complies with the Institute of Personnel and Development★ (IPD) voluntary code of conduct for career consultants (the IPD can tell you about members who follow this code).

Employment Service

This is the name of the government agency which runs local Jobcentres and unemployment benefit offices: you will find your local offices in the phone book under 'Employment Service'. There is also a telephone jobline, Employment Service Direct★.

When you first register as unemployed with a Jobcentre you will be invited to a New Jobseeker's Interview, which is a requirement of claiming Jobseeker's allowance (for more on this, see Chapter 2). After you have been registered as unemployed for three months, you will be called for an interview with an employment adviser; after six months, you may be directed to a Jobclub course, and after 12 months to a Jobplan workshop.

The Employment Service is now operating the New Deal – a government scheme designed to help people make the transition back into work. Several parts of this scheme are relevant for older people, for example the New Deal 50 plus and the New Deal for the Disabled. These are not limited to the registered unemployed: they are also available to those on other benefits and some who are not on benefits, such as carers. A tax-free subsidy is available for individuals who go into jobs or self-employment. The programmes are complex and Jobcentres can give more details.

The local Careers Service office (in the phone book under 'Careers') is also worth contacting. Adult careers advice services are changing rapidly and there is more focus on older people than there used to be. Under 1999 proposals from government, local partnerships will be set up to advise and give guidance, whether on work or non-vocational activities. Careers services and libraries will have details as the partnerships develop.

Special help for older people

Apart from the government programmes under the New Deal there are special groups and agencies in some parts of the country set up specifically to help older people. Some are run by voluntary groups, others by government agencies or local government. The Third Age Employment Network*, which has a membership of over 100 such bodies, provides a list of such groups. You are more likely to find an understanding of what is involved in redundancy, early retirement and age prejudice in employment through the various groups and agencies. A number of them are making good use of the Internet to link up individual job seekers and employers looking for the experience of older candidates.

In late 1999 a new scheme called PRIME* was launched in 28 locations around the country to provide help to over 50s going into self-employment.

If you have special needs or difficulties in finding work because of a disability or health problem, your local Jobcentre can put you in touch with a Disability Employment Adviser. Employment Opportunities* and the Royal Association for Disability and Rehabilitation* (RADAR) also have useful publications.

Your rights as an employee

You need not be so grateful to have a job that you put up with poor treatment from your employer. The first thing to check is that you are actually an employee, rather than an independent contractor. There are advantages to being an independent contractor, particularly for tax. But these are counter-balanced by the obligations and liabilities that bind your employer if you are an employee. In any case, even if you and your employer see your position as one of self-employment, the Inland Revenue may not agree. This can have some unwelcome consequences – see Chapter 16.

The main rights of employees are described below: leaflets on your rights as an employee are available from Citizens Advice Bureaux, Jobcentres or other Employment Service offices. However, in some cases, you acquire these rights only after working for the employer for a minimum period. Table 2 summarises which rights are available to which employees.

Table 2: When you acquire employment rights

No minimum service
Statutory sick pay (not available if aged 65 or over)
Anti-discrimination rights, including rights under the Disability Discrimination Act
Unfair dismissal if sacked for seeking to enforce statutory employment protection
(e.g. covering health and safety, national minimum wage or limits on time at work)
Itemised pay statement
Limits on time at work (see opposite)
Rights in insolvency (but 4 weeks' service to get pay in lieu of notice)

1 month's minimum service
Payment on medical suspension
Written terms and conditions of employment

13 weeks' minimum service
Four weeks' paid annual holiday

1 year's minimum service
Unfair dismissal (not available if aged 65 or over)
Written reasons for dismissal

2 years' minimum service
Redundancy rights (not available if aged 65 or over)

Written terms and conditions of employment

All but short-term employees have a right to get written details of their terms and conditions of employment within two months of starting a job. But, in practice, many employers confirm a job offer by letter, with which they include the terms and conditions. These should cover details such as who the employer actually is, your starting date, job title, place of work, rate and method of payment, hours, holiday pay, pension scheme, notice period, length of employment (if not permanent), grievance procedures and (if there are at least 20 employees) disciplinary procedures.

You do not have to sign any contract you are given, although if you continue to work for the employer once you have received it, you are still likely to be bound by its conditions. The terms set out in the statement can only rarely be altered without the consent of both parties. Note that if a business is being transferred to a new owner the employees must go with it on the same terms and conditions (except for terms relating to employer pension schemes, which are subject to agreement).

Itemised pay statements
All employees are entitled to a pay slip showing the gross pay, any deductions (and the reasons for them) and the net pay.

Time at work
The Working Time Regulations govern the amount of time you can spend at work. You cannot be required to work more than an average of 48 hours a week over a 17-week period (extended in certain circumstances), and further rules cover rest breaks and night working. You are also entitled to one day off a week and, providing you have worked for the employer for at least 13 weeks, four weeks' paid annual holiday. However, there are a number of exemptions, including the following:

- Workers whose working time is not measured or pre-determined, such as managing executives and family workers, are effectively covered only by the rules relating to paid annual leave.
- You can voluntarily agree to disapply the weekly hours limit and collective workforce agreements may also modify the weekly hours, night working and rest break rules. Your holiday rights cannot be disapplied or modified.
- The regulations apply to agency and temporary staff, but not to workers in a few areas, notably transport and work at sea.
- In administering rest breaks, there is some flexibility in some cases (for example, security work or care work).

For more information, contact the Workright Information Line* for a leaflet.

In addition to the Working Time Regulations, you are allowed time off work for some trade union or public duties: for example as a justice of the peace, local councillor or school governor. Time off should be with pay, unless it is for public duties or some trade union activities. The Employment Relations Act 1999 also introduced a right to reasonable time off (unpaid) to make arrangements for a dependant – if, for example, an elderly relative for whom you care falls ill.

Sick pay

Providing you earn at least a minimum amount (£66 a week for the year from 6 April 1999) and are aged under 65, employers must give you statutory sick pay when you are off sick for four or more days in a row, however short a time you have worked for a company, and whether you are part-time or full-time. You get this for the first 28 weeks of any illness (after which you will move on to other types of state benefit – see page 21). Although employers do not have to keep your job open indefinitely, they should treat you sympathetically: the Disability Discrimination Act 1995 (see below) also strengthens the rights of employees in this respect.

National Minimum Wage

A minimum wage of £3.60 an hour (£3.00 an hour for 18- to 21-year-olds and £3.20 for new employees aged over 21 receiving accredited training) applies to all regions, business sectors and sizes of firms. There are very few exceptions, the genuinely self-employed being one. In addition to your basic pay, there are other elements of pay which may count towards the national minimum wage hourly rate, such as bonuses and performance-related pay. However, overtime and shift work premiums do not count, nor do regional allowances that are consolidated into your basic pay. All fringe benefits are excluded, except for accommodation.

If you think your employer is in breach of the national minimum wage, you can complain to the Inland Revenue (which enforces it), an employment tribunal or to the courts. Further details are available from the National Minimum Wage Helpline.★

Anti-discrimination

However recently you started work, it is illegal for an employer to discriminate against you:

- on the grounds of sex, race or marital status
- by failing to give equal treatment (in terms of both pay and conditions) to people of either sex carrying out 'like work'

- because you are (or are not) a union member.

There is no law against discrimination on the grounds of age, although the government has introduced a code of practice on Age Diversity in Employment giving guidance for good practice in recruitment, training, redundancy and retirement. For leaflets describing the code, contact DFEE Publications.* It can be used to back up demands for equal treatment, irrespective of age.

However, under the Disability Discrimination Act 1995, it is illegal for employers with 15 or more employees (except for some public service organisations) to discriminate on the grounds of disability without justification. As well as people who are registered as disabled, this covers non-registered people who have (or who have had) a physical or mental impairment which has had a substantial and long-term effect on their ability to carry out normal day-to-day activities. Leaflets on the Disability Discrimination Act* are available free.

Rights on redundancy
For more on redundancy, see Chapter 2; but note that you have a right to redundancy pay, and paid time off to look for work, only if you have two years service (see Table 2) and not at all if you are over 65.

Rights on insolvency
If your employer is formally insolvent and owes you money, you may be entitled to some payments from the government's redundancy fund. These include up to eight weeks' arrears of pay, up to six weeks' holiday pay, and pay in lieu of notice, subject to maximum weekly amounts (the maximum week's pay was £220 in 1999). If you think you qualify, apply for these payments first to the liquidator or receiver, who will have the necessary application forms.

Unfair dismissal
Your dismissal will normally only be 'fair' if the employer can show that it was due to:

- a reason related to your conduct
- a reason related to your capability or qualifications for the job (including sickness, although this may breach the Disability Discrimination Act – see above)

- redundancy
- a legal duty or restriction which prevents the employment being continued (e.g. you are a lorry driver, but have been banned from driving, and your employer has no other suitable job for you)
- 'some other substantial reason' – e.g. a close relative sets up a business competing with your employer, taking advantage of your connections.

Providing you have one year's minimum service, you should be given written reasons for dismissal, if you request them, within 14 days. If you have worked for one month or more, you are entitled to a week's notice or pay in lieu, unless the contract of employment specified a longer period of notice. After two years, one week's notice is required for each year of work, up to a maximum of 12 weeks. If you feel that you were unfairly dismissed (and are under 65 – if not, you do not get this protection at all), you can take your claim to an Employment Tribunal. You may also have a claim for 'constructive dismissal' if you were placed in an untenable position and forced to resign. You must have one year's service with the employer to qualify for unfair dismissal, although there is no minimum service if you have been dismissed for seeking to enforce, in good faith, statutory employment protection such as anti-discrimination rights, the national minimum wage or the working time regulations. The Public Interest Disclosure Act 1998 also protects 'whistleblowers' in some circumstances.

The factsheet *Dismissal: Fair or Unfair?* is available, along with other useful publications on employment rights, from the DTI Publications Orderline.*

If you work part-time

The rights of part-time employees have improved in recent years. In 1994 the House of Lords ruled that the law discriminated against women, who are more likely to work part-time, to set different minimum lengths of service for full-time and part-time employees to qualify for various legal employment rights. As a result, the government removed all the previous qualifying conditions based on the number of hours worked per week – although the minimum lengths of service still apply.

Another 1994 ruling, this time in the European Court, ruled that part-timers barred from their employer's pension scheme who could prove sex discrimination would have the right to join the scheme. Under the Pensions Act, they can also claim retrospective membership of the scheme for up to two years, but they must do so within six months of leaving the job concerned.

Part-timers may still find that individual employers are less generous to them than to full-time employees, for example in the fringe benefits offered. However, since most part-timers are women the different treatment could be challenged if it is shown to be due to sex discrimination. In addition, further regulations and a code of practice will be issued under the Employment Relations Act 1999 to help ensure that part-timers are treated no less favourably than their full-time colleagues.

If your rights are breached

If you have any concerns about your treatment at work, contact your local Citizens Advice Bureau. You may have the right to take your case to an Employment Tribunal: your Jobcentre can give you the necessary information. You may also be able to get help from ACAS★ – the Advisory, Conciliation and Arbitration Service. For worries about sexual or racial discrimination, contact the Equal Opportunities Commission★ or Commission for Racial Equality★ respectively. A Disability Rights Commission is also being set up.

Chapter 14

Starting your own business

If you decide to set up on your own, you will immediately be beset by choices. Should you set up as a 'sole trader' or start your own limited company? Should you register for Value Added Tax (VAT)? Once you think about all the decisions to be taken, you may wonder whether it is worthwhile! Your attitude towards this sort of question is probably quite a sound indicator of whether you are really suited to self-employment, and could define the sort of business to which you may be most suited, and the help you are likely to need. For example, if your primary interest is in producing something and you find the organisation tiresome, you may need either to set up in the simplest way possible, or make your first task looking for someone to help with the administrative side of the business.

Which method of trading?

'Sole trader'

This does not mean that you have to work alone, but that you are totally and solely responsible for the business. You take all the profits, but you are also personally liable for all debts incurred to the full extent of your means – including personal possessions outside the business, such as your home. Many small businesses start as sole traders and are later turned into limited companies.

Partnership

This is an association of two to twenty people, trading together as one firm and sharing the profits. One or more of the partners may be a 'sleeping partner' who just contributes money. The partnership gets a tax return, but partners also each enter their own share of the pre-tax profits on their personal tax return. All the partners can be held liable for the whole of the firm's debts (except for tax debts), to the full extent of their personal means, in the same way as for sole traders. If one partner absconded, the others would have to pay the absconder's share. Partners pay the same National Insurance contributions as sole traders.

Limited company

A limited company is a legal entity, just as though it were a person, and must be conducted according to rules laid down by company law. These include producing audited accounts which must be filed at Companies House,* and the disclosure of the company's activities to the general public. However, statutory audits are no longer required for companies with annual turnovers of less than £350,000 (although an independent accountant's report is required for companies with turnovers between £90,000 and £350,000).

The shareholders are the owners of the company, but are liable for its debts only to the extent of the face value of their shares. (It is possible for one person to set up a company on his or her own but there must also be a separate company secretary.) If the shares are available to the general public and quoted on the Stock Exchange, then it is a public limited company ('plc'). Private companies – the majority – do not offer shares to the public and style themselves 'Limited' or 'Ltd'.

Franchises

The purchase of a franchise is the purchase of the right to use a particular method to run a particular kind of business. You – the 'franchisee' – are buying expertise and an image, sometimes the right to use and trade under a household name, from the 'franchisor'. You are at liberty to decide the most appropriate method of trading, whether as sole trader, in a partnership or through a limited company.

The entry price can be considerable, and will allow you to trade for a limited period only (typically five years) – it is for you to assess whether the potential rewards are worth it. Becoming a franchisee usually means that you will own the business assets (premises, equipment and so on) – although some franchisors prefer to own them and lease them to franchisees. But you will certainly not own the business method, and are likely to find that the franchisor lays down the essential business techniques you must use.

Which method for you?

The choice may not be clear-cut (and there are other less common options, such as setting up a co-operative). But key considerations will be the question of limited liability, the ease of raising finance, tax, and the administrative burden.

A limited company is clearly preferable if it is important to you to limit your liability (remember, though, that a director's liability is often extended by personal guarantees to a bank or other lender as security for a loan). Banks may prefer to lend to limited companies, and you may prefer to keep your business finances separate from your personal ones.

The rate of corporation tax now payable by small companies is below the basic rate of income tax payable by sole traders. Companies also have the flexibility of paying their directors in a mixture of salary, dividends and pension contributions, in whatever proportion achieves the best balance between corporation tax payable by the company and income tax payable by the director. But National Insurance contributions must be paid by both the company and director on salaries over a certain threshold, and if your business is likely to make losses in the early years, a sole trader has more flexibility to set them against other income. All this means that the choice is often not clear-cut. In addition, the government is concerned that some employees are setting up as companies purely for the tax advantages, and is looking for ways to counter this.

Possible tax advantages may be less important if yours is a very small business with low overheads, which is unlikely to run up debts. In this case, you may be swayed by the consideration that a limited company has to comply with the detailed rules of company law, is likely to cost more to set up, and will probably involve more paperwork. In any case, it is often better to start off as a sole trader – the most flexible form of business organisation with little red tape involved in setting it up.

Partnerships are a slightly different consideration, since they are the standard way of operating in some professions, such as medicine. However, you do have to consider the difficulties of working closely with a number of other people.

You need to be particularly careful if considering buying a franchise. For a franchise to be successful, it needs to combine a successful business idea with a proper level of support and promotion from the franchisor. If a capital sum is payable for an exclusive right to distribute goods or offer a certain service within a given area and no back-up is offered, consider whether you could set up a similar operation yourself and perhaps save a great deal of money.

Cowboy franchisors also exist. They charge a relatively high buy-in fee but offer little or no training or equipment. Or the sum involved may be low – about £5,000 say – but you get very little for it. To reduce the risks, get any potential agreement vetted by a solicitor and check the following points:

- Is the franchisor a member of the British Franchise Association?* Members are bound by a code of conduct.
- What experiences have the other franchisees had? A reputable franchisor should have no grounds to refuse to produce a list of franchisees.

The formalities

If you do not do anything – in other words, simply set up as a freelance – you will technically be a sole trader. If setting up in a partnership, it is wise to have an agreement drawn up by a solicitor covering such things as each partner's share of the profits, how each share is to be valued if a partner wants to withdraw, and what happens on death. Other aspects are: arrangements for holidays, how much each partner can draw, voting rights and what should happen in case of a dispute.

Limited companies must be registered with Companies House,* for which there is a fee. It is important to have professional help in registering a company: check whether your solicitor or accountant has expertise in this. You can also buy companies 'off the peg' through company registration agents: if you do not like the name you can change it through Companies House.

When you register your company, you must submit a 'memorandum of association' which must include details of the name of the company, the objects of the company, the amount of share capital and how it is divided into shares. There are other necessary forms on registration, including details of first directors and secretary and the address of the registered office.

The DTI Publications Orderline★ service produces a number of helpful free guides, including *Setting Up in Business: A Guide to Regulatory Requirements.*

Running the business

Your business name

You can trade under your own name or names. But you may prefer to use a name which attracts attention or says something about the business, and within certain limits you are free to do this. Useful booklets setting out the rules are available from Companies House.★

However, it is illegal to pass yourself or your business off as something which it is not, and if the name you have chosen to trade under is not just your own name, you must indicate the name of the owner(s) on all stationery and display it in your shop, office or place of work.

National Insurance

If you are a sole trader or partner, you must pay Class 2 National Insurance contributions: these protect your right to some state benefits, including state retirement pension and sickness benefit, but not others. Class 2 contributions are £6.55 a week for the year from 6 April 1999, but you can claim exemption if your net yearly earnings from self-employment are below £3,770 (for 1999–2000). You can pay them either by monthly direct debit or by quarterly bills.

People who pay Class 2 contributions must also pay Class 4 contributions, on any earnings between £7,540 and £26,000 (in the 1999–2000 tax year), at a rate of six per cent. These contributions are assessed and collected by the Inland Revenue along with the income tax on your profits.

If you employ anyone you must pay Class 1 National Insurance contributions at 12.2 per cent on all earnings above £83 a week in the 1999–2000 tax year.

National Insurance contributions, of whatever class, no longer have to be paid once you are over state retirement age. The only exception is the Class 1 contributions payable by employers.

If yours is a limited company, you as an individual pay the employee's share of your Class 1 contributions, and the company pays the employer's contribution.

Details of National Insurance for the self-employed are available in leaflets CWL1 and CWL2 from Inland Revenue and Inland Revenue National Insurance Contributions offices.

Value Added Tax (VAT)

VAT is a tax on sales of goods and services, collected for the government by HM Customs and Excise. You may not have to register for VAT if your turnover is (or is expected to be) below a certain threshold, but it may save you money to register voluntarily.

The tax you pay on goods and services that you buy for your business is called 'input tax', and the tax you charge your customers is called 'output tax'. This is how it works: Bill buys raw materials for £235, inclusive of 17.5 per cent VAT: £35 is his input tax. He uses the materials to make goods selling for £450 before VAT, on which he has to charge output tax of £78.75. He deducts his input tax from his output tax and remits the balance (£78.75 – £35 = £43.75) to Customs and Excise, normally once a quarter. If his input tax had been greater than his output tax, he would have been refunded the difference.

The rate of VAT is 17.5 per cent (5 per cent on fuel), but some goods and services such as food are 'zero-rated' – i.e. taxed at 0 per cent – and others, such as most insurance, are 'exempt' – i.e. outside the VAT system altogether. The difference is important. If you produce exempt goods or services, you do not charge VAT on them, but you cannot claim the input tax on them either. If your product or service is zero-rated you can reclaim input tax without putting up your charges. And while trade in zero-rated supplies counts towards your turnover for the registration limit, trade in exempt supplies does not.

Do you need to register?

You must register if your 'taxable turnover' for the previous 12 months reaches £51,000 (from 1 April 1999), or if you expect turnover for the next 30 days to exceed it, or if you buy a business which is already registered. To register, contact your local VAT office (under 'Customs and Excise' in the phone book), which can also supply a range of leaflets.

Once you have registered, you need to keep scrupulous records of all transactions: there are stiff penalties for failing to make VAT returns and payments on time. But there are some schemes which can simplify VAT for small businesses. For example, if your taxable turnover excluding VAT is less than £300,000 a year, you can opt to make annual rather than quarterly returns to Customs and Excise.

If your turnover is below £350,000 a year, you can also opt for a 'cash accounting' basis. This means that the VAT you pay depends on the money you actually receive and pay out in each quarter, not what is invoiced. So you do not have to hand over VAT until you receive it from your customers – a great help, if payment normally takes some time to come through, or if you have bad debts.

Tax

From the tax point of view, there are advantages to being self-employed. For example, you can set more expenses against your income than if you are an employee. However, even if you class yourself as self-employed, the Inland Revenue may not agree. See Chapter 16 for more on tax if you are self-employed.

Keeping records

The accounts you need to keep will depend on the business. If you have a limited company, you will have to pay for annual accounts to be produced and audited (unless your turnover is below a set limit – see page 183); if you are registered for VAT you will have to account for sales and purchases, and if you employ anybody, you will probably need to pay them under the PAYE system. All businesses need to keep some sort of accounts for the Inland Revenue (even if they need not usually send them in – see page 183) in order to prove what their income and expenses are, and you have a legal requirement to keep some types of documentation, for tax purposes. See Inland Revenue booklet SA/BK3 *Self Assessment – A guide to keeping records for the self-employed*.

You can buy printed account books for small businesses which may be suitable, or you can buy blank ledgers and mug up on simple accounting methods for yourself. Computer-based accounting software for small businesses is now widely available, but if you keep your records on computer you must still keep the original documentation backing them up. If you are at all unsure about accounts, ask your accountant to set up a system and teach you how to use it. Some basic points to remember are:

- Always try to collect a written record of any transaction, even if it is only a till note or note on the back of an envelope.
- Never throw any paperwork away unless convinced it is unnecessary – keep copies of invoices sent and received, receipts, cheque-book stubs, bank statements, etc.
- Keep a petty cash book to record out-of-pocket expenses.
- If you employ people, keep a separate wages book to record pay, income tax, National Insurance contributions, etc.
- Keep paid invoices separate from unpaid.
- If you are registered for VAT, there must be a special VAT column in all your records.

Bank accounts

Even if you are working as a sole trader and on your own, it is still worth opening a special bank account for the business. This makes it easier to draw up your accounts and easier to borrow money from the bank, while bank charges on a bank account can be claimed as an allowable expense against tax.

Banks offer a variety of services to small businesses, but their charges for small businesses can be steep. So it is worth shopping around and negotiating before setting up, since it may not be easy to transfer a business account if you have an overdraft or other type of loan.

Licences

Many trades and businesses need to be licensed, for example credit businesses. You can find out which businesses need licences by contacting your local authority planning office or reading *Setting up in Business: A Guide to Regulatory Requirements* from the DTI Publications Orderline.★

The Office of Fair Trading★ also has leaflets describing trading regulations such as the Trade Descriptions Act. Contact your local Trading Standards Department (described as such in the phone book).

Insurance cover

Even if you do not need special insurance you should inform your insurers of your change of circumstances; otherwise they may be entitled not to pay out. But you may also need special cover for:

- business premises
- business stock and equipment
- business interruption, e.g. in case your office is destroyed by fire
- employer's liability, e.g. to cover you if an employee is injured while at work
- public liability to cover damages for injury caused by your business to people or property
- product liability if anything you make, repair or sell causes damage or injury
- professional indemnity if you offer a professional service and you or an employee is negligent (or an employee is fraudulent)
- car insurance – if you use your car for work you will need a policy covering business use
- permanent health insurance (to pay an income if you are out of action, assuming that your income from self-employment is essential to your budget)
- life insurance – to cover you or a key employee if your business could not operate without you.

The Association of British Insurers* publishes a free booklet on insurance for small businesses.

Confidentiality

If you keep or control any data about identifiable living individuals, whether on computer or manually, you will need to register with the Data Protection Registrar.* This applies even if all you keep are the names, addresses and telephone numbers of customers, or suppliers held for business account purposes.

Registering means that your business is listed in a public register of data users and bureaux; you must follow a code of practice, and must reply to requests from people for details of any personal information you hold on them. More information is available from the Data Protection Registrar.

Starting in business

Sources of advice

Government support is largely decentralised and channelled through local agencies such as Training and Enterprise Councils (TECs, called Local Enterprise Councils, or LECs, in Scotland). However, from April 2000 a new Small Business Service will become responsible for co-ordinating government support for small businesses. Most of this support will be for English firms, as business support in Scotland, Wales and Northern Ireland is a devolved matter where separate arrangements apply.

Your nearest Business Link★ centre (or Business Connect★ in Wales, Business Shop★ in Scotland) is the best first port of call for information about both practical and financial help. Each centre is a partnership between TECs, Chambers of Commerce, local authorities, enterprise agencies, and other such bodies. In Northern Ireland, contact the Local Enterprise Development Unit.★

The DTI Publications Orderline★ produces a variety of free leaflets and booklets. One of these is called *A Guide to Help for Small Firms.* It provides lots of useful information including sources of help and advice on finance, innovation and starting a business.

A key source of advice will clearly be your accountant, and, unless you have a cast-iron personal recommendation from someone in a similar line of business, it is worth interviewing several, asking about their areas of expertise and charges. You should find directories of accountants in your local reference library: some directories list accountants' specialisations.

Raising the money

You may need finance for two main reasons: to invest in premises and equipment, and to provide 'working capital' to cover the gap between receipts and payments. Here are some sources of finance to consider:

- Personal finance you contribute (lenders will expect some sort of commitment from you before agreeing a loan).
- Bank loans (or loans from similar lending institutions). Lenders usually want you to secure any loans on business assets, or with personal guarantees from you.

- Bank overdraft – usually cheaper than a loan, because you pay interest only on the amount by which you are actually over-drawn. An overdraft facility is always useful, even if you hope not to use it, and especially suitable if you know that there will be periods of the year when you need to go into the red.
- Venture capital – usually put up by special investment compa-nies for businesses they think will grow. The investor usually buys a stake in the firm, expecting to sell it at a profit when the business has taken off, so there may be little or no interest to pay in the meantime. The British Venture Capital Association (BVCA)* publishes an annual directory of members and the booklet *A Guide to Venture Capital*.
- Investments by private individuals, perhaps through the Enterprise Investment Scheme or other schemes that give tax relief to investors in companies. Such individuals are known as 'business angels'. The National Business Angels Network (NBAN)* is a non-profit-making organisation, with govern-ment support, which aims to act as a catalyst and clearing house to bring together entrepreneurs and investors.
- Investments by friends or family – be sure to document these properly in order to avoid painful disputes in future.

If you are seeking large amounts of finance, it is essential to dis-cuss the possible sources with an accountant, who can also advise on the most tax-effective ways to borrow and the right mixture of finance for your business. You may be able to reduce the amount you need to borrow by leasing equipment.

For certain types of business, factoring can help with finance: you hand over your sales invoices to a factoring company which pays you 80 per cent (say) of the amount you are owed straight away and chases the customer for the rest, generally keeping a percentage for the service.

Guarantees and security

Interest rates charged to small companies are often higher than those charged to the big blue-chip companies, to reflect the extra risks involved. And the lender will want as much reassurance as possible about repayment, often including personal guarantees from you as owner and perhaps insisting that you put up your home as security (so if the business fails, you can lose your home). If your husband, wife or other relative approaches you to give a guarantee for their business, be particularly careful and consult your solicitor. Guarantees may be framed so that they last virtually indefinitely, so even after the original loan has been paid off you could find yourself being held responsible for your relative's financial position, or even losing your own home.

Finding sufficient guarantees can be difficult, and the government Small Business Loan Guarantee Scheme can help if you have already committed all your personal assets as security. The Scheme then guarantees 85 per cent of loans up to £250,000, for businesses which have been trading for at least two years, or 70 per cent up to a maximum of £100,000 for other businesses. The charge is usually 0.5 per cent a year of the whole loan on fixed interest rate lending and 1.5 per cent of the whole loan for variable rate lending. A booklet on the Scheme is available from the DTI Publications Orderline.*

Who should be told?

Limited companies need to be properly registered, but all businesses also need to contact:

- The Inland Revenue – if you have left a job as an employee, send your P45 to your tax office as soon as possible, as you may qualify for a tax rebate.
- The Inland Revenue – for PAYE purposes, if you intend to employ someone.
- The Inland Revenue National Insurance Contributions Agency.
- HM Customs and Excise, if you intend or need to register for VAT.
- Your bank.
- Your insurers (you may need a special policy – see page 190).
- Your mortgage lender.
- Any regulator from whom you will need a licence, e.g. the Office of Fair Trading* if you intend to run a credit business and need a consumer credit licence.

In an attempt to simplify matters for small businesses, the Inland Revenue, Customs and Excise and Inland Revenue National

Insurance Contributions Agency now publish a joint leaflet, CWL1 *Starting your own business?* (available from tax offices). It contains a form that you can use to notify all three organisations when you start your business.

Working from home

Planning permission

Your local authority planning department should have information, but you are unlikely to need permission if:

- the main use continues to be as a family home
- there are no employees
- there are no outward signs of the business, e.g. trade vehicles, business plate.

Above all there must be no 'nuisance' caused – i.e. no cause for your neighbours to complain.

Household bills may rise

If you are at home more, electricity and gas bills will go up, and probably your phone bill too. If you count as self-employed, you can get tax relief on any part of these expenses which was due to business use, and on insurance and cleaning costs.

Insurance

At the very least, you should tell your insurers that you are working from home – if you do not, and later make a claim, they could refuse to pay. You may be charged a higher premium if the risk of insuring you is higher – e.g. if you are a decorator storing flammable materials at home. If you are not using anything more than a computer, say, your existing policy may be adequate but check that your computer is not worth more than the policy's 'single item limit'.

If you use special or expensive equipment, employ people, or could be liable for loss or damage you cause, you will need a commercial policy – see page 190.

Will you pay business rates?

Business rates should not apply unless any part of your house has been altered or fitted with special equipment so that you could not immediately use it as an ordinary family home. If it has, you pay business rates on that part and council tax (domestic rates in Northern Ireland) on the rest.

Your home

If you own your home, it is sensible to tell your mortgage lender – especially if you are insured through them – but as long as it remains a home first and foremost you should not have to pay extra interest. Beware of using part of your home just for work: you may have to pay capital gains tax on it if you make a gain when you move – see Chapter 18.

If you are a tenant, check the tenancy agreement to make sure you are not breaking its terms. If you are self-employed, you can claim tax relief on the rent for any part of the home used exclusively for work.

Part 4

Tax and retirement

Chapter 15

The basics of tax

You may have waved goodbye to the work place but unfortunately this does not mean that you can wave goodbye to tax. Retired people are liable to tax on their income in the same way as anyone else, with one major exception: the benefits of advancing years can mean a lower tax bill because of higher personal allowances given to people of 65 and over.

If you have worked for an employer most of your life and paid tax through the Pay-As-You-Earn (PAYE) scheme, you may not have needed to give much thought to the thorny subject of tax. However, a basic grasp of the subject will help you to:

- make the most of the change that retirement brings to your financial circumstances
- identify ways you can rearrange your finances to make the most of the tax system
- prepare yourself for more direct contact with your tax office (you will find a detailed look at dealing with the tax authorities in Chapter 19).

Most of this chapter is devoted to income tax: the main tax that you will have to pay on your income from pensions and investments. First you will find an explanation of the basics of income tax to give you an idea of how income tax is worked out. Then there is a detailed look at tax on pensions: what is taxed and how you pay the tax. (If you have income from savings and investments, see Chapter 17.)

Once you have got a clear idea of how your income is liable to be taxed, you will find ways of keeping your tax bill to a minimum, looking at the tax-reducing allowances and reliefs you can claim, with practical steps you can take to protect your entitlement to the higher age-related allowances. Finally, there is a look at how tax can affect your changing circumstances in retirement.

The basics of income tax

You do not have to pay income tax on all the money you have coming in (from your pensions, your investments and any spare time earnings, for example). In any tax year – which runs from 6 April in one year to 5 April in the following year – you pay tax only on what the Revenue calls your taxable income. You can get a rough idea of this by taking these three steps:

- Take all the money you have coming in and subtract any tax-free income and any other money you have received which is not liable to income tax – e.g. the proceeds from selling unit trusts (which may be liable to capital gains tax) or a lump sum you took from your pension (which is usually tax-free). This is **your income for tax purposes**.

- Subtract payments you make on which you get full **tax relief**. There are not very many these days – the main ones are some payments to charity, pension contributions, some expenses in employment and some loan interest. See page 207 onwards for details. What is left after deducting these payments is called **your total income**.

- Deduct your personal allowances (see Table 1 on page 210) from your total income to arrive at **your taxable income** – i.e. the income on which your income tax bill is calculated. But this is not the end of the story – see pages 207–14 for some extra payments and allowances on which the tax relief is restricted, in particular the married couple's allowance (if you get it). These do not reduce your taxable income, but you can deduct the amount of relief from your tax bill.

Tax credits

Tax credits, such as the Disabled Person's Tax Credit and the Working Families Tax Credit, were introduced in October 1999. These are means-tested state benefits designed to top up low incomes, but, unlike other state benefits, they are administered by the Inland Revenue and if you are an employee they will usually be paid by your employer through your pay packet. For more information on the Disabled Person's Tax Credit see page 53.

EXAMPLE 1

Will Smith is 64 and married: he has retired from his job as a university lecturer. By the end of the 1999–2000 tax year the money he had coming in will have amounted to £22,600. But he will not pay income tax on all of this. First he takes away sums which are not income: £50 tax-free income from his National Savings Ordinary account, £1,000 he inherited and the £3,000 proceeds from cashing in some unit trusts.

The next things to think about are any deductions: the £600 he paid to Oxfam under the Gift Aid scheme. He cannot deduct his mortgage payments, on which he has already received tax relief by making lower payments to his lender.

Lastly, he takes away his personal allowance of £4,335 which leaves a taxable income of £13,615. He can also deduct the married couple's allowance, but because this is a fixed-relief allowance, he deducts its value once he has worked out how much tax he pays (see Example 2).

1	**WILL'S INCOME FOR TAX PURPOSES**	
	Money coming in	£22,600
	Deduct tax-free income	
	Interest from National Savings Ordinary Account	£50
	Deduct tax-free income	
	Inheritance	£1,000
	Unit trust proceeds	£3,000
	Income for tax purposes	£18,550
2	**WILL'S TOTAL INCOME**	
	Deduct payments qualifying for full tax relief	
	Gift Aid donation	£600
	Total income	£17,950
3	**WILL'S TAXABLE INCOME**	
	Deduct allowances	
	Personal allowance	£4,335
	Taxable income	£13,615

How much income tax?

For the 1999–2000 tax year, there are three rates of income tax, each charged on different slices of your taxable income:

- on the first £1,500 of taxable income, you pay tax at the starting rate of 10 per cent

- on the next £26,500 (i.e. on taxable income between £1,501 and £28,000), you pay tax at the basic rate of 23 per cent (22 per cent in 2000–2001)
- on any taxable income over £28,000, you pay higher-rate tax at 40 per cent.

To get your final tax bill, add up the amounts of tax due on each slice of your taxable income (see Example 2). This will give you your final tax bill unless:

- you can deduct one of the restricted-relief allowances and payments from your tax bill (see page 211)
- some of your income comes from savings and investments. Most types of savings and investment now pay out income 'net', that is, with 20 per cent tax already deducted. If you are a basic-rate taxpayer you have no further tax to pay, and if your top rate of tax is 10 per cent, you can reclaim any excess tax deducted. If you are a higher-rate taxpayer, you pay tax on savings income at 40 per cent, so if you received it net, you will have a further $40 - 20 = 20$ per cent tax on it to pay. The rules for share dividends and distributions from unit trusts and open-ended investment companies (OEICs) are slightly different. This income is treated as being paid net of 10 per cent tax. Your tax liability on it is 10 per cent (even if you are a non-taxpayer) or 32.5 per cent if you are a higher-rate taxpayer. Non-taxpayers cannot reclaim the tax credit – it can be reclaimed only on investment income held in an Individual Savings Account (ISA).

Paying income tax

In practice, most tax is deducted on your behalf at source (i.e. before you get your income) and most tax relief is also given at source (i.e. by making lower payments). If you owe more tax than has been collected at source – for example, you're a higher-rate taxpayer, or you do the odd bit of self-employed work – the extra will be collected either through your PAYE code (see below) or through your tax return. If you owe less tax than has been deducted, you can usually reclaim the overpaid tax.

Pay-As-You-Earn (PAYE)

If you will be receiving a pension from a former employer, it is likely that you will pay your tax through the PAYE system as you did when you were still an employee and received your weekly or monthly payslip. The tax office will therefore continue to send your ex-employer or the pension fund a tax code and to send you a PAYE *Coding Notice* which will enable you to check that what is included in the code is correct. If you are a higher-rate taxpayer or have income that is paid out before tax, it is likely that you will be sent a tax return to fill in which gives the tax office the information it needs to get your tax code right.

EXAMPLE 2

Wilf Smith's taxable income is £13,615. In 1999–2000, the first £4,100 of his taxable income is taxed at 10 per cent – a bill of £150. However, Wilf's remaining taxable income includes £500 in untaxed interest from a National Savings Investment account, and £555 in building society interest from which 20 per cent tax was deducted before he got it. Because enough tax has already been paid on it, Wilf can ignore the building society interest, and the £500 National Savings interest is liable only to 20 per cent tax, i.e. £100. So only £13,615 less £1,500 less £1,055 = £11,060 is taxable at 23 per cent, i.e. tax of £2,543.80.

Wilf's tax before deducting his married couple's allowance is £150 + £100 + £2,543.80 = £2,793.80. The married couple's allowance is worth £197.00, giving a total tax bill of £2,596.80.

		TAX
Wilf's taxable income	£13,615	
Starting-rate band taxable		
at 10%	£1,500	£150.00
Balance of taxable income	£12,115	
less		
National Savings interest		
taxable at 20%	£500	£100.00
Interest already taxed	£555	
Taxable at 23%	£11,060	£2,543.80
Total tax		£2,793.80
less married couple's allowance		£197.00
Tax bill		£2,596.80

Tax on your income

Once you have retired, your main source of income is likely to be the pension you receive, whether it is from the state, an employer pension scheme or a personal pension plan. You may also have income from savings and investments on which you may have to pay tax. Some state benefits are tax-free; the main taxable benefits are Jobseeker's allowance, widowed mother's allowance, widow's pension, incapacity benefit (except short-term incapacity benefit paid at the lower rate) and a few other benefits if you are disabled or sick. Maintenance payments you receive are also tax-free (although before 6 April 2000, some maintenance paid under an agreement set up before a certain date in 1988 may be taxable).

Income from pensions

Some pensions are tax-free, but most are taxable.

State retirement pensions

You will be liable to tax on any of the following:

- **Basic state retirement pension** This is a flat-rate pension paid to anyone who has paid enough National Insurance contributions. You may get an increase to the basic pension if you are a married man whose wife gets no state pension of her own (e.g. because she is not yet old enough to qualify for her own state pension).
- **State Earnings Related Pension (SERPS)** The pension you get is linked to your earnings since 6 April 1978.
- **Graduated pension** This is paid if you were employed between 1961 and 1975.
- **Over 80 pension** This is paid to people of 80 or over who are getting less than the normal state retirement pension.

The £10 Christmas bonus and £100 winter fuel payment are tax-free.

Note that any state pension a married woman receives counts as her income, even if it is based on her husband's National Insurance contributions. However, any increase added to her husband's pension for her is taxable as his income. See Chapter 3 for more details on state pensions.

Although state retirement pensions are taxable, tax is not deducted from them before they are paid. There will be tax to pay only if your state pension, when added to income from other sources (e.g. an employer pension or investment income), comes to more than your allowances and other reliefs. If your only income is the basic state pension, you will have no tax to pay since your income (in the 1999–2000 tax year) will be below the amount of your personal allowances.

The amount of pension which will be included in your income is the total of the weekly amounts payable over the tax year. This applies even if you have chosen to have your pension paid four-weekly or quarterly.

Employer pensions

If you receive a pension from a former employer, the full amount is taxable. Note that if you chose to take a lump sum from your pension when you retired, this is tax-free. Tax on the pension part will normally be collected under PAYE.

When you first receive your employer pension, it might appear that it is being taxed at a higher rate than your earnings were before you retired. This is because the tax deducted will also take into account other taxable income which your tax office expects you to receive before tax over the coming tax year, such as the state retirement pension or investment income. If, by the end of the tax year, you have overpaid tax, the overpaid amount will be refunded.

Personal pensions

The full amount of the pension you get from an annuity bought with the proceeds of a personal pension plan is taxable (unlike annuities you buy of your own accord – see page 144). Many insurance companies deduct tax from each payment under PAYE so the correct amount of tax should be deducted. Other companies simply deduct tax at the basic rate. If your income is too low for you to pay tax, ask your tax office whether the pension could be paid under PAYE.

Pensions from abroad

You are normally liable for tax on nine-tenths of any pension from abroad, whether or not you have it paid in the UK.

Tax on redundancy payments

If you are made redundant, earnings your employer owes you when you leave your job – e.g. normal wages, pay in lieu of holiday, pay for working your notice period, commission – are taxed in the normal way under PAYE, but the following are tax-free:

- any lump sum for any injury or disability which meant you could not carry on your job
- compensation for loss of a job done entirely or substantially outside the UK
- gratuities from the armed forces
- certain lump sum benefits from employer pension schemes
- money your employer pays into a retirement benefit scheme or uses to buy you an annuity (if certain conditions are met).

WHEN YOU RETIRE

Give your tax office advance warning (at least a month if not longer) of your retirement date, and tell them how much and what type of income you expect to get after you retire. This should help the tax office to give you the right PAYE code if you pay tax through PAYE.

The DSS should send you a state pension claim form about four months before you reach retirement age. If it fails to arrive, you should check that the DSS knows the date of your retirement. The form allows you to choose how you get your state pension paid: either four-weekly or quarterly into your bank or building society account, or weekly in cash from a post office.

Other payments are also tax-free if, added together, they come to less than £30,000. These are:

- statutory redundancy payments under the government's redundancy payments scheme
- pay in lieu of notice, in most circumstances, provided your conditions of service do not say you are entitled to it
- other payments made to you, as long as they are not payments for work done, not part of your conditions of service, and technically, at least, unexpected. This would normally cover redundancy payments above the government minimum.

Income from savings and investments

The pension you get is unlikely to be your only source of income in retirement, especially if you have invested any lump sums you got when you retired. Depending on the investments you have chosen, you will have to pay tax on the income you get from them, and if you have gone for capital growth, possibly tax on any capital gain you make. There is also the question of the inheritance tax your heirs may have to pay on the accumulated wealth that you leave them. Chapter 17 covers income tax on savings and investments, together with capital gains tax: inheritance tax is covered in Chapter 33. Later on in this chapter you will see how the investments you choose and how they are taxed can influence the amount of age-related allowances you get if you are 65 or over.

Reducing your tax bill

As explained in 'The basics of income tax' at the beginning of the chapter, you do not have to pay tax on all of the money you have coming in. Apart from choosing investments that pay out a tax-free income, the main way in which you can keep your tax bill down is by making the most of tax reliefs and allowances.

Making the most of tax relief

There are some payments you make which qualify for tax relief.

Payments such as pension contributions and payments to charity under a deed of covenant or Gift Aid are deducted from your income for tax purposes to arrive at your total income. They are valuable to people aged 65 and over, because not only do they give you tax relief at your top rate of tax, but they also reduce the total income on which your age-related allowances depend (see page 213).

The mechanics of getting tax relief vary depending on the type of payment. You may have to claim money back through your tax return; get it back through the PAYE system by having the payments taken into account when working out your income tax code; or hand over less money in the first place.

Many of the payments you can use to reduce your tax bill, such as pension contributions and the payroll giving scheme, are linked to work – whether you are an employee or self-employed. See Chapter 16 for more on these. But if you are no longer working there are still some tax reliefs that may apply.

Note that probably the most well-known form of tax relief, mortgage interest relief on home loans, has been abolished from April 2000. However, the value of the relief had been dwindling over the previous few years, as the rate at which it was given was gradually reduced.

Interest on loans for property you let
Interest on any amount of loans to buy or improve a property you let counts as an expense which can be deducted from the rental income (see Chapter 18).

Interest on a loan to buy an annuity
Provided that the loan was agreed before 9 March 1999, you can get tax relief on the interest you pay on up to £30,000 of loans used to buy an annuity if you are 65 or over and the loan is secured against your only or main home. Relief is restricted to 23 per cent but you get it even if you are a non-taxpayer.

Interest on loans to pay inheritance tax
If you are sorting out someone's estate after their death, you can get tax relief at your top rate of tax for up to 12 months on the interest you pay on a loan taken out to pay the inheritance tax owed on the estate. To get the relief you must actually pay the tax before probate is granted or letters of administration are received.

Gifts to charity
You can get tax relief at your top rate of tax on gifts you make to charity in the following ways (plus payroll giving, explained on page 224):

- by making covenanted payments under a covenant which is capable of lasting more than three years
- by making single donations of at least £250 under the Gift Aid scheme (or £100 donations to poorer countries through the Millennium Gift Aid Scheme, which runs until the end of the year 2000). Note: no mimimum donations from April 2000.

You give yourself basic-rate tax relief by subtracting an amount equivalent to the basic-rate tax on the payments before making them. The charity can then reclaim the basic-rate tax from the Inland Revenue. For example, if you want a charity to be £100 better off under a deed of covenant in 1999–2000, you need to give only £77 – i.e. £100 less the £23 basic-rate tax. If you are a higher-rate taxpayer, you also get higher-rate relief through the PAYE system or through your tax return.

Maintenance payments

If you are legally obliged to make maintenance payments to an ex-wife or ex-husband, you can claim limited tax relief – but, from 6 April 2000, only if either you or your ex-wife or ex-husband were born before 6 April 1935. For tax years before the 2000–2001 tax year, you could claim relief whatever your age.

The relief, if you are entitled to it, is given in a similar way to the married couple's allowance – see page 211.

Making the most of allowances

Allowances depend on your personal situation. You get higher allowances for each tax year in which you are aged 65 or more, provided your total income does not exceed a certain amount (£16,800 in 1999–2000). Allowances save you money in one of two ways:

- Full-relief allowances are deducted from your income before your tax bill is worked out. They give you tax relief at your highest rate of tax.
- Restricted-relief allowances are deducted from your tax bill. The relief is restricted to 10 per cent of the allowance – so, effectively, it is easier to think of the allowance as just a flat-rate amount knocked off your tax bill (or the amount of your tax bill, if less).

Full-relief personal allowances

Everyone automatically gets the personal allowance of £4,335 in the 1999–2000 tax year. In the tax year that you reach 65, your personal allowance is increased, provided your total income is below a certain limit (£16,800 in 1999–2000). If your income is above this level, the amount of the allowance that you can deduct from your income is reduced by £1 for ever £2 you are over the limit. The allowance is never reduced below the level of the basic allowance for people aged under 65. Husband and wife each have their own £16,800 total income limit. Inland Revenue leaflet IR 121 *Income Tax and Pensioners* is helpful.

EXAMPLE 3

Maureen Turner (who is 68 and single) has a total income of £17,700 in the 1999–2000 tax year. She will not qualify for the full higher personal allowance of £5,720 for a person over 65 because her total income is over the £16,800 limit. Instead, she will get her higher personal allowance reduced.

She is over the limit by £900 – i.e. £17,700 minus £16,800. The allowance will be reduced by £1 for every £2 she is over the limit, so she divides the £900 excess by 2 to get £450. She will therefore get a higher allowance of £5,270 – i.e. the full allowance of £5,720 minus £450. However, that is still more than the basic personal allowance of £4,335.

Table 1: Full allowances for the 1999–2000 tax year

Personal allowance	£4,335
Personal allowance (aged 65 to 74)	up to £5,720
Personal allowance (aged 75-plus)	up to £5,980
Blind person's allowance	£1,380

Table 2: Restricted-relief allowances for the 1999–2000 tax year

	Allowance	Value of allowance[1]
Married couple's allowance, additional personal allowance, widow's bereavement allowance[2]	£1,970	£197.00
Married couple's allowance (aged 65 to 74)	up to £5,125	£512.50
Married couple's allowance (aged 75-plus)	up to £5,195	£519.50

[1] Relief is restricted to 10 per cent
[2] Abolished from 2000–2001 tax year

Blind person's allowance You can claim this allowance if you are registered blind. In Scotland or Northern Ireland, where there is no register, the equivalent requirement is that you must be unable to perform any work for which eyesight is essential. If your income is too low for you to use the allowance in full, you can transfer any unused allowance to your husband or wife, whether or not he or she is blind.

Restricted-relief allowances

Married couple's allowance Whether you can get this allowance now depends on your age. With effect from 6 April 2000, the allowance was abolished for couples where both partners were born after 6 April 1935. If either one of you was born before then (i.e. aged at least 65 by 6 April 2000) you can still claim the allowance. If you get married after 5 April 2000, you can also claim, provided one or other of you was born before 6 April 1935. If you are eligible, you can deduct 10 per cent of the married couple's allowance from your tax bill. This is usually deducted from the husband's income, unless his income is too low to use it all. However, you can elect to split the allowance between you or for the wife to have it all. You cannot transfer any extra allowance you get because of your age.

To transfer the allowance, use the boxes provided on your annual tax return, or, if you do not get a tax return, ask your tax office for form 18. You have to do this before the start of the relevant tax year. However, you can transfer unused allowance after the end of the tax year, if you find that the person to whom it was initially given has too little income to make full use of it. There is a box in your tax return which allows you to do this: if you do not get a return, contact your tax office.

If you are getting married couple's allowance and the marriage then ends, through death, divorce or separation, the allowance carries on to the end of the tax year. It is applied first against the husband's income, although if his income is too low to make full use of it, it can then be transferred to the wife.

The value of your allowance depends on your age and income. The allowance can never be less than £1,970 in 1999–2000 (except that in the year you marry you get only one-twelfth of the full allowance for each complete month of marriage). If either partner is 65 or over you get a higher allowance – see Table 2 on page 210 –

unless the husband's total income is above £16,800 (in 1999–2000). If so, your allowance is cut down by £1 for every £2 over the £16,800 limit, until £1,970 is reached. Note that it is always the husband's total income that is used, even though he may qualify only because of his wife's age and even if they have elected for the wife to have some or all of the allowance. In addition, if a husband's total income is over the £16,800 limit, it is his higher personal allowance which will be reduced first, so a married man could have the full higher married couple's allowance but a reduced personal allowance.

EXAMPLE 4

Bert and Molly Jones are 77 and 76 respectively so qualify for the higher personal and married couple's allowances for people over 75. Bert has a total income of £17,300 and Molly a total income of £7,000 in 1999–2000.

Molly will be able to deduct the full personal allowance of £5,980 for people her age. Bert, however, is £500 over the £16,800 limit, which means a reduction of £250 (i.e. £500 divided by 2) in his higher personal allowance from £5,980 to £5,730. He will get the full higher married couple's allowance for people over 75 of £5,195. This gives him tax relief of 10 per cent of £5,195, i.e. £519.50.

Maintenance deduction Until 6 April 2000 it was possible to claim tax relief on maintenance payments you were legally obliged to make to an ex-wife or ex-husband. You can now claim this relief only if you (or your ex-wife or ex-husband) were born before 6 April 1935. If you qualify, the tax relief comes in the form of a 'maintenance deduction' which works in a similar way to married couple's allowance. You get 10 per cent of the minimum married couple's allowance (i.e. 10 per cent of £1,970 in 1999–2000), or if less, 10 per cent of the maintenance you pay, deducted from your tax bill.

Note that special rules used to apply to payments made under a legally-enforceable agreement set up before a certain date in 1988. These rules have been abolished altogether from 6 April 2000, although if you are affected you can still claim the maintenance deduction, assuming you qualify.

Additional personal allowance Until 6 April 2000 you qualify for this allowance if you are supporting a child who is 16 or under (or in full-time education) and you are single, separated, divorced or widowed. You can also claim if you are married, supporting a child and your husband or wife is totally incapacitated (either mentally or physically) throughout the tax year. This allowance will be abolished altogether, whatever your age, with effect from 6 April 2000. However, a new children's tax credit for families with children aged under 16 will be introduced from April 2001.

Widow's bereavement allowance You used to be able to claim an allowance of £1,970 (in 1999–2000) in the tax year of your husband's death and the following tax year. This allowance, too, will be abolished from 6 April 2000, although if your husband died between 6 April 1999 and 5 April 2000 you will carry on receiving it until 6 April 2001 (unless you remarry before that date).

Claiming allowances

Although allowances are not actually sums of money that you can claim, you do need to let your tax office know which allowances you qualify for so that they can be taken into account when working out your tax bill. If you get a tax return each year, use that to claim your allowances. Otherwise, write to your tax office telling them which allowances you think you can claim and why.

How not to lose your age-related allowances

Total income' for the purposes of working out your age-related allowances is broadly your gross income less outgoings that qualify for full tax relief. It doesn't include any tax-free income, but it does include the before-tax amount of any building society or bank interest. If it looks as though you will exceed the total income limit (£16,800 in 1999–2000), there are steps you can take to protect those allowances.

First check the payments that you can deduct from your income for tax purposes to make sure that you cannot reduce your total income in this way. For example, do you make payments to charity? You could save yourself tax by doing so under a deed of covenant or the Gift Aid scheme. Then examine your investments.

If you have investments which produce taxable income you would almost certainly benefit from exchanging them for investments that are tax-free – provided you do not sacrifice more in return than you would gain in tax savings.

Beware of making a taxable gain on a life insurance policy (e.g. by cashing more than five per cent a year of the amount you invested in a single premium bond). This gain will swell your total income for the purposes of calculating your age allowance.

If you are married and one of you is over and the other under the total income limit, consider putting joint investments, such as building society accounts, into the sole name of the partner who is under the limit. In the example of Molly and Bert (Example 4), Bert could qualify for the full amount of his higher personal allowance if he agreed to transfer joint investments producing £500 (or more) of income into Molly's name only.

GROSSING UP

When working out whether your total income will be over the total income limit, your calculations should use gross, or before-tax, figures. With 20 per cent tax deducted from savings, for example, you will need to divide the amount you receive from a building society account by 0.8 to get the gross amount. To gross-up any payments you make after deduction of basic-rate relief such as covenants to charity, divide by 0.77.

Chapter 16

Tax if you carry on working

Keeping your tax affairs in order is fairly straightforward if you work for an employer, because under the Pay-As-You-Earn system the right amount of tax should be deducted from your pay before you get it. But in tax terms there are advantages to being self-employed. Self-employed people can deduct more expenses to reduce their taxable income and they have more scope to reorganise their affairs so that they pay less tax. Later in the chapter you will find an explanation of how to deal with tax in self-employment, but first we look at tax if you are an employee.

Employed or self-employed?

The Inland Revenue is fairly strict about whom it will class as self-employed. In general, you are on dangerous ground if all (or nearly all) your income comes from just one source, and you are paid on a regular basis without having to send in an invoice. But you will usually count as self-employed if you can answer 'yes' to all the following questions:

- Do you have final say about how your business is run (for example, where you work and the hours that you work)?
- Do you put your own money at risk?
- Do you bear any losses, as well as keep the profits?
- Do you provide the major equipment which you need for your work (e.g. a van, machinery, computer)?

- Are you free to employ others, and if so, do you set their terms of employment and pay them out of your own pocket?
- Do you have to correct unsatisfactory work in your own time and at your own expense?

If you answered 'no' to some of these questions, but you still think you are self-employed, see Inland Revenue leaflet IR56 *Employed or Self-Employed?* and contact your local tax office. You can ask for a decision in writing on whether you count as self-employed.

Tax if you are an employee

Pay-As-You-Earn (PAYE)

PAYE is a way of collecting tax bit by bit over the tax year. The Inland Revenue works out for you a PAYE code which indicates an estimate of the amount of free-of-tax pay you are entitled to over the tax year. Any excess over this free-of-tax pay is taxed.

You are sent a Coding Notice which tells you how your PAYE code is calculated: your employer is told what your code is, and uses it, together with various tables supplied by the Revenue, to deduct the right amount of tax from your pay. Each pay-day, your employer gives you one fifty-second or one-twelfth (depending on whether you are paid weekly or monthly) of the free-of-tax pay, deducts some tax-allowable payments you make, such as pension contributions, and then pays out the rest after tax.

A PAYE code usually consists of a number and a letter: the number shows how much free-of-tax pay you are allowed in the whole tax year, and the letter shows what allowances you are getting. Example 1 opposite shows how the letter and number are arrived at.

Changes to your PAYE code

The Coding Notice (if you get one) will normally be sent out in January or February each year, and applies to the next year starting on 6 April. The Inland Revenue may also send you a notice if there is a change in tax rules, if you query your code, or if your circumstances change.

EXAMPLE 1

Susan Jones is aged 66, single, and has carried on working part-time for her previous employer, earning £8,000 in 1999–2000. She has deferred her state pension, but has an income from her investments in British Government stocks, the income from which is paid out before tax. Her Coding Notice shows first her allowances: since she qualifies just for the full amount of age-related allowance for someone of her age, the total is £5,720.

Then the Notice shows her deductions, e.g. any taxable perks from a job, any untaxed income such as state retirement pension or untaxed investment income, any higher-rate tax due on investment income, and any underpaid tax from previous years. In Susan's case, the only deduction is the £700 to account for the untaxed income from her British Government stocks.

Finally, to get to Susan's code, her Coding Notice shows how her deductions are taken away from her allowances, i.e. £5,720 – £700 = £5,020. The final digit is knocked off and replaced by the letter P, which indicates that she gets the full age-related allowance for someone of her age, giving her a PAYE code of 502P. This tells her employer to give her £5,029 (since the last figure is always assumed to be 9) free of tax each year, so about £5,029/12 = £419 of her pay each month will not be taxed.

For example, you might start to draw your state pension, which is paid out before tax. If so, tell your tax office immediately: if you do not get a new PAYE code, you will have paid the wrong amount of tax at the end of the tax year. If you have paid too much, your PAYE code will be adjusted so that less tax is deducted on future pay-days. If you have paid too little, and the underpayment is large, in order to avoid a large drop in your income, your code may be adjusted to what it should have been had you paid the right amount of the tax from the beginning of the tax year, and any underpayment will be collected through the next year's PAYE code or through a tax bill at the end of the year.

Income from several sources

If you have more than one source of income taxed under PAYE, you will normally get a PAYE code for each source, although your allowances and deductions will if possible be included in the code for the main source. So if, say, you have an employer pension from one job, untaxed income from investments and are also working for an employer, you will probably get a code for both your job and the pension, and tax on your untaxed investment income will be collected through one of your PAYE codes.

In some cases you may get no free-of-tax pay, for example because you have lots of untaxed income. If so, your tax office may tell your employer (or pension provider) to add a notional amount to your income before the PAYE on it is worked out. The effect is that all the tax you are liable to pay is collected from this source. In this case, you get the letter K in your code.

Changing jobs

When you change jobs, your old employer should give you a form P45. This shows your PAYE code and details of the tax deducted from your total pay for the year to date. Give this to your new employer on your first day so that the correct amount of tax can be deducted from your pay.

If you do not do this, and your earnings are above the PAYE limit (about £83 a week, £361 a month in 1999–2000), your employer will give you only the 'emergency code', operated on a 'week 1' or 'month 1' basis. The emergency code assumes that you are entitled only to the basic personal allowance, and the 'week 1' or 'month 1' basis means that your employer takes no account of any free-of-tax pay due from the beginning of the tax year to the time you start work. Your employer will send a P46 form to your tax office, which will contact you to sort out the correct code. Once you have been allocated a proper code any tax you have overpaid will be refunded to you.

Temporary work through an agency

If you work through an agency, say as a temporary accountant, you will be treated as an employee (normally of the agency) and taxed under PAYE. But there are exceptions to this rule: you may be able to work through an agency and still be treated as self-employed if you are an entertainer, model, subcontractor in the building industry, or if all your work is done at or from your own home.

Other temporary or casual jobs

Income tax will not be deducted unless your earnings are more than about £83 a week (£361 a month). If you are paid more than this, you are taxed as described under 'Changing jobs', above.

If you are off sick

Statutory sick pay paid by your employer and any sick pay from your employer's own sick pay scheme are normally taxable under PAYE. But if the amount you get is lower than the amount of free-of-tax pay you are entitled to, your employer will refund some of the tax you have already paid in each pay packet.

If you have been unemployed

If you are unemployed and have been living on benefits with no other taxable income for a full year, your total taxable benefit will be below your allowances, so there will be no tax to pay. But if you have been unemployed for only part of the tax year, when you return to work your benefit office will give you a new form P45. This will allow your employer to deduct the right amount of tax straight away.

Increases to your income

As well as your pay, any other 'remuneration' your employer gives you, such as taxable fringe benefits and expenses, will increase your income for tax purposes. However, some fringe benefits and expenses are tax-free.

Taxable fringe benefits

Whether or not you actually pay tax sometimes depends on your income, but the following perks are taxable whatever your income:

- rent-free or low-rent accommodation (unless you either have to live there to do your job properly – e.g. as a publican – or you need to live there to do your job better, and it is customary for the job)
- assets transferred to you, such as a second-hand computer your employer gives you
- payments made for you, and debts, credit and charge card bills settled by your employer (although you can claim tax relief if these are to cover business expenses)
- travel and other vouchers
- any 'profit' you make on mileage allowances if you use your own car for work and your employer pays you more than the actual cost (or a Revenue-approved figure).

However, other benefits are taxable only if you are paid at a rate of £8,500 or more a year (or, if you worked for part of the year only, if your earnings would have come to this amount over a full year), including taxable fringe benefits and expenses. These benefits are:

- company cars and vans, free petrol and diesel
- loans of money, if you pay less than the 'official' rate of interest prescribed by the Treasury – though these are tax-free if the total maximum balance outstanding on all your cheap or interest-free loans does not exceed £5,000 at any time in the tax year
- loans of physical objects such as computers or furniture
- private medical or dental insurance.

Tax-free fringe benefits

These perks are tax-free whatever your income:

- your employer's own goods or services which you get free or at a discount, provided they do not cost your employer anything to provide
- your employer's contributions to an 'approved' or 'statutory' pension scheme
- the cost of providing life insurance and sick pay, provided the scheme meets certain conditions
- fees and subscriptions paid by your employer to various 'approved' professional bodies
- the first 15p-worth of luncheon vouchers each working day
- free or subsidised canteen meals if they are provided for all employees
- in-house sports facilities, if open to staff generally and used mainly or wholly by employees
- essential travel, accommodation and subsistence payments if you are temporarily absent from your normal workplace for up to 24 months. Travelling expenses for your spouse may also be tax-free if your health is such that he or she has to accompany you on trips abroad
- routine health checks or medical screening for you or your family
- clothes needed specially for your work and paid for by your employer

- relocation expenses of up to £8,000 when you have to move to a new job or are transferred, whether or not you sell your old home
- genuinely personal gifts, such as retirement gifts and awards for long service of 20-plus years – but not gifts or awards of money
- gifts from business contacts, providing you get no more than £150 from each source
- Christmas party or similar annual functions that are open to all staff and cost no more than £75 a head a year
- the value of entertainment (e.g. business lunches) provided by someone other than your employer
- shares you get through an approved profit-sharing or share option scheme
- new shares bought under a preferential scheme through your job: any benefit you get from receiving more shares than members of the public will not be taxed as income, provided certain conditions are met
- awards from staff suggestion schemes – up to a £5,000 maximum
- books and fees paid for by your employer for some external training courses, and some extra travel and living costs
- retraining courses for employees who are leaving (if certain conditions are met)
- counselling services provided to redundant employees
- contributions made by your employer to an Individual Learning Account for you (see page 168)
- computer equipment provided for you by your employer, provided the taxable value is no more than £500 – anything over £500 is taxable – and provided the benefit is not restricted to directors
- subsidised transport on public transport or works buses, available to employees generally
- some perks for people who cycle to work
- taxis paid for by your employer to take you home if you work until 9pm or later (within limits)
- free parking at or near your workplace
- travel and subsistence payments when public transport is disrupted or for severely disabled employees incapable of using public transport.

Tax-free expenses paid by your employer

In order to qualify for tax relief, expenses have to be incurred 'wholly, exclusively and necessarily in the performance of the duties of your employment'. This rules out things like the cost of formal clothes which you could wear outside work, even if you would never choose to, and travel to and from work. The expenses which do count as tax-free ('allowable' expenses in tax jargon) are:

- liability insurance, or legal costs paid by your employer if you are taken to court in a work-related case
- the cost of fees and books (and sometimes extra living and travel costs) for work-related training
- the cost of cleaning and repairing protective clothing and uniforms necessary for your job
- the cost of maintaining and repairing factory or workshop tools and instruments; also the cost of replacing them, less the proceeds of selling the old ones, providing the new ones are not inherently better than the old
- the cost of necessary reference books and stationery used strictly for your job
- a proportion of your home's heating and lighting and possibly telephone, cleaning and insurance costs, if it is a condition of your work that you work at home
- interest on loans (not overdrafts or credit card bills) to buy 'equipment' necessary for your job
- fees and subscriptions to professional bodies 'approved' by the Revenue
- travelling expenses that are incurred strictly in the course of your work, including any running costs of your own or a company car which are attributable purely to your work
- occasional late-night journeys home or extra travel costs if public transport is disrupted by industrial action
- travel costs of your wife or husband travelling with you on a business trip, if your health is so poor that it is unreasonable to travel alone
- reasonable overnight expenses – such as papers and phone calls home – if you stay away from home overnight on business, providing that the payment does not exceed £5 a night (£10 a night outside the United Kingdom)

- expenses of entertaining customers if you can claim the cost from your employer
- agents' fees (within limits) if you are an actor or theatrical performer taxed under PAYE.

Any other expenses are added to your earnings from the job, for tax purposes. If you get a fixed expense allowance, and do not spend all of it on tax-free expenses, you are taxed on the difference.

Deductions from income

There are some payments you make which you can deduct from your income before working out your tax bill. These deductions therefore save you tax. Chapter 15 explains the main tax-allowable payments, but there are also some which are linked to your work.

'Allowable' expenses

In trades where it is customary to provide your own tools or clothing (e.g. plumbing) many trade unions have agreed a fixed deduction with the Revenue for upkeep and replacement – e.g. £70 a year. You can claim the whole amount even if you do not spend that much, and if you spend more, you can claim more.

If you have to pay expenses to do with your work, and you are not reimbursed by your employer, you can also deduct these from your income from that job, provided the expenses are 'allowable'. The expenses you can deduct are broadly the same as those listed as 'Tax-free expenses paid by your employer', except for the travel costs of a wife or husband travelling with you, overnight expenses, late-night travel and the costs of business entertaining, all of which must be paid by your employer in order to be tax-free.

Pension payments

Within limits, you can get tax relief on contributions to employer pension schemes, personal pension plans or retirement annuity contracts (old-style personal pensions), and on Additional Voluntary Contributions either to an employer scheme or a separate free-standing scheme.

Payroll giving schemes

These are schemes run by employers allowing you to give money to charity free of tax. The maximum you can give this way in 1999–2000 is £1,200 a year (with no maximum from April 2000).

Vocational training costs

Until 6 April 2000 you can claim tax relief on some payments for your own training. From 6 April 2000 this tax relief is being replaced by subsidies to Individual Learning Accounts (see page 168).

How you get the relief

Payments to employer schemes and payroll giving schemes are normally taken direct from your salary before the tax is deducted, so you get tax relief at your top rate of tax automatically. You get basic-rate relief on vocational training and personal pension plan contributions by paying smaller amounts; higher-rate tax relief on these, and tax relief on contributions to a retirement annuity contract is given to you through your PAYE code or tax return.

Tax if you are self-employed

Chapter 14 looks at the different ways in which you can be self-employed. This section gives an introduction to how you will be taxed if you are a 'sole trader' or member of a partnership; if you have set up a limited company, see pages 230–1.

Sole traders and partners pay tax at the same rate as individuals, on the business profit for the accounting period ending in the current tax year. Because you may not know exactly what your profits are until after the end of the tax year, you pay tax estimated on the basis of your previous year's tax bill, in two instalments 'on account', with a final balancing payment after the end of the tax year.

Working out taxable profits

Your taxable profits are broadly your takings for the year less your allowable business expenses; you also need to take into account changes in the value of your stock, any money owed by you and to you, money spent on capital equipment, and any losses you make.

Business expenses

An expense is allowable only if it is incurred 'wholly and exclusively' for the business – a less stringent definition than for employees. The main allowable expenses are:

- the cost of goods bought for resale
- the cost of raw materials
- running costs such as advertising, delivery charges, heating, lighting, postage and phone bills, renting and cleaning your place of business, business rates, the cost of small tools and special clothing, stationery, relevant books and magazines
- accountant's fees and bank charges on business accounts
- VAT on allowable business expenses if you are not VAT-registered
- wages, salaries and employers' National Insurance contributions for employees
- if you work from home, a proportion of your telephone, heating, lighting, cleaning, council tax and insurance bills, plus a proportion of your rent if part of a rented home is used exclusively for business
- interest and arrangement fees on overdrafts and business loans
- contributions to some trade and professional bodies
- cost of travel and accommodation, and some meals, on business trips
- travel between different places of work
- running costs of your own car (or a proportion if you use the car for private purposes, too)
- some bad and doubtful debts, legal costs of recovering debts
- some legal costs
- business insurance premiums
- reasonable charge for hire of capital goods, including cars (this is restricted for cars costing more than £12,000 when new).

Stock values

You can claim as a business expense only the cost of raw materials and goods for resale that you actually sell during your accounting year. To work out stock values, you should usually base this on the cost to you – you can only use the price you charge your customers if you expect to sell the stock for less than it cost you. If stock is unsold at the end of the year, you can carry forward the cost and deduct it when you sell the stock.

Money owed

You must keep your accounts on an 'accruals' basis. This means that your books must be kept according to the dates that your invoices are raised and your expenses are actually incurred (even if payment is considerably later).

Capital allowances

You are not allowed to treat the cost of buying capital assets as a business expense for the year in which you buy them, nor can you claim depreciation, but you may be able to claim capital allowances instead. These have the effect of spreading tax relief for the cost of capital equipment over a number of years. Broadly, capital equipment is anything that cannot be used up within a year of purchase – this includes vans, cars, computers and machinery, and some types of property.

The cost of capital equipment you buy goes into a 'pool' of expenditure. Each accounting year, you can claim up to 25 per cent of the value of the pool at the end of the year as a 'writing down allowance' and deduct that amount from your profits for tax purposes. The pool is reduced by what you claim. If you sell something in the pool, its value (usually the sale proceeds) must be deducted from the pool before working out your writing down allowance for the accounting year in which the items were sold. If the proceeds come to more than the amount of the pool, the excess – called a 'balancing charge' – is added to your profits for the year.

You can claim less than 25 per cent of your pool as an allowance. Do not claim more of your capital allowance than you need to reduce your tax to nil (and remember to use up your personal allowances first – see Chapter 15). Any capital allowances left unclaimed are carried forward to next year's pool of expenditure and can reduce tax in later years.

From time to time the government makes available a higher initial allowance instead of the normal writing-down allowance. For example, small and medium-sized businesses could claim a first-year allowance of 40 per cent on expenditure on some machinery and plant (not cars) in the 24 months ending on 1 July 2000.

Separate pools

Items bought partly for business and partly for private use have their own pools (you get a proportion of the capital allowance in line with the business use). This includes cars (but not lorries or vans); any car costing over £12,000 must have its own pool. There is a maximum writing down allowance of £3,000 for each individual car pool in any year.

You can opt to have a separate pool for items of capital equipment which you expect to sell or scrap within five years – a computer, for example. The advantage of doing this is that, if you sell the item during that time for less than what is left in the pool, you can deduct the difference – the 'balancing allowance' – from that year's profits.

Using your losses

It may not be all doom and gloom if you make a loss – you can use the loss to reduce other tax, due either now or in the future. Watch out, though, for strict time limits on doing so. You can normally do one of three things:

- **Set the loss against future profits** You set the loss against profits from the same business in the following accounting year. Any losses left over can be carried forward to the year after, and so on.
- **Claim immediate income tax relief** You can ask for the loss to be set against any other income (or capital gains once your income has been reduced to nil) you have for the current tax year.
- **Set the loss against income and capital gains for the previous tax year** (provided the business was carried on in that year).

In addition, any loss incurred in the first four years of trading can be set against income from any source arising in the previous three years. If you make a loss in the last 12 months of trading it can be set against profits from the same trade arising in the previous three years.

Starting up

Your accounting year need not run from 1 January to 31 December, nor need it coincide with the tax year. Your first accounting year does not have to cover exactly 12 months, but once you have chosen a year end, changing it can be tricky – check with your tax office. If yours is a seasonal business, you may want to arrange a year-end in a slack period.

Table 1: What your tax bill is based on in the opening years of a business

	Tax is initially based on
First tax year of business	Actual profit from the date you start up until 5 April. If the first accounting period ends after 5 April, a proportion of the profits is calculated on a time basis
Second tax year	Profit in the 12 months ending with the accounting date in the year, or if there is under 12 months before the accounting date, the profit in the first 12 months, or if there is no accounting date in the year, a proportion of the profits calculated on a time basis
Third and following tax years	Profit in your accounting year ending in the current tax year

Table 1 shows what your tax bill is based on when you first start up. If these rules mean that you are taxed on the same profits in two successive tax years, you may qualify for some 'overlap relief', which can be deducted from your profits in the last year of the business (or possibly earlier if you change your accounting date).

Paying the tax

Leaflet CWL1 (from any tax office) contains a form which you can use to tell the Inland Revenue, HM Customs and Excise and the Inland Revenue National Insurance Contributions Agency that you have started up. You also have to notify your tax office that you have taxable income by 5 October after the end of the tax year, following which you will be sent a tax return (if you have not had one already). The tax return enables you to work out any tax due, which must be paid by 31 January or, if later, three months after the date on the return. You can ask the Revenue to work out the tax for you if you send back your return by the 30 September following the end of the tax year in question.

After that, tax is due in three instalments: on 31 January during the tax year in question; on 31 July just after the end of the tax year; and the following 31 January. The first two payments are 'payments on account' and are based on your tax bill for the previous year (or an estimate if your first trading period has not yet ended). The third and final 'balancing payment' is due the following 31 January at the same time as the tax return, and will cover any tax outstanding. So if you pay tax for your first year on 31 January following the end of the tax year, the first instalment for the following year will be due at the same time.

You do not need to send in accounts. If your total turnover is less than £15,000 a year, you only have to give three lines of figures on your tax return – total turnover, allowable business expenses and your net profit. But you must be able to back up your accounts with proper records, should your Tax Inspector challenge them.

Partnerships

Profits from a partnership are worked out in the same way as profits for a trade or business, and taxed like those of other businesses.

The same rules for the opening years apply for each partner when he or she joins the partnership. The taxable profits of the partnership for each accounting period are shared out between the partners in line with their shares under the partnership agreement for that period. Each partner's tax bill then depends on his or her other income, deductions and allowances.

So if, for example, the profits are £40,000 and there are two partners sharing the profits equally, each partner will pay tax on £20,000. But if one partner pays tax at the basic rate, and the other is a higher-rate taxpayer (because he or she has lots of other income, say) the tax each pays on their share will be different. In effect, each partner is treated as if they run their own individual business based on their share of the partnership profits.

If you employ someone

When you take on staff, as well as taking on all of an employer's obligations to comply with health and safety requirements, and other legislation for protecting employees' rights, you take on responsibility for:

- deducting income tax from your employees' pay under PAYE (assuming that your employees earn more than the basic personal allowance – about £83 a week, or £361 a month, in the 1999–2000 tax year)
- deducting Class 1 National Insurance contributions from your employees' pay and paying Class 1 contributions as an employer. Again, these payments apply only if your employees earn more than a set limit – £83 a week in 1999–2000.

When an employee starts

You need to tell the relevant tax office – this will be a PAYE office, and may be different from the office dealing with your business; your own tax office should tell you where it is. You will be sent a *New Employer's Starter Pack* telling you what to do, which encloses all the forms you will need. The first step is to ask your employee for his or her National Insurance number and form P45: you can use the PAYE code shown on the P45 to work out how much free-of-tax pay to deduct. Your PAYE office will let you know if the code needs to be changed. If the person has not got a P45, you need to send form P46 to the PAYE office, and in the meantime use the 'emergency code' to deduct the tax.

Month by month

You will also be sent tax and National Insurance tables. By using these with the employee's PAYE code, you will know how much tax and National Insurance to deduct. You then need to send these deductions off to the relevant Accounts office, usually quarterly.

At the end of the tax year

You need to complete a form telling your PAYE office how much you have paid each employee during the year and what deductions you have made: a copy also goes to the employee.

Companies

Much of what has been said about how businesses are taxed applies to limited companies too. However, there are some important differences: the main ones are listed opposite.

Corporation tax

Companies do not get personal allowances, of course, and instead of paying income tax, they pay corporation tax. This is charged (in the 1999–2000 tax year) at two rates:

- a full rate – 30 per cent
- a small-company rate – 20 per cent. This is payable on all profits up to £300,000. Above this, the rate of tax gradually increases, according to a complex formula. The full rate applies on all profits over £1.5 million.

From April 2000, companies with profits of up to £10,000 will pay corporation tax at 10 per cent; above that, the rate will increase on a sliding scale until the 20 per cent rate applies at profits of £50,000.

Business expenses

The salaries paid to company directors are an allowable business expense, like other salaries, and so are deducted in calculating profits. Any surplus profits can be voted to directors as bonuses, on which they pay individual income tax – but this is a complex area in which you will need help from an accountant. Any part of the surplus that is not paid out is called 'retained profit' and subject to corporation tax.

Capital allowances and losses

These are the same for companies as for sole traders and partners, but cannot be set against the directors' or shareholders' income from other sources: they apply only to the company's income.

Accounting periods

A company may choose any date it likes for its accounting period. However, profits are taxed by reference to the year which runs from 1 April to 31 March. If the accounting period is different, the trading profits of the two periods will be split on a time basis. Other income and any capital gains are not split in this way: the actual date received determines which year they are taxed in.

Tax if you are a director

If you are a company director, you are technically an employee, even if you own shares in the company. So you will be paid under PAYE, pay Class 1 National Insurance contributions and your company will have to pay employer's Class 1 contributions. However, for the purposes of working out whether you pay tax on fringe benefits you will always be classed as earning at a rate of £8,500 a year or more (see pages 219–20), whatever your actual salary.

Capital gains

Businesses and companies, like individuals, may make capital gains, e.g. on the sale of a business property. These are taxed as described in Chapter 17, with some exceptions – an important one being that companies, unlike individuals and sole traders, do not qualify for the annual tax-free amount.

On the other hand, several reliefs exist from which businesses can benefit. For example, tax due on any gains made by individuals – but not companies – may be deferred if the proceeds are reinvested in the shares of 'qualifying' unquoted trading companies. You may also be able to defer capital gains tax if you dispose of 'qualifying' business assets, providing you reinvest an amount equal to the disposal proceeds, or if you give away business assets in an unquoted company (e.g. to a younger family member).

Retirement relief is currently available if you own at least a five per cent stake in a company and are over 55 or retire through ill-health, but it is being phased out.

Note that while sole traders and partners pay capital gains tax, companies pay corporation tax on any capital gains (although this is calculated in the same way as capital gains tax).

When you need an accountant

If you have set up as a company, you will need an accountant in order to comply with the accounts and auditing rules for limited companies. If you have set up in any other way, this is not essential. But it may be advisable, because accountants should be versed in all the latest rules and regulations and should be able to advise you on the various options open to you. In addition, they are likely to have a knowledge of how the Revenue will interpret the rules in practice. See page 191 for how to find an accountant.

Chapter 17

Tax and investments

Tax has an important impact on the return you get from your investments and, as explained in Chapter 15, the investments you choose and how they are taxed can influence the amount of age-related allowances you get if you are 65 or over. However, tax is not the only consideration when picking ways to save and invest. The other factors you should take into account in your retirement planning are dealt with in Chapter 10. Table 1 tells you how the investments discussed in that chapter are taxed.

The most common tax you will have to pay on your investments is income tax, which is charged on the income they produce. The other main tax to watch out for is capital gains tax, which you may have to pay on the profit you make from selling shares and unit trusts, for example. The rules for this tax are explained later in the chapter. Then there is inheritance tax. Although this does not directly affect the return you get on your investments, it may affect the value of your accumulated wealth that you pass on to your heirs. You will find an explanation of how this tax works in Chapter 33.

How investment income is taxed

Income you receive from savings and investments is treated rather differently from other income. The various types of investment fall into one of four categories:

- **Tax-free** There is no tax to pay on the income from these investments, though you may have to meet specific conditions to keep the tax-free status.

- **Taxable** You will be paid the income without having tax deducted but unless you are a non-taxpayer, tax will be due. Tax is payable at 10 per cent if you are a starting-rate taxpayer, 20 per cent if you are a basic-rate taxpayer, or 40 per cent if you are a higher-rate taxpayer. The tax is collected either through your tax return, or through PAYE on other income.

- **Taxed** The income is normally paid with 20 per cent tax already deducted. This meets the tax liability of basic-rate tax-payers, but non-taxpayers can either reclaim the tax or register to have the income paid without tax deducted. To register, complete form R85 from the bank or building society, or get leaflet IR110 *A Guide for People with Savings* from your tax office. Higher-rate taxpayers have to pay a further 20 per cent tax, either through their tax return or PAYE, to bring the total paid up to 20 + 20 = 40 per cent. If you pay tax at a top rate of 10 per cent, you can reclaim any excess tax deducted before you get the income.

- **Taxed with a tax credit** This applies mostly to income from shares, unit trusts, OEICs and investment trusts. These have a 'tax credit' of 10 per cent deducted from the income before you get it. Starting-rate and basic-rate taxpayers have no further tax to pay, but non-taxpayers cannot reclaim the 10 per cent tax credit. If you pay tax at the higher rate, you will have to pay extra tax at a rate of 32.5 per cent, but the tax credit counts as tax already paid.

Married couples

If you are married and own investments in joint names – a building society account, for example – the income will automatically be treated as if it is paid to you in equal shares, with each of you paying tax on half the income. However, if you own the investment in unequal shares, the income can be taxed accordingly. You both have to make a joint declaration to one of your tax offices setting out how the capital and income are shared between you, using form 17. The different tax treatment applies from the date that you make the declaration. You cannot choose the proportions in which the income from joint investments will be taxed. You can make a declaration only to be taxed according to your real shares in the capital and income.

Table 1: How investments are taxed

	for income tax	for capital gains tax
Annuities you buy yourself	taxed[1][2]	no capital gain
Bank deposit or savings account	taxed[2]	no capital gain
• British Government stocks (gilts)	taxable/taxed	tax-free
Building society account	taxed[2]	no capital gain
Corporate bonds	taxed	normally tax-free
Enterprise Investment Scheme shares	tax credit	tax-free
Friendly Society insurance policies	tax-free[3]	tax-free
Friendly Society tax-exempt savings plan	tax-free	tax-free
Gifts – see British Government stocks		
Guaranteed income bonds	tax-free[4]	tax-free
Index-linked gilts – see British Government stocks		
ISAs (Individual Savings Accounts)	tax-free	tax-free
National Savings Certificates (fixed-interest or index-linked)	tax-free	no capital gain
Investment trusts	tax credit[5]	taxable[5]
Life insurance savings policy	tax-free[3]	tax-free
National Savings Capital Bonds	taxable	no capital gain
National Savings Fixed Rate Savings Bond	taxed	no capital gain
National Savings Income Bond	taxable	no capital gain
National Savings Investment Account	taxable	no capital gain
National Savings Ordinary Account	tax-free/taxable[6]	no capital gain
National Savings Pensioners Bonds	taxable	no capital gain
OEICs (Open-Ended Investment Companies)	tax credit[5]	taxable[5]
PEP (Personal Equity Plan)	tax-free	tax-free
PIBS (Permanent Interest-Bearing Shares)	taxed	tax-free
Shares	tax-credit[5]	taxable[5]
Single premium insurance bond	tax-free[4]	tax-free
TESSA (Tax Exempt Special Savings Account)	tax-free	no capital gain
Unit trusts	tax-credit[5]	taxable[5]
Venture Capital Trusts	tax-free	tax-free

[1] Only part of the monthly income is taxable – see page 144.
[2] Non-taxpayers can register to have income paid without tax deducted.
[3] Tax-free unless you cash in early and are a higher-rate taxpayer – see page 143.
[4] Usually tax-free to basic-rate taxpayers but proceeds may push you into the higher-rate band or mean you lose age allowance – see page 138.
[5] Income comes with tax credit, any capital gains on disposal chargeable to capital gains tax.
[6] The first £70 of interest (or £140 if it is a joint account) is tax-free.

Special rules for some investments

Tax-free investments

Some investments are tax-free only if you meet certain conditions, which are usually linked to the amounts you can invest and the amount of time for which you have to invest. These are ISAs, TESSAs, PEPs, and Venture Capital Trusts. Income from the Enterprise Investment Scheme is taxable, but there are other tax advantages. See Chapter 10 for the details.

British Government stocks (gilts)

Interest from all new holdings of gilts is now paid out gross (before tax). However, you can choose to have it paid out after deduction of 20 per cent tax, or, if it is already paid out after tax (net), you can go back to having it paid gross. You can change between having your interest paid gross or net of tax, at any time, by contacting the Registrar's Department of the Bank of England.*

Life insurance

The proceeds you get from life insurance policies (including Friendly Society policies that are not tax-exempt) are free of basic-rate income tax in your hands. This is because the life insurance fund has already paid some tax which cannot be reclaimed even by people who are not taxpayers. If the policy is 'non-qualifying' (explained below) and you are a higher-rate taxpayer, you may also have some extra tax to pay.

There are currently two types of policy for tax purposes:

- **Qualifying policies** These include regular-premium policies, such as most endowment policies. Provided you keep these policies going for at least 10 years (or three-quarters of the term of the policy if less), there will be no extra tax to pay: if you do not meet these conditions, and are a higher-rate taxpayer, you have to pay tax on the gain (i.e. proceeds less contributions).
- **Non-qualifying policies** These include single premium insurance bonds and some guaranteed income bonds. Higher-rate taxpayers may have some tax to pay on withdrawals, but at present you can withdraw up to five per cent a year of your original investment and put off paying the tax until you finally cash in the policy.

WARNING

If you are aged 65 or over, a non-qualifying life insurance policy may affect your age-related allowances. Even if you do not have to pay tax on an insurance gain from a non-qualifying policy (because you are not a higher-rate taxpayer), a taxable gain is added to your 'total income' for the purposes of working out whether you are entitled to the higher age-related personal and married couple's allowances. So before cashing in a policy, check that it will not reduce your allowances.

Capital gains tax

As explained in Chapter 10, it is likely that you will be investing for capital growth as part of your longer-term investment strategy. But capital growth means capital gain, which for some investments means the possibility of paying capital gains tax.

The main investments which attract capital gains tax are shares, unit trusts, OEICs and investment trusts unless they are held in a PEP or ISA. You make a capital gain on these (and other 'assets') when you sell them or give them away for more than you paid for them (or for more than their value when you were given them). Some gains are tax-free and with others – e.g. shares you have sold at a profit – you do not have to pay tax on the whole of your gain because of the various deductions you can make.

Tax-free capital gains from investments are summarised in Table 1 on page 235. Other tax-free gains:

- your only or main home (see Chapter 18)
- private motor cars
- prizes, betting and lottery winnings
- sterling cash or foreign currency for your own use – e.g. on holiday
- compensation for personal or professional wrong or injury
- possessions with a predicted useful life of more than 50 years, if the disposal proceeds are £6,000 or less. There is also some tax relief if the proceeds are between £6,000 and £15,000
- gifts to charities, 'national heritage bodies' (e.g. some museums), local authorities, government and universities.

Gifts between a husband and wife are free of tax when made, but when the recipient finally parts with the gift, any capital gains tax will be worked out according to the period both partners owned the asset.

Working out your gains for tax purposes

To work out the gain (or loss) you make on an asset which is not tax-free – the profit you make from selling shares, for example – you need to do the following calculations:

1 Take the final value
Take the final value of the asset when you dispose of it – i.e. its sale price or, if you gave it away, its market value.

2 Deduct the initial value
From the final value, deduct the asset's initial value when you got it – i.e. the price you paid for it or its market value if you were given it or inherited it. See also the 'Tip' below.

Tip

Only gains made since 31 March 1982 are taxable, so if you acquired assets on or before then, you can choose to use the market value on 31 March 1982 as the initial value instead of the real initial value when you actually acquired the asset. However, if you do this, you cannot deduct expenses you incurred before 31 March 1982 in your calculations. It is worth using the March 1982 value if your expenses were minimal and the value of your asset was greater on 31 March 1982 than when you bought it. If the value of your asset on 31 March 1982 was less than its value when you acquired it, you would be better off using the real initial value.

---

3 Deduct allowable expenses
Once you have taken the initial value from the final value, deduct any allowable expenses that you incurred when acquiring or disposing of the asset – e.g. stamp duty and commission costs when buying or selling shares. You can also deduct any money you have spent on increasing the value of the asset (unlikely with most investments) but you cannot deduct maintenance costs.

If these three steps give you a plus figure, you have made a gain for tax purposes. If they give you a minus figure, you have made a loss for tax purposes, which you can set against gains either in the same or future tax years. Carry on to see if you can reduce your gain.

4 Deduct indexation allowance

This is an allowance that makes sure that you do not pay tax on gains that are simply the result of inflation. It only applies if you owned the asset before 1 April 1998 – gains made after that date may qualify for *taper relief* instead. A gain can be reduced or eliminated by your indexation allowance, but you cannot use your allowance to turn a gain into a loss, or to increase a loss.

Indexation allowance is equal to the increase in price of the asset and any allowable expenses in line with increases in the general level of prices between March 1982 and April 1998, as measured by the Retail Prices Index (RPI). To work out your indexation allowance, multiply the initial value and each allowable expense by an indexation factor (worked out as follows to three decimal places):

$$\frac{162.6 - X}{X}$$

162.6 is the RPI figure for April 1998, when indexation allowance ceased. X is the RPI for the month in which the initial value or expense was incurred.

Tip

Any tax office should be able to tell you the indexation factor for the month you need.

---

5 Deduct losses made in the same year

Gains after indexation are called chargeable gains, and any losses after indexation are called allowable losses. You can deduct a loss made on disposing of one asset from gains made on disposing of another. Any losses that are not needed to reduce your gains (before taper relief) to zero can be carried forward to future years: by contrast you need only use enough of your losses brought forward from previous years to reduce your gain to the level of the *tax-free slice* (see below). Again, this is your gain *before* taper relief, so in order to minimise your tax bill you should set your losses first against those gains that qualify for the least taper relief.

6 Work out your taper relief

Taper relief reduces the gain according to the length of time you hold an asset (see Table 2) after 5 April 1998 (when it was introduced). Taper relief is more generous for business assets, and if you held the asset immediately before 17 March 1998 you can add an extra year to the period that qualifies for relief. So if, for example, you bought a holiday cottage in 1990 and sold it in September 2000, you would have held it for two complete years after 5 April 1998; you would qualify for an extra year because you owned it before 17 March 1998, making three years' relief. Only 95 per cent of the chargeable gain (after deducting any losses) would be taxable.

7 Deduct your tax-free slice

Now add together all your gains (after indexation, losses and taper relief) for the tax year. The result is your total taxable gains, from which you can deduct your tax-free slice. This is the amount of taxable gains you can make each year before you pay tax – for 1999–2000 it is £7,100. If it does not reduce your chargeable gains

Table 2: How much tax relief

Years* asset held	Percentage of gain chargeable to tax	
	Non-business assets	Business assets[1]
0	100	100
1	100	92.5
2	100	85
3	95	77.5
4	90	70
5	85	62.5
6	80	55
7	75	47.5
8	70	40
9	65	32.5
10	60	25

[1] Proposals to tax business assets more favourably were put forward in 1999.

to nil (or a minus figure), you will have to pay capital gains tax. Note, however, that if you are married, each partner will have a tax-free slice to deduct from their own gains.

WARNING

Keep careful records of losses. You have to inform the Inland Revenue about any losses within five years and ten months of the end of the tax year in which they were made, i.e. by 31 January 2006 for losses made in 1999–2000. You can do so either on your tax return or by sending a separate letter. If you fail to tell the Revenue, you will not be able to deduct them later on.

How much capital gains tax?

Taxable capital gains are taxed as if they were investment income. This means that the amount of gains on which you have to pay tax is added to your taxable income and taxed (in 1999–2000) at 20 per cent if the total is below the basic-rate limit (£28,000 in 1999–2000) and at 40 per cent on any amount above that limit.

Paying capital gains tax

If you receive a tax return, you can give details about any gains on that. If you don't get a tax return, you must tell your tax office that you have made a capital gain by 5 October after the end of the tax year in which the gain was made. You will then be sent a tax return. You only need to give full details of your gains if, in total, they came to over £7,100 (in 1999–2000) and arose from total disposals of over £13,000, but do not forget to claim any losses.

The notes accompanying the tax return will tell you how to work out how much tax is due (see Chapter 19 for how the tax return works). The tax has to be paid, together with any income tax due, by 31 January following the end of the tax year, at the same time as the latest date for sending in your tax return.

EXAMPLE

When she retired in May 1990, Charlotte Smart used £10,000 of the lump sum she received from her employer pension scheme to buy shares. In December 1999, her shares are worth £25,500, so she decides to get out while the going is good and sells them. To see how much capital gains tax she will have to pay, Charlotte first calculates her gain for tax purposes:

Charlotte's gain for tax purposes	
Final value of shares	£25,500
less	
Initial value of shares	£10,000
less	
Expenses on selling	£ 470
Gain for tax purposes	£15,030

To calculate the indexation allowance, Charlotte first needs the indexation factor. Her tax office tells her that this is 0.288. She multiplies the initial value of her shares by this factor, i.e. £10,000 × 0.288 = £2,880.

Charlotte then deducts this from her gains for tax purposes to arrive at her gains after indexation:

Gains for tax purposes	£15,030
less	
Indexation allowance	£ 2,880
Gains after indexation	£12,150

At this point, Charlotte should deduct any allowable losses she has made. However, the gain on her shares is the only gain she has made in this tax year and she has no losses either from this or previous tax years. The gain doesn't qualify for taper relief because she has not owned the shares for long enough. The last thing to deduct is therefore her tax-free slice (which in the 1999–2000 tax year was £7,100) to arrive at her net taxable gains on which she will pay tax:

Gains after indexation	£12,150
less	
Tax-free slice	£7,100
Net taxable gains	£5,050

When she adds her gain of £5,050 to her taxable income of £13,700, she finds that she is still within the basic-rate tax limit of £28,000. Her capital gains tax bill is therefore £1,010 (i.e. 20 per cent of £5,050). Note that Charlotte could have saved all this tax had she sold only enough of her shares in December 1999 to bring her gain to just below the tax-free slice. By selling the rest after 5 April 2000, she could have set her 2000–2001 tax-free slice against the remaining gain. However, she would have risked a fall in the share price during the wait – and this assumes that she is unlikely to make any other taxable gain in 2000–2001.

Special rules for shares and unit trusts

If you own one lot of the same type of shares in the same company (or units in the same unit trust), and you acquired them all at the same time, there is no problem deciding which date you use for the initial value when you come to working out the taxable gain. However, if you acquired shares (or unit trusts) in the same company at different times and then you sold them at different times, the Revenue has special rules for deciding which shares you disposed of, how much they cost you, and what your indexation allowance is. If this affects you, you can telephone for the free Inland Revenue helpsheet IR284.*

Chapter 18

Tax and your home

If retirement has brought with it thoughts of moving to a smaller home, investing in a second home, or simply making the most of the one you have got, tax will be one of the factors that you will need to take into account. The other more personal factors are dealt with in Part 5 of this book, where you will find information on what to consider if you are on the move, plus all the practical aspects of being a homeowner.

Buying a home is by far the biggest single transaction you are likely to make. In this chapter you will find information about the tax position on the money you make from your home – whether it is by renting a room, letting a whole property or by getting your home to pay you an income with a home income scheme. There is also an explanation of how capital gains tax can affect your home – or other property – when you sell.

Mortgage interest relief

If you have a mortgage on your only or main home, you used to be able to get tax relief on the interest you paid on the first £30,000 of the loan. However, the amount of tax relief you get has gradually been restricted, and the relief will be abolished altogether from 6 April 2000. The abolition of mortgage interest relief may lead you to reassess your mortgage – and whether you should have one at all. For more on this, see Chapter 10.

Making money from your home

In general, you will have to pay income tax on money you make from your home whether it is income from letting, or income you get from a home income scheme. There may also be capital gains tax to pay when you come to sell your home – see pages 247–9. Below are the effects on your income tax bill.

Letting a room

If you have decided to supplement your retirement income by taking in a lodger, you can take advantage of the 'Rent-a-Room' scheme. The rent your lodger pays you (including any money your lodger pays you for meals) will be tax-free up to a set limit, which in 1999–2000 is £4,250 (or £2,125 if someone else lets out rooms in the same property).

If your lodger pays you more than £4,250 a year, you have a choice of how the money is taxed:

- you can choose to pay tax on the amount above £4,250 (but you will not be able to deduct expenses – see below) *or*
- you can agree to pay tax on the whole of the income you receive less expenses. If you do this, the first £4,250 will not be tax-free. It is worth choosing this method only if you have substantial expenses.

Letting your home

If you have decided to travel for a while, you may need to let your home while you are away, or you may decide to let a holiday home to boost your income. Here are the tax rules for income you get from letting your main home or a second home. (For the capital gains tax implications, see page 247.) Also see Inland Revenue leaflet IR150 *Taxation of rents.*

Reducing your income from letting

All the income from the letting is liable to income tax. However, before adding your income from letting to your other income for tax purposes, you can deduct certain expenses, the most common of which are:

- rent, rates, council tax, water rates, ground rent, feu duty (in Scotland)
- normal repairs and decoration
- management expenses as a landlord (e.g. stationery, phone bills, the cost of rent collection)
- the cost of insurance
- legal and professional fees, e.g. fees for renewing a tenancy agreement
- estate agent's fees, accommodation agency fees and advertising costs
- costs of services you provide (if the rent includes them)
- lighting and heating bills (if you, rather than your tenant, pay them)
- wear and tear – you can either claim the actual cost of what you have had to replace or a fixed amount, which is normally 10 per cent of the rent (less council tax). In some (limited) cases you may be able to claim capital allowances instead, but not for furniture or equipment in residential accommodation.

Interest on property you let

Interest on a loan to buy property which you let is treated as an expense of the business and deducted from your rental income. If you rent out part of the home you live in, and you have a mortgage, you can claim business interest relief on part of the loan, depending on how much of the house you rent out, and for how long. If, for example, you let out one of ten rooms for the whole year, you could claim one-tenth of your interest as a business expense and deduct it from your rental income.

Your home, your business

If your letting falls into one or other of the following categories, the income will count as earnings from a business and will be taxed accordingly:

- You run a guest house or bed and breakfast business.
- You supply services beyond those normally supplied by landlords, such as regular meals and room-cleaning for tenants. In this case, the provision of services may be treated as a separate business.

- You let furnished holiday accommodation in the UK (i.e. it is available for at least 140 days during each 12-month period, actually let for 70 of those days, and during the 12-month period there must usually be at least 7 months when no one tenant occupied the property for more than 31 days at a stretch).

The main benefits of being taxed as a business are that you are more likely to be able to claim capital allowances and that you can set off losses from these businesses against your total income, and not just other income from property. However, you will have to keep separate accounts and (except for furnished holiday accommodation, which has its own section) enter the income under 'Income from self-employment' on your tax return.

Home income schemes

If you own your own home, and you do not fancy sharing it with a lodger, you can use the value of your home to help boost your income with a home income scheme. Limited tax relief used to be available but has been abolished except for loans agreed before 9 March 1999. See Chapter 5 for more on home income plans and similar 'equity release' schemes.

Capital gains tax on your home

You need worry about capital gains tax only when you come to sell your home, and you will not have to pay it if the home is your main home and you have lived in it for most of the time that you have owned it. But there are steps you will need to take if you own a second home, or have let your home or part of it.

More than one home?

If you have two homes, only your main home is exempt from capital gains tax when you come to sell. You can choose which home you want to be regarded as your main one – it does not have to be the one in which you spend most time, though in most cases you must live in it at some stage.

Unless it is obvious to both you and the Inland Revenue which is your main home, you should write to the Revenue within two years of acquiring the second home to tell them which is your main home for capital gains tax purposes. If you miss the two-year deadline, your main home will be decided for you. If you do not like the decision, it is up to you to prove that the one that has been chosen is not in fact your main home. However, if you have a home in London where you have been living and working for 20 years but also have a holiday cottage in Suffolk, for example, it is unlikely that the Revenue will choose the holiday cottage as your main home, and even if they did, it would be easy to prove that the London home was, in fact, your main home.

Things to consider before deciding which home to nominate as your main home include: which one you are likely to sell first (especially if you are likely to move into the other home); which one will make the bigger gain after indexation (see Chapter 17 for how to work this out); and likely changes in house prices. See Inland Revenue helpsheet IR283, *Private Residence Relief.*.

A home you let

You will not lose any exemption from capital gains tax if you have lodgers who share your living rooms and eat with you. And if the home you let has also been your main home for the whole time you have owned it, the whole of the gain you make when you sell will be exempt, even if you let it out while you were away, provided all your absences count as qualifying absences. These include:

- any absence before 31 March 1982
- absence in the first year if you could not move into your home because of building work or because you had not sold your old home
- absences while you were living in a home that went with your job
- most job-related absences
- absences in the three years before you sell the home
- any other absences of not more than three years in total, provided you live in the home before and after the absences.

If you were absent from the main home you let for any other reason, the Revenue will work out the portion of the whole gain from selling your home, which relates to the time for which it was let. It is this portion (which, broadly speaking, is the fraction produced by dividing the time you let the home by the time you owned it) on which you will be liable to capital gains tax. The portion which relates to the time when you lived in the home yourself is still exempt from tax. However, there will be no capital gains tax to pay, even on the portion that relates to letting, if this is less than £40,000 and it is smaller than the portion of the gain relating to the time when you lived there.

If you let part of your home, the same rules apply, though the portion of the gain for the part you let will take into account the number of rooms or floor area as well as the time you let this part of the property.

If you work from home

If you are self-employed and use part of your home exclusively for business, the part you use will not be exempt from capital gains tax for the period you use it. However, most people will be able to show that they do not use it exclusively for business.

Chapter 19

Dealing with the tax authorities

The tax system has been through a major programme of change. The core of this programme has been the changeover to what is called self-assessment, but the programme also covers the streamlining and simplification of Revenue working methods and procedures, reorganisation of the office structure, and greater use of information technology. However, it is self-assessment which has made the biggest difference.

Self-assessment means that the responsibility is now on you, the taxpayer, to provide all the information needed to assess your tax. This does not necessarily mean that you will have to work out the final tax bill yourself, but you will have to provide the information needed to do so in a set format, through the self-assessment tax return.

If your tax affairs are straightforward and the tax you owe is collected at source – e.g. through PAYE – self-assessment will not have much impact. However, if you have untaxed income, have several sources of income and/or capital gains, or are self-employed, in a business partnership, a company director or a higher-rate taxpayer you will be affected.

The Inland Revenue has made a concerted effort to improve its services. The initiatives it has taken include a taxpayer's charter which sets out how you can expect to be treated in your dealings with the tax office, a self-assessment telephone helpline, and improvements to the system for dealing with mistakes and problems. This chapter starts with how to find your tax office, and how the information flows backwards and forwards between taxpayers and the Revenue; which forms you have to fill in, and when and how you pay the tax. If you think you have paid too much (or too little) tax, you will find advice on getting problems sorted out. Finally, this chapter looks at how to appeal.

Finding your tax office

The tax office which deals with your tax affairs is not necessarily the one nearest to where you live. It largely depends on which tax office deals with your major source of income.

If your main income is from a pension from an employer which is taxed under the PAYE scheme, your employer will be able to give you the name and address of your tax office. This is likely to be the same one that dealt with your tax affairs while you were still an employee. However, if the pension fund that pays your pension is in a different office from your employer, your tax office may well be the one which deals with that area.

If you are self-employed, your tax office depends on your business address. If your main income is from your investments or the state pension, your tax office will be the one which deals with the area in which you live.

Collecting tax

Your tax inspector is concerned with assessing how much tax you should pay, not with the collection of it. Tax collection is the responsibility of the Collectors of Taxes. In the past these have been located in separate offices, but they are being brought under the same roof as tax inspectors.

General enquiries

If you just want to make a general enquiry, or you want to get hold of one of the free Inland Revenue explanatory leaflets, you do not need to go to your own tax office. Instead, you can telephone any tax office or a tax enquiry centre (in the telephone book under 'Inland Revenue') or visit their web site. If your enquiry is specific to your own tax affairs, it is always best to write to your own tax office.

The taxpayer's charter

This states clearly that taxpayers are entitled to expect the Inland Revenue:

- **To be fair** The Revenue should treat everyone with equal fairness and impartiality and you should be expected to pay only what is due under the law.
- **To be helpful** The staff at your tax office (and any other Revenue officials) should be courteous and assist you in getting your taxes right by providing clear information.
- **To help you understand** your rights and obligations.
- **To be efficient** The Revenue should be prompt, accurate and keep your tax affairs confidential. Information obtained from you should be used only as allowed by the law. The Revenue should also strive to keep both your expenses and those of your tax office down.
- **To be accountable** Standards, and how well the Revenue lives up to those standards, should be made public. Taxpayers should be told how to complain, and be able to have their tax affairs re-examined. A complaint can be made to an independent Revenue Adjudicator,★ or your MP can refer you to the Parliamentary Commissioner for Administration.

In return, you the taxpayer have an obligation to be honest, to give the Revenue accurate information, and to pay your tax on time.

Giving and getting information

One of your obligations as a taxpayer is to give the Revenue accurate information. You have a legal responsibility to keep certain types of record to back up this information, although these are things such as bank statements which you are likely to keep in any case. Records must be kept for 22 months after the end of the tax year, or for just under six years if you are self-employed.

The Revenue issues various forms. These follow a rough chronological pattern (although in special circumstances you may get some forms at any time during the year). If you pay tax under PAYE, January is likely to bring you your PAYE *Coding Notice*. In April, most tax returns are issued. Then, probably in about June and December, you may get a *Statement of Account*.

Because of the sometimes onerous duty of filling in a self-assessment return, the Revenue tries to avoid putting people on to the self-assessment regime if possible. So, if you are due a tax refund, you may be sent a kind of simplified tax return (the R40). In addition, if you are taxed under PAYE, but the Revenue wants to check that your tax code is right, you might be sent form P810.

Coding Notices

If you pay tax under PAYE – e.g. you get a pension from a former employer, or you do part-time work for an employer – you may receive a *Coding Notice*. This is basically the Revenue's way of telling you which allowances you are getting and how much untaxed income it thinks you are receiving – i.e. what has gone into working out your tax code, which determines how much tax you pay under PAYE. See Chapter 16 for details of how your PAYE code is worked out.

It is easy to see what allowances you are getting because they are listed and explained in an accompanying leaflet. If an allowance you can claim does not appear on your Coding Notice, you are not getting it and you should write to your tax office pointing this out.

Note that restricted-relief allowances have to be adjusted for the right amount of tax to be collected. Under the allowances column of the notice, you will see the full amount of any married couple's allowance, widow's bereavement allowance or maintenance deduction to which you are entitled. However, deducting the full amount of the allowance would give you tax relief at your top rate of tax. So, in the other column you will see an entry called 'ALLCE RESTRICTION', which is how the Revenue makes sure that you get relief at 10 per cent only. To check that the amount of the allowance restriction is correct, subtract the amount of the allowance restriction from the amount of the allowance shown in the left-hand column, and multiply the result by your top rate of tax. The answer should be the same as 10 per cent of your allowance.

If you qualify for a reduced age-related allowance because your total income is above the age allowance income limit (£16,800 in 1999–2000) you will also see 'EST INCOME £', which is an estimate of your total income. If this is not correct, you will not get the right amount of age-related allowance.

There are other adjustments if you owe tax from a previous year which has not already been collected. The amount shown in the right-hand column next to 'UNPAID TAX' will not be the same as the amount you owe: it is actually the amount which, when multiplied by your top rate of tax, will bring in the tax due.

If you think any of these figures are wrong, you should write to your tax office telling them why.

Your tax return

You may not get a tax return at all if your affairs are simple and you are taxed under PAYE. But even if you never received a tax return while you were still working, you may get one once you have retired. There are two main reasons for this. First, if you are likely to have untaxed income coming in (from your state pension, for example), tax needs to be collected on it, or your tax office will have to take it into account when working out your PAYE code. The other reason is to make sure that you get the correct amount of any age-related allowances that you are entitled to. Even if you don't get a return, you are legally obliged to inform the tax office by 5 October after the end of the tax year in question if you had taxable income, on which you have not already paid tax, or capital gains.

The tax return is made up of a core tax return which covers the most basic information, plus separate 'schedules' which you need to fill in if, for example, you are employed, self-employed, have income from property, or have income from abroad. Your tax office should send you the schedules it thinks you need automatically, but the Inland Revenue★ has an orderline that you can phone to order other helpsheets.

The forms generally ask you to put the totals of various types of income or payments – to give your total income from building society accounts, for example, rather than to list all the separate accounts. They come with extensive notes and helpsheets which tell you what to enter, and the self-assessment helpline or local tax enquiry centre should help if you have difficulty.

You then have a choice. Providing you send back your return by 30 September (i.e. within six months of the end of the tax year), you can ask your tax office to work out the final tax bill, based on the information you have given.

If you miss this deadline, or decide to work out the tax yourself, the Inland Revenue issues various tax calculation guides which tell you how to work out the tax: there are several versions for people in different situations. You enter the tax due on your tax return and send it off with the tax due by 31 January (i.e. within ten months of the end of the tax year). Note that if the tax is less than £1,000, and you have income taxed under PAYE, you can ask for it to be collected through PAYE in the coming tax year, rather than paying it as a lump sum now.

There is a fixed penalty of £100 if you fail to send in your return by 31 January (plus further penalties if you miss later deadlines). You also have to pay interest and possibly a surcharge on any tax outstanding (the Revenue may pay you interest if you overpay your tax).

Checking your tax return
The Inland Revenue checks all tax returns for obvious errors, such as a simple mistake in adding up. If an error is spotted, your tax office will write to you – you will not be penalised for innocent errors. However, the Revenue will also 'enquire' – investigate more thoroughly – into a cross-section of returns. It has a year to do this, running from 31 January after the end of the tax year in question. An enquiry does not necessarily mean that the Revenue thinks a return is incorrect.

Statements of account

If you owe tax that the Inland Revenue cannot collect at source, e.g through PAYE, it is payable in instalments. A statement of account is a notice telling you the Inland Revenue's estimate of an instalment of tax you are due to pay. You are likely to get one only if you have income that is received before tax is deducted, such as untaxed investment income or income from property, or are self-employed.

'Payments on account', as these instalments are known, are payable by 31 January during the tax year and by 31 July just after the end of the tax year. Of course, you will not know exactly how much tax is due until the end of the tax year. So the instalments are based upon your previous year's income – each instalment is simply 50 per cent of the income tax and Class 4 National Insurance contributions for that year.

If, when you fill in your tax return later on, you find that your payments on account have led to an under-payment of tax, you have to pay the amount due by 31 January following the end of the tax year, at the same time as the latest date for sending in your return. If you have overpaid tax, you can either claim a repayment straightaway, or ask for it to be set against your next tax bill – see the example below.

You do not have to make payments 'on account' if your tax bill for the previous tax year was below £500 or if most (at least 80 per cent) of your tax is collected at source, e.g. through PAYE. Note, however, that it is up to you, to some extent, to decide how much to pay 'on account'. If you think that your income is likely to fall, for example, you can make an estimate of how much the instalment should be and enter this on your tax return or use form SA303 (supplied with the statement of account). It's not up to your tax office to approve this amount, but if you get it wrong you will have to pay interest on the amount underpaid (and possibly a penalty if you have been fraudulent or negligent). If you overpay tax, you may be paid interest.

EXAMPLE

George Edwards finally retired in 1999 after several years as a self-employed consultant. He got his first statement of account for the 1999–2000 tax year in January 2000, which was 50 per cent of his last tax assessment (£3,600), i.e. £1,800. He paid another £1,800 on account in July 2000.

George received his tax return for the 1999–2000 tax year in April 2000. The latest possible date for returning this was 31 January 2001. However, when he had worked through it in December 2000, he found that his tax bill for 1999–2000 was only £2,400 – he had overpaid tax by £3,600 – £2,400 = £1,200. George had a choice. He could either ask for a repayment straight away or set the £1,200 against his next tax bill.

The next tax bill George was due to pay was his January 2001 statement of account, i.e. 50 per cent of his 1999–2000 tax bill. This was £2,400 x 50% = £1,200, cancelling out the repayment due. So in the interests of simplicity he did not ask for an immediate repayment.

His next payment on account, in July 2001, is a further £1,200. In practice, however, George should not have to make payments on account much longer: he is due to start receiving a personal pension soon, which will be paid under PAYE. The Inland Revenue can collect any tax that is due (e.g. on untaxed investments) through PAYE in future.

> **Tip**
>
> If you are a non-taxpayer and get share or unit trust dividends from which tax has been deducted, you do not need to wait until the end of the tax year to claim the tax back. Ask your tax office for a tax claim form as soon as the tax deducted comes to at least £50 (repayments are not made during the tax year for smaller amounts). Once your tax office knows you are in this situation you may find that you get sent an R40 tax claim form automatically for the next year.

Solving problems

If you think there is something wrong about your tax affairs, for example your tax code has not taken account of an allowance you can claim, or you think you have paid too much tax for another reason, it is always best to write to your tax office. However, you can also contact them by phone.

Letters to the tax office

If you are moved to write to your tax office, it will probably be for one of two reasons: to point out their mistake, or to confess to a mistake you have made.

Pointing out mistakes

When you write to your tax office, explain briefly what you think is wrong and why. To help your tax office deal with your letter efficiently, always quote your tax reference number (shown on any correspondence or form that you have received from the Inland Revenue). If you cannot find your tax reference, give your National Insurance number.

You should get a reply to your letter within 28 days, although if you have written to reclaim tax, it may take longer if they have to issue a cheque. If you do not get a reply within this period, it is worth telephoning your tax office to see what is happening. Again, it will help if you can quote your tax reference number and/or your National Insurance number.

Confessing to mistakes

If you have made a mistake in the information you gave to the tax office, you must write and tell them as soon as possible. If your mistake meant that you did not pay enough tax, you will have to pay all the tax you owe and you may be charged interest on it.

If your mistake meant that you paid too much tax – for example you forgot to deduct a tax-allowable payment or claim an allowance – you can make a claim for the tax you have overpaid. The time limit for this kind of claim is five years from 31 January following the tax year in question.

Letters from the tax office

If your tax inspector thinks there is something wrong with your tax affairs, or if your tax office needs more information in connection with your tax return, for example, they may write to you. If you think what they are requesting is reasonable (most requests should be), give the information requested if this is possible. If you have not got the information – you need a certificate from your building society, for example – let the tax office know that the matter is in hand and give an estimate of when they can expect to receive the information.

Dealing with unhelpfulness

If you think that your tax inspector is being unreasonable – for instance you think that points you made in a previous letter have been disregarded – write a letter repeating your position. If this fails, write directly to the officer-in-charge, whose name should appear at the top of any correspondence from your tax office. The officer-in-charge should reply personally, and should either agree with you or set out fully the reasons why your argument is not accepted.

If you are still unable to get any satisfaction from your tax office, write to the Regional Controller who deals with your tax office (names and addresses of Regional Controllers are available from any tax office). Mark your letter for his or her personal attention, set out concisely and clearly your grounds for complaint against your tax office and ask for an investigation. If you still have no joy, you can refer your complaint to the Revenue Adjudicator's Office.★ The adjudicator will be able to look at your case impartially while still having access to all the files. Alternatively, try your MP, who may refer your case to the Parliamentary Commissioner.

Dealing with mistakes

If your tax office gets something wrong and you find that you owe tax as a result, you may not have to pay the tax you owe. This will apply only if:

- you have taken reasonable care to keep your affairs in order – for example you have dutifully filled in all your tax returns – and it was reasonable for you to believe that you did not owe any tax
- you were told about the arrears more than 12 months after the end of the tax year in which the Revenue received the information that should have told it that more tax was due.

See Inland Revenue leaflet COP 1 *Mistakes by the Inland Revenue.*

Getting help

Self-assessment has been a marketing bonanza for financial advisers. If you think that you need advice, remember that anyone can call themselves a 'tax adviser', so look for a Chartered Institute of Taxation (ATII) or Association of Tax Technicians (ATT) qualification. But you should not *have* to pay for help to deal with self-assessment. Try one of the Inland Revenue's tax enquiry centres first: also see the *Which? Tax-Saving Guide.* Help the Aged* also offers tax services.

Appeals

You can lodge a formal appeal if you are in dispute with your tax inspector because the Inland Revenue has refused to grant you an allowance or deduction to which you think you are entitled, or because you do not agree with the way in which your self-assessment return has been amended. Your case will go to a hearing of the Commissioners of Tax. General Commissioners deal with most cases while Special Commissioners deal with cases which require tax expertise. You can request that your case be dealt with by the Special Commissioners instead. Regardless of who hears your case, you can be represented by a lawyer or accountant if you wish, though this can be expensive.

If you do not agree with the Commissioners' decision on a point of fact, you have no further appeal, but you can complain about maladministration – see 'Dealing with unhelpfulness', above.

If you do not agree with the Commissioners' decision on a point of law, you can take your case to the High Court in England and Wales, the Court of Session in Scotland or the Court of Appeal in Northern Ireland. Before you take this route, it is worth weighing up the possible costs of pursuing your case against the amount of tax in question – and the interest that you may have to pay if you lose.

Part 5

Day-to-day living

Chapter 20

Where to live in retirement

For many people, retirement is synonymous with moving to a long-dreamt-of cottage in the country with roses round the door and a garden to potter about in. However, unless you have been forced to live in an area you actively dislike for the sake of your job, you should put a lot of careful thought into the matter before you pack up and go. It is a good idea to make a list of the advantages and disadvantages of your present house or flat and its locale, bearing in mind the following points:

- Do you have family nearby? Do you lead an active life in the community, with long-term friends whom you see regularly?
- Are facilities such as the library, health centre, post office, church and so on within easy reach? Do you normally travel to them by car? Remember that there may come a time when you are no longer able to drive; are the facilities on main routes that are likely to be well served by public transport?
- How quiet will you find the area when you are at home all day? Is there much traffic? Your current neighbours may be quiet, but how much would you suffer if they were to be replaced by noisier ones? Might it even be *too* quiet? You might find you like to see other people going about their business if you have been used to plenty of social contact in your working life.
- Is your home light enough, warm enough, small or large enough? (See also Chapters 22 and 27.)
- Is the garden sufficient for your needs now? Will it be hard for you to manage in later years?

Staying put

If you still live in the house in which you brought up a family, you may have been finding it too big for your needs. However, if you and your partner will now both be at home all the time, you are bound to need more room than when you were out at work. No matter how devoted you may be, you will need space to follow your own interests; one of you may need a quiet room in which to study, while the other might be doing upholstery, keep fit, carpentry or any number of potentially noisy or untidy pursuits. A separate room each is a tactful solution.

You will also probably want sufficient space to have relatives and friends to stay in comfort. Ideally, you should be able to have people to stay for a week or two without it proving a strain for anyone.

If you have a large house you may discover it is too expensive to keep. However, if you are particularly attached to it you could consider taking in lodgers. If you live near a university or large teaching hospital you might be able to find postgraduate students, perhaps from abroad, who will probably be more mature and responsible than younger undergraduates. Such students can bring a good deal of interest into your life, as well as extra income. Make careful enquiries to the university first as to your legal position when you want your lodgers to go.

Another option for raising cash from your home is an equity release scheme. These are covered in Chapter 5.

Adapting your home

Unless your home is already perfectly suited to the needs of older people, it is best to adapt it before you retire so that you do not have the worry of major alterations later when your income is reduced. If the house is old, consider having a survey done to identify potential troublespots so that you can carry out any necessary repairs to cut down on future expense. See Chapter 21 for more on surveys.

If you live in a house with two or more storeys which has only one bathroom, it is a good idea to install another one on a different floor. Both bathrooms should be suitable for older people, with grab rails on the bath and perhaps a handrail by the lavatory. A shower is more economical than a bath and may be more accessible for people with mobility problems.

Check that the electrical wiring is in good order and consider having more fittings put in so that there is good lighting throughout the house, particularly on the stairs. If need be, reorganise the kitchen so that you do not have to bend or stretch too far to reach any of its components.

The crime prevention officer from your local police station will visit free of charge to give you advice on security; time the visit before that of your electrician as you may be recommended to install outside lighting. Most importantly, fit a smoke alarm on each floor – most cost £10 or less and are simply fitted by means of two or three screws.

For more ideas and information on adapting your home see also Chapters 22 and 27.

Gifted housing plan

If you feel that your house will in due course become too much for you to cope with, you might wish to consider the 'gifted housing' scheme run by Help the Aged.★ You give the house to the organisation but continue to live there, freed of all responsibility for upkeep of the house and garden and for payment of buildings insurance and council tax. Help the Aged will house you for life: if you wish to move later it will find you a home within one of its housing developments. For more details obtain their *Gifted Housing Plan* booklet.

Moving elsewhere in the UK

If you do decide to move, most of the points outlined above are equally applicable to your choice of a new home. It may be that you are now liberated to move near to family members, in which case there is a focus for your choice of area. However, if you are thinking of moving to a part of the country where you have perhaps enjoyed several holidays, or which simply appears suitable for retired people, a good adage is: 'look before you leap'. Picturesque locations can be bleak in winter, and an isolated area may lack amenities. The best way of getting a realistic picture is to rent accommodation for several months at the most unappealing time of the year and, while there, to keep within the level of income you will have to live on rather than splurging out on holiday treats.

If after this experience you still want to move to your dream home in the country, bear in mind one final but major point: public transport in country areas is constantly diminishing (and increasing in cost), and the village shop is fast disappearing since the majority of country-dwellers use their cars to reach the supermarket. In some areas, the traditional village community is vanishing as commuters make up the bulk of the population, while holiday homes stand vacant for the greater part of the year. Elderly people who have grown up and spent their lives in the area usually have a network of family and old friends who will help them get into town or to the doctor; will you, as newcomers, want to rely on the goodwill of relatively recent acquaintances if you are no longer able to drive? Or will you be able to afford taxis?

Moving to an area which has traditionally been popular with older people, such as one of the south-coast towns, brings different problems. If the town has a large older population, its welfare services may be severely strained: GPs may be reluctant to accept any more pensioners on to their lists, and waiting lists at, for example, hearing aid clinics may be very long. Consequently, careful research into areas such as health provision is vital before you actually begin to look for a new house or flat.

If you can afford to, you may wish to buy your next home a few years before you retire so that you can begin to take your place in the community while you are still employed. This does have its advantages in that you will not find unaccustomed leisure coinciding with new surroundings and a dearth of social life, but your work commitments will limit the time that you are able to spend house-hunting and making a careful choice of area.

Buying a flat
If you decide to scale down from a house to a flat in order to economise, there are some points you should check up on. The repair of the building as a whole can be a minefield: if the leasehold tenants share the ownership of the freehold there may be frequent meetings (and frequent disagreements) on the subject of what maintenance work needs to be done. On the other hand, if the freehold belongs to a separate landlord, there may be a different set of problems: sometimes a service charge is levied to cover maintenance, with the proviso that if the set charge is not

sufficient the leaseholders will be jointly responsible for the extra cost. This sort of arrangement can be a licence for an unscrupulous landlord to pocket the service charge year after year while doing negligible maintenance, then suddenly charge you for extensive repairs. Sometimes the landlord may hand over maintenance to a management company, which may not be properly run.

Guard against falling foul of such situations by taking a thoughtful look at the condition of the property as a whole and asking a few of the current tenants about the way in which the flats are managed. Ask, too, for detailed accounts of the expenditure on the building over the last few years. Some service charges include central heating and hot water; if you are planning to spend your winters in the sun, you would be letting yourself in for unnecessary expenditure by taking on such a lease.

Always make a very detailed examination of the charges that will be imposed and the legal obligations of the leaseholders and freeholders before buying. Costs can escalate and flat-owners should be aware of their legal rights both to information on how service charges are made up and their ability to challenge unreasonable charges before a Leasehold Valuation Tribunal. These basic rights are set out in a free leaflet *Leasehold Retirement Housing* available from the Leasehold Advisory Service★ which can also offer free advice on any leasehold issue.

If you will need a mortgage to buy the flat, check whether you will actually be able to get one. The resale value of a leasehold property decreases towards the end of the leasehold period, and you may find it difficult to get a mortgage on anything with a lease of less than, say, 60 years. It is now possible to force a landlord to sell the freehold or to extend the lease, but this is not always straightforward. The Leasehold Advisory Service can give further information. There are proposals to introduce a new 'commonhold' form of tenure for flats which would enable individual flat owners to own and manage the whole building collectively from the outset.

A further point to bear in mind is the soundproofing of the flats; walls and ceilings may be thin and future neighbours noisy. Try to look round the flat in the evening and at a weekend when most of the other tenants will be at home.

Council tenants

If you wish to give up a large council house and move to more suitable accommodation you may be able to effect an exchange or transfer. Homeswap is a computerised matching scheme for local authority and housing association tenants. Contact HOMES★ (Housing Organisations Mobility and Exchange Services) for a leaflet. Some councils keep an exchange list for homes within their area, while most councils and housing associations participate in the HOMES mobility scheme which puts your council or housing association in touch with other landlords who may be able to offer you a home or put you on their waiting list. This scheme is principally for those who have an urgent reason for moving, such as being near a relative who needs help, but there is a Tenants Exchange Scheme with which you can register, whatever your reason for moving. Leaflets on these two schemes are available from housing authorities.

If you have a disability, note that under the Disability Discrimination Act 1995 it is an offence for a disabled person to be treated differently on housing lists, such as those of council housing departments, accommodation bureaux and estate agents.

Sheltered housing

You may decide to opt for sheltered housing, which is now available in many areas of the UK. This usually consists of a development of living units – houses, flats or bungalows – which are sold to people only above a certain age, probably 55 or 60. There is a resident manager or warden, and each unit normally has an alarm system whereby a resident can call for help if needed. However, they are intended for residents who can look after themselves.

You should buy sheltered housing, whether new or second-hand, only if the builder is registered with the National House Building Council;★ the builder will have had to comply with the NHBC's Sheltered Housing Code of Practice. All sheltered housing now being sold should be handled under a management agreement that will protect residents' rights. As soon as you pay a reservation fee the builder must provide you with a Purchaser's Information Pack (PIP), which will confirm in detail the type of lease, service charges, insurance, the warden's duties and reselling restrictions (for example, you can sell only to people over a certain age).

Check how experienced the management organisation is: if the scheme is not a new one, find out what the increases in service charges have been in previous years. All schemes have a sinking fund to cover the cost of long-term repairs; contributions to this may be included in the service charge, or may be deferred until the property is sold. If they are to be deferred, ask how major repairs will be funded if they become necessary before there is sufficient money in the fund.

Apart from the legal obligations involved, find out how generous the communal facilities are. Some include laundry rooms and common rooms for functions. Make sure, too, that the units are well designed for the needs of older people.

Lists of sheltered housing developments are available from the Elderly Accommodation Counsel* and Retirement Home Specialists.* There may be a small charge with the latter two organisations. *A Buyer's Guide to Retirement Housing*, published by Age Concern* at £4.95, will give you more details, and Help the Aged, has a retirement property service.

For details of residential and nursing homes see Chapter 27.

Moving abroad

You may feel that you want to leave the British weather well behind you along with your job, but a move to sunnier climes can bring problems of its own. You need to weigh up the pros and cons even more carefully than when considering a move within the UK: while an ill-planned move at home can lead to the expense and stress of a second upheaval, a sojourn abroad can also leave you some rungs down the British property ladder.

The advice given above on having a trial period of residence also holds good for moving overseas. Make sure you see the area at all times of year and, if there are British people already in residence, find out their opinions. Compare the prices of a wide range of goods and public transport, checking the availability and comfort of the latter. Most important of all, research the local health facilities. Are they of a reassuringly high standard, and are there special facilities for the older person? Are you eligible for free health care? If you have private health insurance in the UK, would it cover you in your chosen country?

If you do not already speak the language of the country you are planning to live in, how well will you be able to learn it before you move? If your grasp of it is only limited you will be restricted to the company of other expatriates for your social life. Bear in mind that in time of stress or ill-health you will probably find it harder to express yourself, so do not regard learning the language as one of the aspects of moving abroad that can wait until last.

Check what the pension arrangements are. You can normally receive your UK state pension in any country, but you would not be entitled to subsequent increases unless you are living in a European country, the USA, or a few other countries (not including Australia and New Zealand). However, in European countries and some countries that have a special agreement with the UK, you may be able to claim an overseas benefit, provided (in most cases) that you have paid National Insurance contributions in the UK. Ask your local Benefits Agency Office for leaflet GL29 *Going abroad and social security benefits*. You should also find out how changes in exchange control regulations would affect pension payments, dividends and banking arrangements.

For advice on conditions of residence, local tax regulations, your legal position as a foreign resident and whether you will need a work permit if you plan to take on any sort of job, enquire first at the embassy or consulate of the relevant country.

Note that even if you regard your move abroad as permanent, you will still count as a UK resident for tax purposes if you make visits back to the UK which average 91 days or more in a tax year. And even non-residents may have to pay some UK tax, for example on investment income arising in the UK, or inheritance tax on gifts made (e.g. on death). For details, consult Inland Revenue booklets IR20 *Residents' and Non-Residents' Liability to Tax in the United Kingdom*, and IHT18 *Inheritance Tax – Foreign Aspects*, available from tax enquiry centres and tax offices.

Chapter 21

Moving home

You have made the decision to move house, decided on the area you want to live in – now it is time to set the ball rolling. This chapter takes you step by step through the whole process of buying and selling, from choosing a property through to moving. For buying and selling in Scotland see pages 284–5; for information on renting see pages 285–7; for how to sort out a trouble-free move, see pages 287–92. Consumers' Association★ also produces *Which? Way to Buy, Sell and Move House* and *Which? Way to Buy, Own and Sell a Flat.*

Getting a mortgage

If you need a mortgage, you may wonder whether your age could be a hindrance. Although some lenders still require mortgages to be repaid by retirement age, many are now more flexible, looking instead at what people can afford to pay. Some lenders have special deals for older people. More of a problem may be deciding what type of mortgage is suitable.

Types of mortgage

The two most common types are repayment and endowment mortgages. With a repayment mortgage, your monthly repayment is split into two – part reduces the amount you owe, the rest is interest on the amount still owing. With an endowment mortgage, you pay interest on the loan, together with premiums for an investment-type life insurance policy. The policy matures at the end of the mortgage term to pay off the loan (though there is no guarantee that it will produce enough interest to do so). You then keep any money left over.

Taking out a new endowment is not a good idea for people approaching retirement. You are stuck with paying the endowment premiums until the policy matures – an inflexible long-term commitment which is something you should avoid at this stage of life – and you'll get very poor value if you cash it in early. Also, endowment policies are very expensive for older borrowers.

If you have a repayment mortgage, your lender may insist that you take out a mortgage protection policy to repay the mortgage if you die during the term of the loan. With endowment mortgages, you do not need any extra life insurance.

However, repayment and endowment mortgages are normally set up to last over a period of at least 20 years – otherwise the cost of repaying the loan, or building up a big enough investment to repay it, will make the monthly payments very high. Unless you need to borrow only a small amount, this could be a problem for you if you expect your income to fall once you retire. But there are alternatives to consider.

Using an existing endowment policy

If you already have an endowment policy in force, e.g. from an earlier mortgage, do not cash it in – you could get a very poor return. Instead, look for a lender who will let you use it to repay the new mortgage – lenders make a lot of money from the commission on selling new endowment policies (although they now have to disclose a lot more information about the costs involved), but you should be able to use an existing one.

Using an existing pension plan

Lenders may be prepared to give you a loan on the understanding that you will repay it on retirement using the tax-free lump sum from a personal pension plan (or occasionally, an Additional Voluntary Contributions scheme – see pages 77–8). However, this option will reduce your income in retirement – do not take it unless you are happy that you will have enough pension to live on.

Interest-only mortgages

An increasing number of lenders are prepared to offer these mortgages, which are both flexible and keep your monthly outgoings low. As the name suggests, you pay interest only on the loan – it is up to you to decide how and when to repay it, e.g. by using the proceeds of a Personal Equity Plan (PEP) or Individual Savings Account (ISA). They are sometimes marketed specially for retired people, with no obligation to repay the capital until the house is sold or the borrower dies. A variation is the 'shared appreciation mortgage', where instead of interest the lender takes a share in any growth in the property's value.

Fixed-rate or variable interest?

Fixed-rate mortgages, where the interest rate is fixed for, say, two years, are now common. After the fixed-rate period is over you pay the standard mortgage rate. Beware of deals that tie you into the lender's variable rate for several years after the end of the fixed-rate period. There are potential problems – if interest rates generally fall after you have taken one out, you could lose out, and there are usually stiff penalties to discourage you from repaying the loan for the first few years. Lenders may also insist that you buy other products, such as house insurance, through them. But if you can find a deal without too many strings, and think that interest rates are more likely to rise than fall, then they offer certainty – useful if you are living on a fixed income.

House-hunting

If your family has left home you may well consider moving from a large house with its responsibilities into a small house, bungalow or flat. See Chapter 20 on the practical considerations.

Estate agents

You may have a very clear idea of the sort of property you want. To get an impression of the type of property and price ranges handled by various agents, have a look at the advertisements in the windows or in the local paper. Do not restrict yourself to just one agent. Enquire of all the agents in the locality, and see if there are any, perhaps not so close, which specialise in the type of property you want.

Be prepared to spend time initially calling in or ringing up regularly in order to establish a good relationship with the agents. The better the contact you have with agents, the more likely they are to remember you when a suitable property comes their way.

WARNING

Estate agents are paid by the seller, not the buyer, so do not expect them to have your interests foremost in their minds. And be aware that estate agents are keen to sell financial services, or introduce clients to financial organisations (for which they get commission). You may get a good deal, but there is evidence to suggest that, particularly in the past when buyers were easy to come by, a few have discriminated against people who decline financial services.

The estate agents will give you details of available properties which they think may be of interest. Photographs of properties serve as a rough guide, but they can be misleading and should be regarded with caution. For instance, a house may have been trimmed of its less attractive surroundings. The Property Misdescriptions Act 1991 makes it illegal for estate agents and other property sellers to give inaccurate descriptions of properties. Regulations extending the scope of the Estate Agents Act 1979 also mean that estate agents may be banned from estate agency work if they discriminate against potential buyers who do not buy financial services from them, misrepresent the value of a house, or fail to pass on details of offers to the seller (in order to favour a purchaser who will earn them more in insurance commission).

If you have a problem

If you have a complaint about an estate agent, write in the first instance to the head office. If this does not lead to a satisfactory conclusion and your agent is a member of the Ombudsman for Estate Agents (OEA),★ write to the Ombudsman – but you must do this within six months.

If your estate agent is not a member of the OEA, find out if he or she belongs to a professional body: the National Association of Estate Agents (NAEA),★ the Royal Institution of Chartered Surveyors (RICS)★ or the Incorporated Society of Valuers and Auctioneers (ISVA),★ the professional services department of which deals with complaints. If so, write to the appropriate body, explaining the problem: they may be able to help. Another option, if you suspect that any law has been broken, is to contact your local Trading Standards Department (the address will be in the *Yellow Pages*), or to write to the Office of Fair Trading.★

Property shops

Some areas of the country have property shops, displaying details, including photographs, of houses and flats. The seller pays for this, usually around one to two per cent of the selling price. You can get particulars of any property you think looks suitable and arrange to see it.

Moving to a new area

It is not easy to house-hunt at a distance, although if you have access to the Internet it is becoming easier as more and more estate agencies set up their own websites – *www.NAEA.co.uk* is a good place to start. If you are not on the Internet, you can call on an agent in your home town and ask if it has contacts with fellow agents in another area. The *Estates Gazette* publishes a monthly regional directory of agents (also available on the Internet at *www.egi.co.uk*). If you are moving to another area, ask at the library what papers cover the district, and on what day property adverts appear.

Some agents are linked to a regional or national computer. You register your requirements with one agent, and receive details of properties matching your specifications that are currently on the books of all the others. Big chains of estate agents may have their own system for doing this, while the National Homelink Service is operated by members of the NAEA.★ This provides a referral service for anyone moving from one area to another. The Homelink member in your present locality will contact another Homelink member in the area to which you are moving, giving details of your requirements. The names and addresses of Homelink agents in any area can be obtained from the NAEA.

Relocation or homesearch agents act solely on behalf of buyers, and vary from individual consultants to fairly large organisations. They offer various services, ranging from finding a suitable property (for purchase or rent), through to overseeing the sale of your home and making removal arrangements. You can find them in the *Yellow Pages* under 'Relocation agents'; there is also an Association of

Relocation Agents.* It is usual to be asked to pay a 'retainer' of anywhere between £150 and £500. A further fee, usually of 1 to 1.5 per cent of the purchase price, is payable on exchange of contracts (or 10 to 15 per cent of the first year's rent for rented properties).

Surveys

The valuation

If you are applying for a mortgage the lender will ask a local surveyor to carry out a mortgage valuation survey to help assess the amount they are willing to lend. The cost (which you pay) depends on the value of the property. It is not a structural survey and does not guarantee that the house is structurally sound and without defects, so it is important to pay for a proper survey, too.

The offer of a loan may be altered or withdrawn after the valuation. You would then need to start again with a different property or a different lender. The valuer can include a recommendation to the lender not to make a loan unless specified work is carried out, or he or she can advise the lender to withhold an amount (£5,000, say), which will be paid out when the work has been carried out satisfactorily.

A house- (or flat-) buyer's report

This should provide a good idea of the general condition of a property, but it won't include an inspection of areas that are not easily accessible (because they are covered by carpets, for example). This is usually carried out by the surveyor when doing the mortgage valuation. It costs roughly twice as much as a valuation.

Full building survey

This is the most detailed and expensive option and should be carried out by a qualified surveyor who specialises in this kind of work. Your solicitor or a friend may be able to recommend one to you, or you may be able to use the surveyor who is doing the mortgage valuation if he or she is properly qualified. It is preferable to use a surveyor local to the property being inspected since he or she may know of any relevant conditions in the area which might affect it.

Discuss with the surveyor how comprehensive a survey you want carried out and ask how much you would need to spend to put the house in good order. Bring to the surveyor's attention anything about the property, the neighbourhood or the sellers that you think could create problems. The extent of the survey will depend on the age and condition of the property – and how much you can afford. You should obtain written confirmation from the surveyor, setting out the extent of the inspection. Expect to pay several hundred pounds, at least three times as much as for a valuation.

Survey for a flat

A survey for a flat, particularly if it is in a converted house, should cover an inspection of the whole building. This should include the roof, foundations, drains, gutters and so on; also any communal services such as electricity, water or gas supplies or anything that you will be liable for under the terms of the lease. If you can, give the surveyor a copy of the lease, so that he or she can comment on your responsibilities for repairing and decorating the flat and for contributing towards the cost of maintaining communal parts of the buildings.

Selling your old home

You can either handle the sale yourself (if you have the time and energy to do so), or commission an estate agent to do it for you. An estate agent will do most of the work for you, but his or her fees will probably be the largest single cost of moving home – typically, anything from 1.5 to 3 per cent of the sale price.

Selling through an estate agent

Although it is a costly business, there are advantages to selling through an estate agent. They take some of the work and worry from the seller, they have good facilities for publicising the sale and ready access to more would-be buyers. They also offer better security if you are living alone: for example, you can ask for the agent's representative to accompany all viewers.

It is a good idea to visit several agencies to get some idea of the costs involved. Choosing the cheapest estate agent is not necessarily the best option; it is also important to find one who can sell your home quickly and efficiently. Recommendation and personal experience count for a lot. If you are buying and selling in the same area, you could sign up with a few agents as a buyer, before you try to sell, in order to get an idea of which one offers the best service.

How estate agents charge

Commissions vary widely across the UK. There are also various types of agreement, which affect how much you pay:

- **Sole agency** – in return for agreeing to sell through only one agent, you are charged a relatively low rate.
- **Multiple agency** – you instruct as many agents as you like, but pay only the one who comes up with the buyer. In return for the flexibility, charges are higher.
- **Joint agency** – you sign up with two agents only – both agree to the arrangement and to who gets the commission. This is likely to be the most expensive option.

Some estate agents make a charge (up to £200) for the marketing and administrative costs incurred, irrespective of whether they manage to sell your home. This is more common north of the Midlands. However, if they do sell the property, the commission is likely to be lower than with a 'no sale, no fee' agreement.

If you need to sell quickly, multiple agency may be best. If you go for this, sign up with at least three agencies. Otherwise, the amount you save with a sole agency makes this the best option. If the agent you have signed up with does not sell your property quickly, you have the option of leaving and instructing another agent on a sole agency basis. Telling each agent at the outset that you will reconsider after, say, six weeks, should encourage them to 'push' your property in that time. But unless you have got a 'no sale, no fee' agreement, you will probably have to pay each agent's marketing and administration costs – sale or no sale.

WARNING

Beware of an estate agent requesting 'sole selling rights'. This is quite different from the normal 'sole agency' agreements many estate agents offer because it means that if you sold your home other than through the agent – through your own newspaper advert, for example – you would still have to pay the agent commission.

Never accept wording that says that agents' fees will be payable for introducing a buyer who is 'ready, willing and able to buy'. If the sale does not go through, but the buyer was prepared to buy, you will still have to pay.

Once you have decided on the type of deal, negotiate the cost and terms (easiest when the housing market is stagnant): as well as bargaining for a reduction in the commission, you may be able to get add-on costs such as advertising waived. Whatever agreement you make with the agent, you should get it confirmed in writing.

Legal matters

As soon as you start house-hunting seriously, you should organise someone to do the conveyancing – the legal and administrative work involved in buying or selling a home – so that whoever you choose can be ready when you decide to make an offer or advise on any legal snags. You have three options: appoint a solicitor or a licensed conveyancer, or do it yourself.

The choice between a solicitor and licensed conveyancer is very much a matter of personal preference. Both should be able to provide a full house-buying service and carry out the necessary legal work for you: both are free to charge what they choose but must give you advance information on the basis of their charges. It is worth getting estimates from more than one solicitor or conveyancer before contracting someone. Many charge a flat fee for all the work involved. In addition to the basic fees, you will have to pay for disbursements – expenses incurred in dealing with the purchase, such as bank charges for transferring money, and other sundry costs – as well as Land Registry fees, local authority searches and stamp duty.

You could save money by doing the conveyancing yourself. It is worth considering if you are buying or selling freehold (but not leasehold) property and have got the time and confidence.

Making an offer

When you decide that you want to buy a particular house or flat, put your offer in writing to the estate agent, with a copy to the seller. The offer does not commit you, provided it is made 'subject to contract', so you can still withdraw if, say, a survey decides you against continuing with the purchase. If there is any objection to the deal being on a 'subject to contract' basis, do not proceed; and do not sign any kind of contract at this stage without taking legal advice.

When you make a firm offer the estate agent may ask you to pay a deposit (£200, say). You are under no obligation to do this, as such deposits have no legal standing and can be withdrawn at any time. If you do pay a deposit, make sure that you get a receipt stating that the deposit was paid 'subject to contract', so that if the purchase should fall through the deposit is returned in full.

Before exchange of contracts

Once an offer is accepted, the house is then 'under offer'. Check that the estate agent at this point withdraws the property from the market until exchange of contracts. This will avoid 'gazumping' – the seller accepts a later, higher bid. You are not protected against gazumping until you have entered into a binding contract.

As soon as an offer has been accepted, the seller's conveyancer draws up a draft contract. The seller will be asked to answer an enquiry form about the property. This asks standard questions about boundaries, restrictions and so on.

Agreeing amendments to a draft contract can take time. It may take a while to obtain a mortgage offer or to get the results of local searches. Once all the necessary information about the property you plan to buy is received, a good solicitor or conveyancer will be happy to go through all the paperwork with you. Do not be afraid to ask questions on any points that are still unclear. It is important to make sure that everything is right now – it will be too late to change things after exchange of contracts.

Sometimes an offer may be accepted with the proviso that exchange of contracts should take place within, say, a month: otherwise the property may be put on the market again. If two or more people want to buy the same property, the seller will sometimes tell the solicitor or conveyancer to send out a second set of contracts to the would-be buyers' solicitors. The buyers then have to race each other – the first to send a deposit and signed contract gets the house. Solicitors and conveyancers are required to tell you when there is a contract race.

Exchange of contracts

Once contracts are exchanged, buyer and seller are locked into a legal agreement from which neither side can withdraw without penalty. At this point a deposit has to be paid by the buyer to the seller – usually 10 per cent of the purchase price, but a lower figure can sometimes be negotiated. The deposit is non-refundable and is used as security to ensure the contract is complied with and the purchase is completed. The amount will be deducted from what has to be paid at completion.

Insurance

Nowadays, most contracts expect the seller to continue insurance cover until completion. However, older contracts are sometimes still used, under which insuring the property becomes the responsibility of the buyer from the date contracts are exchanged. You should therefore check the insurance requirements with your conveyancer before exchange. You may need to keep your buildings insurance cover on your existing home until completion, in case the buyer defaults.

Let your insurer know in writing before you move. The cost of insurance varies, depending upon where you live, so you may be charged a higher premium or get a refund; the move might provide a good opportunity to change insurer (you should get a refund for the unexpired portion of your existing policy). See Chapter 22 for more on house insurance.

If you are getting a mortgage, the lender will make it a condition that the property is insured (the mortgage valuation will say how much it should be insured for). The lender will probably be keen to arrange the cover – they get commission for doing so. Lenders cannot force you to buy insurance from them but they will want to check that the policy provides adequate cover for their security, and will often charge a fee, usually £25, for the administrative costs of doing so. Lenders are allowed to offer additional discounts in return for you agreeing to buy their home insurance. Be very wary of accepting such deals – the lender's insurance is often expensive and you may be tied to it for several years.

Completion day

The date for completion is agreed at the time contracts are exchanged and is specified in the contract. As a purchaser, do not agree to a completion date unless you can meet it – you will have to pay interest from the agreed date until completion actually takes place, and you may be liable to pay damages to the seller and any other sellers if there is a chain of sales held up by your delay.

On the date of completion, the seller has to give vacant possession – that is, to move out on or before the day with all furniture and belongings. Meanwhile, the buyer must be able to pay the remainder of the purchase price. This is usually done through the solicitor or other conveyancer, so if you are buying you need to send the money to them in good time for any cheques to clear. When the final payments are made, the deeds will be handed over, including the conveyance or transfer to the buyer. If you have a mortgage, the title deeds of the property are kept by the mortgage lender as security for the money being lent.

Tip

A buyer has to pay stamp duty on the transfer of any house or flat where the purchase price is more than £60,000. The rate of duty is one per cent on the total purchase price paid, rising to 2.5 per cent if the purchase price is above £250,000 and 3.5 per cent above £500,000. These figures include the first £60,000, whereas no duty is payable if the transfer is £60,000 or less – so if you are buying a property for just over £60,000 you could save over £600 by agreeing to pay the going price for items such as carpets separately, bringing the purchase price below the limit. Tell your conveyancer if you agree to do this as the contract should record the price division.

The house-buying chain

You will probably be trying to buy one property and sell another – and ideally, to keep the timing of the two closely linked. If your ability to buy your new home depends on someone purchasing your old one, you are involved in a 'chain' of sales and purchases.

In an effort to speed up the whole process of buying and selling a property, the government and others have now made a number of proposals, including sellers' packs containing key information about the property. However, until their proposals take effect, you have the following options if you find yourself caught in a chain:

- selling first and moving into rented property before buying a new home
- if your seller has dropped out, find another buyer quickly (perhaps reducing the price to do so)
- take out a bridging loan to finance short-term ownership of two properties
- use a part-exchange scheme.

'Part-exchange schemes' have become more common, while bridging loans have fallen out of favour. However, each of the options can be costly, so it is important to explore them all to see which is most suitable for you.

Bridging loans

Bridging loans from banks and building societies cover the period between paying for your new home and getting the proceeds from the sale of your old one. There are two types of loan:

- **Closed** – you borrow for a fixed time because the completion date for selling your home has been set.
- **Open-ended** – when you are unsure when your home will be sold. Banks and building societies are less willing to offer these because of the uncertainties involved, and many refuse to give any open-ended loan. Do not consider getting one unless you can afford to pay for both homes, for, say, six months.

As well as interest on the loan (at three to four per cent above the current bank base rate), there is usually an arrangement fee to pay on top.

Part-exchange schemes

A number of estate agents and property developers offer these schemes as an alternative to bridging loans. They agree to buy your home, which is valued to produce a quick sale (it may be lower than the valuation for an 'open market' sale). The agent or developer then buys it at a price generally at or somewhat below their valuation.

You are then free to buy your new home, while the estate agent sells your old one. Generally, if the agent sells it for more than the valuation they keep the extra.

Buying and selling in Scotland

The Scottish system differs from the English system in a number of important ways.

In many parts of Scotland, most estate agency is carried out by solicitors. Properties are usually advertised at 'offers over £x', often referred to as the 'upset price', and often with a closing date. Any offers received up to that date will be considered. You need to get a mortgage (and a full building survey, if you want one) before making an offer.

In both buying and selling property in Scotland you should be aware to involve a solicitor (there are as yet no licensed conveyancers in Scotland) much earlier in the process than in England.

Offers in Scotland are not 'subject to contract'. You can 'note your interest' with the selling agent: this does not commit you to buy, it simply notifies the selling agent that you wish to be kept informed of developments. But if you make an offer and it is unconditionally accepted, there is a binding deal – the seller has to sell, and you have to buy. Offers are submitted in writing and include details such as the price offered, what is included in the price, and the date you want to move in. The offer may be conditionally accepted, with proposed changes in terms. This may lead to a series of letters between the solicitors (these letters are known as 'missives'), until agreement is reached and moving day fixed. You probably won't have to pay a deposit: you pay the full price when you move in.

This system has pluses and minuses. Valuations and surveys are done before the buyer makes an offer – so if you make a few unsuccessful bids, the costs could mount up before you have even found a place to buy. On the other hand, the system does seem to speed things up and remove some of the uncertainty of buying and selling a home.

If you buy a house or flat in Scotland intending it as your residence or principal residence, you will acquire Scottish domicile. This may affect, among other things, the way your property is inherited on your death.

If you do have a disagreement with a Scottish estate agent, the Ombudsman for Estate Agents★ may be able to help (see page 274). Scottish members of the OEA have to abide by a Code of Practice which has been drawn up specially for Scotland. For a disagreement with a solicitor, contact the Law Society of Scotland,★ which also publishes various free guides. Buying and selling in Scotland is covered in depth in *Which? way to Buy, Sell and Move House.*

Renting

If you decide to rent a house or flat, start by looking in the local papers, but do not forget to ask friends and neighbours too. Many estate agents now handle rented accommodation and there are letting agencies that specialise in this. Be prepared to pay them a fee – two weeks' rent, say, in addition to the deposit (usually equivalent to one month's rent) and the first rent payment.

Tenancy agreement

It is advisable to rent property that has a proper tenancy agreement, so that both you and the landlord are clear about your legal rights and responsibilities. Note that if you are a lodger who shares a property with its owner, and the owner has unrestricted access to your room (e.g. for cleaning), you are usually regarded as a licensee rather than a tenant: the difference is important since there is little legal protection for licensees.

If you are in any doubt a Citizens Advice Bureau or solicitor may be able to help, and you may find useful *The Which? Guide to Renting and Letting*, published by Consumers' Association.★

The main types of tenancy agreement, for private-sector tenancies created on or after 15 January 1989, are as follows. Note that all tenancies starting after 27 February 1997 are assumed to be assured shorthold tenancies unless otherwise specified.

Assured tenancies
These tenancies can be either for a fixed term – i.e. for a number of years or months – or capable of lasting indefinitely, but with either party able to terminate the agreement at set intervals. The key points are:

* You have security of tenure (although you can lose this through actions such as repeated failure to pay the rent). The landlord cannot evict without a possession order.

- The rent charged is a matter for agreement between the two parties involved. This is known as an 'open market' rent.

Assured shorthold tenancies

These are fixed-term tenancies. They are popular with landlords because:

- Tenants have no security of tenure – the landlord has an absolute right to recover possession six months after the beginning of the tenancy, provided the correct procedure is followed.
- Although the tenant has the right to refer the rent initially payable to a rent assessment committee, the committee may reduce the rent only if it is significantly higher than the rents of other comparable properties.

Housing associations

Housing associations are non-profit making bodies established to provide affordable accommodation, and they are now a major provider of housing. Although much of their funding comes from the state, they are treated as private sector. A housing association tenancy agreement set up on or after 15 January 1989 will be either an assured tenancy or an assured shorthold tenancy, as described above. However, tenants of registered housing associations have the benefit of a 'tenant's guarantee', which is an assurance from the landlord of good standards of management.

Tenancy problems

Before a landlord can evict you, even from an assured shorthold tenancy after the fixed term has expired, he or she has to obtain a court order. You also have legal protection against landlords taking less formal steps to get you out, such as threats and intimidation.

If you want to leave a property, on the other hand, you must give the landlord the minimum notice as specified in the tenancy agreement.

Disabled people have some protection against discrimination in property matters, if the discrimination relates to the person's disability and is unjustified. Offences under the Disability Discrimination Act 1995 include refusing a tenancy or offering less favourable terms to a disabled person, offering different facilities, evicting a disabled person or giving different treatment on housing lists. However, these rules do not apply to landlords who let out rooms to no more than six people in their own homes.

Where to go for help

If you have a problem with a landlord or with the tenancy agreement, go to a Citizens Advice Bureau, a solicitor, a law centre or a local housing advice centre. There is also an Independent Housing Ombudsman Scheme,* which covers housing associations (and private landlords may join on a voluntary basis). You can phone the Ombudsman to check whether your landlord is a member.

The Department of the Environment, Transport and the Regions (DETR)* publishes a series of housing booklets, explaining the law and your rights as a tenant in detail. These are available from local libraries, housing advice centres and Citizens Advice Bureaux or direct from the DETR.

Moving home

Moving home can be both stressful and expensive. As well as organising the removal arrangements, you also need to inform large numbers of people and organisations (a checklist starts on page 290). Moving from a home in which you have brought up a family brings an extra difficulty: it can involve clearing not just your own accumulated belongings, but the discarded possessions of children who have flown the nest.

One advantage, on the other hand, is that if you are no longer working full-time, you may have more time in which to organise the move. Another advantage is that being able to move at a less popular time, such as mid-week when removal firms tend to be less busy, will give you a better choice and may even cost less.

Choosing a removal firm

Cost is one of the main considerations when choosing a removal firm, and it can vary by hundreds of pounds. How much you will have to pay depends on how far you are moving, how many possessions you have and how much packing you want the firm to do.

Find out the names of removers – both local firms as well as the larger national companies – by looking in the *Yellow Pages*, by asking the British Association of Removers (BAR)* and the National Guild of Removers and Storers for a list of their local members, or by sounding out friends. Do not choose on cost alone; find out how many people would be allocated to the job, check the small print (for example, the remover's liability if something went wrong) and ascertain how they would deal with awkward and valuable items.

Getting quotes

As soon as you have some idea of the moving date, ask the removal firms to send someone round to give you a quote. They should look right round your property, including the loft, garage and garden, to see what quantity and type of furniture and belongings are involved. Tell them if you are planning a clear-out – this could reduce the quote.

Get each quote in writing. (If you accept a verbal quote the firm could alter it after the move.) It is worth getting at least three quotes before deciding. Check how long a quote will remain binding on the company: it may have to be accepted within, say, 21 days and the work done within, say, three months. Some firms provide estimates – these are only a guide to the final cost, not a binding price, so it is wise to clarify the position at the outset.

When getting quotes you should point out to the removers any belongings that may need special packing, or may present problems in handling or transporting. Point out any built-in cupboards or shelves that will need dismantling and decide if you want to take the carpets with you. Lifting and laying fitted carpets may cost extra.

What does the quote include?

Some firms will quote a basic figure, then add on things like packing boxes, insurance and VAT. If you want to put your possessions into storage, most firms will give you a quote for the actual removal, plus the weekly cost of storage in a warehouse.

Most removers offer a variety of packing and unpacking alternatives. You may think it worth the cost of paying for all the packing, unpacking and moving to be done by experts, so that all you have to do is supervise the work. This is the most expensive option. You can do some or all of the packing yourself (most removal firms can sell you the materials) but be aware that the mover does not take responsibility for what he does not pack. You also need to allow plenty of time in advance.

> **Tip**
>
> It is important that you read the contract before you sign on the dotted line, so that you know what the firm is promising to do. If there is anything you are unhappy with take it up with the firm and consider altering the contract before you sign.

Generally, payment has to be made in advance or on the day of the move. When you accept the quote you are expected to give a firm date for the job: having booked a date, you would have to give reasonable notice if you wanted to change it; otherwise, the company might well charge a cancellation fee.

Moving abroad

You have the choice of sending your goods individually or as 'groupage' or 'LCL' (Less than Container Load) – meaning that your belongings make up a part-load in a container. Charges and packing costs are lower for shared loads, but you don't have as much control over when the move is made, since the firm has to take account of the wishes of at least one other customer. However, shared loads may be easier to arrange for popular routes. In either case, check where your possessions will actually end up – will they be delivered door to door, or just to the nearest port of entry?

You will need to be particularly careful when deciding what to take. It may not be worth taking electrical or electronic equipment, if this is not compatible with voltages or other standards overseas. Some surprising items may be banned or subject to special regulations: cane furniture is apparently viewed with grave suspicion in some countries. On the other hand, you may be able to buy some goods before you go free of UK VAT. A specialist removal firm should be able to advise: FIDI* (Fédération Internationale des Déménageurs Internationaux) is the international trade association for such specialists, and BAR* (British Association of Removers) has an overseas group of members affiliated to this organisation.

Insurance for the move

Removal contracts usually limit the removal firm's liability for lost and damaged goods, so you will need extra, more comprehensive, insurance. While your belongings are in transit they may be covered by your existing house contents insurance policy. Check with the insurer beforehand – if it does not provide you with adequate cover you may be able to extend your policy. Alternatively, the removal firm may offer, or in many cases insist on, its own insurance. This usually costs around five to ten per cent of the removal costs.

What to do if things go wrong

If anything gets broken or damaged, try to make a written note of it at the time, and ask the removers to sign it. Complain in writing to the removal firm. If you get no satisfaction, write to the British Association of Removers* (BAR), if your removal firm is a member. If you are still not happy you can go to court or arbitration. If the firm is a member of BAR it will subsidise the cost of arbitration, which is binding on both parties.

Who to tell about your move

Services

Arrange to have service meters read before you move. If this is not possible, make a note of the readings yourself. This can help if there are disagreements when the bills arrive. Arrange for the disconnection of appliances such as cooker and washing machine and make arrangements for them to be connected in your new home.

- **Gas, electricity and water** Each utility (find the address/phone number on your bill) will need to know the completion date, your account number and new address. Give seven working days' notice. Remember that you now have a choice of gas and electricity suppliers. For a list contact OFGEM.* You are responsible for water rates until completion date. If you have paid in advance you can claim a portion back. To have the water reconnected in your new home contact the new authority, giving at least two days' notice.
- **Telephone** As for gas and electricity – contact your telephone company or dial 150 for your local BT office. If moving to a new area, contact the local sales office. If you take over the existing number there will be no charge. Contact BT* for a

Home Mover's pack. If moving within the same exchange area you can usually take your existing number with you. If your new home does not have the modern plug-in sockets, they will have to be installed. Both BT and the cable companies can install these sockets so it is worth shopping around for the best deal.

If you are to have a new telephone line, shop around for the best deal from BT and the cable company operating in your area. To find out which cable company operates in your area contact the Cable Communications Association (CCA).* A cable company may be much cheaper than BT for a brand new connection. In parts of Scotland companies such as Scottish Telecom and Atlantic Telecom, for example, use radio instead of cable.

- **Mail** For a charge, you can get your mail redirected. Fill out form P944 from any post office – give at least five working days' notice. Leave your new address – or leave sticky labels with your new address printed on them – at your old home in case any mail does slip through.

Finances

Let any of the following organisations with whom you have an arrangement know of your change of address.

- **Banks, building societies and investments** If moving to another area, you may want to transfer your account to a local branch. It may be a good idea to wait until after you have moved, in case payments go astray at this crucial time. Give companies with whom you have standing orders and direct debits your new address and account number. If you have investments, tell institutions of any changes to accounts which receive direct payments.
- **Credit cards** When paying the last bill before moving, note your change of address on the back of the payment slip. If you have given someone 'continuous authority' to deduct money from your credit card account (like a standing order), give the company your new address.
- **Pensions and benefits** For state pensions, notify your local

Benefits Agency office and if necessary nominate a new post office at which to cash your payments, using form P80MA (from post offices). If you receive other pensions, including any from a previous employer, make sure the payers know your moving date (and new bank account details if applicable).

- **Insurance** Send your new address and the policy numbers to the company. With car insurance, you must tell your insurer, intermediary or broker before you move or your insurance may not be valid. The premium may change if you move to a different area.

- **Tax** Write to your tax office, quoting your National Insurance and tax reference numbers (find the address on your PAYE Coding Notice or tax return, or ask your employer or pension provider).

- **Council tax** Tell both your old and new Council Tax Offices. You have to pay Council Tax from the day you move into your new home. If you have paid in advance at your old one, you are entitled to a refund.

- **Loans and rental companies** Rented TVs and videos can usually be taken with you and your account transferred. Give the rental company your new address. Also notify TV Licensing, via the post office, or write to: Barton House, Bristol BS98 1TL. There is a section on your TV licence to complete and send in.

- **DVLC** Complete and send the sections on your driving licence/registration document to DVLC, Swansea, postcode SA99 1BN for the licence and SA99 1BA for the registration document.

- Tell your **accountant, solicitor, investment adviser or stockbroker, trade unions/professional bodies**. Also notify your **doctor, dentist, optician,** magazines and other **subscriptions, newsagent** and **dairy** (remember to pay any outstanding bills). At your new address, register with a new doctor and find a dentist as soon as possible – see Chapter 30.

Chapter 22

Security and safety in the home

From reading the papers, it may seem that older people are not safe in their own home. This is not so – it is just that these incidents often receive considerable, and sometimes dramatic, publicity, which tends to give a distorted impression of the facts. Statistically, your chances of being a victim are slim – crime against older people is, in fact, rare. However, fear of crime still can have a debilitating effect on the quality of life of many people. A sometimes neglected, but even more important factor, is everyday home safety, which is covered on page pages 300–303.

Many crimes and accidents are preventable if you take the right precautions. Help the Aged* and Age Concern* both publish free leaflets on steps to take. There is an extra incentive to sort out your security when it comes to insuring your home. Insurance may be cheaper if you are adequately protected, and the insurer may even insist on particular safeguards. For more on insuring your home in retirement, see pages 303–309.

Emergencies

Do not be inhibited about ringing the emergency services in situations of urgency at any time of day or night. They will assess your case over the phone and will respond immediately if necessary. If they do not think it warrants an emergency call-out, they may recommend that you contact your local police station or doctor for further advice.

Contacts

Keep a list of useful phone numbers near to the phone:

- the local police station
- your doctor
- neighbours, particularly those with keys to your house
- a locksmith
- the gas, electricity and water companies
- two plumbers (for quotes)
- two electricians (for quotes).

The best way to find a tradesperson is to go on personal recommendation. Ask friends and neighbours if they can give you the name of someone reliable. Otherwise, it is wise to choose a member of a trade association – you are more likely to have some comeback if something goes wrong.

A secure home

The basic principle of home security is to make your property as unattractive a target as possible to the opportunist thief. Burglars like to work unseen. Take a look at your house from their point of view. Can they easily get round the back of the house, or work hidden from view behind trees or fences, for example?

Many thieves manage to enter houses by finding doors or windows which are not shut properly. Even if you are leaving the house for only two minutes, lock the doors and windows.

Free security advice

A crime prevention officer (CPO) is a police officer specially trained in crime prevention techniques. He or she will conduct a free security survey of your home and give you impartial advice. Also, tell the CPO if you have any ideas or comments on local crime-related issues – your feedback is important. Ring your local police station and ask to be put in touch with the CPO.

A watchful eye

Contrary to popular belief, most burglaries take place during the day when people are out at work. People at home during this time can do particularly valuable work in keeping an eye out for anyone acting suspiciously in the locality. If you see anything out of the ordinary, make a note of the person's description and contact the police. Do not be tempted to get involved in any situation yourself.

Get to know your neighbours, and agree to keep an eye on each other's houses. Take the phone numbers of those people you trust, and give them yours. A Neighbourhood Watch scheme is a voluntary group of local residents working in liaison with the police. Such schemes are designed to help prevent burglary and other crimes in the area. They can also be good sources of free advice. If you are in a Neighbourhood Watch area contact your local coordinator – he or she will probably have a good idea of any current crime problems. If you would like to help start up a local Watch, contact your crime prevention officer at the local police station.

Locks and bolts

Door locks

There are two main types of door lock. The most secure locks are Kitemarked to British Standard (BS) 3621 and have to pass a number of stringent physical tests.

Cylinder rim locks fit on to the surface of the door and the frame, and are usually operated by a lever inside and a key outside. Buy one that has a 'deadlock' device – the bolt automatically locks each time the door is closed (though be careful about locking yourself out). A **cylinder rim nightlatch** is a basic type of lock and should not be used as the only lock on any exit door.

DISCOUNTS

Some of the large do-it-yourself superstores offer discounts for the over-60s on certain days. If you need to buy any locks, lights or other items for the house, you should be able to save some money by using one of their discount cards. Even if you buy elsewhere, the other store may be prepared to match the discounted price.

A **mortice lock** fits into the width of the door – always use a 5-lever version on any exit door. They do not automatically deadlock, so you have to remember to lock them each time you go out (you can also keep them locked when you are in but leave the key in the lock). A **mortice sashlock** is a mortice lock with a handle, commonly used on back doors but also appropriate for some front doors. Again, look for a 5-lever (as opposed to a 2- or 3-lever) lock.

For a high level of door security, fit two locks to the main exit doors, front and back – a Kitemarked mortice lock (or mortice sashlock) and a cylinder rim lock higher up. Two locks help to spread the load and look formidable from the outside. If there is room for only one lock, choose a Kitemarked cylinder rim lock. You will need to be particularly careful if any door has glass panels: make sure that at least one lock is out of reach of the panes, and preferably fit laminated glass for extra security.

Other security measures for doors

Consider replacing weak back doors that have plywood panels with solid doors. Once you are satisfied that your door is strong, several other pieces of door furniture can be used to secure it in addition to locks, and to help you see who is calling. A **door chain** allows you to open the door slightly to check a caller's identification. Buy the sturdiest chain you can find and secure it with screws that are at least 30mm (1¼in) long. You can also buy metal **door limiters** that are, in effect, heavy-duty door chains. A **door viewer** is a small wide-angle lens fitted through the door, so that you can see the identity of callers before opening the door. Some are clearer to see through than others, so have a look through them in the shop first. **Security mortice bolts** or **surface-mounted sliding bolts** will help to strengthen the top and bottom of the door, and **hinge bolts** (sometimes called **dog bolts**) will protect the hinged side of the door from being forced.

Window locks

Fit locks to all downstairs windows and any upstairs windows where a burglar might be able to gain access via a flat roof, porch or balcony. The type of lock will depend on what your windows are made of, how they open and close, and whether you want the lock to show from the outside. Most are operated by a standard key. Window locks are fairly easy to fit by using a screwdriver. You should also fit locks to the top and bottom of patio doors.

Fire security

Remember that you may need to get out of the house quickly in case of fire, so do not barricade yourself in to the extent that you cannot get out in a hurry or others cannot get in to help you. If you are indoors, keep keys handy and make sure everyone in the house knows where they are. If double glazing is fitted, at least one window should open wide enough for you to escape through it.

Spare keys

Be careful with your spare keys. Never keep them in an accessible place – say on a string tied to the inside of the letterbox, or under an outside doormat or flowerpot – however convenient it may be. When you go out, do not leave any exterior keys in an obvious place; otherwise, if someone did break in they would be able to carry out goods through a door.

If you lose your door keys, change the locks as soon as possible – keep the name of a locksmith handy. The local crime prevention officer may recommend a master locksmith.

If possible, find a nearby relative or neighbour who you trust and give him or her a set of keys in case you lock yourself out or need help while you are indoors. Remind your relative or friend not to label the keys with your name and address.

Alarms

Burglar alarms

A burglar alarm is a good deterrent and can give you peace of mind, but of course it cannot guarantee that you will not be burgled.

There are two types of standard burglar alarm: bell-only and monitored. **Bell-only alarms** have a central control panel linked to a number of different types of sensor. If the alarm is switched on and any of these sensors detects an intrusion, the bell on the outside of the house (and the siren inside) will ring for 20 minutes or so, attracting attention and scaring off any burglar. Most alarms consist of a combination of sensors that guard the main doors and windows, plus a number of movement detectors (called passive infrared or PIRs). Many control panels operate via your own four-digit code number, although it is possible to buy some that are key-operated. A bell-only alarm will cost from around £450 up to about £1,000, depending on size.

A **monitored alarm** has similar components to a bell-only alarm, except that when the alarm is triggered a signal is sent to a 24-hour monitoring centre, who will call out the emergency services if they believe there is an intrusion. You will have to pay more for a monitored alarm – usually well over £1,500 plus an annual monitoring fee to the control centre.

Burglar alarms can be adapted to fit any property – the installers will generally come up with their own design of the components. But first you should think carefully about what you want the alarm to protect and exactly how you want to use it, and make this clear to the installers. For instance, you may want to have the alarm set when you are in the house. Always get at least three quotes for an alarm from installers – choose a selection of local and national firms and check that the company is approved by one of the five alarm inspectorate institutions recognised by the police, and make sure the installer confirms that the system conforms to BS 4737.

Be wary of any maintenance contracts: some may tie you to a contract for several years, with rapidly increasing annual fees. You do not have to have a maintenance contract with a bell-only alarm, but you probably will with a monitored alarm. Look for a contract that lasts for only one or two years (this information may well be hidden in the small print).

Never buy an alarm from a door-to-door salesperson. And if your insurance company has made an alarm a condition of the policy, check that the type you plan to buy meets with their approval.

Social alarms

A social alarm which you wear round your neck or wrist or clipped to clothing lets you call for help at any time from anywhere in the house.

Leaving the house

If you are going on holiday, remember to cancel the milk and the papers, move items such as the computer and video out of view of the windows, set a timer switch (or two) so lights come on in the evening, and lock away garden tools and ladders. Tell friends that you are going to be away and ask them to keep an eye on your home.

Storing valuables

If you have important documents, spare cash, jewellery or other small valuables that you do not need to keep at home, put them in a safety deposit box at a bank. Do not keep large amounts of cash at home – burglars like nothing better. Photographs of any other valuable items, such as antiques, will help the police to trace them if they are stolen. For televisions, videos and cameras, use an ultraviolet marker pen (available from stationers) to write your postcode and house number on each item.

Exterior lighting

Exterior lights can illuminate dark corners and alleyways. You can buy lights that stay on all night (often called dusk-to-dawn lamps) but they may work out quite costly to run unless you use a low-energy fluorescent light bulb. Other types switch on when they sense someone crossing their beam and stay on for a few minutes (they have a passive infra-red sensor that detects movement). Both will illuminate your entry and exit, and should help to deter an opportunist thief.

Fitting most exterior lights involves drilling holes in an exterior wall and wiring up the light to the internal electrical circuit. If you are not confident of your own skills, use a reliable electrician.

VICTIM SUPPORT SCHEMES

Victim support schemes offer free support and advice to anyone who has suffered as a victim of a crime. Counsellors will visit you in your home and offer practical and emotional help. You can contact them through your local police station or via Victim Support.*

Letting people into your home

Always use the door viewer and chain when answering the door. Some officials, such as gas or electricity meter readers, may call on you unannounced. Always insist on seeing an identity card with a photograph first, even if the caller is in uniform. If in doubt, shut the door on them and ring their company to check identification. If you are still suspicious, ring the police.

In general, do not let salespeople in but deal with them on the doorstep. If you do let someone into your house, stay with them and do not let them wander around alone.

Anyone with a legitimate reason to call on you should carry an ID card, and will willingly display it. Do not let anyone you do not know – adult or child – into your house, even if they claim it is an emergency.

Safety

Falls are by far the most common type of home accident involving older people, and make up about two-thirds of all cases needing treatment. These figures increase for those aged 75 and older, in particular people who live alone and women who suffer from osteoporosis. Falls and injuries most commonly occur on stairs and outside steps.

Preventing falls

Illuminate your home well – you need relatively high light levels as you grow older. You should aim for similar lighting levels in all rooms. Choose large areas of light colour when decorating, and use matt paint – shiny surfaces can dazzle. For people with poor sight, contrasting colours on edges and steps will make navigation easier. Consider fitting light switches with a large rocker pad.

Keep spare light bulbs handy (low-energy bulbs need changing less frequently), and use table lamps in poorly lit places. If the stairs are steep, add an extra handrail to the inner wall. Make sure that there are no rucked-up carpets or loose corners that you could trip over, and run appliance cables as close to the wall as possible, not across the room and never under the carpet. For a rug on a slippery floor, fit small stickers to the corners to prevent it sliding across the floor. In the kitchen, mop up any spills immediately, and do not overstretch to reach high cupboards. In the bathroom, rubber mats and extra handrails in or near the bath are useful to prevent slipping. If you are using a ladder, place it at a safe angle to the wall and do not lean out from it when at the top. Make sure that someone else is on hand in case you fall, preferably supporting the ladder at the bottom.

Electrical safety

Most electrical appliances are now sold complete with a fitted plug. If not, there are a number of 'easy-to-wire' plugs on the market that make the task slightly simpler. When fitting a plug follow the instructions carefully; use the correct fuse as recommended by the manufacturer and check that the cable is securely fixed. Some plugs have special handles or mouldings for easy grip. Replace any plug with signs of scorching or burning, or the flex if it is worn. Do not overload power points by using multiple adaptors – each socket should carry no more than 13 amps in total.

Do not use any electrical appliances in the bathroom that have an ordinary 3-pin plug. Any appliances for use there should be specifically designed for the bathroom and permanently wired into the mains.

If any electrical appliance shows signs of wear or a fault, have it checked by an electrician or dispose of it and buy a replacement. Keep access to the fuse box clear.

For general electrical advice, many electricity companies have telephone information lines, including some specially targeted at older people – look in the phone book under 'Electricity'. If you are worried about the wiring circuit in your home, ask if they offer a free visual wiring check of the mains circuit – some may charge a small fee. Otherwise, use a reliable electrician, but get at least two estimates first.

Gas safety

If you are worried about gas safety, there is now a free Health and Safety Executive Gas Action Line.★ You can get gas detectors for home use – look for those bearing the Kitemark BS 7348. They will detect gas leaks and sound an alarm, but need to be permanently wired into the mains rather than plugged into a socket. A further hazard is carbon monoxide, a non-detectable but toxic gas given off if wood, coal, oil or gas is burned without sufficient oxygen. You can obtain carbon monoxide detectors, kitemarked to BS 7860, or card indicators. See Chapter 24 for more details on gas services.

Fire safety

Smoke alarms

Smoke alarms are cheap, easy to fit and will alert you if there is a build-up of smoke in your home. They have saved many lives in recent years. The best advice is to fit as many as you can afford (bearing the Kitemark BS 2740). There are types for deaf people (available from the Royal National Institute for Deaf People*), with a vibrating pad beneath a pillow or a flashing light.

If you are fitting only one or two alarms, place them in communal areas such as at the bottom of the staircase, in a hallway or an upstairs landing, preferably in the centre of the ceiling. Do not fit smoke alarms in the kitchen or bathroom – they may go off accidentally. Once you have fitted an alarm, test it monthly and replace the batteries every year.

Heaters and fires

If you use any electric, gas, paraffin or solid-fuel fires or heaters, make sure that they all have secure fireguards and are placed well away from any bedding, clothes or curtains and cannot be knocked over. Never leave clothes drying in front of any fire or heater, and do not sit too close to one. If you use a fuel-burning fire, the room should be well ventilated to avoid carbon monoxide poisoning, so make sure that airbricks and ventilators are not obstructed. Do not move any portable fire or heater when it is on or alight and switch heaters off at night.

Smoking in the home

If there is a smoker in the house, ensure that there are plenty of ashtrays around where they cannot be knocked over easily. Never leave a burning cigarette in the ashtray – always stub it out properly and make sure the contents of any ashtray are cold before throwing the ash and stubs in the bin. Be wary of falling asleep while holding a cigarette – this is how many fires begin. Old foam-filled furniture in particular may be highly flammable. Smoking in bed is particularly dangerous and should be avoided.

Electric blankets

Some electric blankets can be left on all night, while others must be switched off before you get into bed. Whatever type you have, follow the instructions carefully, and make sure that the blanket is kept in good condition, stored without creasing when not in use and serviced every few years. Never attempt to repair one yourself. If a blanket shows signs of damage or wear, return it to the manufacturer.

Dealing with fires

Closing internal doors helps to prevent a fire spreading quickly. Be wary of tackling a fire, even if it is very small; the best idea is to get everyone out of the house and then ring 999. Fire safety experts do not recommend small fire extinguishers for home use, as you may waste time trying to tackle the fire. They also need regular servicing. If you feel you must have one, contact your local fire brigade's fire prevention officer for a Home Office leaflet detailing the different types of extinguishers available.

Fire blankets are good for smothering flames such as those caused by a chip-pan fire – choose one that is Kitemarked to BS 6575. Never throw water on to burning oil or fat fires.

House insurance

By the time you reach retirement, you will almost certainly have plenty of experience of insuring your home and belongings. However, when you retire there are some special considerations to take into account, particularly if you have generally insured through your mortgage lender in the past and are now faced with choosing a policy yourself. One advantage of being retired is that you may qualify for a special age-related discount. *The Which? Guide to Insurance* published by Which? Books* covers this subject in depth.

If your home were burned to the ground, could you afford to rebuild it? That is an extreme case, but if the answer is no, then you need **buildings insurance**. If you have a mortgage to buy your home, your lender will insist on it but it makes sense even if you do not have a mortgage. If you live in a block of flats or a tenement property, your insurance responsibilities will be explained in your lease. You may also need buildings insurance if you are a tenant and your rental agreement states that insuring the fabric of the property and/or any fixtures and fittings is your responsibility.

What is covered

Buildings insurance covers the fabric of your home (the bricks and mortar, windows, roof and other integral parts) as well as fixtures and fittings (such as kitchen units and central heating boilers). In this chapter, 'house' generally means either house or flat. Buildings insurance is not a maintenance contract: it is intended to provide cover for *specific* damage or loss as a result of *specific* occurrences, not to pay for your running repairs. A condition of buildings insurance is that you keep your property in a good state of repair and take reasonable steps to prevent damage to it.

Are you adequately insured?

The guiding principle of insurance is that you can claim for what you lost and no more. This means that there is absolutely no point insuring for more than you need to because it will be a waste of money. 'Over-insuring' does not mean that you can claim for more than you stand to lose as a way of making money. If your insurer suspects that your claim has left you better off than before (this is called 'betterment' in the insurance industry's jargon), your claim will be reduced. For example, if your portable television is stolen and you claim to replace it with a state-of-the-art model with a huge screen, your claim will be reduced to the amount you would need to buy another portable.

Another more general principle is that you get what you pay for. If you insure for less than you need to, i.e. you are 'under-insured' – payment of any claim will usually take into account the fact that the premiums you paid were for a lower amount of cover. If, for example, you insure the contents of your home for £15,000 but the cost of replacing them is £20,000, any claim you have to make will be reduced in line with your under-insurance (i.e. only 75 per cent of your claim will be met). Similarly, if you make a claim to replace something as new – your three-year-old camera, for example – but the insurance you bought gives only 'indemnity' cover (where the insurance will pay the value of the item at the time you lost it), your claim will be reduced to the figure you would need to buy a three-year-old camera.

Valuing your contents

You have to insure for the cost of replacing all your possessions. Rather than make a guess, add up the cost of replacing everything in your home – many insurers provide checklists to help you do this. Most house contents policies are index-linked so that the amount you are insured for keeps pace with inflation. However, this will not take account of new possessions or fluctuations in the value of antiques, so review the sum you are insured for periodically.

With some policies the premium depends on the number of bedrooms in your house (including bedrooms that you use for another purpose: as an office, for example). These 'bedroom-rated' policies may provide unlimited cover, in which case you do not need to work out how much to insure for. However, most do have a maximum limit which, for contents cover for a three-bedroom house can be as little as £20,000 or as much as £35,000. Even so, you should still check that you do not exceed the limits

Two types of cover are available – indemnity and new-for-old. **New-for-old** means that your insurer will pay to replace damaged items with new ones. **Indemnity cover** means that the insurance company will pay you only the actual value of items damaged or lost. So, if you had a ten-year old cooker destroyed in a fire, with new-for-old cover you would get the price of a new cooker, whereas indemnity cover would give you only the value of a ten-year old cooker.

Most house contents insurance policies offer new-for-old cover, except for clothes, linen, pots and pans and, sometimes, bicycles. If you decide to cover some or all of your possessions on an indemnity basis you can calculate the value as follows. Take the current price of the item, and divide it by the number of years you would expect it to last for. Multiply this amount by however many years old it is, and deduct the result from the current shop price. This calculation gives you the value less a deduction for wear and tear.

Jewellery, antiques and valuables

If you have valuable items worth over a set amount, these will be covered only if you have informed your insurers that you want them covered. Definitions of valuables vary – check your policy.

Having a valuation is important when you need to make an insurance claim for any valuables, and to play safe you need to update valuations every three years or so. However, the insurance valuation for jewellery, 'collectables' or fine art could be as much as twice the amount you paid for it – or up to four times as much for rare or hard-to-replace items. The valuation reflects the amount you might have to pay, if you needed to buy a replacement or get a copy made. When getting a valuation, always make clear you want a valuation for insurance purposes.

You can get valuations from auction houses, jewellers and antique dealers: look out for qualifications such as those from the Royal Institution of Chartered Surveyors,★ the Incorporated Society of Valuers and Auctioneers★ or the National Association of Goldsmiths.★ Some valuers hold on to the goods for a week or so to research them. It is also helpful to have photographs, preferably taken from more than one angle.

Cover in the garden

If retirement for you means creating the garden you have always wanted, you should be aware that cover for possessions in the garden will be limited with most policies.

As part of your possessions, house plants and their pots should be covered by a contents policy. However, it is very unlikely that plants growing in the garden, unsecured window boxes and other plant life outside the house will be covered by a standard policy. If you want to insure things left out in the open – including expensive terracotta pots, garden furniture and other garden ornaments – check whether your insurance covers you and ask your insurer to extend your cover if necessary.

Special requirements

If you want cover for something unusual, such as a powered wheelchair, consult the *Insurance Buyer's Guide* (Kluwer Publishing – try your local library) or an insurance broker or advisor (see page 150). Note that with any type of insurance, you are legally obliged to tell your insurers of anything which might affect the risk they are taking on, whether or not they ask you about it. So if, for example, you plan to take in paying guests, take a long holiday or take up a hobby involving special or hazardous equipment, such as glass-blowing over a naked flame, make sure you inform your insurers. The same applies if you are carrying out building work.

Valuing your buildings

You need to insure your buildings for how much they would cost to rebuild, including the cost of removing rubble and architects', surveyors' and other fees. This can be quite different from the likely resale value of your home, which could be much more or much less. The rebuilding cost is calculated from the floor space of your home and standard rebuilding cost tables. A version of these tables, and advice on how to calculate the rebuilding cost of your home, are available in an information sheet called *Buildings insurance for homeowners* from the Association of British Insurers.*

When you have a mortgage, your mortgage valuation usually recommends an appropriate amount of insurance. Virtually all buildings insurance policies then automatically adjust your cover each year to keep pace with rising (or falling) building costs. Even so, you may find that over the years the sum insured grows too much or too little and you become over- or under-insured. So recalculate the sum (or get professional advice from a surveyor) every five years or so. This is particularly important once you have paid off your mortgage, since you have no mortgage valuation to guide you.

Legal liability

If you find that you, or an elderly relative, need help in the home it is particularly important that you check what insurance cover you have. A standard buildings insurance will cover you for any legal liability as owner of the home, your contents cover for liability as occupier or for personal liability claims. So, if your cleaner trips on a poorly-fitted carpet and breaks a leg, you may find that you can claim from your house insurance any damages you are legally obliged to pay.

LONG HOLIDAYS

Beware – various types of cover, such as theft cover, may be withdrawn or limited if you go away on holiday for a long time (usually defined as 30 days) or if you rent out all or part of your home. There may also be special conditions to observe, such as draining the water system.

Money-saving tips

- Most house insurance policies come in two parts – insurance for buildings and insurance for contents – but you do not usually have to buy both from the same insurer. You can save money by buying the cheapest of each type, but check that there are no gaps between the two types of cover.
- Many companies offer discounts or special policies to people who are retired or over a certain age. These companies include

Age Concern,★ Cornhill Direct, Eagle Star, GAN, General Accident, Help the Aged,★ Ideal, Iron Trades, Royal Sun Alliance, Saga★ and Towry Law. A 5 or 15 per cent discount at age 50 or over is a common saving. Teetotallers or people in certain professions or trade unions can also often get discount from some insurers.

- You could get a discount on the cost of a policy by agreeing to pay a certain amount (a 'voluntary excess') towards a claim, in addition to any compulsory excess.

- Many insurers offer discounts on house insurance if you fit extra security devices, such as locks or alarms, to your home. But you must be scrupulous about locking up every time you go out: otherwise you could find your claim refused.

Problems with claims

Many claims are not settled in full because of 'wear and tear'. If, say, a roof collapses in a storm, and you claim on your insurance, the insurer may argue that the roof collapsed partly because of the storm and partly because it was old and in poor condition and would have collapsed soon anyway. The insurance company will then make a deduction for wear and tear.

Some buildings policies guarantee not to make a deduction for wear and tear. However, with all policies you still have a duty to maintain your property in 'reasonable repair'. If you do not do this, your insurance company can refuse to pay your claim.

Many other claims are reduced because insurers say that the estimate provided for a repair was too high. If your claim is not accepted in full, and you still think you have a case:

- First complain to the head of the company. Be cautious about accepting any offers of less than the amount you are claiming. You are sometimes asked to complete a form agreeing to 'full and final' settlement. Do not do this if you think you may need to claim more.

- If the dispute is over the cause of the damage, get together evidence to support your case. For example, if there is a dispute over what caused something to break, find out how old the item was and its normal natural life. If necessary, get expert witnesses, such as electricians, builders and so on, to look at the damage and give an opinion.

- If the dispute is over the value of damaged items, and you do not have any receipts or valuations, get new estimated valuations by describing the items to experts – e.g. proprietors of antiques shops, electrical goods shops. Find photographs showing the items or try to get witness statements from people who have seen them.

- If the disputed loss is very large, you can hire a loss assessor to collect evidence on your side. Loss assessors usually work for a percentage of the final insurance payout. Contact the Institute of Public Loss Assessors.★

- If the insurance company sends a loss adjuster to examine the damage, ask for a copy of his or her report. Insurance companies are not required to show you this, but some will do so. (A loss assessor works for you; a loss adjuster works for the insurance company.)

Complaints schemes

As well as the option of going to court, there are two main complaints schemes for house insurance disputes – the Insurance Ombudsman Bureau★ and the Personal Insurance Arbitration Service (PIAS).★ Both are free and most companies belong to one or the other (it will say which in your policy document), although the Ombudsman is by far the most effective. But with both schemes you should have taken up your complaint at the highest level within the company, first.(Note that in due course insurance complaints will be handled by a new Financial Services Ombudsman Scheme currently being set up.)

Chapter 23

Your rights as a householder

A dispute with a neighbour, or a problem with a builder or the local council may become something more than a minor irritation once you are newly retired and at home at times of the day when you would previously have been out. Needless to say, it is best to try and sort matters out in an amicable way if you can. However, it is helpful to know the legal position in case things get difficult. As well as the information in this chapter, Consumers' Association★ also produces *150 Letters that Get Results*, giving practical information on resolving common consumer problems.

Neighbours

Being good neighbours is not always easy, especially if you are living close together and have very different lifestyles. Legally speaking, you have certain rights and interests in relation to your property and, in turn, your neighbours have rights and interests of their own. Inevitably at times these will conflict, causing tensions or sometimes even a serious dispute.

Nuisance

The law says that an occupier of property is not allowed to use it in such a way as to interfere with other people's reasonable enjoyment of their property. Loud music or barking dogs may fall into this legal category of 'nuisance', as might an offensive smell or irritating smoke.

But the mere fact that you find something a nuisance does not mean that the law is being broken. The law accepts that a fair amount of give and take is necessary in everyday living. For example, in a semi-detached property or a block of flats a degree of noise penetration is unavoidable; you have to put up with what is reasonable. And you must react reasonably too, and not, say, turn up the volume on your television to drown the rock music from next-door's stereo.

Someone who is especially sensitive to a particular form of nuisance is not entitled to a legal remedy in respect of behaviour that would not be a nuisance to other people. For instance, if you like to have a nap in the afternoons when children are frequently playing loudly in a neighbouring garden, you have no right to complain if other people going about their various activities would find the noise level tolerable.

If you are seriously disturbed by noise nuisance you can complain to your local council: contact the environmental health department. After investigating your complaint, the council can serve a notice on the neighbours, forbidding further unreasonable noise. If the noise continues, your neighbour can be fined. The council may also have powers to confiscate equipment, such as a hi-fi, in some cases. Alternatively, you can go direct to the magistrates' court (sheriff court in Scotland). If you win, your neighbours can be fined if they continue to be noisy.

A newly introduced law in England and Wales gives more power to councils to deal with trouble-makers living in local-authority housing. The law also covers other social landlords such as housing associations.

It is important to take into account the type of neighbourhood. If you live in a rural area you must expect to put up with 'country smells' – up to a point, anyway. If, say, a neighbouring farmer chooses to put his manure heap right next to your hedge when there are alternative sitings which would avoid this kind of offence to neighbours, it is reasonable to expect the farmer to take action to improve the situation. In a similar way, if you live close to a factory or industrial site in an urban area, you must expect to put up with a degree of noise and possibly the emission of fumes or smoke. However, smoke control laws strictly limit what may be emitted from factory chimneys, and in the first place it may be worth contacting the environmental health department of your local council. If noise from an industrial site or roadworks is disturbing you, note that local councils have power under the Control of Pollution Act to serve a notice restricting hours of working and the type of machinery used. It could be that restrictions were imposed before the works started.

If your neighbours are keen gardeners, they may be in the habit of lighting bonfires now and again. In general, there are no restrictions on when bonfires can be lit. Whether it is a nuisance depends on whether the fires interfere with the use and enjoyment of your property, and whether they are more frequent than the ordinary person would consider reasonable. If you cannot persuade your neighbour to do anything, say by moving the fires to a different part of the garden, you could take the matter up with your local council – keep a detailed diary and get statements from others affected first. Your local council has powers to serve a notice requiring the fires to be stopped (though this is unlikely) or perhaps to be lit less frequently. If your neighbours ignore the notice, the council could take them to the magistrate's court, which could impose a fine if they were found guilty. You can bypass the council and go straight to the court to ask for a 'nuisance order' if you wish – but remember that if you do you will need to prove your case.

Neighbours who let weeds and shrubs thrive can be even more of a bane at times, but there is no law which says that people must be tidy. However, your local council has powers to clear up areas within its control, if it considers a highly visible mess is ruining the 'amenity' and beauty of the neighbourhood – you may be able to get the council to shift the rubbish if this is the case (these powers exist in England, Scotland and Wales). If the rubbish attracts vermin the council will certainly act. The council can serve a notice requiring the removal of the mess, and your neighbours could face a considerable fine if they do not comply.

If you are having problems with your neighbour, try contacting Mediation UK★ which can put you in touch with local counselling services, which aim to resolve conflicts without having to go to court. But if an informal approach fails and you have to take formal action yourself, it will help to keep a written record of specific incidents to back up your case.

Boundaries

Trespass

Each time they cross over your property without your permission your neighbours are trespassing. If a friendly word does not stop this, you are perfectly entitled to bar their way. Note, however, that you are under a legal obligation to ensure that people who come on to your land – including trespassers – are reasonably safe. If you are faced with repeated acts of trespassing you can take them to court, get an injunction and claim compensation. The amount you recover will depend on the amount of inconvenience you have suffered and whether your property has been damaged.

If the next-door neighbour's dog is plaguing you by coming into your garden, you must provide your own fencing to keep it out; as a general rule, pet owners do not have to erect fences to keep animals in. Unless the deeds of the property put the obligation to maintain a fence on you, the position is different in relation to farm animals: in this case, the farmer must prevent livestock from trespassing, and pay for any damage if it does.

Overhanging branches

If branches from a neighbour's tree overhang your property, you are entitled to cut them off at the point where they cross the boundary. Branches laden with ripe fruit may have particular appeal; however, strictly speaking, the branches and their fruit continue to be your neighbour's property, and so you should either throw them back or provide your neighbour with an opportunity to collect them. A word of warning before you start chopping: make sure that the tree is not subject to a Tree Preservation Order – you can check with your local council (in Northern Ireland, the Department of the Environment). If it is, you will need its authority first. If you live in a Conservation Area, give the council six weeks' notice of any intended action so that it can decide whether you need planning permission to fell the tree.

Tree roots

Sometimes tree roots may affect foundations and cause subsidence. Usually it is not the roots themselves that cause damage but the fact that they are absorbing water from the soil, which contracts, causing foundations to shift. The person on whose land the tree is growing will be responsible for the damage, as long as this is the cause. If you are insured for this it will be far simpler to claim on your insurance than to pursue a claim against your neighbour.

Boundary in the wrong place

It sometimes emerges from examination of the deeds to a property (the documents which prove ownership) that a boundary wall or fence has been erected in the wrong place. For instance, it may happen that your fence encloses a strip of land that appears on the deeds as belonging to your neighbour. If the true owner has not asserted his or her right to the land over a long period – usually 12 years – it becomes your property. It is not necessary for you to have lived at the property for the entire period: you can take advantage of your predecessor's uninterrupted possession of the land in calculating the relevant period.

A right to light

If trees in your neighbour's garden are blocking out sunshine, and so restricting the natural light you enjoy through your windows, there may well be nothing you can do about it because, generally speaking, there is no right to light. But there are two ways in which a right to light can arise. First, it may be expressly granted in the deeds to your property (the documents which prove ownership). Secondly, it may be permanently acquired through long enjoyment over an uninterrupted period of twenty years. It is not the house as a whole that benefits from this, but particular rooms. Even if you have acquired a right to light in one of these two ways, and have enjoyed bright sunlight through a window for over twenty years, you will probably be without a valid claim where a partial obstruction from, say, an overhanging tree as opposed to some artificial structure now partially obscures the light you enjoy.

Walls and fences

Walls and fences can lead to problems when neighbours aren't sure who is responsible for their upkeep. But if you are planning to construct a new wall on a boundary, or repair or excavate near an existing wall, you must give adjoining owners notice of your proposals. The Party Wall etc. Act 1996 provides a way of resolving difficulties if your proposals aren't accepted.

The basic rule is that the person who puts up a fence is the person who owns it. But that will not help on a housing estate where the builder erected all the fences. Where this is the case you will have to look at the deeds, which may clarify the position.

As a fallback position, there is a legal presumption that close-boarded fences with supporting posts every so often, and timber lap fences or chain-link fences built similarly, are assumed to belong to the owner on whose side the supports are. The reason for this is that the landowner is assumed to put a fence as near the boundary as possible; if the supports protrude over the boundary the landowner will be trespassing on the neighbour's land.

Repairs to a neighbour's fence

If your neighbour's fence is in danger of collapsing and, for instance, ruining your herbaceous border, you cannot automatically require him or her to mend the fence; however, in the case of many estates, where the deeds allocate ownership of a fence, the owner may be responsible for repairs. In any event, if damage actually occurs you can claim the cost of putting it right.

Neighbours' access for repair work

If the side wall, say, of your neighbours' property is close to the boundary between the two properties, they may wish to place a ladder in your garden or on your path in order to paint the side of their house or repair guttering. You are not automatically bound to agree to this unless the deeds to your property specify that your neighbours are entitled to access for such purposes; without such a provision or your express authority they will commit an act of trespass in entering on to your land. However, in England and Wales, the Access to Neighbouring Land Act 1992 gives your neighbours the right to seek a court order permitting them to enter your land for the purpose of carrying out works that are reasonably necessary for the 'preservation' of their property.

Getting work done on your home

Most of the problems people experience with building work relate to the **cost**, the **quality of work** and/or the **time** taken to complete it.

Cost

Quotation or estimate?

There is no clear distinction legally, and the fact that one or other term is used need not be decisive. The critical question is whether the price or charge given in the estimate is intended to fix the liability of the customer (making it a quotation), or a rough-and-ready, if informed, guide to the price ultimately to be charged (making it an estimate). Given the difficulty in determining this, it is wise to clarify at the outset whether the figure represents the limit of your liability or merely an informed forecast of the likely cost.

Where no price is specified

If you have not agreed a price – say, in an emergency when you have been anxious to get the work done as soon as possible – the contractor is entitled to a reasonable price for the job done. If you feel you are being overcharged, you are not bound to pay what the builder asks but can pay a smaller sum in settlement. To ascertain what a reasonable price for the job would be, obtain estimates for the work from other contractors, or contact a trade association for guidance.

If you are going to have any major building work carried out, it would be sensible to draw up a contract at the outset to help avoid problems later. The Royal Institute of British Architects produces standard contracts for various types of work. You can buy them from Riba Publications Limited.★

Quality of the work

When a contractor agrees to do work for you, he or she is entering into a contract. Quite apart from the provisions expressly agreed in any contract, for example those concerning price or type of materials, there are various implied obligations the builder must fulfil, which are set out in the Supply of Goods and Services Act 1982 (these are common law obligations in Scotland). Essentially, the contractor agrees to carry out the work to a reasonable standard using materials of satisfactory quality within a reasonable time. If he or she fails to meet any of these obligations, you have a claim for breach of contract.

If the work is defective, you should normally give the contractor an opportunity to put it right, unless circumstances are such that you have reasonably lost faith in his or her ability to do the job properly. If this is the case, you are entitled to get another contractor to finish the work. Before selecting someone else, you should get two or three estimates for the balance of the work – if need be, this will enable you to demonstrate later that you have paid no more than is reasonable. If you are prepared to have the original contractor back, you should send him or her copies of these, stating that unless the job is completed satisfactorily within a specified time, you will be engaging one of these contractors, and will claim from him or her any extra costs you incur as a result.

The time factor

If it is important that you get the work done by a particular date, you should get the contractor's written agreement to this, and also state in writing that 'time is of the essence'. Doing this strengthens your legal position, because in the absence of an agreement of this sort, the law will not regard time of completion as being of critical importance.

Where no date for completion is specified, the work must be completed within a reasonable time; if it is not, you can claim compensation for any additional expense and inconvenience you are put to as a result (the cost of meals out if you cannot use your kitchen, for example). If, on the other hand, a specific date for completion has been agreed, and you have made time of the essence, you have the option of ending the contract and getting in another contractor if the work is not completed in accordance with the time specified. Having done so, you are entitled to claim back any extra costs (and compensation for any substantial additional inconvenience) from the original contractor.

Problems with your local council

Your local council has extensive responsibilities for the provision and maintenance of services in your area. When facilities or services are not up to scratch, you may want to complain to those responsible, or even make a formal claim for compensation if you have had an accident as a result.

Litter

The law on litter control has been tightened up and there are tougher penalties to deter offenders. What is more, local authorities, transport operators, government departments, schools and other educational establishments now have a legal duty to keep the land they control free from litter and refuse. Local authorities can also designate privately owned land – for example, supermarket car parks – as litter control areas.

If you feel that litter control is inadequate on roadways or other places to which the public has access in your area, take up the matter with your local council. If you are still not satisfied, you may apply to the magistrates' court (sheriff court in Scotland), applying for a litter abatement order against the body under a duty to clear litter from the area concerned – the local council, say, if it is a public road. You must give them five days' notice of your intention to apply for the order before doing so. Similar provisions exist in Northern Ireland.

Dog mess

Local councils have a duty to clear dog mess from public places. In addition, in England and Wales local councils can use 'poop scoop' by-laws to designate areas where owners must clean up after their dogs – anyone who fails to do this will face a fine. Councils can also use by-laws to set up dog-free zones – children's play areas, for example. Under Scottish law, owners who allow their dogs to foul designated areas, for instance public roads and recreation areas, are liable to pay a fine. In Northern Ireland, dog owners permitting their dogs to foul the footpath may be fined.

Uneven pavements

Local councils are responsible for maintaining the pavement. If you feel the state of a pavement – or road – is a hazard to the public, you should report this to the council (highways department) and ask them to carry out appropriate remedial works.

It does not necessarily follow that because you have an accident on a pavement you can hold the council responsible and make a claim against it for any loss or damage you suffer. You will have to be able to show that the council was negligent – or careless – in carrying out its duty. This will depend on such factors as:

- how long ago the council did anything to the pavement
- whether the hole or the defect was obvious
- what sort of maintenance and inspection programme the council has
- whether there have been any previous complaints or trouble
- whether you were taking care to look where you were going.

It will often help when making a claim if you have been able to take photographs of the scene of the accident, for instance a close-up shot demonstrating unevenness in a pavement. It is also a good idea if possible to get evidence from a witness who can support your claim; this person need not necessarily have seen the accident – but if he or she can give evidence as to the state of the pavement this may help. If you have suffered injury, it is important to get a medical report from your doctor as soon as possible.

You may not only have suffered injury, but damage to clothing and perhaps additional travel expenses too. You should claim compensation ('damages') for all these things. Do not be surprised if the council (or its insurers) rejects your claim at first; more often than not you will have to persevere – remember, it is for you to prove your claim. Incidentally, you may be told that as the difference in height of the sections of pavement was less than 22mm (1 inch) your claim cannot stand. This is not the law – whether the council is liable to compensate you will depend on a consideration of all the circumstances.

If your injuries are at all serious, or the circumstances complicated, you are likely to need help from a solicitor who deals with personal injury cases. In England and Wales, ring the Law Society's Accident Line Scheme★ and you will immediately be put in touch with an Accident Line solicitor in the area. Legal Aid is no longer available for personal injury cases, so ask about methods of payment when choosing a solicitor. Solicitors will work on a 'no win, no fee' basis if they think you have a good chance of winning. The cost of going to law may also be met by legal expenses insurance; even if you don't think you have such insurance, check your household insurance, since legal expenses insurance may be included as an option. It is also possible to buy legal expenses insurance after the event, to cover the costs of losing if you need to go to court.

It is worth knowing about the Legal Advice and Assistance Scheme – better known as the Green Form Scheme in England,

Wales and Northern Ireland. Under the Scheme you can get up to two hours of free advice if your disposable income and capital fall within certain strict limits. In Northern Ireland those ineligible for free advice may qualify for advice on payment of a contribution related to their means. The same is true in Scotland, where assistance is more extensive and may continue until a decision is made to take formal legal action. You can find out more about the Green Form Scheme from leaflets available at solicitors' offices and your local Citizens Advice Bureau.

Chapter 24

Basic utilities

Being able to keep warm, cook, have running water and use the phone are things that most of us take for granted. But if being at home all day means running up phone or fuel bills that you cannot afford, or if your hands become too stiff to turn on the tap, life at home can become very difficult.

The companies that provide gas, electricity, water and the telephone offer a wide range of services, some specifically designed for older people, that will help you budget, cope with bills and use your appliances safely.

Choosing the right company

Gas and electricity

Just as you can already shop around to get the cheapest phone service, you can now choose your gas and electricity suppliers. Other companies act as 'brokers', offering to set you up with a new supplier (Saga,★ the holiday company, is one such company).

Shopping around between energy companies should help you to save money, although you should be careful that the new supply company offers services that meet your needs. To find out which companies are offering gas and electricity services in your area, contact the relevant regulator, OFGEM★ (the Office of Gas and Electricity Markets). For electricity companies in Northern Ireland, contact OFREG★ (the Office for the Regulation of Electricity and Gas).

Changing gas and electricity suppliers should be a fairly straightforward process. There is no need to have new pipes or meters put in and the gas and electricity used stays the same. All you have to do is sign a contract. However, you do not have to change supplier if you do not want to. You can choose to remain a customer of British Gas or your existing electricity company simply by doing nothing.

It is worth noting that if you do change gas and electricity companies, you may no longer be entitled to compensation payments – e.g. for missed appointments – you might have qualified for had you stayed with British Gas or your existing electricity supplier (see 'Appointments', on pages 330–1).

Telephone

Telephone services are another area where you have a choice of service provider. Shopping around can bring big savings, but you need to do your homework – not all the competing phone companies are always cheaper than British Telecom* (BT). BT and cable companies are called 'direct' operators because you connect to their network direct to your home. To find out which cable company operates in your area, phone the Cable Hotline.*

With 'indirect' operators you continue to pay line rental to BT, but you dial a special code number before you make a call, which gives you access to cheaper rates on some or all calls. As well as all costs, some indirect operators charge a subscription fee which you have to pay on top of your BT line rental.

Special services

Gas

As a standard condition of their gas supply licences, all gas companies must offer special services to older, disabled or chronically sick customers. Most do this through a 'Gas Care scheme', involving your name and address being kept on a register along with details of any special requirements you might have. For example, if you let the scheme know that you cannot get around quickly, the meter reader will wait a bit longer for you to answer the door. These Gas Care schemes are free, voluntary and confidential. With some schemes, those on the mailing list receive a newsletter detailing all the extra services that older people are eligible for.

Your gas company should be able to give you information over the phone and send you the relevant leaflets in the post. If you are a

British Gas customer, ask for the leaflet *Our Commitment to Older or Disabled Customers* which gives details of the special services available to retired people.

Your gas company energy efficiency advisers (see 'Cutting your bill', on pages 328–9) should be able to help if you are having difficulty with the controls on your appliances. For example, some gas appliances can be adapted to make the knobs easier to turn. Controls marked in ways to help people with poor sight are also available. These adaptations are free.

Electricity

Every company that supplies electricity has to publish a special code of practice for elderly and disabled people – you should be able to get a copy by calling the customer services number on the reverse of your latest bill, or at your local showroom. Some companies run care schemes similar to those run by the gas suppliers (see above). The codes of practice set out the different ways you can pay your bill, the rules about disconnection, and the special facilities and services available for elderly or disabled customers.

Telephone

BT produces two leaflets detailing its special services: *Special Help for People who are Older or Disabled*, and *The BT Guide for People who are Older or Disabled* (available in braille, large print and audio tape). Such services include Typetalk, which enables those with hearing difficulties to communicate via a relay operator who types the hearing person's reply into a textphone. Leaflets are available from BT Sales.★ If you cannot use the phone book because of a disability or medical condition, you may be able to use BT Directory Enquiries★ free of charge (phone 195 to register).

Water and sewerage

The water regulator OFWAT★ has issued each water company with guidelines relating to older customers – for example, bills may be made available in braille, large type or audio tape. Many companies offer special services or keep records of elderly people with particular needs. However, you often need to register for these schemes before you can benefit – so contact the customer services number on your last bill to find out more.

Meters, bills and disconnection

Newly retired people tend to find that they use their heating, cooker and other appliances more than when they were at work all day, so fuel bills are likely to go up.

Payment options

If you are newly retired you may find yourself adjusting to life on a smaller income, so careful budgeting is important.

Gas and electricity

There are five main options for paying and budgeting for the gas or electricity you use, regardless of the company you are with:

Monthly or quarterly bills

Each month or quarter you receive a bill for energy you have used in the previous month or three-month period. This is a good way to pay if you are sure you will have enough money to meet the bill. If somebody else – for example, your son or daughter – deals with your finances, ask the company to send the bill straight to them. In most cases you pay less if you agree to pay by direct debit, or make a 'prompt' payment (i.e. pay in full within a set time limit, usually within 10 days of receiving a bill). As well as saving you money, paying by direct debit can be convenient if you find it difficult to get out of the house.

Payment plans

With a payment plan you pay a fixed amount each month, agreed with the company in advance. The advantages of this are that you do not get big winter bills and you know how much money to set aside. Some companies also have weekly or fortnightly payment plans – ask for details. Sometimes, however, the company's estimate of how much energy you are likely to use in a year is wrong, and you could find at the end of the year that you still owe them money or that they need to refund some to you. If you are using a payment plan, check the figures on the bills you do receive against your meter and let the company know if you think you are using much more or much less energy than was estimated.

Stamps

Electricity stamps are gradually being phased out. For the latest information, call the customer services number on your last bill. Gas stamps are accepted by British Gas for both gas and electricity bills but will not be available from the new gas companies. Where stamps are still available, they can be purchased from electricity or gas showrooms and – in some areas – post offices. You can buy as many or as few stamps as you want, whenever you like, and use them towards your bill. Contact the company to find out the exact details.

Pre-payment meters

These meters take special keys, cards or tokens (which you have to charge up with credit in advance); coin meters are being phased out. The advantage of a pre-payment meter is that you do not build up a debt, but check the cost; the standing charge may be more than double that of paying by direct debit. A token, key or card meter avoids the problems of having large sums of cash around, but you have to be able to get credit charged on to your card (or whatever) easily. The range of outlets is steadily increasing and in most areas will include post offices, selected stores and petrol stations. These outlets may have special opening hours and some may even be open for 24 hours (usually petrol stations only). Always check that outlets are local and convenient for you before considering this option.

Paypoint

Paypoint is a national network that allows customers of utility and service companies to settle their bills in cash. It operates through a number of outlets close to homes and shopping centres, such as newsagents, service stations and convenience stores. As well as simple cash bill payments, customers can buy tokens and charge smart cards or keys to use in pre-payment metering and budgeting schemes.

Telephone

Phone bills from BT come every three months – you can pay them by direct debit, phone, at any post office, bank, or BT shop. If you pay by quarterly direct debit you will receive a discount on your line rental of £1 per quarter. You could also choose to spread your payments by opening a budget account and making monthly payments by direct debit from your bank account, although there is no discount for this. BT is able to send most customers bills listing all calls made. Other telephone service companies offer a range of payment options: check before you subscribe.

Water and sewerage

In most cases, your water bill is an average annual amount based on the rateable value of your home. Water and sewerage bills can be issued annually, half-yearly or every three months. Most companies do not bill customers monthly, but all will accept a monthly payment plan they have agreed to. Most will accept payment by direct debit or any of the other popular methods. However, most companies do not give a discount for direct debit or prompt payment and water savings stamps have been phased out. Contact your local company (or companies – in one or two areas there are different companies for water and for sewerage) for full details of the payment options available to you.

You can have a water meter installed so that your water bill is based on the volume of water that you actually use. See 'Cutting your bill', on pages 328–9.

Estimated accounts (gas/electricity)

Your gas company or its agents should call and read your gas meter at least once every two years. If you change gas supplier, your new company may arrange for another meter-reading company to come and take readings. Your electricity company should read your meter every six months, although this timespan does vary from company to company. For any quarter where your meter is not read (you still get a bill every three months) both gas and electricity companies will estimate how much energy you have used based on your past consumption, printing a letter **E** next to the meter reading figure on your bill.

You do not have to pay an estimated bill that is wrong. When you get an estimate, check it against the actual reading on your meter. If it is wrong send the bill back giving the actual reading or call the number given on your bill. The company will send you a new bill based on the correct meter reading.

If the company does not agree that your bill is wrong, but you still think you are right, do not pay the part of the bill which is in dispute. Pay the rest, and ask the company to investigate further. Contact the relevant watchdog (see the last section of this chapter) if you and the company still cannot agree on the bill.

The Gas Consumers Council* has produced a free guide, *The Meter Beater*, to help you if you have a query about reading your gas meter. The address and phone number of your local office will be on the back of your gas bill and in the phone book.

If you can't pay your bill

Gas/electricity
If your bill arrives and you cannot pay it, do not panic but do not ignore it – tell the company straight away. It should make every effort to help you pay the bill over time before it can legally disconnect you. Disconnection may be used only as a last resort. If you have difficulty in meeting your bill, you could agree with the company that you will pay in one of the following ways:

- Pay a set amount each week, fortnight or month towards the debt and the energy you are still using. The company has to set the repayments at a rate you can afford.
- Have a pre-payment meter fitted. The meter will be set so that each time you put in your money or token it will take some money to pay off the debt.
- If you are receiving means-tested benefits, you can have money for your bill deducted from your benefit before you get it. Check with your company.

Remember these are things that the company *has* to do – if you are not offered a way to sort out your problem that could be suitable for your circumstances, complain to the company straight away. If that does not work, contact the Gas Consumers Council* or OFGEM* for help (OFREG* for electricity companies in Northern Ireland).

The gas and electricity companies will not disconnect pensioners who cannot pay their bills during the winter months (between 1 October and 31 March for gas, 1 October and 1 March for electricity), so if you and the adults you live with are all pensioners, and you have trouble paying a high winter bill, tell the company straight away and you will be able to sort out the debt problem without the worry of being left in the cold.

Water
By law you cannot be disconnected for non-payment of your water bill, although the water company can pursue you through the courts for payment.

Telephone
The phone companies do not have the same rule as gas and electricity companies – but they should only disconnect people as a last resort. Once again, contact them as soon as you think you may be struggling to pay the bill, and they will try to sort out some method of payment which you can manage.

Cutting your bill

It is worth shopping around to find the cheapest gas, electricity and telephone companies. There is now a greater quantity of different packages on offer than ever before. Real savings can be made if you choose the one that is right for you and your usage level. For example, some of the energy companies are offering packages with either no, or very low-standing, charges. These are good for people with low usage rates.

In the case of the telephone, if you use the phone very little or alternatively a good deal, you might also be able to reduce your phone bill. Ask the company for details of special schemes for low and high use. For example, BT has a Light User Scheme – designed for people who receive calls rather than make them. A rebate on your line rental is available (£12.72) if your call bill over the quarter is less than £10.81. Alternatively, if you make a lot of calls you can save money by joining BT's free Friends & Family scheme whereby you save 10 per cent on call charges to 10 numbers you nominate – call BT for details.

Look out for articles in *Which?* comparing company prices and for the new range of *Which?* factsheets that outline the latest information on the tariffs and services on offer.

Introducing energy saving measures into your home can also help you save money. All gas and electricity companies should provide advice on energy efficiency – each should run an advice phone line and publish a leaflet on the subject, and many will arrange for an expert adviser to visit your home at no charge to you. If you are receiving certain social security benefits, you may be able to get financial help with the costs of energy efficiency measures such as draught proofing and insulation. The Energy Action Grants Agency★ (which administers the Home Energy Efficiency Scheme), the various Care and Repair★ organisations and the Energy Savings Trust★ all provide advice and assistance.

If you only use a little water and yet live in a house with a high rateable value, you might be able to cut your water bill by asking for a water meter to be installed. From April 2000, meters can be installed free of charge: if you later change your mind, you should be able to revert to your original method of payment without charge. Your local water company should be able to advise you on whether switching to a water meter would make sense in your particular case.

Breakdowns

If your service is interrupted

In the case of gas, TransCo★ (previously British Gas) owns pipes and most meters, and can turn off your supply in order to do work, or if there is an emergency (if gas is leaking, for example). The company should give you ten days' notice that your supply will be turned off if it is going to carry out routine work on the pipeline and five days if it is going to work on meters, but in an emergency it can happen without warning. If the suspected leak (or other danger) is inside your home, TransCo can enter without your permission to stop the leak.

All utility companies have similar rules about the amount of notice they must give to customers for non-emergency stoppages. Members of care schemes may get special advance warning. If you are not given this notice then you are entitled to compensation: £20 if your electricity company did not give two days notice and £10 if your water company did not give 24 hours notice. If your supply is interrupted for more than 24 hours (or 48 hours for water, in some cases), you will also get compensation. You should get £10 for disruption of water supplies, and £40 if your electricity is discontinued – and the same amount again for each service every working day until the supply is restored (there is no standard figure for gas stoppages). Some water companies have now also agreed to pay out compensation in the event of drought-related supply restrictions.

If you need repairs done

All the utility companies should give a high priority to essential repair work for older people (as the telephone services should do if you are disabled and immobile). So, when you need the appliance repaired urgently, remind them that you are a retired person and explain your situation.

Visits by company staff

Checking out callers

With the exception of meter readers, staff will rarely call unannounced. If someone does call at your home saying they are from one of the utility companies, always ask to see their identity card. If you have poor sight you can agree a confidential password in advance that they will use whenever they call on you. Contact your company for details or to arrange a password. In the case of British Telecom, employees carry an identity card bearing their name and photograph which you can check by calling BT Security.*

Appointments

If someone from British Gas has made an appointment to see you and they do not turn up you are entitled to compensation of £11. Such compensation is not automatically available if your gas supplier is not British Gas. However, you could suggest that you be given this as best practice.

BT and all of the water and electricity companies must state whether your appointment is for the morning (usually defined as before 1pm) or the afternoon, and, in the case of the electricity companies, must give you a more precise appointment if you ask for one. If the company fails to keep an arranged appointment you are usually entitled to compensation: water companies must pay you £10, while an electricity company must pay you £20. BT's customer service guarantee scheme also allows you to claim compensation for delays in installation and repair, missed appointments and repeated loss of service.

Using gas safely

Carbon monoxide, a highly poisonous gas which kills about 40 people every year, can be produced by faulty, badly installed, or poorly maintained gas appliances. It is difficult to recognise because it has no colour, no smell and no taste and its symptoms (headaches, sickness and dizziness) are easily mis-diagnosed or ignored.

However, there are several simple steps that you can take to minimise the risks:

- When choosing a new appliance, ensure it has been tested for safety. If buying a second-hand appliance, make sure the dealer gives you a written guarantee and a copy of the user instructions.
- Always get a Council for Registered Gas Installers (CORGI)★ registered expert to install your appliance – never be tempted to do-it-yourself. When an appliance is fitted, ask where the ventilation is and never block it – if any additional building work is done on your home, ensure that this ventilation is not restricted.
- Ensure that your gas appliances and flues are checked and serviced regularly (see sections on 'The law on gas safety' and 'Servicing', below).
- Buy a carbon monoxide detector. There are a range of types currently available, but check that they meet the British Standard – for more advice contact your gas supplier or the Gas Consumers Council (GCC).★

The law on gas safety

If all the people living in your home are pensioners, disabled or chronically sick then you are entitled to a free annual safety check by a CORGI★ registered expert – contact your gas supplier and ask to be put on its gas care scheme.

If you are a tenant, then by law your landlord must have any gas appliances checked for safety at least once a year, and get any faults repaired by a CORGI★ registered gas installer.

Servicing your appliances

Even if you have had a gas safety check, you should still have gas appliances serviced regularly. Appliances such as central heating boilers, gas water-heaters and fires should be serviced every year. Always have your gas appliances installed, serviced and repaired by an expert (this is the law, not just good advice). Some of the new supply companies and British Gas offer gas appliance, central heating and boiler servicing as an optional extra when you sign up. These service contracts cost between £30 and £120 per annum, depending on the level of cover required and the company you are with. You can buy your servicing contract from any company, not necessarily one linked to your gas supplier. For details on servicing contact your gas supplier (British Gas Servicing in the case of British Gas customers) or any other CORGI★ registered installer.

If you smell gas

Turn off the gas at the mains straight away (the lever is usually near your meter – make sure you know where it is). Open doors and windows to let the gas out and then phone the TransCo★ emergency service. TransCo is responsible for making the installation safe and will undertake minor repairs that can be completed within half an hour (costing less than £4). A TransCo helpline★ gives details of CORGI★ registered installers who should be contacted for any further repair work.

If your gas appliances have to be turned off

If a gas engineer finds that one of your appliances is dangerous, by law he or she must disconnect it and you will not be able to use it again until it is made safe. However, if because of a breakdown in your supply you are left without heating, hot water or cooking, TransCo will sometimes be able to help – for example, by lending you an electric heater, kettle and so on.

Complaining

Complain if one of the utility companies does not deliver a decent service. They have all set up systems to deal with complaints from customers, and most publish leaflets to direct you to the right person.

Gas

For problems with gas supply or accounts, your first contact should be with the Customer Services department of your gas supplier, details of which are given on the back of your bill. If you are not happy with the way they handle your complaint or with the result, you can take your complaint to a watchdog. The Gas Consumers Council★ (GCC) is an independent body representing the interests of gas consumers. The address and phone number will be on the back of your gas bill. They are able to take up complaints about any gas matter, including disputes about bills, disconnection, broken appointments, repairs and service work. If the GCC cannot help you, they may involve OFGEM★, the gas and electricity regulator.

Electricity/water

If you are not happy with the service from your electricity or water company, contact the company's customer service team who will consider your complaint. If you are not satisfied with their response, contact the relevant watchdog: OFGEM★ for electricity (OFREG★ in Northern Ireland) or OFWAT★ for water (the DoE Water Service★ oversees the water industry in Northern Ireland and the Water Industry Commissioners in Scotland★ deals with complaints in Scotland). They too will accept complaints by phone, although they prefer complicated disputes to be set out in writing.

Telephone

If you have got a complaint about British Telecom, your first line of action should be to write to your local office, go to your local BT shop or call BT customer services.★ If you are then unhappy with the way your complaint has been handled, ask the Customer Services Manager to look into your complaint personally. Finally, if you feel that the complaint has not been dealt with to your complete satisfaction you can call BT's Complaints Review Service.★ If complaining to BT is getting you nowhere, go to OFTEL,★ the independent industry watchdog.

For queries or complaints about the services of any other phone company, call the company's Enquiries line. As with BT, if you remain dissatisfied once you have taken your complaint up formally with the company, you can contact OFTEL, who can try to help you resolve your complaint. However, note that they do not have powers to force companies to take a particular course of action.

Chapter 25

Getting around

This chapter covers car ownership in retirement, as well as other forms of transport. See also Chapter 27 for additional information about transport for less able-bodied people.

You and your car

In retirement your priorities as a car owner may alter, and couples who have had two cars in the past might now find the second unnecessary. If your local public transport is cheap and accessible, there may be no need for a car at all. At retirement your level of income may change, making a smaller, cheaper car more desirable. The type and frequency of car journeys you take may alter: previously, you may have spent much time driving on the motorway while you may make only brief local trips now. You are also likely to value different features in a car as you grow older: practicalities such as ease of getting in and out will become more important and reliability might be higher on your list of priorities, too.

If you are faced with paying for everything after giving up a company car, you should consider what you can afford if you have to budget carefully.

Annual running costs

To calculate the true cost of motoring, add up the following annual expenses:

- servicing and repairs
- fuel – divide annual mileage by average miles per litre, then multiply by the average price of a litre over the year

- annual depreciation – check car price guides
- road tax (Vehicle Excise Duty)
- insurance
- membership of a motoring/breakdown organisation
- any annual loan repayments.

Vehicle Excise Duty

From 1 June 1999 you will pay less road tax on a less powerful car – £100 a year if the engine size is 1100cc or less, rather then the full £155. From autumn 2000 a completely new system of graduated Vehicle Excise Duty rates will be introduced for new cars. The rate you pay will depend on your car's rate of carbon dioxide emission. You may want to bear this in mind when you next change your car.

Depreciation

If you intend to change cars every few years depreciation should figure significantly in your calculations, especially if you intend to buy new: thousands of pounds can be wiped off a new car in just a couple of years, but thereafter the decline slows dramatically. Depreciation is generally greatest on large cars. Details for all makes and models are given in car price guides available from newsagents. *Which? Car*, published every June, picks out the fast and slow depreciators.

You lose most money if you buy a new car and replace it every two or three years. It makes sound financial sense to buy a second-hand car over two years old and replace it every few years (cars have become far more reliable over recent years, so buying a used car need not be a risky proposition). However, if you choose a new car consider holding on to it for five years or so to absorb the impact of the initial depreciation.

Insurance

The good news is that insurance premiums generally go down as you get older. However, if you become disabled or have certain illnesses, some insurance companies will refuse to cover you or will ask for an inflated premium. This is by no means the case with all companies, so shop around to find the best price.

If you have been driving a company car you may encounter problems getting a no-claims discount equivalent to your driving record when you take out your own policy. A letter from the fleet manager should be evidence enough.

Many insurance companies ask for a medical certificate before renewing the policy every year after the age of 70 (or 73, or 75). Most of these rely on self-certification (you declare yourself to be fit to drive), but some require full certification based on a medical examination, for which the driver usually has to pay (doctors set their own fees for such certificates).

Rust is likely to become a potential problem once cars are over six years old. Most corrosion warranties are for six years, and the chance of rust increases after that time: 6 per cent of six-to-eight-year-old cars have some rust.

Buying a new car

Ready cash may increase your chances of obtaining a significant discount on the price of a new car – up to about 10 per cent or more – but even if you cannot pay cash you should still be able to get a discount if you shop around.

Buying a car can be time-consuming, especially if you are determined to get the best price, but a thorough approach can save you a lot of money, so it is worth putting in a bit of effort. Do some research before you start visiting dealers: be clear about what exactly you want, but it is best to be flexible about the exact model if you are offered a good deal. Adopt a firm line with dealers and state what you want from the outset. Don't pay for anything you are not happy with. *Always* take a test drive and make sure the demonstration model is of the same, or a similar, specification as the car you are considering. Note that some features, especially power steering, can radically alter the way a car drives.

You may get a good deal on special editions, ex-demonstration models and cancelled orders. Models about to be replaced may be offered at temptingly low prices, too. It may seem convenient to trade in your old car – first read price guides (available from newsagents) to determine its value and assess the discount on the new one. Though many companies have switched to all-inclusive prices, bear in mind additional costs such as delivery and number plates, which could add up to several hundred pounds.

If you qualify for the higher rate of the mobility component of the Disability Living Allowance or War Pensioners' Mobility Supplement you can use the Motability* car finance scheme. You hand over all or part of your allowance, plus (sometimes) a down-payment, to lease or buy the car. This can work out cheaper than buying conventionally. The Motability scheme can also be used for second-hand cars, for those cars with special controls and for powered wheelchairs.

Buying a second-hand car

Do all you can to establish that the car is what it seems: carry out as thorough an inspection as possible (or pay a mechanic or the AA* or RAC* to do one) and satisfy yourself that the documents are in order and that the seller is legally entitled to sell the vehicle. If the seller's name and address are not on the top of the registration document the car may not belong to them, or they could be a dealer posing as a private seller.

Check all MOT certificates carefully and ensure the mileage details and dates correspond – criminals can wind back a car's odometer to knock thousands of miles off the true figure, a practice known as 'clocking'. Inspect the car's Vehicle Identification Number (VIN) plates for signs of welding or tampering, which could indicate a stolen vehicle – there are usually two: one under the bonnet and one inside, often on the floor by the driver's seat.

If you are suspicious about a car contact AA Used Car Data Check or the HPI Register,* which holds details of cars with finance payments outstanding, stolen vehicles and insurance write-offs. A check costs about £30.00.

The sale price depends not only on the age and condition of the car, but also on where you buy it. The same vehicle will command a higher price if sold by a dealer rather than privately; prices are lowest at auctions. However, your legal comeback is reduced in the two cheaper markets. A private sale does not confer Sale of Goods Act rights, although the car must 'correspond with the description', and an auctioned car is sold 'as seen' – and that is on the basis of the briefest opportunity to inspect it. With a dealer you not only have full Sale of Goods Act rights but the car may be sold with a warranty.

Thinking about features

Options and extras

Most car manufacturers offer a range of features which make a car easier to operate. These may be optional extras or may be standard features on the more expensive models in a range. Traditionally the preserve of large luxury cars, these features are increasingly being offered on both smaller cars and less upmarket models.

- Automatic transmission, which, together with power steering, saves a lot of effort
- Power-assisted steering
- Central locking and electric windows
- Height-adjustable seats and steering wheels
- Adjustable seat height.

Smaller cars fitted with automatic transmission and power-assisted steering (among the few optional extras that do not depreciate) are always in demand by used-car buyers, and tend to hold their value well.

Design features

Cars vary quite considerably in their design specifications. When retired, you may want to take into account a new set of considerations: how easy is it to get in and out of the car? Is there adequate leg room? Are the driving position, seat height and seat belts comfortable? These are factors that may be significant over the course of a long journey. To evaluate a prospective purchase from this point of view, use the checklist below.

For **access** take note of:

- shape of door catch and effort needed to operate it
- door height, width and ease of opening/closing
- height of door sill
- height of seat off ground
- obstruction by steering wheel.

For **comfort** and **ease of use** assess:

- distance from driving seat to pedals, height of pedals off floor and pedal spacing

- movement and effort needed to shift gears
- shape and position of handbrake and effort needed to use it
- configuration of dashboard and controls
- access to ignition.

For **ease of using the boot or hatch** look at:

- size and height of boot aperture
- effort to open or close boot or hatch.

Remember when buying a car not to rely on an appraisal of design features alone. *Always* take a test drive. RICA★ publishes detailed information on a range of cars for elderly and disabled people, while the Mobility Advice and Vehicle Information Service (MAVIS)★ can advise on car choice and adaptations.

Your driving licence

The Driver and Vehicle Licensing Agency (DVLA)★ will normally send you a reminder to renew your licence about three months before it expires on your 70th birthday. All licences issued by the DVLA are now in a photocard format with a separate paper counterpart showing additional information, for example endorsements. If you do not have a photocard driving licence you will be sent a separate application form (D750) with your reminder.

If you do not receive a renewal reminder form (because you have moved, say) you may apply to renew your licence by completing form D1, available (like form D750) from post offices.

After you reach 70, you must renew your licence every three years. You must declare any physical or mental conditions which may affect your ability to drive safely. These are listed on application forms and on form D100 (available from post offices).

The DVLA may ask you to complete a medical questionnaire and give consent for them to obtain a report from your GP. Depending on the information you give on the questionnaire, they may require you to be examined by a local medical officer. The report is paid for by the DVLA, but you will have to pay any travelling expenses.

It is possible that you will then be issued with a medically restricted licence. The medical restriction might be in terms of time, for example a licence issued for only one or two years where a disability is progressive, or restricted to a type of vehicle, such as a car with modified controls.

Fit to drive?

Danger signs

Be objective about your capabilities and suit your driving to your skills. While experience counts for a lot, the physical and mental effects of ageing bring with them a higher risk of accidents. Eyesight steadily declines from about the age of 50, starting with longsightedness and involving loss of contrast sensitivity, less ability to adapt to the dark and tendency to suffer more from glare. Stiffness in the neck and back leads to difficulty looking around properly.

Reaction times also become slower as you get older and you become more prone to fatigue, which reduces concentration and slows reflexes further. Older people find it harder to make judgements in fast-moving traffic and to assess other vehicles' speeds. Confusion over complicated junctions and signs is also more likely.

As your driving abilities decline, plan ahead for the future, first looking to have a car you can operate easily, and later considering the options if you finally have to give up driving. For more information see the 'Getting around' section of Chapter 27.

Sensible driving

You can take a refresher lesson with a driving instructor who will give you a general impression of your driving and offer some useful tips. The Institute of Advanced Motorists★ offers members a reassessment drive – essentially the same as an advanced driving test but without a pass or fail at the end. The Royal Society for the Prevention of Accidents★ also offers a graded test (which needs regular updating) that gives you a guide to your competence. The AA★ publishes a leaflet giving advice for older drivers, which offers plenty of useful tips. Assessment centres around the country can advise you on your ability to drive and the type of equipment that might help you (services and charges vary). A free guide to the centres is available from the Mobility Advice and Vehicle Information Service (MAVIS)★.

Staying behind the wheel

Simple conversions and add-on features such as extra-wide mirrors and easy-release levers for the handbrake, as well as manufacturers' options such as automatic transmission and power-assisted steering can make driving possible for years after it becomes difficult to operate a conventionally equipped car.

The Mobility Advice and Vehicle Information Service (MAVIS)*, run by the Department of the Environment, Transport and the Regions, along with other assessment centres, can give free advice to any older driver worried about continuing to drive. They can give details of mobility centres where you can have your abilities expertly assessed and try out a range of car adaptations.

Orange/blue badge scheme

If you cannot walk or you have extreme difficulty walking you should be able to get an orange badge from the social services department of your local council (Regional and Island Councils in Scotland, DoE Roads Services Division in Northern Ireland). A new Europe-wide parking badge scheme has been introduced, and if you qualify you will now receive a 'blue' badge; the existing orange badges will gradually be replaced by blue badges as they come up for renewal.

For both schemes, you need a medical certificate that describes the nature of your disability and makes it clear that the disability severely limits mobility. The badge can be displayed on any car you travel in, whether you are the driver or a passenger. You are entitled to park for up to three hours on single and double yellow lines (except in some parts of central London), and without a time limit in Scotland. You can also park free of charge for any length of time at street parking meters and places where other cars can park only for a limited period.

Other forms of transport

Air travel

A few airlines offer reduced fares for retired people, so check with your travel agent or airline to see what is available. However, do not leap to the conclusion that these are necessarily the cheapest fares to be had. Provided you book in advance there are a number of cheap tickets you can buy, notably the Advanced Purchase Excursion fares (Apex and so on). Most of these cheap fares have certain conditions attached, which may involve travelling on particular days or within a set period, for example. They may offer no refund at all in case of cancellation.

Because of the strictures that are imposed on such tickets, it is imperative that you take out insurance to cover yourself against the risk of failing to travel on the appointed date.

The discounted fares that are advertised in newspapers are another source of cheap flights. These can be extremely good value, but you should take a cautious approach and adopt the following precautions:

- Check on the airline that will be carrying you. The fewer planes an airline has the longer a delay is likely to be.
- Don't pay the whole fare until you have received the ticket – just pay a small deposit and use a credit card if possible so that you are covered by the Consumer Credit Act.
- Check with the airline's reservation office that your booking is secure and do the same for your return journey as soon as you reach your destination.
- Check on the restrictions on the ticket and if you are not able to change flights take out insurance to cover yourself against an alteration of plans.

Rail travel

A Senior Railcard costs £18 a year for those over 60. Get an application form from any staffed station or rail-appointed travel agent. The Senior Railcard gives you a one-third discount on First Class and Standard fares (this excludes peak-hour journeys made wholly within London and the south-east on weekday mornings). Reductions are also available on some additional fares: see your station or travel agent for details.

If you have a Senior Railcard you can also buy a Rail Europe Senior Card for £5 which will give you a discount, usually of about 30 per cent, on rail and sea travel throughout most of Europe. You can get details from some mainline stations, travel agents or Rail Europe.*

Coach travel

Coach travel is usually cheaper than rail travel, but journey times tend to be longer and seating less spacious than on most trains. However, many coaches now have washrooms, toilets and refreshments on board.

The biggest coach company is National Express (known in Scotland as Caledonian Express), while many independent coach operators cover smaller networks: see your travel agent for details. You can reserve a seat on a particular coach if necessary. Seats tend to be cheaper midweek, and you can get reductions of approximately one-third on the price if you have a coachcard (£8 for one year or £19 for three years).

Bus travel

The concessions available to people travelling by bus vary from area to area and are generally the responsibility of the local authority. Senior citizens are nearly always eligible for a reduction, and there may be separate schemes for disabled people. Local bus operators may also have their own schemes for bus passes, and there may be local schemes for passengers with limited mobility. Contact your local transport authority for details of what is available.

Taxis

If you don't use your car much, using taxis may actually cost you less than maintaining your own vehicle. In Greater London, if you have difficulty using public transport, you may qualify for a special taxicard to cut the cost. Contact the taxicard section of the London Mobility Unit.★ Other local authorities may run 'Dial-a-ride' or similar schemes: contact the transport planning or social services department of your local authority.

Powered wheelchairs, scooters and buggies

A powered wheelchair may help you get around locally. A useful guide to choosing one is available for £2.75 from the Research Institute for Consumer Affairs★ (RICA).

Chapter 26

Holidays

Types of holiday

Tour operators

Nowadays, packages for the over-55s include adventures to exotic worldwide locations as well as more restful holidays. Certain operators also run packages especially for the retired holidaymaker, such as British university and college study breaks, singles festivals, dancing holidays, cruises, wildlife tours, religious tours, garden tours and walking tours, wedding anniversary breaks and winter sun holidays of six months' duration.

The Holiday Care Service* can give useful advice on holidays for disabled people and people with limited mobility.

Touring holidays in Britain

Bed-and-breakfasting can be one of the cheapest types of holiday as well as the most varied. But don't rule out staying in hotels. Consumers' Association* publishes both *The Good Bed and Breakfast Guide* and *The Which? Hotel Guide*, with details of over 1,000 establishments in each Guide.

Self-catering

You should be able to find holiday self-catering accommodation in pretty well any part of Britain you wish to visit. Several companies offer a range of accommodation from the simple and comparatively inexpensive to luxury homes sleeping six to eight – a good option

---

TIPS

- You are likely to get bigger discounts if you make your booking on the day. Hotels often offer weekend deals.
- Pick your season – there are fewer bargains in the busy summer season or at Easter.
- The Scottish, Wales and Northern Ireland Tourist Boards* publish free booklets listing short break rates at hotels in the UK. They can also send details of operators offering discounted package breaks. Guides from the English Tourism Council* are on sale in bookshops.

---

for a family holiday with grandchildren. Many have been checked by the relevant tourist authority and given an appropriate grading. The best place to look is in the classified columns of the Sunday papers, where you should find advertisements placed by companies and by cottage owners themselves.

Self-catering abroad can be booked through most of the major holiday firms and can also be arranged privately. France offers a particularly wide choice in holiday homes, especially among gîtes – rural properties which range from converted barns to grander accommodation. The owner generally lives nearby and will usually help with advice on local services – but not necessarily in English. Various tour operators offer gîte holidays.

Retreats

A retreat can enable you to spend time in quietness and contemplation. For details of over 200 retreat houses in Britain and Ireland, apply to the National Retreat Association.*

Farm holidays

Farm holidays are increasingly popular; you can go as a paying guest in the farmhouse itself or rent a caravan or cottage. Bed-and-breakfast rates are usually good value, and some farms will provide an evening meal as well.

For a choice of over 1,000 farms that have all been inspected by the tourist authorities, buy *The Farm Holiday Bureau Guide: Stay on a Farm* from bookshops, tourist information centres or the Farm Holiday Bureau UK Ltd.*

Caravanning

Caravanning is an ideal way of touring without having to worry about what the accommodation at your destination will be like. The Camping and Caravanning Club★ offers family membership for £27.50 plus a £4 joining fee (the latter waived if you join by direct debit or credit card), and members over the age of 60 qualify for a 20 per cent discount on site fees.

The Club offers insurance and a foreign touring service, and each new member's pack contains a touring safety guide with advice for beginners. You can also obtain a listing of hire companies for caravans, motor caravans and extendable caravans – these are ideal for retired people as they are lightweight and have less wind drag, making them easier to transport. An annual guide called *Your Place in the Country* lists 91 full-facility club sites all over Britain, while the two-yearly *Big Sites Book* contains details of 4,000 sites, 2,000 of which are certificated – that is, they are small sites where only CCC members can go.

Timesharing

The activities of some salespeople have given timesharing a very bad name. The basic idea of timesharing is that you buy the use of a certain property, often abroad, for a certain period at a certain time of year. If you do not wish to use that time yourself you can lend it to friends, sub-let it or swap it for time at another timeshare property elsewhere and, if you have bought the timeshare in perpetuity, you simply leave it to someone in your will as you would any other property. Timeshare should not be regarded as an investment – resale prices can be as little as 40 per cent of the original price and you still have to pay for flights, food and maintenance fees, as well as exchange fees if you want to swap. Do your sums very carefully – you might be better off with package holidays.

Depending on location and period, a timeshare will cost from four to five figures to buy. The second-hand value of most timeshares is far less than new, so consider buying from a reputable resale agency. But however you buy, do your homework and make sure you know the resort into which you are buying. The maintenance charges should be checked very carefully to see exactly what they represent and whether they are linked with a cost of living index. You should also make careful enquiries as to the resale value of the property, which may be a good deal lower than the initial purchase price; also note that it can be very difficult to resell a timeshare property. In some countries you might become liable for direct taxation as a timeshare owner, so this is another area to investigate.

Within the European Union, timeshare resorts must conform to rules laid down by an EC directive on timeshare. The Directive requires prospective purchasers to be given specified information, regulates the contents of the contract, and gives consumers the right to cancel within a minimum cooling-off period of 10 days, during which no deposit may be demanded by the seller. There is also the UK Timeshare Act 1992, which gives you a 14-day cooling-off period.

Be particularly careful if you sign a contract outside the UK as you are unlikely to be protected by UK law. If you run into problems, you may have to go to a foreign court which could cost you a lot of money and trouble.

You should resist the sort of presentations that are attached to offers of lavish prizes and free holidays, even in Britain, and avoid signing any contract until you have had it checked by a solicitor. Never produce your credit card to a sales person as identification – you could come under heavy pressure to use it to put down a deposit. The trick is to resist all blandishments, pressure and promises and consider the purchase as coolly as you would with any other large item.

A checklist of points to consider when buying a timeshare, called *The Timeshare Guide*, can be obtained from the Department of Trade and Industry.* Many reputable timeshare companies belong or are affiliated to one of two exchange organisations: Interval International Ltd* and RCI Europe Ltd,* which give access to holiday resorts in nearly 100 countries and offer short breaks, cruises and coach tours. The Office of Fair Trading* has produced a report on the industry which can be obtained free of charge by application in writing. The trade organisation for timeshare developers, exchange organisations, resale companies and so on is the Organisation for Timeshare in Europe*. This organisation offers a free advice and conciliation service to anybody who has dealings with its members.

Holiday peace of mind

No matter what sort of holiday you are planning, there are certain basic guidelines to follow in order to be prepared for all eventualities.

Money

Never carry more cash with you than you need – and do not be lulled by a holiday atmosphere into being more careless than you would be at home. Do not carry your wallet, passport or indeed anything else of value in your back pocket and never leave your money on display. Carry a shoulder bag across your body, or preferably wear a money belt under your top layer of clothing. Leave jewellery at home or, if you must take it, in the hotel safe or tucked away in your rented accommodation.

If you are unfortunate enough to meet with a mugger, do not play the hero – hand over your money without argument. Pack a copy of your insurance policy in your hand luggage so that you can check the procedure if necessary, and keep a list of emergency phone numbers to ring in the event of theft.

Insurance

It is advisable to take out comprehensive insurance appropriate to your needs. Tour operators often insist on insurance as a condition of booking, but note that you do not have to take out the insurance package they offer; you may well be able to find a cheaper one elsewhere that will give you satisfactory cover. However, if you are travelling independently you may not be entitled to compensation for mishaps tours operators could be considered liable for. Note that a few companies increase their premiums for people over 65, though you should be able to shop around for reasonable rates.

Read the small print carefully and ensure you will be covered for the following eventualities:

- loss of your deposit or cancellation of the entire holiday
- the cost of curtailing or cancelling your holiday in the event of serious illness or death in your family
- loss of money, baggage and personal effects
- the cost of emergency purchases if your baggage is delayed

- personal liability cover in case you cause injury to another person or damage to property
- compensation for any inconvenience caused by transport cancellations or delays
- medical treatment, hospitalisation, ambulance service, emergency dental treatment, special transport home, the cost of prolonging your stay and that of a companion who may have to stay with you.

In the personal liability and medical categories the sums become astronomical: allow £1,000,000 for the former (but £2,000,000 in the USA), and £500,000 inside Europe and £1,000,000 for the rest of the world for the latter.

Paying for at least part of your holiday by credit card could provide some medical cover while you are travelling (but not during your stay). This should not be considered as an alternative to medical insurance. If things go wrong, under the Consumer Credit Act you should be able to claim from the credit card company as well as the tour operator (though you will get money only from one). But your holiday must cost more than £100 per person; the credit card slip should be made out to the operator, not the travel agent; and note that debit cards, charge cards and most gold cards do not offer this protection.

Peace of mind while you are away

The Home Office has published a leaflet, *Peace of mind while you're away*, giving advice on preventing burglaries while you are on holiday. Free copies are available from police stations.

Health

For travellers abroad, the Department of Health★ issues a useful leaflet called *Health Advice for Travellers* (T5), which gives advice on precautions to take and how to cope in an emergency. This leaflet also contains form E111, which entitles you to free or reduced-cost emergency treatment in EU countries. You must take this to a post office for processing. However, it is still advisable to take out insurance that will cover medical expenses (see above).

Get medical advice well in advance of your trip, as some courses of vaccinations need to be given over a few months. These are usually cheapest from a GP. Alternatively, try a British Airways Travel Clinic.* These clinics provide advice, immunisations and a range of first-aid and preventive equipment, such as needle and syringe packs and water purifiers.

The Medical Advisory Service for Travellers Abroad (MASTA)* gives information on immunisation, malaria medication and the latest health advice on journeying abroad. If you telephone the organisation and give details of your trip you will receive a printed health brief. MASTA also supplies a range of goods, such as mosquito nets and repellents, water purifiers and sterile packs of syringes and dressings.

Do not forget to pack any medication that you take regularly. Make sure that it is clearly labelled with both the trade name and generic name, and find out if there are any restrictions on taking it in or out of the UK or the country you are visiting; a back-up letter from your doctor may be useful.

In addition, take a simple first-aid kit with you. If you are going to a hot climate, use plenty of high-protection sun screen – and beware of ice-cream, seafoods, salads, fruit (unless you can peel it yourself) and water (which also means ice). Avoid buffets laid out at room temperature – go for foods from the menu that have to be freshly cooked.

When travelling by air, wear loose-fitting clothes, drink plenty of liquid and remember that alcohol consumed in the air has much more effect than it does on the ground. Allow a couple of days for resting and acclimatisation when you arrive.

Complaints about holidays

The following information covers holidays arranged by a tour operator.

Always try to get problems sorted out on the spot. Speak to the tour rep if there is one. Otherwise, try the manager of your accommodation and the tour operator's office locally or in the UK. Complete a complaint questionnaire while still in the resort. If you still aren't satisfied, take it up with the tour operator within 28 days of your return. Collect names and addresses of witnesses or people who have suffered similar problems, and take photographs if appropriate.

Write to the tour operator as soon as possible. Tell them what went wrong, how it reduced the value of your holiday, and state what sort of response you are expecting. If you are looking for compensation, put a figure on this. The amount will depend on your situation, but here are the three main elements to consider:

- The difference between what you paid for and what you got (for example, the cost of the three-star hotel you booked compared with the two-star hotel you were moved to). If only certain days of your holiday were affected, you should claim just for that proportion.
- Loss of enjoyment, disappointment, inconvenience etc. Take into account what your holiday cost and how much of it was affected.
- Out-of-pocket expenses (for example, the cost of eating out if you are not given an adequate means to cook on a 'self-catering' holiday).

Only in extreme cases are you likely to recover the full cost, but in many cases you should be awarded compensation for loss of enjoyment, plus reimbursement of extra costs incurred.

If you are not happy with the operator's response, write back stating why. If they make an offer you think is too low, keep any cheque they send (but do not cash it) and continue the correspondence until you get a more satisfactory outcome.

If an exchange of letters does not get you what you want, consider other ways of settling the dispute.

The small claims procedure was designed to be a fairly quick, straightforward and cheap alternative to the full county court. It is kept informal and you can argue your case in person without having to use a lawyer. It can be used for claims up to £5,000 in England and Wales. The limit on small claims is £750 in Scotland and £1,000 in Northern Ireland, but both these limits are currently under review. These limits apply to the total claim, not each individual's – if, say, you were claiming for a ruined family holiday.

If your tour operator belongs to ABTA,* you can use the independent arbitration scheme operated by the Chartered Institute of Arbitrators.* It relies totally on written evidence. You must apply within nine months of your return from holiday, and the decision is binding on both parties, so you can't go to the small claims court

later if you do not like the decision. The Association of
Independent Tour Operators (AITO)★ also has a scheme for settling customers' disputes with its members, run by an independent
mediator.

You can also join Which? Personal Service,★ which offers individual help and expert advice if something goes wrong with goods
and services you've bought, including holidays.

Chapter 27

Caring for elderly parents

While retirement can bring the bonuses of more leisure and, one hopes, sufficient income to enjoy it, problems may be lurking in the wings. Very many people in middle age find that their parents (or other relatives) increasingly need help as their health and strength diminish. Sometimes this can happen suddenly as illness strikes or one parent dies, leaving the other unable to cope. At worst the situation may arise when, for example, you yourself have family worries, expenses with older children, a difficult menopause or other health problems.

Although it would be misguided to try to cross all the bridges before coming to them, a certain amount of forward-planning would be prudent, and could save time, money and problems later on, whether you are already a carer or suspect that you might one day become one.

Taking decisions

You and your partner should decide how much time you could devote to looking after elderly relatives if the need arose. It may be that you are working and will be for some time to come, or you may have to take into account your own health and ability to cope with any stress that might occur as a consequence of becoming a carer. The temptation to try to 'take over' your parents' lives may be difficult to resist, but as far as possible the decisions should be theirs.

Which home?

If your parents are considering moving, discuss with them in some detail where they might go, whether it is to be nearer to you or not.

This decision, at least, should certainly involve you even if they are still very active.

The availability of local social services and of public transport, the helpfulness of neighbours, ease of access to doctor, dentist and shops, and aspects such as whether hills have to be climbed regularly all need to be considered, particularly if your parents will not be living near you.

If your parents move in order to be closer to you, your involvement will clearly become more immediate and you will need to consider your commitment carefully. If one parent is widowed there will be a particular need to keep an eye on the survivor, if he or she is determined to stay on at home. But even if your parents are still together, you will probably find an increasing amount of time will be spent visiting them and lending a hand. Unless there is a big job that requires your assistance, frequent short visits are probably best if they live nearby – and of course, they will most likely be able to help you.

Staying put

Many elderly people are anxious to remain in their own homes, particularly if they have lived there for a long time, know the district and have friendly neighbours, a sympathetic doctor, and so on. But with increasing age and frailty it is important to help them make the right provisions for doing so. It is surprising how much *can* be arranged if necessary. See the section on 'General safety and convenience' later in this chapter.

Some areas have home improvement agencies, run by voluntary organisations, housing associations or the local authority. They give advice and practical help, particularly to elderly and disabled people, on house repairs, improvements and adaptations. This can include small jobs, such as putting in a handrail, to having the house surveyed, applying for grants and loans to fund improvements, and finding and overseeing a reliable builder.

There are around 250 agencies across the UK. Contact their national organisations for addresses: Care & Repair (England),★ Scottish Homes (Scotland),★ Care and Repair Cymru (Wales)★ and Care and Repair Northern Ireland.★ The Anchor Trust★ also offers information and leaflets. RICA★ has produced a booklet called *Adapting Your Home* with information on equipment and tips to make a home easier to live in (for a free copy, send a large s.a.e.). For details of grants available for home improvements see 'Living under the same roof', below.

Various financial schemes designed to help people stay in their own homes exist. Help the Aged* has a 'Gifted Housing Plan', for example, which allows you to donate your home to them while continuing to live there. The charity is responsible for the maintenance of the property during your lifetime. More information is available through Help the Aged Housing Division;* and see also Chapter 20.

Another option may be to raise money on the home to provide an annuity or capital, while the owner continues living in it. Equity release or home reversion schemes might be considered, but it is essential to take good legal and financial advice before making any commitment; for more details see Chapter 5.

Age Concern* publishes a book *Using your home as capital 1999–2000: A guide to raising cash from the value of your home* (£4.99 inc postage and packing).

Living under the same roof

It may be that you are considering whether your elderly parent(s) would be better living with your family – or whether you should move to their home. This should be a family decision taken jointly after a long, hard look at all the options.

An existing house could be extended: one of the provisos for successful integration between different generations is plenty of living space, so they can be independent from one another while having, say, an alarm bell installed in case of need. This option depends on the financial situation – perhaps on parents being willing and able to put their own money into it – and on planning permission being obtainable. Building on an extension could improve the value of the house; it could be designed for maximum convenience, taking into account any existing or possible future disabilities. You might wish to investigate the possibility of grants for such work: the Department of the Environment, Transport and Regions* produces a booklet (No. 96HC202/C) called *House Renovation Grants*, or ask your local authority housing department for up-to-date information about grants including renovation grants, Home Repair Assistance (not means-tested if you are adapting your home for an elderly person to live with you) and Disabled Facilities Grants. The Age Concern★ factsheet No. 13 *Older Home Owners: Financial Help with Repairs and Adaptations* may also be of use (it covers home improvements too).

It could be worth pooling resources – money from your own house and that of your parents – to buy a bigger property with amenities to suit everyone. Or, if your parents live in a big house and the area is convenient for jobs, schools and so on, discuss with them whether you might move in there after a certain amount of conversion.

If accommodation is tight, the situation can be that much more difficult. You may be in a position where you feel you have to offer a home to a widowed mother or father and it can produce poor reactions from the rest of your family. Not only might there be physical considerations to cause resentment – children having to share a room, for example, when they have been used to their own space – but emotional ones, too. For example, the 'generation gap' could lead to your children and their friends being openly criticised for behaviour the elderly consider inappropriate.

Parents moving in with you should bring some of their own furniture, especially the bed. Any small possessions which also mean 'home' should also be included, and an electric kettle and ring would enable them to make a snack or drinks without always having to use the main kitchen (make sure that these are safely sited to eliminate the risk of scalds and burns and that a fire blanket is readily available).

No one of any age likes to feel useless, so encourage parents to contribute – perhaps helping to prepare meals or doing some gardening or shopping. It is a good idea to involve them – to boost their morale, and as a help to you to set against the extra work of having another family member living with you.

Sheltered or retirement housing

Sheltered housing, sometimes called retirement housing, usually consists of a group of self-contained bungalows or flats where elderly people who are still active can live independently, yet the development is under the care of a warden who keeps an eye on the properties, any communal rooms and the welfare of the residents. This is particularly reassuring if your parents live some distance from you. The housing department of the local authority or Age Concern* should be able to provide appropriate addresses and information on the requirements which have to be met in order to qualify for their schemes, as well as details of costs, etc. (Age Concern Factsheet No 10 *Local authority charging procedures for residential and nursing home care* is useful.)

In the private sector, many private companies and some housing associations and councils build sheltered houses or flats for sale. There is a service charge to cover the cost of a warden and maintenance. Further information can be obtained from Age Concern's free factsheet No. 2 *Retirement Housing for Sale* or its book *A Buyer's Guide to Retirement Housing* (£4.95 including postage and packing). Or contact the Anchor Trust,* the Elderly Accommodation Counsel (EAC),* the New Homes Marketing Board* or Retirement Home Specialists.* See also Chapter 20.

Another option, if the developer agrees, is to buy a 'life share' in a sheltered housing scheme – that is, the purchaser buys sheltered housing at a percentage of the asking price and lives in it for life, after which the entire value of the property reverts to the finance company putting up the money. This option requires good legal advice. Some councils and housing associations provide shared ownership schemes in which you buy a proportion of the property's value – normally 25 per cent, 50 per cent or 75 per cent. You usually pay rent on the remainder. To find out if there are any schemes in your area you should contact your local council, local housing association or the Elderly Accommodation Counsel*.

Abbeyfield very sheltered care houses are another possible choice nationwide. These accommodate up to ten older people in individual bed-sitting rooms with their own furniture; residents have a great degree of independence. The aim is to create a happy family atmosphere with some meals taken communally but also with plenty of privacy, overseen by a housekeeper. Although Abbeyfield houses are normally for active people, there are now some registered care schemes which cater for the more frail. More details are available from the Abbeyfield Society.* With charitable housing associations often offering a licensee arrangement, any proposed contract should be carefully checked by a solicitor, particularly with regard to security of tenure, so that your parent fully understands his or her rights as well as those of the housing association.

Residential and nursing homes

There may come a point where a parent needs so much help and supervision that you have to consider giving up work or placing him or her in residential care. This is an extremely difficult decision. The carer may enjoy working and while doing so, be able to make a significant financial contribution – to exchange this for the confining task of nursing an elderly person is not a decision to be taken lightly. It could be a bad option not only for the carer, but for the person being cared for.

Very often in such a situation it is a good idea to involve someone outside the family to help and advise. A talk with a social worker or someone at Age Concern★ or from a local branch of the Carers National Association★ could help in the formulation of a decision acceptable to everyone. It might, indeed, be better for all concerned, not least the elderly person, if he or she went into residential care close by, if a suitable place were available and financially viable, where visits and outings with the family could be frequent. However, this may not always be acceptable, certainly at first, by the person who has to make the move.

Charities such as Age Concern,★ the Elderly Accommodation Counsel★ and some private organisations offer useful leaflets and advice on choosing a home and financing a place, or you could consult the local authority housing department or the social services for information about homes in the area. The local telephone directory gives a list of local homes under 'Social Services – Homes for Adults'. Or try the Community Health Council for information (address in the phone book). Age Concern's factsheet No.29 *Finding Residential and Nursing Home Accommodation* is helpful (Age Concern also publishes a book, *Finding and paying for residential and nursing home care* (£6.99)). Voluntary organisations such as the Salvation Army also run homes; more information is available from the *Charities Digest*, which you should be able to consult at a local library. See also Chapter 9 on financial help for people living in a residential care home or a nursing home.

Look round several residential homes and try to take your parent to visit when you have narrowed down the selection. He or she may have to wait for a vacancy at the homes they like best, but also note that both private and voluntary residential homes can choose to whom they offer accommodation.

Everyone will have their own priorities, but points to note are:

- Situation – is the home within safe and easy walking distance of shops, post office, doctor's surgery, bank, library, etc?
- Are there any hills to climb en route and is the site level? Is it in a pleasant area with not too much noise from main road, factories, etc?
- Is public transport readily available? How frequent are the services and where do they go? Is there a concession for elderly people on local transport and what are the fares?
- Do the other residents seem congenial and reasonably active? Is it a mixed-sex home (these can often have a better atmosphere)?
- Are the staff pleasant and what is the quality of the catering?
- Are outings and other social activities arranged?
- Are pets allowed, and can residents bring some of their own possessions?
- Is there a guest room, and can visitors obtain meals? What is the cost? How available is the room?
- Is the home near enough for your parent's own doctor to visit?
- Are shop mobility schemes available? (See 'Getting around', on pages 363–5.)

If your parent is very frail or disabled, a move to a nursing home will probably be necessary as residential homes normally cater for reasonably active clients. Try to talk to some of the residents privately; look at the lavatories and kitchens; find out how regimented the home is: do the residents have to get up and go to bed at particular times?

General safety and convenience

Whether your parent lives with you or on his or her own, look together at safety precautions and general convenience. The tidier a house can be kept the safer and more convenient it will be.

- Could a change be made from a coal fire to gas or electric central heating? (Budget schemes are available for paying installation and running costs.)
- Special care should be taken with gas appliances, open fires and the guarding of cookers and kettles.

- Bathing or showering should be made as easy as possible, with grab rails and aids for getting in and out (the social services can advise on and fit these).

- Install a smoke alarm to alert your parent in case of fire (obtainable quite cheaply from DIY shops) and make sure the batteries are checked regularly.

- Ensure that there are non-slip backings on any mats or rugs (the fewer the better), adequate lighting on stairs and landings, and a fire extinguisher or safety blanket ready to hand.

- Adequate locks on doors and windows, a door peep-hole and/or some form of alarm (see below) could provide reassurance (always assuming that the locks can be easily undone in the case of fire) See Chapter 22.

RICA★ has produced a free booklet called *Equipment for an Easier Life* (send a large s.a.e.).

The police are always ready to help with advice on security, perhaps via a home visit – contact the crime prevention officer at the local police station. It may be possible to get financial assistance to help with the cost of door and window locks, door chains and so on once a need has been identified: get in touch with the housing department of the local council. Age Concern★ and Help the Aged★ also give advice and offer leaflets on security problems. Generally useful are Help the Aged's leaflet *Security in Your Home* and Age Concern's factsheet No. 33 *Crime prevention for older people*. For more on home security see Chapter 22.

An elderly person living alone is likely to welcome a community (or social) alarm system as a means of getting help quickly and easily whenever it is needed. Many local councils run schemes, usually through their housing or social services departments, for both council tenants and home owners. The user needs to wear a small pushbutton on a neckcord or wristband, or clipped to clothing. When pressed this sends a radio signal to a unit (plugged into the mains and a modern telephone socket), which then automatically dials out to programmed telephone numbers. With council schemes, the call will go through to a 24-hour communication centre where, depending on the service offered, the operator will try to speak to the user through the system (most of the units have loudspeakers built in). If the user needs someone to go to him or her, the operator will send one of the scheme's staff or will contact the user's local friends or relatives. Some councils will take on people who live outside their area and have bought a compatible alarm.

Most councils charge for the service and have eligibility rules, but if your parent is, say, 75 and lives alone, he or she is very likely to qualify if there is a scheme in the area. If not, there are other options. Housing association and commercial schemes operate in a similar way to that of councils. Alternatively, you can buy alarms that can be programmed to dial friends' numbers direct.

Which? (March 1997) has a report on 13 different alarm systems. The results are given in more detail – along with advice about obtaining and using systems – in *Guide to Community Alarms*, a booklet available from RICA★ (£2.75). The Information Department of the Disabled Living Foundation★ can also advise.

Financial and legal matters

Your parent may appreciate help and advice from you about his or her financial affairs. The first step is to see exactly what money is available. See Part 2: Your finances in retirement earlier in the book to help you work out your parent's situation in terms of pension and tax. He or she may be entitled to the higher tax allowances for older people whose incomes are less than a certain amount – the 'age-related allowance' – see Chapter 15. Other tax allowances may also apply. *The Which? Guide to Money* also contains a useful section on 'Your Finances in later life'. When your parent has listed current expenditure on food, heating, clothes, repairs and so on, prepare a budget together, writing down and totalling basic expenses and seeing how much is left over for other items such as holidays, newspapers, TV and video rental.

Certain benefits may be claimable, such as disability living allowance; if your parent is reluctant to apply, thinking of financial aid from, say, the DSS as 'charity', you will have to be persuasive that he or she has a right to receive it. Age Concern★ produces *Your Rights: A Guide to Money Benefits for Older People* (£4.25), a booklet that lists all the welfare benefits to which elderly people are entitled. Also see leaflets FB 2 *Which Benefit* – this contains a useful summary of all the social security benefits – and FB 31 *Caring for someone?*, which gives details of benefits for carers. Both are available from social security offices and post offices. The Citizens Advice Bureau, too, can advise on money matters.

Power of attorney?

You might like to think about taking out an 'enduring power of attorney' so that you would be able to manage your parent's financial affairs and property in the event of his or her becoming mentally incapable of doing so. Although a sensible measure, this may be psychologically unacceptable to your parent, who may still feel in full control. However, it may be an acceptable solution, at least for a time, to enter into an arrangement where cheques are signed jointly and your parent does not therefore need to feel so threatened by the idea of being 'taken over'. The deed must be drawn up while your parent can still understand the implications, and it can be modified, if preferred, to take effect only if and when he or she can no longer cope. You can obtain more detailed information from the Public Trust Office, Protection Division,★ or the Supreme Court in Scotland.★

Wills

It is also advisable to ensure that your parent has made a will. You may feel reluctant to bring up the subject, but many elderly people feel easier in their minds when a will has been made and they know that their property will be disposed of according to their wishes. Once done, the matter can then be forgotten until the will is needed. See Chapter 32 for more information.

Getting around

Different cities, authorities and voluntary bodies offer their own individual schemes for elderly people who require help to get about because they are disabled or have no means of transport, so get in touch with an organisation such as Age Concern★ or a local DIAL UK★ to see what is available in your parent's particular area.

Short distances
* *Door to Door: A Guide to Transport for Disabled People* is produced by the Royal Association for Disability and Rehabilitation

(RADAR)* (price £8.00). It covers all forms of transport, including buses, trains, taxis, cars, etc., for both local and longer distance journeys. It also gives contact points for services across the country. The National Federation of Shopmobility* can provide information on schemes available in your area.

- Orange/blue badges are available, giving parking concessions to disabled or blind people or their drivers. Enquire about these at the local social services department (Regional and Island Councils in Scotland, DoE Roads Services Division in Northern Ireland). A new Europe-wide parking badge scheme has been introduced, and if you qualify you will now receive a 'blue' badge; the existing orange badges will gradually be replaced by blue badges as they come up for renewal. To qualify for a blue badge the person must fulfil certain criteria which these departments can outline. The badge is given to the *person* rather than the vehicle, so it can be displayed on a friend's car, taxi, etc. if the disabled person is travelling in it. Conditions will vary locally, but these will be explained when the badge is issued. For more information about the blue badge, see Chapter 25.

- RADAR* has produced *Access in London* (£7.95).

- Concessions are available for elderly and disabled people on public transport. These vary regionally: local transport authorities will tell you about their schemes. A Disabled Persons Railcard and a Senior Railcard, which enable concessionary fares to be purchased, are available from staffed railstations and rail-appointed travel agents. (See Chapter 25 for further details.)

- Many councils issue concessionary tokens for use on public transport and sometimes these can be used towards the cost of a local taxi fare. In some areas there are Taxicard schemes for disabled residents – for details, contact your local authority (regional council in Scotland).

- Some volunteer bureaux (and a very few social services departments) run Social Car schemes using volunteer drivers, for a charge. Journeys commonly involve hospital or surgery visits, but some schemes will take you anywhere you want to go. The WRVS and British Red Cross* also provide transport, mostly for health or welfare purposes. Many disability groups and other organisations such as Age Concern★ will hire out minibuses or take passengers – check with your local group.

- Some Age Concern★ offices in cities have wheelchairs on loan for a few hours so that an elderly person can be wheeled to the shops if he or she finds walking too difficult.

Longer distances and general information

- The Confederation of Passenger Transport★ offers a free booklet, listing members who hire out special vehicles for disabled people and advising how to get the best from other bus and coach services.
- Motability★ can help with information on leasing or buying a car or electric wheelchair for people receiving the higher rate of the 'getting around' part of the disabled living allowance.
- Tripscope★ is a nationwide telephone-based travel and transport information service for people with mobility difficulties. It can tell you how to get from A to B, no matter where A and B are, taking into account your disability. It also offers assistance with any aspect of travel in the UK and abroad and can answer any transport-related questions, from wheelchair hire to accessibility of lavatories. It can supply a free information pack explaining the scope of the organisation.
- The AA,★ National Breakdown★ and RAC Response★ offer special roadside assistance and recovery for disabled motorists.

When one parent dies

A parent left alone by the death of a spouse has certain problems to face – just as a carer trying to cope on his or her own does.

In the case of a widow or widower, the spouse's death has often been the major factor in dictating a change of lifestyle. However, this is a decision which should not be taken hastily and any new long-term arrangements should be carefully organised. Once the funeral and sorting out of legal and financial matters are over, there is often a feeling of flatness or restlessness as well as grief – just the wrong time to move or make radical rearrangements, although a holiday or period of staying with a son or daughter could be a good idea.

The problems may not be the same for widows as for widowers who decide that they want to continue living in the marital home.

An elderly woman left alone may find herself worrying about filling in official documents or forms, sorting out household and garden maintenance problems (especially if they require some strength), and all the many tasks that her husband may have been responsible for. It will be necessary to make sure that she can manage the practical tasks around the house and that all the installations are safe. An accident to someone living alone could be that much more serious than with a partner in the house.

If she does not drive, this could be very confining, particularly if she lives in an isolated area. There could be volunteer transport available, or a neighbour willing to offer lifts. It may be possible to organise some volunteer or paid-for gardening help.

The problems for a man on his own might be slightly different. He may not have been used to doing any housework or cooking – and he may not feel like bothering with meals. You may be able to arrange domestic help, either through the social services or privately, which would have the advantage of providing someone to keep a discreet eye on his welfare as well as giving him a helping hand. It is preferable, if you can pop in quite often, not to take over the domestic side of his life entirely as his wife might have done. You will probably not have time, and he might well enjoy the extra activity. Practical advice on how to organise things may, however, be appreciated.

Help with cooking and planning nutritious meals will be essential for his continuing good health, and a well-filled cupboard of canned and packaged foods will be invaluable. He may have a freezer, so he could stock up with a few ready-prepared meals for when he does not want to cook. If he also has a microwave, keeping himself fed should be fairly simple. Remember that the milkman can deliver basic foodstuffs as well as milk – a boon in bad weather or if your parent is ill. See also Chapter 28.

Men or women can feel that catering for themselves and eating alone involves no pleasure, so this is an area which needs watching if a daily regime of biscuits and scrappy snacks is not to take the place of well-balanced meals. If you live at a distance, it may be necessary to enlist the help of a neighbour or home help to keep an eye on things. There may be a lunch club that your parent could go to once or twice a week or a friend nearby who might like to take a turn-and-turn-about lunch every week. Lunch clubs, as well as being provided by social services departments, are often run by voluntary organisations. Age Concern★ has its own clubs, sometimes providing transport with provision to take wheelchairs. They can supply a list of all clubs in your parent's area.

· Before the situation arises when one parent is left alone, it is a good idea to suggest tactfully activities and interests that are *not* joint ones, so that when the time comes, there is a ready-made group of friends and acquaintances to offer company and something to do. The social life of couples can be very different from that of a single partner; old friends may appear not to want to meet a widow or widower, either because the constant reminder of death depresses them or because they feel that three is an awkward number. For all these reasons individual hobbies and interests are a good investment for the future.

Passing the time at home can sometimes be difficult for someone living alone and the days may hang heavily. Make sure that your parent's radio and television work properly, and that newspapers and magazines are available. Joining the local library if it is not too far away is a must if your parent is not already a member. A neighbour may be able to change books if it is difficult to get there. If your parent has a tape recorder, this is a good way to record letters for distant friends and relatives and many elderly people also enjoy recording their reminiscences. An active elderly parent will probably want to continue gardening. The September/October 1997 edition of *Gardening Which?* includes a feature on the therapeutic effects of gardening ('Gardening Home'). The November 1998 edition features tests on a range of tools for easier gardening. There is also a guide to gardening equipment for disabled people available from the Disability Information Trust.★

Being a carer

Whether or not your parent lives with you it is important to be on the alert for health problems. In any case you may have to ensure that physical check-ups – at the optician, dentist, chiropodist and so on – take place regularly and that your parent is having an adequate and nutritious diet.

Remember that some symptoms which are often put down simply to 'getting old' are, in fact signs of treatable illness which can be, if not cured, at least alleviated. This applies more if the symptoms appear gradually rather than suddenly; in the latter case, medical advice should be sought immediately.

If symptoms persist, encourage your parent to have a thorough check-up. In some cases a change in personality such as irritability, rudeness and difficult behaviour or extreme withdrawal and gentleness may indicate the onset of illness, particularly if such behaviour is uncharacteristic. Such infections as bad colds or flu can be serious in elderly people and sudden lack of energy or extreme tiredness should be taken seriously. It is better to call the doctor if in doubt, rather than dismissing such things as minor ailments. See Chapter 31 for more on health problems.

Medication

If medication is prescribed, make sure that your parent is taking it regularly (and not taking proprietary medicines at the same time) and that he or she can undo bottle caps easily. Discreet inspection of the medicine cabinet may reveal a variety of prescribed and over-the-counter pills and potions, some of them completely out-of-date.

There are various memory aids to help elderly people take their medication at the right time. Ask the pharmacist for more details and see also 'Medication problems' in Chapter 31. It is particularly important to ensure the correct and correctly spaced dosage if your parent had been in hospital and has been given new medication with which he or she is unfamiliar.

Incontinence

If your parent is incontinent the problem can be alleviated. Help may be available via the social services in the way of laundering bed linen, and a local continence adviser or district nurse can offer practical advice on obtaining a commode, other types of appliance available, incontinence pads and protection of bedding, and so on.

There are also ways of helping to control incontinence and the district nurse or adviser should be able to suggest these. Sensible measures would be to make sure that the lavatory or commode is easily accessible and, while not cutting down on the amount of fluid drunk over 24 hours, to offer drinks in the morning rather than before going to bed. Age Concern* produces a free factsheet No. 23 *Help with incontinence*. You could also contact the Continence Foundation* helpline or write for their factsheets and leaflets.

WHERE TO GET HOLD OF WHAT

Aids and appliances for people who need them are available from different sources, depending on where you live. For example, you might get grab rails and bath aids from your local social services, incontinence pads and walking frames from the GP via the district nurse and the physiotherapist attached to the practice respectively, and commodes from the British Red Cross* or your health authority. This type of equipment is on show at 40 centres in the UK – contact the Disabled Living Centres Council* for details. Contact your GP or the social services in the first instance, or telephone the local branch of Age Concern.* See also *Equipment for an Easier Life* (a guide to products and where to get them) – single copy available free, with a large s.a.e., from RICA.*

Alzheimer's disease

Mental problems can be more difficult to deal with than physical ones, but they are now much more widely recognised than they used to be and there are many more sources of information and help, such as the National Association for Mental Health (MIND).* Again, Chapter 31 has more information about dealing with these problems but Alzheimer's disease is a very common problem in elderly people and deserves a special word in this chapter as it is the cause of so much worry and stress to carers.

Although obviously this does not apply to all elderly people who occasionally become muddle-headed and less 'sharp' than they once were, early signs of Alzheimer's disease can be confusion, forgetfulness (not being able to remember the right word, not recognising familiar faces, becoming mixed up over dates or times, for example), wandering off, and having fixed delusions and changes in personality. These pointers, especially if they happen gradually, can alert a carer or relative as to what may be happening and the parent's GP should be contacted so that a diagnosis and specific advice can be obtained, perhaps from a geriatric specialist or psychiatrist.

Symptoms that occur suddenly signal a need for urgent medical attention. If your parent is going to need protracted care, it is important to find out at an early stage what support would be available from the social and medical services and to have a frank discussion with everyone concerned over how much – or how little – care you are in a position to give in these circumstances.

Do your best to simplify life for your parent. Make sure that clothes are easy to put on – trousers and skirts with elasticated waists, sweaters which can be worn either way round and loose dresses. If your parent lives with you, you could lay the clothes out in order ready for putting on each morning. Cut down on the number of pots and pans, crockery and dishes in use to avoid confusion, and ensure that medication is easily checked and taken.

If wandering off is a problem, make sure that your parent carries a card with your name, address and telephone number, and a back-up number of someone else for extra reassurance.

If your parent is very confused, he or she may not recognise the difference between night and day and may get up and even dress at any time of the night. Instituting a regular routine during the day with set hours for meals, bathing and going out can provide a framework within which both carer and parent can work – not the least important being regular exercise so that the parent is more likely to be tired and sleep well. Remember that a change – going on holiday, moving house – can cause extra disorientation and confusion in an elderly sufferer, and be ready with extra support if possible.

Alzheimer's disease can, more than almost any other problem for carers, cause immense distress. Not only are the physical manifestations trying and wearing, but the psychological ones too. To see a parent on whom one has relied and whom one loves become a different person, who may not even recognise close members of the family, is enormously upsetting. However, it is essential for carers to protect their emotional state by, first of all, doing everything practical to help the parent, and then accepting that the present condition is brought about by illness and that the real affectionate, loving and competent parent is the person they remember before the illness struck. Nevertheless, carers will need all the emotional as well as practical support that can be called upon.

Minimising stress

Not the least of the problems attached to being a carer is the stress it can bring because you yourself may be at a stage where you may have family, health or financial problems. Causes of stress can be very small – irritating mannerisms and reactions in your parent which, repeated on a day-to-day basis drive you mad – or far more serious if your parent is ill or disabled and needs constant physical help and emotional support.

It is most important to try to cut down the stress factors on you and your family in order to avoid possible damage to your own health and disruption of daily life.

Local social services

These can be extremely helpful; consider involving them at an early stage. A social worker can be consulted direct, either by phone or in writing, and will be able to advise on a particular problem or point you in the direction of the right person to deal with it. There is usually an emergency service in case of need. Even if your parent might qualify for social services help, there is variation from area to area in the services available, whether or not you have to pay for them – and the waiting time to be assessed for help. These are some of the services:

- **Meals on Wheels** – or other for people who have no one to provide lunch for them and are incapable of getting it for themselves.
- **Home carers or care assistants (used to be known as home helps)** (usually for elderly people living in their own homes).
- **Laundry service** for linen.
- **Installation of an alarm system**.
- **Installation of a telephone** free of charge if it is deemed to be vitally necessary.
- **Aids** to make the home more manageable, such as ramps, rails, bath aids – these are normally provided free of charge. The British Red Cross★ lends various items such as commodes and wheelchairs, the Disabled Living Foundation★ can advise on all types of aid equipment and the Carers National Association★ produces a useful factsheet called *Making Life Easier: A Guide to Aids and Equipment*.

- Provision of **respite or short-term residential care**.
- **Care attendants**, who can take over from a carer who is looking after someone at home.

Local social service departments (social work departments in Scotland, health and social services boards in Northern Ireland) will provide information on all the services they offer and also about other services in the area which can help elderly people or their carers. See Chapter 30 for more on local authority home care services.

Sitting service schemes

Such schemes may be available, depending on the area, and could be provided by the district health authority, local authority or voluntary organisations, or jointly. Your health visitor or social worker will be able to advise you. Not much help is available for night-time, but a friend or relative might relieve you for the occasional night. Private care might also be a possibility, although this is expensive.

Respite care

All carers should be able to enjoy breaks from the responsibility of care. Carers need not only annual holidays but regular shorter breaks each week. Respite care for elderly people can provide time for holidays, and voluntary organisations as well as official ones should be able to help on a week-by-week basis.

Holidays

Such organisations as BREAK★ are able to provide holidays for people, whatever their degree of disability, although there is a charge; this gives carers the opportunity to take their own holiday. The Holiday Care Service★ gives free information on which holidays would best suit elderly or disabled people, according to their needs. It can also provide information on schemes for volunteer helpers to accompany a disabled person.

Local carers' association

There might be a carers' association in your area, probably a branch of the Carers National Association,★ which will provide much support and helpful advice on alleviating strain.

Looking ahead

Carers naturally become depressed sometimes and bogged down in the everyday business of caring. They may feel resentful that the rest of the family are not doing enough to help, and see themselves in a situation that can only get worse. Many dread the death or increasing illness of their parent and wonder how they are going to cope.

It cannot be emphasised enough that not only must carers have free time but, during this time, peace of mind in the knowledge that their parent is being kindly and safely cared for by someone else. The cultivation of a good self-image is important too – after all, giving compassionate care to another person is a very important job and should be recognised as such.

Sport and exercise can be a great release for a carer under stress, and you might think of joining an adult education class. It is also a good idea to prepare for the time when you will no longer be a carer, either by taking up some form of retraining for work or a leisure activity which will be enjoyable later on.

Part 6

The good health guide

Chapter 28

Healthy eating

Most people's eating habits are now very different to those of several decades ago. One of the main reasons, of course, is that a far greater variety of fresh and processed foods is available than ever before. Patterns of health and disease have also changed: people are living longer and are more likely to suffer from what are often referred to as 'diseases of affluence', such as coronary heart disease, strokes, various cancers and diabetes.

Although there has been a welter of apparently conflicting advice in the media over the years on what you should or should not be doing in order to keep healthy, there is a consensus that the key factors are to:

- eat a healthy diet
- exercise regularly
- keep off smoking
- keep alcohol intake to a moderate level.

There is also agreement that these strategies are important at all stages of life. For instance, a report by the Department of Health (1992) reviewed all the evidence about diet and health for those over 65. It concluded that good nutrition is essential to help maintain health, reduce the risk of certain diseases and promote recovery from illness, and that it is appropriate for most people as they get older to adopt similar patterns of eating and lifestyle to those recommended for younger adults.

The recipe for healthy eating

Eating for health broadly means focusing on the three groups of foods on pages 378–9, and concentrating in particular on the first two groups.

Even if you are healthy and active try making changes in line with the following healthy eating guidelines. You don't have to change everything at once. Decide on priorities, make gradual alterations and experiment with different recipes and meals – remember that even small changes can be of benefit.

Fruit, vegetables and salads

Fruit and vegetables provide a variety of vitamins and minerals, and are an especially important source of vitamin C. Eating more fruit and vegetables can help to prevent constipation as they provide dietary fibre; evidence suggests that they may also play a role in reducing the risk of certain cancers. Fruit and vegetables are high in fibre and low in calories, so are ideal for filling up on if you are trying to lose weight.

Tips

Aim to eat **five portions of fruit and vegetables a day:**

- Start the day with a glass of fruit juice.
- Snack on fruit or raw vegetables such as carrots and celery between meals.
- Choose fruit salads, stewed or baked fruit or fresh fruit and yogurt for dessert.
- Use less meat and add extra vegetables, beans and lentils to stews, casseroles and soups.
- Don't overcook vegetables as this destroys some of their vitamins (see the section on vitamins).
- Keep a supply of canned fruit and vegetables (but check the label to see if they have salt, sugar, or syrup added).
- Keep a supply of frozen vegetables – they are quicker and more convenient to prepare than fresh ones. A survey for *Health Which?* magazine found that their vitamin C content was just as good and sometimes better than that of some fresh vegetables.

Breads, cereals, potatoes, rice and pasta

These are sometimes referred to as starchy foods or **complex carbohydrates**. Many people think of them as fattening foods to be avoided, especially if you are trying to lose weight. In fact, the recommendations are to eat more – this applies especially to older people, who tend to eat only small helpings of them. If you are dieting it is much better to cut down on fatty foods (see the section on page 384 on weight gain), which provide approximately twice as much energy (calories) as starchy ones.

Eating more breads, cereals and potatoes has a number of benefits. From them you will gain a variety of vitamins and minerals (such as B vitamins, calcium and iron) and essential fatty acids (types of polyunsaturated fatty acids needed by the body in small amounts). In addition, wholemeal/wholegrain breads are a good source of fibre. Starchy fibre-rich foods are filling and satisfying, so eating more of these will make you less inclined to reach for fatty and sugary snacks and foods.

Tips

- Have thicker slices of bread and eat bread with your meals. Wholemeal bread has more fibre than white but if you do not like it stick to your favourite type – the important point is to eat more.
- Start the day with breakfast. Choose a low-sugar, high-fibre cereal.
- As well as bread and potatoes, try different types of rice and pasta or use other cereals and grains.

Meat, fish and dairy products

In the past everybody was encouraged to eat plenty of these foods because of their high protein content, and many people still consider them to be the most important part of a meal. Studies now show that most healthy people eat far more protein than they actually need. Foods high in protein do provide vitamins and minerals but they can also be high in fat and saturates, and we now know that high-fat diets are associated with increased risks of heart disease and certain cancers (breast, colon and prostate). Fat is also a concentrated source of energy (calories) that can lead to extra weight gain. At the moment in the UK our daily energy intake is about 42 per cent fat; a better target is 35 per cent. Eating more fruit, vegetables and starchy foods will mean that you have less room for high-fat and other foods anyway.

Tips

- Choose lean meat and remove any visible fat. Poultry contains less fat than red meat but leave the fatty skin.
- White fish is low in fat – unless you fry it or add fatty sauces.
- Meat products like sausages, burgers and pâtés often contain large amounts of fat. Check the nutrition label.
- Milk and dairy products are an important source of calcium and vitamins; try using semi-skimmed or skimmed milk and low-fat yogurts and cheeses in place of full-fat ones – they contain just as much calcium and are a good way of reducing fat intake.
- Try having a vegetarian meal at least twice a week based on beans, lentils or nuts which contain more fibre. Beans and lentils are low in fat.

Fibre, fat, sugar and salt

Nutritionists agree that we all need to boost our fibre intake, and cut down on fat, sugar and salt.

Fibre

Fibre is what gives seeds, fruits, roots, stems and leaves of plants their structure.

It is a mixture of indigestible carbohydrates that pass through the body unabsorbed. Some types of food naturally contain more fibre than others, but processing also affects the fibre content: refining cereals such as wheat (e.g. to make white flour) involves removing much of the fibre from the outer husk of the grain.

Dietary fibre (also known as roughage) keeps your bowels functioning healthily and regularly. It combines with water to add bulk to the stools and greatly assists the passage of digestible materials and waste products through the intestines. It helps to prevent constipation and diverticular disease, and there is some evidence that it protects against bowel cancer. Fibre can be broadly separated into two types: insoluble and soluble, and all plant foods contain a mixture of both. These differ in some of their effects: **insoluble fibre** provides the most bulk, reducing the time taken for food to pass through the gut; and **soluble fibre** has been shown to have a modest effect of lowering blood cholesterol, especially if your cholesterol is already high. Whole-grain wheat and rye are rich sources of insoluble fibre. Oats, barley, beans and lentils, however, contain a significant proportion of soluble fibre. Fruit and vegetables contain roughly half and half of each.

Eating more fibre also improves the overall balance of your diet – helping to reduce the amount of fat and increase the amount of starchy-carbohydrate you eat. More fibre can also mean more nutrients: choosing whole-grain foods, fruits, pulses and vegetables will increase your intake of some vitamins, minerals and other substances thought to have positive health benefits.

Although raw bran is high in fibre, adding it to foods is to be discouraged because of its high phytate content. Phytate binds in the gut with certain minerals like calcium, zinc and iron from other foods so that their absorption is reduced. (Other wholemeal foods also contain some phytate but its effect is compensated for by their rich mineral content and the fact that processing reduces the amount of phytates present.)

Tips

- Increase your fibre intake gradually: unpleasant side effects such as wind decrease once your body gets used to having more fibre.
- Drink plenty of fluids, preferably water.
- Choose wholemeal breads and cereals and have more beans, lentils, fruit, vegetables and salads.

Fat

All types of fat contain the same amount of calories, and so should all be used sparingly. The difference between them lies in their chemical make-up. All fats are a mixture of different fatty acids, which give them different properties and effects.

- **Saturated fatty acids** (saturates): encourage the body to produce more LDL (or 'bad') cholesterol, increasing heart disease risk. Some cancers (e.g. bowel and breast) have been linked to high intakes of saturates. Main sources: dairy products, meat and meat products, biscuits and hard fats (such as butter and lard).

- **Monounsaturated fatty acids** (monounsaturates): replacing saturates in your diet with monounsaturates seems to have a good effect. It reduces bad (LDL) cholesterol, and maintains or slightly increases 'good' (HDL) cholesterol. Main sources: olive oil, rapeseed oil, blended vegetable oil (check the label), avocados and nuts.

- **Polyunsaturated fatty acids** (polyunsaturates): these are better than saturates but not as good as monounsaturates. Current advice is to replace saturates with a mixture of poly- and monounsaturates. However, there are two main types of polyunsaturates: omega-3 and omega-6. Omega-3s that come from fish oil can help to reduce your risk of a heart attack because they reduce the risk of your blood clotting. Try to eat at least two portions of oily fish, such as mackerel, pilchards or trout, a week. Omega-6 polyunsaturates (main sources include polyunsaturated margarines and spreads, and corn, sunflower and soya bean oils) bring down total cholesterol, but they do this by decreasing both good and bad cholesterol.

- **Trans fatty acids** (trans fat): are thought to be at least as bad as saturates and have been linked with heart disease and rheumatoid arthritis. Some trans fats are found naturally in dairy products, but most come from artificially hydrogenated polyunsaturates, and are found in some margarines, biscuits and cakes.

Tips

- Cut down on total fat by limiting saturates, using some polyunsaturates (margarines, oils, oily fish) and having the rest of your fat as monounsaturates such as olive oil.
- Use oils rather than hard fats for cooking as they are low in saturates.
- Change to a reduced-fat spread or margarine which is low in saturates and high in polyunsaturates.
- Cut down on frying, use less fat in cooking and spread less fat on bread and toast.
- Go easy on crisps, chocolate, mayonnaise, cakes, biscuits and pastries – all high-fat foods.

Sugar

As some people get older they find they want to add more sugar to their foods and eat more sweetened foods. The problem with consuming lots of sweet foods is that they decrease the appetite for other foods, are not very nutritious, and, of course, cause tooth decay. Sugar provides only calories, but no vitamins, minerals, protein or fibre. Avoid sugar and sweet foods particularly if you have diabetes or are trying to lose weight.

Intense **sweeteners** such as aspartame, acesulfame-k and saccharin are much sweeter than sugar and are used in a variety of foods like drinks and yogurts or as a table-top sweetener. Although the government is satisfied that they are safe it is probably not a good idea to eat large amounts of any one type of sweetener. They can help you to lose weight only as part of a calorie-controlled diet.

Tips

- Aim to cut out sugar in drinks and breakfast cereals.
- Use less sugar in recipes.
- Sucrose, dextrose, maltose, invert sugar, syrup and caramel are all forms of sugar – check labels.
- Honey and brown sugar are no better than white sugar.
- Sugary foods are often high in fat as well (cakes, biscuits, chocolates).

Salt

Countries with high salt intakes such as the UK have higher average levels of blood pressure than countries with low salt intakes. Blood pressure increases with age and high blood pressure is a risk factor for heart disease. If you are taking medication for high blood pressure you may have already been advised to eat less salt.

Tips

- Avoid adding salt to foods during cooking or at the table. Some salt is needed by the body but this can easily be obtained from the salt present naturally in foods.
- Season foods with lemon juice, herbs and spices – you will soon get used to the taste of less salty foods.
- Canned and processed foods are often very salty, so choose brands which have less or no extra salt added. More than half the salt we eat is added by manufacturers during food processing (note that salt is the same as sodium chloride – check labels).
- Salt substitutes still contain some salt.

Special needs as you get older

Your energy (calorie) requirements as you get older will depend on your health and lifestyle. Some people may need to alter the quantities they eat due to changes in these; this does not necessarily mean that you have to eat less, as many people are more active in retirement than they were when working.

Weight gain

Keep a check on your weight. Being overweight is associated with reduced mobility, diabetes and hypertension and puts extra strain on joints. Obesity is usually measured using the body mass index (BMI) which is weight in kilograms divided by height in metres squared. Check your BMI and aim for a weight within the recommended healthy range. A BMI between 20 and 25 is considered healthy; between 25 and 30 is a sign of being overweight, and over 30 is defined as obese. If you need to lose weight set yourself a realistic target, such as one or two pounds a week. Change your diet in line with the healthy eating recommendations, filling up with more fruit, vegetables, salads and starchy foods and cutting down on fatty and sugary ones. Increase your level of physical activity and exercise, and get plenty of support and encouragement from those around you. Join a slimming group or ask your GP to refer you to a dietitian if you need extra help. Unfortunately, there is no easy way to lose weight; it is much better to lose it gradually and get used to a healthy, sensible diet.

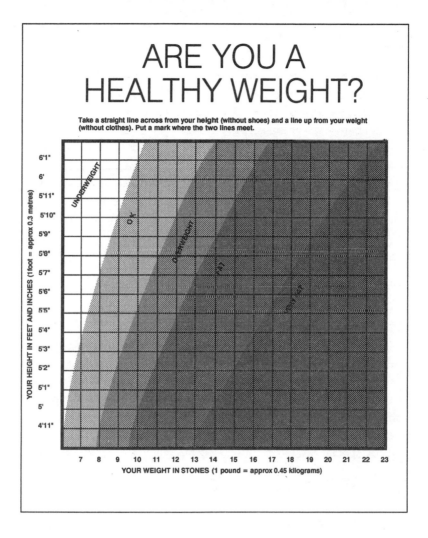

ARE YOU A HEALTHY WEIGHT?

Take a straight line across from your height (without shoes) and a line up from your weight (without clothes). Put a mark where the two lines meet.

Maintaining your weight

Some people lose their appetite and interest in food as they get older, perhaps as a result of illness, depression, problems with teeth, bereavement or certain drug treatments, or because they are living alone. It is not just the amount that you eat that is important, but the type and variety as well. Poor food intakes over a prolonged period can lead to weight loss, increased susceptibility to infections and illness and nutritional deficiencies. If you experience a sudden loss of appetite or unexplained weight loss check with your GP.

Tips

- Have small regular meals and snacks, using a variety of different foods.
- If you don't feel like cooking, remember that cold meals and snacks can be just as nutritious.
- Choose milky drinks and fruit juices rather than tea, coffee and soft drinks.
- If your appetite is very poor you may need to take a vitamin supplement. Choose a multivitamin and mineral supplement. (Very high doses of some vitamins can cause health problems, so stick to the recommended dosage and take one which provides amounts close to or just below the Recommended Daily Amount (RDA) – it should tell you this on the label.)

Catering for one

Cooking and catering for one need not be expensive and time-consuming if you plan your meals and shopping in advance. If you have a freezer buying larger quantities is often more economical than buying smaller amounts; some foods can be divided into individual portions and frozen, or you could buy larger quantities with friends or neighbours and divide them between you. Look out for special offers on foods and buy vegetables and fruits that are in season. If you are cooking stews, casseroles and soups, prepare a larger quantity and freeze what you don't need immediately in individual portions.

You may not feel like bothering to cook just for yourself. Quick and/or easy meals like sandwiches, beans or scrambled eggs on toast, jacket potatoes and salads can be just as nutritious as a full meal, but try to make sure you include a variety of foods. Experiment with new recipes and try different foods.

Stocking up

It is a good idea to keep various storecupboard foods in case you are ill or unable to get to the shops. Useful items include UHT long-life milk, long-life fruit juices, canned fruit and vegetables, dried fruit, canned fish, meat, beans, rice puddings and custards, crackers, breakfast cereals, oats, rice and pasta. If you have a freezer keep some bread, meat, fish, frozen fruit and vegetables and individual portions of meals. Make a regular check on stocks.

Most milkmen will deliver a range of foods to your doorstep, such as bread, eggs, potatoes, yogurt and fruit juices. Local authority social service departments and voluntary agencies often run luncheon clubs, day centres and pop-in clubs – your local library or social services department should be able to provide you with details of these. If you are really not able to cope with cooking you may be able to get Meals on Wheels delivered to your home.

Cooking skills and equipment

Retirement may prove a good time to improve or master new culinary skills. There are plenty of cookery classes available, including ones especially for men. Enquire about adult education classes in your area at your local library.

If you have physical problems cooking or preparing foods a range of special equipment and appliances is available to make things easier. Details are available from the Disabled Living Foundation.*

Vitamins

Vitamin requirements for older people are generally similar to those for younger individuals. However, you should make sure you maintain a good intake of vitamin C, which is found in fruit and vegetables, particularly blackcurrants and citrus fruits and their juices (oranges, grapefruit, lemons). For most people there is no need to take vitamin supplements; a healthy, varied diet should provide all the vitamins you need.

The vitamin content of fruit and vegetables decreases during storage and cooking (especially vitamins A, C and some B vitamins). To conserve the vitamins as much as possible don't soak vegetables and avoid overcooking them – boil them lightly in a small amount of water and use a saucepan with a lid, or stir-fry, microwave or steam them. Don't add baking soda.

Calcium
Bones become weaker and less flexible as you get older, partly because less calcium is deposited and partly because more is lost

from the bones. This loss of bone (see Osteoporosis in Chapter 31) is a major problem because it means that bones are more likely to fracture following a fall, for example. Although the role of dietary calcium in the development and prevention of osteoporosis is uncertain, it is known that calcium is important. Make sure you are eating enough calcium-rich foods. These include all types of milk, yogurt, Cheddar cheese, sardines, whitebait, spinach, parsnips, baked beans, almonds, white bread and dried figs.

Most people get all the calcium they need from their diet, but if your appetite is poor or you don't eat any dairy produce, a calcium supplement may be appropriate. Take one which gives at least 500mg per day (there is no advantage in taking extra high doses). If you are already taking a multivitamin and mineral supplement check the label to see if it contains any calcium and, if so, how much.

Vitamin D

Vitamin D is involved in the regulation of calcium absorption and is obtained from exposure to sunlight and a few dietary sources (fatty fish, margarine, eggs, liver, evaporated milk, skimmed milk powder and some breakfast cereals which have extra vitamin D added). Try to get outside during the day – walking or gardening are good ways of doing this. Remember to use sunscreen if you are going out for long periods during the summer. Anyone who is housebound or unable to follow this advice may need a vitamin D supplement and should consult the doctor.

Cod liver oil was often taken in the past as it is a particularly good source of vitamins A and D. Most people's diets now provide enough of these vitamins, so it is not necessary to take extra in this way. Both vitamins can be toxic in excess, so if you want to take cod liver oil stick to the recommended dosage and don't take other vitamin supplements which contain either vitamin A or D.

Fluid and alcohol

Drink at least six to eight cups of non-alcoholic drinks a day. It is important to have enough fluid even if you don't actually feel thirsty. Tea and coffee are diuretic (they increase the production of urine) and not good sources of fluid. Water is best.

As far as alcohol is concerned, there is evidence that a low amount of alcohol can have health benefits to people over 40 by reducing the risk of heart disease. The benefits can be gained by one to two units of alcohol a day for men and women. There is no increased benefit in having more. Also, to reduce the negative risks of alcohol (for example stroke, high blood pressure and some cancers), daily consumption should be limited to no more than three units a day for women and four units for men.

Food labels and safety

Food labels

Food labels can be confusing and misleading. Here are some points to watch out for:

- **'Use by'** dates are found on highly perishable foods; don't eat food which is past its 'use by' date unless it has been cooked or frozen to extend its life.
- **'Best before'** means that foods will be at peak quality until this date – after this they are still safe to eat (if stored according to instructions) but their quality may deteriorate.
- Ingredients are listed in order of weight, so that the main ingredient will be listed first.
- Beware of health claims on foods, like 'Healthy' and 'Good for you'. There are few regulations controlling the use of these.
- Check foods with claims like 'low-fat', 'high-fibre', 'sugar-free'. There are no statutory definitions for these claims, so you need to check whether a product that claims to be, for example, low-fat, really is what it says by comparing it with similar products.

Convenience foods

This term covers a huge variety of different products. They are not necessarily 'junk foods': products like canned and frozen fruit and vegetables can be just as nutritious as fresh. See under 'Fruit, vegetables and salads' page 378.

Storing foods safely

Store foods safely to minimise the risk of illness due to food contamination. Make sure that your fridge and freezer are the correct temperatures, between 0°C and 5°C and –18°C, respectively. Keep foods covered. Cooked foods should be stored on higher shelves in the fridge and raw ones on the lower shelves so that the raw food (such as poultry) cannot contaminate food that is not going to be cooked again before it is eaten. Keep eggs in the fridge.

Food preparation

Follow the basic rules:

- Wash your hands before and in between handling food.
- Clean work surfaces before you start and continue to clean as you go.
- Don't use the same knife or chopping board for raw and cooked foods.
- Don't eat raw eggs or products containing uncooked eggs.
- Follow cooking instructions on food labels – this is especially important for cooked-chilled foods, which must be properly reheated.
- Make sure that meat (including burgers) and poultry are properly cooked: when you prick the thickest part of the meat the juices should run clear.
- Left-over cooked food should be chilled quickly, covered, and then refrigerated or frozen.
- Reheat foods once only and heat thoroughly.
- Keep pets away from food and food preparation areas.

Chapter 29

Exercise

What does retirement mean to you? More freedom, more activity – travelling, gardening, visiting new places, getting on with all those things you meant to do but couldn't because you were working?

Or does it mean getting older? An inevitable deterioration? Being unable to cope with everyday tasks which require strength, not being able to keep up with younger people, feeling stiffness in the joints, becoming more dependent on others, not being able to meet up with friends, succumbing to the conditions of old age such as high blood pressure or heart problems? Sounds depressing, doesn't it? Even if you are already suffering from any of these problems, none of them means that you have to succumb to old age and inactivity – some are even reversible. Now is the time to make sure you are still going strong in your 90s.

Do you think you are fit? The chances are that if you have been doing a sedentary job and driving rather than walking, you are not. Nowadays you often do not have to exert yourself physically unless you put your mind to it. Lifts carry you upstairs, cars and buses take you to work. Unless you have been going out of your way to take regular exercise, over the years your muscles will have been getting weaker, and your stamina deteriorating. You may not find it so easy to take up the activities you are looking forward to, or keep up the ones you're already doing – but that does not mean you can't, or shouldn't.

What is fitness?

If you are thinking about skipping this chapter because you are too old, too unfit or too unhealthy to consider exercise, or because you have had to give it up because of illness or injury – don't. The benefits of exercise can be enormous, and you don't have to suffer to feel them.

Strength and endurance, stamina and flexibility are all part of being fit. Together these things give you the ability to lift and carry, keep up a fast pace while walking uphill, or reach something on the top shelf of a cupboard. Much of what we call ageing is nothing more than the results of being inactive, and losing these aspects of fitness. If your muscles are not used they shrink, and become less powerful, making it harder for you to do things you could do easily when you were younger. Weaker muscles mean you are more likely to fall, and because bones also get weaker as you age, you are more likely to break something if you do.

You may find you put on weight when you get older, but, more importantly, the proportion of muscle and bone to fat may change, so that there is more fat. Dieting may mean you lose fat, but unless you exercise you could lose muscle and bone as well.

Although fitness tends to decline with age, there is no reason why many older people shouldn't be as fit or fitter than others in their 20s, 30s and 40s, particularly if the younger age groups aren't taking any exercise.

Stamina

This is what we need to walk or run, and keep it up over any distance. Most unfit people can manage to run a short distance – to catch a bus, for example. But muscles need oxygen to keep working, or they will get painful and you will get tired. Unless you have got stamina your body will not be able to get oxygen to your muscles quickly enough. Aerobic exercise (designed to increase the amount of oxygen to the blood) improves the way your body uses oxygen, your cardio-vascular system. People who have not been exercising aerobically will find they get tired more easily as they get older, but aerobic training can keep your body using oxygen efficiently. Aerobic exercise includes walking, jogging, swimming, dancing, climbing stairs, gardening and cycling. In order to reap the benefits you need to puff a little, and work up some sweat, but not to the extent that you are completely out of breath – you should still be able to carry on a conversation.

Strength and endurance

Strength is what you need to lift – including lifting your own body weight from a chair, for example. Endurance is what you need to carry what you have lifted. Strength training will make your muscles become bigger and more powerful. You do not have to lift heavy weights to do this – even squeezing a tennis ball regularly can help improve your arm muscles so that you will always find it easy to pull a plug out of a socket. Swimming and gardening are good starting exercises for building up strength (though be careful of your back at first when digging). This sort of training also helps to strengthen bones. Strength can help protect against back pain (and against falling).

Suppleness

Suppleness means that you can move all your limbs through a full range of movement without difficulty. If you are flexible you will find it easier to bend your knees to pick something off the floor, and to stretch your arms above your head to reach something off a shelf. Swimming is a good way to get all your joints moving, while keeping them supported, but daily stretching exercises will help (see 'Getting started' on pages 396–8).

The benefits of exercise

Apart from ensuring that you can keep fit enough to live an independent and active life, exercise can have a positive, preventive effect on many of the conditions associated with growing older.

Coronary heart disease (CHD)

If you are physically inactive, you are more likely to suffer from coronary disease. Exercise can prevent the onset of the disease – the more you do, the more protected you are. What is more, if you keep up the exercise you are protected for as long as you persevere with the activity. This is a result of improvements in the way your cardiovascular system works (see 'Stamina', opposite), and a strengthening of your heart muscle. Exercise can also keep down the build-up of harmful cholesterol in your arteries.

As exercise can also help control your weight, it can influence your likelihood of suffering heart problems related to obesity. If you have had a heart attack you should not necessarily avoid exercise: it has been shown that exercise can have a protective effect. Ask your doctor (and see under 'Heart attack' in Chapter 31).

High blood pressure

Exercise can have a similar effect to beta-blocking drugs, although it does not work in exactly the same way. The Health Education Authority (HEA)★ has two sets of recommendations. At least 30 minutes of activity at moderate intensity on at least five days a week will achieve health benefits. At least 20 minutes of vigorous activity on three or more days a week will maximise aerobic fitness and help reduce mortality. If you already have high blood pressure you should speak to your doctor before exercising – certain exercises might not be suitable for you, for example those involving lying on the floor.

Respiratory diseases

People with respiratory diseases such as asthma, bronchitis or emphysema often think that their condition means they cannot exercise. It is true that the amount of exercise that can be done is limited, but as exercise can improve these conditions it should not be avoided altogether. The amount of exercise you are capable of gradually increases, with the benefit that your capacity for everyday tasks increases too. Asthma attacks can be brought on by exercise in some cases, but warming up gently and using an inhaler can avoid this. Swimming in an indoor pool is less likely to provoke an attack because the air breathed is warm and moist.

Back pain

The less physically fit you are, the more likely you are to suffer from back pain. If the muscles in your back are weak, you are more likely to hurt yourself when you attempt to put stress on them – by lifting something heavy, for example. Strengthening stomach and back muscles helps prevent injury.

If you already have back pain, exercise can help reduce and manage it, depending on the type you suffer from.

Arthritis

Exercise can be of benefit whichever type of arthritis you have. In the degenerative forms of arthritis (osteoarthritis) exercise can increase muscle strength and counteract the effect of the wasting of muscles that happens after joint disease and injury. The range of movement in the knee can be improved, for example, making it easier to rise from a chair. For inflammatory joint diseases (rheumatoid arthritis) the range of movement in joints can be maintained by exercising while joints are inflamed. When inflammation has gone down, you can work on restoring strength and endurance. Exercise can help correct and reduce the deformities that might occur, and improve everyday activities.

Osteoporosis

Bones get weaker progressively after early adulthood, as they lose their mineral content. For women this happens even faster after the menopause. Weaker bones are more susceptible to fracture – older people are more likely to break bones if they fall. One of the reasons for the loss of minerals is physical inactivity. Exercise can help make bones stronger, even after the menopause. Men also benefit, as exercise has been shown to protect against hip fractures. The best type of exercises to do are those for strength, but even regular walking can have a good effect.

Exercise makes you feel good

The main thing to remember is that exercise can be a fun part of your life. Try to view it as part of your life, not a daily chore. Look at it as a way to increase your social life, to take advantage of the outdoors and to make sure that you can enjoy life to the full for years to come. Most people who take regular exercise claim they feel better for it and there is evidence to back this up.

Apart from the social aspects of exercise, it seems there is a chemical reaction which can make you feel happier. Substances called endorphins released into the brain may help give a sense of well-being, so exercise can help you combat stress, anxiety, tension and aggression. It can help you fight depression and tiredness, and make you sleep better.

Getting started

One of the most important things you can do to get your body moving and used to exercise is to walk more. If you try to walk, as briskly as you can, for half an hour a day, you are well on the way to improving your stamina and your strength – particularly that all-important strength in your legs which will help protect against falls (swing your arms too, to help work your upper body). Walking can easily become a part of your everyday routine if you walk rather than drive, or get off the bus a few stops early or take the stairs instead of the lift. Once you have got into the swing of walking you might want to join a walking or rambling club.

Do not try to exercise too hard too soon, as that might easily result in injuries or strains. Before you start exercising it is advisable to do some warm-up exercises to loosen up your joints – particularly because as you get older muscles get stiffer, and tendons and ligaments get weaker. Even before you do some gardening it is advisable to warm up. Try circling your shoulders backwards and forwards, and then circling your whole arm. Stretch your arms out in front of you, and circle your wrists in one direction, then the other. While sitting, bend and straighten first one leg, then the other, in front of you. Lift your feet from the floor, one at a time, and circle them in one direction, then the other. A little gentle marching on the spot, or walking up and down the stairs a few times, will get your cardio-vascular system working.

Exercise includes sports such as bowling, ballroom dancing and golf. Make the most of the advantages of being retired. You will find that your local leisure centre offers concessions for swimming off-peak, for example. Contact your local authority to find out about other concessions in leisure amenities.

If you feel very wary of starting exercise, or if you know you are suffering from a particular condition, check with your doctor first. This is especially important if you want to take up any weight-bearing exercising for strength, or exercise involving strenuous aerobic activity.

A target to aim for is five or more occasions of moderate activity, lasting up to 30 minutes, each week, but you can take your time in working up to this. Any moderate physical activity is better than none, and as frequent exercise brings the most health benefits, you will need to get into the habit. Start by aiming to exercise at least once a week. Table 2 (overleaf) divides activities into light, moderate and vigorous. You should aim to be reasonably fit before you do the more vigorous ones. To make yourself aware of how much you are achieving when you start exercising, make a chart of how you are doing. Monitor how far or fast you walk, and how long you can continue for without feeling tired, for example.

Table 1

Activity	Stamina	Suppleness	Strength	Comment
Aerobics	***	***	**	A lot depends on the teacher; can be pricey
Badminton	**	**	**	Most sports centres have courts
Circuit training	***	***	***	A lot depends on the quality of the routine/class
Climbing stairs	**	*	**	You don't need a gym
Cricket	*	**	*	Sociable; find a club
Cycling (hard)	***	*	**	Wear a helmet
Dancing (ballroom)	*	**	*	Good for co-ordination
Dancing (disco)	**	**	*	Not just for the young
Digging the garden	*	*	***	Mind your back
Golf	*	**	*	Start by taking lessons
Jogging	***	*	*	Use grass, not road; wear proper shoes
Rope-skipping	***	**	*	Not just for boxers
Rounders	**	*	**	Or try soft-ball
Rowing	***	*	**	Mind your back
Soccer	**	**	**	Keep on running
Squash	***	***	**	Wait till you're fit
Swimming (hard)	***	***	***	Best all round
Tennis	**	**	**	Find all-weather courts
Walking/rambling	**	*	*	Hill walks can score ** for strength
Weight training	*	**	***	Make sure you're properly supervised
Yoga	*	***	*	Start in a class

KEY *** very good ** some effect * little or no effect.
Your skill and how hard you play will also affect the rating

Aim to improve all aspects of fitness – stamina, strength and endurance, and suppleness. Table 1 lists different forms of exercise, comparing their effectiveness in each of these areas. Sport England★ can put you in touch with the governing body of the sport or activity you choose.

Table 2

Light activities	Moderate activities	Vigorous activities
long walks (2 miles plus) at an average or slow pace; lighter DIY (e.g. decorating), table tennis, golf, social dancing and 'exercises' if *not* out of breath or sweaty; bowls, fishing, darts and snooker	long walks (2 miles plus) at a brisk or fast place; football, swimming, tennis, aerobics and cycling if *not* out of breath or sweaty; table tennis, golf, social dancing and exercises if out of breath or sweaty; heavy DIY actvities (e.g. mixing cement); heavy gardening (e.g. digging); heavy housework (e.g. spring cleaning)	hill walking (at a brisk pace); squash, running; football, tennis, aerobics and cycling if out of breath or sweaty

Chapter 30

You and the health service

Good health

Staying healthy and enjoying good health throughout retirement is the ideal. Health is about maintaining physical and mental well-being, not just the absence of illness. The title of this chapter may conjure up images of hospitals, doctors and nurses, but services which improve health are provided by a whole range of different professionals, employed by different organisations, including Health Authorities, Local Authorities, National Health Service Trusts, independent contractors and private agencies. Such different organisations can have very different priorities. This chapter aims to explain who provides what and where you can find them.

The National Health Service (NHS)

To get the best out of the NHS, it pays to know how the system works. In addition, a good relationship with the doctors and other medical staff you come in contact with would help.

General practitioners

Your first port of call for health matters is your general practitioner (GP). He or she is the central figure in the 'primary care' team – the group of professionals from various health disciplines who work from a surgery or health centre. This team might include a district nurse, health visitor, practice nurse, community psychiatric nurse, therapists, social worker, receptionist and medical secretary. So choosing a GP is one of the most important health decisions you ever make. The checklist in the box opposite will help you decide what your priorities are when you are looking for a new GP.

Your relationship with your GP is crucial as he or she will not only diagnose and treat your problems but control your access to other NHS services. If you need specialist help your GP will have to write a letter of referral. In some areas there is direct access to some services, such as physiotherapy.

Choosing your GP

You do not have to give a reason for changing your GP. All you need to do is to turn up at the new practice and ask to be registered, as long as they are willing to accept you – they may not if you live outside their catchment area. Consider the following:

- Get personal recommendations from friends and neighbours.
- Contact your local Health Authority for its list of doctors, which provides information about each practice, the doctor's sex and age or date of qualification, services the practice provides and who else works there. Your local library may also have a list.
- Read the practice leaflet to see what services are provided by the practice. Even though practices have to produce leaflets by law, to explain who works at the practice and what services are on offer, the quality of leaflets varies enormously.
- Get a pre-registration interview with the GP. Some GPs may be willing to talk to you before you register to discuss your needs and see if you get on. Some practices may prefer you to see the practice nurse instead. If you do not manage to get an appointment, talk to the practice manager.
- Contact your local Community Health Council. They are the patients' statutory representative in the NHS and may be able to point you in the right direction. (They are called Local Health Councils in Scotland and Health and Social Services Councils in Northern Ireland.)

Remember that after all this, the practice may turn you down. If you cannot find a GP who will take you on contact your Health Authority which has a duty to find you one.

When you are making your final decision keep in mind:

- **Age:** would you prefer an older GP or one who has qualified more recently?
- **Sex:** would you prefer a male or female doctor? By joining a group practice you may be able to get access to both.
- **Special interests:** would you like a GP with an interest in a particular condition, e.g. diabetes?
- **Location:** is it important to have a practice within walking distance or on a certain bus route?
- **Services:** do you want services such as counselling and complementary therapies to be available? Would you like to be able to see a nurse about minor problems?
- **Surgery hours:** are evening or weekend clinics important for you? Do you prefer an appointment system or an open surgery where you just turn up?
- **Facilities:** do you need wheelchair access?
- **Out of hours care:** you may find that your GP is not the one you will get to see, if you have an emergency night call.

Health checks

All newly registered patients must be offered a check-up within 28 days after being accepted by a new practice. These checks will usually be carried out by the practice nurse. If you are not well enough to visit the surgery the nurse can visit you in your home. All patients over 75 must be offered an annual check-up, again at home if you cannot visit the surgery. The check-up includes assessing your mental and physical condition, mobility and physical environment.

Community Health Services

These are provided by employees of Community Health Service Trusts, but they can often be found at GP practices. With many health care problems it is teamwork between a range of different providers which gives you the best package of care. You can be referred to them by your GP. The name community services just indicates that they provide services in health centres, GP or dental practices or directly to you at home, rather than at hospital.

District nurses (community nurses)

District nurses are qualified nurses but are also specially trained to care for people at home. Although most of their time is spent in people's homes, they also work in GPs' surgeries, residential homes and health centres. They carry out a diverse range of duties apart from nursing, such as advising on healthy living. District nurses can also provide further sources of information such as voluntary groups. You are most likely to be referred to a district nurse by your GP, although social workers, home helps and relatives can also request help from one on your behalf. To get in touch with a district nurse ring your GP's surgery or contact the Community Health Services Trust.

Community psychiatric nurses

Community psychiatric nurses provide counselling, help and support to people in the community who have mental health problems. They are registered nurses, either in mental illness or learning disability nursing. They can assess the psychiatric needs of an individual and their social and physical requirements. They also provide help and support for family members.

Community psychiatric nurses work with GPs, social workers and doctors who specialise in psychiatric medicine. They operate in regional areas and can be contacted directly, or through your GP or the social services. Some work in specialist teams, such as those involved with caring for elderly people with psychiatric conditions.

Chiropodists

Chiropodists treat foot problems such as ingrowing toe-nails and corns. Chiropody is available to everyone under the NHS but priority is given to women over 60 and men over 65, disabled people, pregnant women and children.

Chiropodists who work for the NHS are state registered, after completing three years' training. There are long waiting lists so many people opt to see a chiropodist privately. You can contact the Society of Chiropodists and Podiatrists★ to get details of local practitioners. Members have to be state registered and have the initials SRCh after their name.

Domiciliary care

Care assistant schemes use trained helpers to help elderly or disabled people live in the community, for example helping people get up, wash and dress themselves, prepare meals and go shopping. Find out from your local social services department whether there is a scheme in your area.

Specialist nurses

These are qualified nurses who can advise on certain topics such as incontinence. You can be referred through your GP. Specialist nurses sometimes run clinics in the GP practice. Ask your GP what specialist nurses work in your area.

Occupational therapists

Occupational therapists work in the community, visiting patients at home to advise on how to cope with daily living, including giving advice on equipment and aids and their installation. Occupational therapists work for the social services department or in hospitals where they are involved in the rehabilitation of disabled people and preparing patients before they are discharged, for example from elderly care wards.

Physiotherapists

Physiotherapists help keep people mobile and rehabilitate others after injury, surgery or stroke. They are involved in treating a wide range of conditions from incontinence, through rheumatism and arthritis to muscular pain. They use methods such as manipulation, massage, exercise, ice and acupuncture. They can treat you in your home or at hospital.

You can contact a physiotherapist through your GP or local hospital physiotherapy department, which may operate an open access system, which means that you do not need your GP to refer you. Physiotherapists also practise in the private sector.

Speech therapists

Speech and language therapists work with patients with all types of speech problems, for example as a result of head injuries and strokes. Speech therapists work in hospitals and in the community; you can be referred to one via your GP or district nurse.

Dietitians

Dietitians work in hospitals and in the community, including GPs' surgeries, health centres and homes for the elderly. The dietitian's role is to assess patients' nutritional status, educate them and help them make informed decisions about their diet. They are especially important in advising patients on therapeutic diets, for example for diabetes. You need to be referred by your GP to see a dietitian.

Other community services

Dentists

Dentists can choose to work privately or to have a contract with the Health Authority to see patients on the NHS. Some dentists carry out both private and NHS dental work.

There are two main types of dentist:

- general dental practitioners
- community dentists – based in health centres.

You may also be referred by your GP or dentist to the dental department of a hospital, which carries out specialist treatment.

Registering with a dentist

The dental contract means that once you have registered with a dentist you are on that list for 15 months. When you register with a dentist, the contract with your old dentist ends automatically. You become entitled to all the dental care you need to maintain the health of your teeth and gums on the NHS. This does not include cosmetic treatment. If you are not registered with a dentist, he or she may accept you as an 'occasional patient'. You are then entitled to a limited range of treatment on the NHS. However, there is evidence that in some areas of the country it is difficult to register with a NHS dentist.

Health Authorities maintain lists of dentists in your area if you have problems finding a local NHS dentist.

Paying for dental treatment

You pay 80 per cent of the cost of NHS treatment, unless you are eligible for free or reduced-cost treatment. The most you can be asked to pay for any one course of NHS treatment is £330. A 'course' is whatever treatments are needed to bring you up to full dental health. The charges for private treatment are far higher with no limit on the costs, so ask for an estimate first.

Certain people get free dental treatment, including those on income support and those who hold an HC2 exemption certificate. Certain war pensioners may be able to get a refund of charges. Other people may get help paying for dental treatment because they are on a low income. Further details are in the Department of Health leaflet HC11 *Are you entitled to help with health costs?*. Dentists also provide certain services that are free for everyone, including home visits and repairs to dentures.

Opticians

Opticians may have a contract with the Health Authority to provide services on the NHS.

There are four different types of opticians:

- Ophthalmic opticians – sometimes called optometrists, they test eyesight and examine eyes for any medical problems. They prescribe glasses or contact lenses to correct vision but refer any medical problems to your GP or eye doctor (opthalmologists).
- Dispensing opticians – they make up your glasses but cannot prescribe them.
- Ophthalmologist – they are doctors specialising in the treatment of eye disorders.
- Orthoptists – they work with ophthalmologists, usually in eye hospital departments.

Eye tests are especially important for older people as they can help detect glaucoma. They also give early warning of conditions such as hypertension and diabetes. The risk of eye problems increases as you get older – most blind/partially sighted people are elderly. Conditions such as glaucoma are far more successfully treated if they are identified early – i.e. before any symptoms show. So routine eye examinations are vital and are now free to the over-60s.

Any deterioration in your eye-sight should always be checked – don't assume 'it's just old age'.

Choosing an optician

You can book an appointment with any registered optician for an eye test. You can find a list of registered opticians from a variety of sources, including your local library and the *Yellow Pages*, and your Health Authority will have a list. Check first that the optician provides NHS treatment.

Paying for optical services

Since 1989 'free' NHS eye tests have been available only to certain people, including those on income support, people with an HC2 certificate, people registered as blind or partially sighted, diagnosed diabetic or glaucoma patients, anyone over the age of 60, anyone of 40 or over who is a parent, brother, sister or child of a person with diagnosed glaucoma, patients in the Hospital Eye Service, people needing complex lenses who would get a voucher for them. If you have an HC3 certificate you may not have to pay the full cost of your eye test. Holding the HC2 certificate also entitles you to help with the cost of glasses or contact lenses. A range of different values of voucher are available depending on your prescription. Check with your Health Authority or GP or look at leaflet HC12 from the Department of Health.

Pharmacists

Pharmacists dispense prescriptions and can give you advice about medicines and a wide range of health problems. They are the most accessible of all health professionals. Most pharmacists work in chemists and some in hospital pharmacies.

Men and women over 60 automatically qualify for free prescriptions. Exemptions are also made for people with a specified medical condition confirmed by their doctor, those with HC2 certificates and those receiving a War Pension and who need a prescription for the disability for which they get the pension.

If you have regular prescriptions it might be cheaper to get a four-monthly or yearly prescription pre-payment certificate. You can pick up an application form for these from post offices, pharmacists, or from your Health Authority.

Going into hospital

You may be able to claim for the cost of travelling to hospital for treatment as an in-patient or as an out-patient or when you are discharged from hospital. If someone needs to accompany you for medical reasons, their fares may be paid as well.

Your travel expenses will be fully paid if:

- You are automatically entitled to health benefits (e.g. you are on income support) or have an HC2 certificate.
- You live in the area covered by the Highlands and Islands Development Board in Scotland and have to travel at least 30 miles (or more than 5 miles by water) to get to hospital (you can find out about this scheme at your GP's surgery.

If you are entitled to help with your travelling costs, you will receive the payment when you get to hospital. You have to find the cheapest form of transport to the hospital.

If you have an HC3 certificate you may be entitled to some help with travelling costs. The amount you pay will depend on the maximum amount stated on your certificate. To claim, get form HC1 *Claim for help with health costs.*

If you have difficulty travelling to hospital you may be entitled to go by the hospital car service. Ask your GP about this. NHS ambulance services provide transport for those who are medically unfit to travel by other means. You do not have to pay for this.If you receive mobility allowance you can use it to help you with your travel needs. There are also travel passes which allow disabled or elderly people to use public transport free or at a reduced rate. In many parts of the country there are Dial-a-Ride schemes which provide transport for disabled people. Ask your local social services department or your GP.

If you are visiting someone else in hospital you may also qualify for help with travel costs if you are on Income Support. To claim, get form HC1 *Claim for help with health costs.*

Your pension in hospital

If you are receiving a state pension, tell your Social Security office if you are going into hospital for in-patient treatment on the NHS and let them know the discharge date as soon as possible.

If you live in a local council residential home and you are going into hospital for in-patient treatment on the NHS, your retirement pension may be reduced immediately. If you have been in hospital for more than six weeks when it becomes due it will be immediately reduced. To check how much your pension will be affected ask for leaflet GL12 *Going into hospital?* from the Benefits Agency. If you live in your own home your pension is not affected until you have been in hospital for six weeks.

Patient's Charter

The Patient's Charter was launched in 1991 and highlights the rights of all patients. At the time of writing this Charter is to be replaced with a new NHS Charter which will set standards of care you can expect but will also state what the NHS can expect from you: your responsibilities.

Private treatment

Some people decide to be treated privately rather than on the NHS. It is important to remember that private health care is not and does not claim to be a complete replacement for the NHS. Do not assume that your private health insurance will cover all your needs – read the small print very carefully. See below for points to consider when choosing your policy. The NHS covers all medical and surgical treatments including emergencies, while most private treatment is for straightforward, non-emergency surgery such as hip replacements, varicose vein removal and hernias. These operations can be those with the longer waiting lists, so going private may ensure faster treatment.

Private treatment does have some advantages over the NHS, including choosing your own consultant and sometimes your hospital. The food, internal decoration, privacy and visiting arrangements may all be better in private hospitals.

PRIVATE MEDICAL INSURANCE: WHAT'S COVERED

Private medical insurance is designed to pay the bills for private treatment of 'acute' conditions – which means short-term and curable disorders. In general, policies do not cover the treatment of long-term illness which cannot be cured, such as asthma, diabetes and multiple sclerosis, conditions commonly referred to as 'chronic'

Here are the main things you can usually claim for. There may be various limits on the amounts you can claim for in each category, so read the small print very carefully:

- Accommodation and nursing charges – often the biggest part of the bill.
- Surgeons' and anaesthetists' fees; operating theatre fees.
- X-rays: dressings and drugs while you are an in-patient.
- Consultants' and physicians' fees.
- Radiotherapy, chemotherapy, physiotherapy and other specialist treatment.
- Home nursing charges if the consultant recommends home nursing and it follows on from in-patient treatment.
- Out-patient and day care treatment, but only if this is linked to a stay in hospital.

The most expensive policies may also include cover for:

- Cash benefits if you stay in hospital as an NHS patient.
- Treatment while travelling abroad, but not if you go abroad specifically to get treatment. (The USA and Canada may be excluded.)

What the brochures don't tell you

There are other important issues to consider when deciding whether or not to opt for private health care that may not always be obvious from the brochures.

PRIVATE MEDICAL INSURANCE: WHAT'S NOT COVERED

Insurance probably won't cover you for all your needs. Here are some typical exclusions:

- Health problems you have already got or had. You can occasionally be covered for pre-existing (or foreseeable) conditions but only if the insurer agrees to cover them when you apply. Some policies cover pre-existing conditions once you have had no treatment for them for one or two years.
- Incurable conditions. Insurance covers diseases, illnesses and injuries which can be cured: long-term illnesses such as diabetes are not covered, though initial treatment and relief of acute phases may be. The terminal stages of cancer may not be covered.

- AIDS. Some policies are now specifically excluding AIDS and related conditions, but you may be covered for initial diagnosis and limited stay in hospital.
- Routine treatment, such as dentists' and opticians' services and preventive screening. Some policies entitle you to a discount on the cost of general check-ups.
- Complementary medicine, though some policies pay for osteopaths and chiropractors if your GP refers you.
- Some hospital and nursing home accommodation costs – if you are a patient partly for domestic reasons, for example geriatric care.
- Some out-patient costs, e.g. glasses, hearing aids, medicine.
- The services of your GP (such as the fee for filling in your claim form).
- Renal dialysis.
- Self-inflicted injuries or suicide attempts.
- Alcoholism and drug abuse.
- Cosmetic surgery, unless it is needed after an accident.

It is very important to look at each policy on its merits. The list of exclusions does preclude many of the things which affect people as they get older, related to chronic problems. The consultants who work in the private sector are usually the same consultants who work in the NHS (many have a part-time contract with the NHS which also allows them to do private work). Private patients will usually see a consultant. NHS patients should always be in the charge of a consultant but they may be treated by a less senior doctor, under supervision.

- If you have complications you may sometimes be better off in an NHS hospital, as they are more likely than private hospitals to have the back-up facilities to hand, though some private hospitals built near NHS hospitals, or on the same site or as the private wing of an NHS hospital should have quick access to full back-up facilities.
- Private hospitals do not always have a resident doctor, so there could be a delay in an emergency – for example, at night if a doctor had to be called to the hospital.

If you are paying out of your own pocket for private health care, ensure that your bill is broken down in sufficient detail for you to see how much you are being charged for each item. Shop around for the best deal for your circumstances.

Paybeds

Some NHS hospitals have private paybeds. About one in ten private operations is done using these beds in NHS hospitals. Like any other private patient, patients in paybeds pay for both their accommodation and for private treatment, but they have the advantage that NHS back-up facilities and staff are on hand in an emergency. Some of the beds are on private wings, but most are private rooms on ordinary wards, so the surroundings may not be as good as in a private hospital.

Community care changes

The second major consequence of the 1990 NHS and Community Care Act was the 'new community care'. It placed the onus on Local Authorities to find out what services were needed to enable people to live in their own homes, after the closure of long-term care institutions. The closure programme had seen a growth in the private sector provision of nursing and residential care homes, mostly paid for out of the social services budget.

As of 1993, Local Authorities (social services department) have had a duty to assess people who need community care and to state their criteria for eligibility for assessment.

The assessment is in two parts:

- A care assessment – this considers the needs and wishes of an individual and his or her carer, if there is one. If it is decided that care is needed and those needs can be met, the provision of the care will be arranged. This 'package of care' should be designed to meet the individual's needs.
- A financial assessment to see how much, if anything, the individual has to pay for the services. For care in residential or nursing homes the local authority will follow national rules, but for care in the home, the local authority will decide its rules.

To find out what is available in your area, you need to talk to your Health Authority. The split between Health Authority and Local

Authority responsibilities in terms of providing health vs. social care is at its most controversial here. Increasingly, you will be expected to pay for services you may have thought you were entitled to as part of state provision. It is difficult to specify exactly what services these are as they differ from area to area and depend on what agreements were reached between Health and Local Authorities over who should pay for what. Anything that falls on the Local Authority side, you will be means-tested for.

The leaflets mentioned in this chapter are available from your local Benefits Agency offices; you should also be able to find them at doctors' and dentists' surgeries, hospitals and post offices.

Chapter 31

Health problems

Although there are a number of changes in the body that occur as a normal part of ageing, it would be totally wrong to regard ill-health, loss of mobility and a decline in mental agility as an inevitable result of growing old. In fact, most people are capable of staying fit and active well into their eighties. Even those who do have to cope with a new health problem, such as arthritis, high blood pressure or heart disease, are usually able, with the right medication and a few adjustments to their daily routine, to enjoy their retirement to the full.

There is bound to be some deterioration with advancing years, but, in most people, this natural decline can be slowed right down, simply by staying physically and mentally active.

Stay physically active

As you grow older, you will notice a slight loss of flexibility and muscle strength, as well as a reduction in endurance (stamina). However, taking regular physical exercise should help maintain the heart, lungs, muscles and circulation in the best possible condition, making it easier to perform normal daily activities like shopping and housework without becoming unduly breathless or tired. This exercise routine will also keep balance and coordination in good working order, reducing the chance of a fall indoors or out.

There is no need to push yourself too hard – in fact, it would be dangerous to exercise over-strenuously. Just choose an activity that you enjoy, that gets you moving about, without making you gasp for breath or causing your joints or muscles to become stiff or sore. Also, you should check with your doctor before you start a new activity, and stop exercising at once if you suffer any warning symptoms of heart strain, such as chest pains, dizziness or palpitations.

Even for someone who is housebound, a routine of stretching and loosening-up exercises can do much to stop the joints stiffening up, and help keep you independent and mobile. Ask your doctor, nurse or health visitor to recommend a suitable programme of home exercises, and see Chapter 29.

Stay mentally agile

As with physical performance, there also tends to be a slight deterioration in certain mental functions with advancing age. For example, many elderly people notice some difficulties with short-term memory, finding it more difficult to remember a new name or telephone number.

However, a general more serious decline in mental function, known as dementia, is not a normal characteristic of ageing and is always the result of a disease (see the section on dementia in the Health Problems A–Z).

To maintain mental vigour, it is important to keep the brain constantly stimulated with a variety of new ideas and activities. The more you use your mind, the more likely you are to remain mentally agile. This is why it is so important to plan ahead before you retire, to ensure your increased leisure time does not leave you bored and frustrated.

Preventive measures

Doctors and scientists who have studied the effects of ageing on health and fitness have yet to agree on the exact nature of the biological processes involved. One theory is a progressive decline in the body's immune system so that it is no longer able to defend itself as efficiently against bacteria, viruses and the growth of cancer cells. Alternative mechanisms include the gradual build-up of toxins inside the body; or the wearing down of the templates that control the copying of different types of cell, allowing errors to occur during tissue regeneration.

SMOKING

People who are trying to give up smoking may have difficulty doing so on their own unless they are highly motivated and have a specific reason for giving up. Not only is nicotine a powerfully addictive drug but many people suffer quite unpleasant side effects from withdrawal. To help overcome these effects there are nicotine substitutes in the form of chewing-gum and skin patches. Counselling and various self-help measures (videos, for instance) may also be encouragements while you are giving up.

What is agreed is the influence of lifestyle factors such as smoking, poor diet, lack of exercise, excessive alcohol consumption and over-exposure to strong sunlight – all of which are known to accelerate the degeneration caused by ageing of body organs and tissues, including the skin, bones, nervous system and circulation.

Although genetic inheritance also influences the ageing process in a way that is obviously beyond your control, adopting a healthy lifestyle can significantly reduce your risk of developing many of the diseases that are more common in older people. The importance of lifestyle is discussed in more detail under each of those health problems where it represents a significant underlying cause.

IMPORTANT NOTE

It is important to seek medical help for any persistent, recurrent or unexplained symptom. Unfortunately, many elderly people suffer their symptoms in silence, blaming their aches and pains, blurred vision, deafness, dizziness, falls – to name just a few of the more common complaints – on getting older.

Do not regard any troublesome symptom as being a normal part of ageing. Often the cause is a particular disease, treatment of which may relieve that symptom, making life a lot more fulfilling.

Health Problems A-Z

Angina

Angina is a transient pain or tightness which occurs in the chest and sometimes spreads to the neck, jaw or arms. Typically, the pain comes on suddenly during exercise, although it may be brought on by stress, extremes of temperature, or eating a large meal.

Descriptions of angina vary from a mild discomfort to a heavy, crushing pain, and sometimes it is mistaken for indigestion or acid reflux. Other symptoms that often accompany an angina attack include sweating, nausea, dizziness and breathing difficulty. The pain usually eases with rest; if symptoms persist this may be due to a heart attack, where the heart muscle is permanently damaged.

Angina is caused by a lack of oxygen and nutrients reaching the heart muscle, usually because the coronary arteries which encircle and supply blood to the heart have become clogged up with fatty deposits – a condition known as atherosclerosis. This narrowing of the coronary arteries prevents the normal increase in blood flow that should occur when extra demands are placed on the heart, such as during exercise. Atherosclerosis tends to increase in severity with age, which is why angina is more common in elderly people. Women are protected from atherosclerosis by their oestrogen hormones until the menopause, when there is a sudden decline in oestrogen production.

Treatment of angina includes drugs to widen the coronary arteries (nitrates, calcium channel blockers) and drugs to reduce the heart's demands for oxygen by slowing the heart rate (beta blockers). Surgical procedures such as angioplasty (insertion of a catheter with an inflatable balloon tip into the narrowed arteries to flatten the fatty deposits) or bypass grafting (attachment of a blood vessel to divert blood flow around the blockage) are successful in relieving symptoms in many people.

Self-help measures for angina sufferers include stopping smoking to help increase blood flow through the coronary arteries; exercising regularly but only until the symptoms come on; relaxation measures to reduce stress; avoiding exercise on hot or very cold days, or soon after a meal; and losing excess weight to put less strain on the heart.

Anxiety

The main causes of anxiety in older people are worries about health, money, or loss of independence. While anxiety is a perfectly normal reaction to any problem or fear that cannot readily be resolved, it can become a disorder in its own right if it is preventing the individual from thinking clearly or rationally, sleeping properly, or carrying out everyday activities.

Many elderly people live alone and because there is no one to share their worries with on a regular basis, they are more vulnerable to a build-up in anxiety. Therefore, the first step is to find someone to talk things through with, perhaps a friend, a relative, a neighbour, the vicar or your doctor or health visitor.

If there are persistent or recurrent symptoms related to anxiety, such as difficulty falling asleep, loss of appetite, a feeling of suffocation, constant trembling, or a sense of impending doom, it is important to seek professional help. A variety of measures can relieve anxiety, including relaxation exercises, regular physical activities, meditation or counselling. The National Association for Mental Health (MIND)* may be able to offer advice.

Tranquillisers can also be very effective in the short term, but these do not help the individual to overcome the underlying reasons for the anxiety. Also, if they are taken regularly for longer than a couple of weeks, there is a risk of addiction.

Arteriosclerosis

Hardening of the arteries – arteriosclerosis – is a group of disorders which cause a progressive thickening and loss of elasticity of the artery walls. The most common of these disorders is atherosclerosis, a condition where the arteries become clogged by a build-up of fatty deposits.

The risk of atherosclerosis increases with age, but there are a number of lifestyle factors which speed up the development of fatty deposits inside the arteries. These contributory factors include tobacco smoking, lack of exercise, excessive alcohol consumption and eating a lot of foods containing large amounts of saturated fat and cholesterol.

Common disorders which may be caused by atherosclerosis (discussed under their own separate headings) are angina, heart attack, dementia, leg ulcers, stroke and transient ischaemic attacks.

Back pain

The most common cause of back pain in elderly people is osteoarthritis of the spine. In this condition, wear and tear of the joints between the vertebrae (spinal bones) leads to narrowing of the spaces between the joints and overgrowth of bone around them.

As a result of this joint degeneration, the spine becomes painful, stiff and often tender over specific areas. Movements such as bending over or getting out of bed can prove difficult, mainly because of the stiffness that develops in the lower spine.

A sudden attack of severe back pain in someone over the age of 60 is occasionally due to collapse of one or more vertebrae that have been weakened by osteoporosis. In this condition, which mainly affects women after the menopause, the bones lose their normal density and become more fragile. The spine has to carry a considerable load as it is the main supporting column of the body; it is therefore not surprising that vertebrae affected by osteoporosis sometimes compress and crumble.

Anyone with persistent back pain should be careful over their choice of painkillers: they all have their potential side effects which are more likely to develop the older you are and the longer you take them. Codeine and dihydrocodeine are very effective pain relievers, but often cause constipation; aspirin and other anti-inflammatory drugs may cause indigestion, peptic ulcers and a variety of other adverse effects that you should discuss with your doctor; paracetamol is a relatively safe painkiller, but should never be taken in excess because of the risk of liver damage.

For those people with osteoarthritis of the spine, there are a number of important self-help measures in addition to medication. These include exercises to strengthen the supporting abdominal and spinal muscles – swimming is a particularly good activity in this respect; a heating pad to relax any painful muscle spasm; a corset to act as a lumbar support; a firm mattress or a board under the mattress to provide support at night; and a resolve to lose any excess weight if you can to reduce the load on your spine. The Back Care Association* may be able to offer further advice.

It is not a good idea to rest your back all the time. Prolonged sitting or lying will only make the discomfort and stiffness due to osteoarthritis worse. Ask your doctor, nurse or health visitor which exercises you can safely do to keep your spine mobile and the supporting muscles firm.

Finally, see your doctor as soon as possible if your back pain is getting worse, or if you develop symptoms of pressure on a spinal nerve, such as weakness, numbness, pins and needles, or problems with bladder or bowel control.

Bereavement

Bereavement, which is a natural reaction to the death of someone you loved or were close to, is a traumatic experience whatever your age. However, because older people are more likely to suffer the loss of their partner or a close friend, bereavement is a relevant issue in any discussion of health problems after retirement.

Although bereavement itself is not a disease, it can cause a variety of symptoms that may be mistaken for the onset of mental illness and, because it is such a stressful life event, it is important to take precautions to prevent any long-term effect on health and well-being. Symptoms that may occur as the result of bereavement include numbing of emotions, outbursts of grief, feelings of hostility even towards the individual who has died, seeing or hearing the dead person, and guilt about not having done more for the person when he or she was alive. Realising that all these responses are perfectly normal will help in the recovery process as you slowly come to terms with what has happened.

To protect your own health, try not to bottle up your emotions; keep busy to avoid brooding, but don't take on too much; look to friends and family for comfort and support but don't allow them to overburden you with their grief; and even if you don't feel like it, eat at least one proper meal each day and take some exercise.

For those people who are unable to cope or who become severely depressed or agitated, their GP may prescribe antidepressants or a short course of tranquillisers. A number of organisations offer practical help and advice to the bereaved, including CRUSE Bereavement Care,★ the National Association of Widows,★ and Age Concern England,★ all of which have branches all over the UK.

Blindness

Blindness may be the result of a variety of disorders; in elderly people the most common causes are damage to the retina due to diabetes (diabetic retinopathy), cataracts (opacities developing in the internal lens of the eye), untreated glaucoma (abnormal build-up of pressure inside the eye), stroke (where the haemorrhage or blood clot damages the part of the brain which responds to visual information) or degeneration of the central part of the retina (macular degeneration).

It is important to consult a doctor as soon as possible in the event of any loss of vision or persistent visual disturbance, such as seeing coloured haloes around lights. However, because loss of vision is usually a gradual process which may pass unnoticed, regular eye checks are essential. These are free for those over 60. Anyone with a close relative who has suffered from glaucoma should mention it to the optician because this eye condition can be inherited; in any case, pressure checks are a routine part of an eye test for an elderly person.

Treatment of blindness will obviously depend upon the underlying cause, for example surgical removal of a cataract which can be replaced by an artificial lens, or laser therapy to seal damaged blood vessels on the retina in someone with diabetic retinopathy.

Anyone who is left with a permanent severe defect in their vision should ask the GP to register them as blind or partially sighted, which will entitle them to a range of visual aids as well as certain benefits from the DSS. The Royal National Institute for the Blind (RNIB)* can also offer advice.

Bronchitis

A productive cough that brings up sputum (also referred to as phlegm or mucus) may be due to an attack of bronchitis. This condition, which may come on after a cold or flu, is due to inflammation of the bronchi (the main airways inside the lungs). As a result of the inflammation, the normal production of mucus in the bronchi is increased; it often becomes discoloured due to the infecting viruses or bacteria, and the white blood cells that are fighting them.

For an acute attack of bronchitis, the doctor may prescribe a course of antibiotics to deal with any bacterial infection present. To relieve the cough, take an expectorant to make the sputum easier to shift, but avoid a cough suppressant which will only prevent the airways being cleared of excess mucus.

Also, use a steam vaporiser because a moist atmosphere will be less irritating to the airways, and drink plenty of fluids to help thin the mucus.

Chronic bronchitis is mainly a disease of smokers and those who have been exposed to high levels of air pollution. It is defined as a productive cough on most days for three months or more every year. Tobacco smoke and air pollutants have an irritant effect on the bronchi, increasing the production of thick, sticky mucus which clogs up these airways. In addition to the productive cough, there is likely to be wheezing, tightness in the chest and breathing difficulty on exertion.

The problem is mainly due to an increase in the size and activity of the mucus-producing glands and a greater susceptibility to chest infections. Just stopping smoking should improve the situation although the longer the individual has smoked, the more severe the lung damage is likely to be.

Measures to deal with a sudden flare-up of symptoms in chronic bronchitis are as described for acute attacks. In addition, the doctor may prescribe a bronchodilator, usually as an inhaler, to try to open up the obstructed airways, but these do not work as well in chronic bronchitis as they do in asthma.

Anyone with the tendency to develop bronchitis as a complication of a cold or flu should visit the GP for treatment as soon as the symptoms emerge in order to reduce the chance of a bad attack. Because older people are more vulnerable to respiratory complications with flu, vaccination each autumn against flu is routinely recommended for everyone over the age of 65.

Cancer

Cancer is not just one disease; there are many different types, each of which starts by involving a specific organ or tissue in the body. If you develop any of the symptoms listed in the box, arrange a visit to your doctor straight away – early diagnosis means that treatment is more likely to be successful.

Unfortunately, many people are scared to report symptoms they think might be due to cancer. This is foolish for two main reasons: their symptoms will often be due to a harmless or non-cancerous condition which will not only respond to treatment, but also allay their fears; and in those few cases where the diagnosis is cancer, any delay in treatment reduces the chance of a successful cure.

CANCER WARNING SYMPTOMS

Any of the following symptoms may be an early-warning signal for cancer:

- Changes in a mole on the skin.
- A new lump or bump.
- Mouth ulceration lasting longer than one month.
- Persistent change from normal bowel habit.
- Unexplained weight loss.
- Vaginal bleeding after the menopause.
- Hoarseness lasting several weeks.
- Coughing or vomiting up blood.

There have been a number of advances in the treatment of cancer, with improved surgical techniques and a wider variety of powerful anti-cancer drugs available. In addition, doctors are now better able to control the complications that sometimes accompany cancer, such as pain, nausea, constipation, cough or difficulty swallowing.

The cancer screening tests offered to women on a regular basis – cervical smear and mammography (breast X-ray) – are usually only recommended up until the age of 65. However, if any woman has passed this age without having had either of these checks, she should ask her doctor whether the screening test is still advisable. You can also continue having breast screening for as long as you want – ask your GP. Cancers of the cervix and breast may not cause any obvious symptoms until they have reached an advanced stage.

BACUP (the British Association of Cancer United Patients)* can give further information on general and specific queries to do with cancer.

Colds and flu

For most people, catching a cold or a dose of flu is no more than a temporary inconvenience. These viral infections may cause a variety of familiar symptoms, including sore throat, fever, dry cough, aches and pains, runny nose, weakness and swollen glands. The main difference between a cold and flu is that the latter typically makes you feel too ill to do anything other than stay in bed, and lasts a few days longer.

Traditional cold and flu remedies, like paracetamol or aspirin to relieve discomfort and bring down a temperature, plenty of fluids to replace those lost with the increase in sweating, and inhalations to ease nasal congestion, are helpful whatever your age.

However, for older people, a cold or flu is potentially a lot more serious. Complications such as bronchitis, pneumonia and pleurisy are more likely to develop, and if there is any long-term heart or lung disorder the risks are even greater.

It is therefore advisable for all people over the age of 65 to ask the doctor about receiving an annual flu jab, which is designed to provide immunity against the influenza viruses expected to be around that year. This immunisation is normally given in September or October.

In addition, if cold or flu symptoms do start, it is important to visit the doctor if any complications seem to be developing, such as a productive cough, chest pain, breathlessness or wheezing.

Constipation

Everyone has their own characteristic bowel habit, and for some a bowel movement only once or twice a week is perfectly normal. The proper definition of constipation is either having to strain to open the bowels, or a decrease in the usual frequency of bowel movements.

Although constipation may affect people of any age, it becomes more common with advancing years. One reason for this is the tendency for older people to eat fewer high-fibre foods; another is the influence of physical activity on bowel function – those who take less exercise as they get older are more prone to constipation.

A number of drugs can also cause constipation including iron pills, painkillers and cough medicines that contain codeine, and certain antacids, all of which are commonly taken by older people. In addition, a significant number take a laxative routinely, in the mistaken belief that they need to have a daily bowel movement, and this can lead, paradoxically, to a lazy bowel.

Self-help measures to relieve constipation include taking more exercise – even a gentle stroll can help; eating more fibre-rich foods such as fresh fruit and vegetables, beans and pulses, whole-grain bread and cereal; and drinking six or more glasses of water or soft drink each day. If these remedies fail to help, seek medical help.

Deafness

Deafness can be a serious handicap because it acts as a barrier to normal conversation, isolating and depressing the sufferer as a result. However, for many elderly people, it may be possible to improve their hearing significantly, so deafness should not be treated as a normal part of getting old.

The first step is to overcome any embarrassment and admit to the GP that you actually have a hearing problem. Sometimes the cause is simply a build-up in ear wax, and hearing can be restored to a satisfactory level by having the ear canals syringed with warm water. This is usually performed by the GP or practice nurse.

Your GP may need to refer you to an ear, nose and throat clinic or hearing aid centre for a full assessment of your hearing, and to see whether a hearing aid might help. However, be warned that in some parts of the country there are long waiting lists for this service on the NHS. Also, however sophisticated the hearing aid, it will only be able to amplify those sound frequencies you have difficulty detecting; it will not give you perfect hearing.

Other measures to help you communicate include asking people to speak slowly and clearly, and to avoid shouting at you, which only distorts the words being spoken. Keep any background noise like the television or radio to a minimum. It may be worthwhile taking a lip-reading class to acquire the basic skills. Further advice may be obtained from the Royal National Institute for Deaf People (RNID),★ the British Deaf Association,★ and the Council for the Advancement of Communication for Deaf People.★

Finally, there has been a lot of adverse publicity about the sale of hearing aids through advertisements in magazines or newspapers. This is because they can be very expensive, and they may not work properly for you if they haven't been designed to suit your particular pattern of hearing loss.

Dementia

Dementia is not a specific type of illness: it is a general term for grossly impaired mental function which may result in loss of short- and long-term memory, altered personality, disorientation and confusion, disruption of speech and comprehension, erratic moods and behaviour, wandering, and an inability to carry out simple everyday activities like washing and dressing.

The most common cause of dementia is Alzheimer's disease, which accounts for about 75 per cent of cases in people over the age of 65. Another common reason for loss of normal mental function is a stroke or series of minor strokes that may not necessarily have caused any physical disability such as paralysis. Parkinson's disease and long-term alcohol abuse may also lead to forms of dementia.

Dementia is not a normal part of ageing and anyone who develops symptoms of mental deterioration should be seen by his or her GP for a thorough evaluation. Occasionally, these symptoms are the result of a disorder which can be treated successfully, for example certain types of anaemia, an infection or even depression, in which case normal mental function can usually be restored.

Unfortunately, however, there is no cure at present for conditions such as Alzheimer's disease. Research into Alzheimer's has suggested several possible causes, for example the excessive build-up of a protein in the brain, which is actually being produced to stimulate nerve cell regeneration as part of a natural mechanism designed to compensate for the effects of ageing. Other theories put forward include the toxic effects of an accumulation of aluminium inside the brain; or an abnormal response to a viral infection.

New drugs are being developed which may improve memory and intellectual ability in some sufferers, but their use is still experimental, and clinical trials are under way to establish whether they are really that effective.

For anyone who has to care for someone who is suffering from dementia, here are a few useful self-help measures that may make life a little easier:

- Establish a daily routine with a fixed schedule of events.
- Make sure that clothes are easy to put on.
- Keep doors and windows locked if the sufferer is likely to wander.
- Do not move objects to new places in the home.
- Help the person keep a diary and a daily checklist of tasks.
- Be patient in the event of stubbornness or aggression, and remember that this is due to the condition.

- Claim benefits from the DSS such as attendance allowance.
- Arrange with your GP temporary care in hospital or a nursing home so that you can take a well-earned break.
- Contact the Alzheimer's Disease Society* for support and advice.

There is more about Alzheimer's disease in Chapter 27.

Dental problems

With a daily routine of brushing and flossing, most people should be able to keep their natural teeth into old age. However, older people have to take extra care of their teeth as the gums tend to recede with age, exposing the neck of the tooth, which has no protective enamel.

Ask your dentist or dental hygienist to check your brushing technique if you are unsure, or use a disclosing tablet, which shows how effectively the teeth have been cleaned by colouring any plaque left behind. Dental floss can be useful in removing particles of food lodged between the teeth, but take care not to cut into the gums.

If there are large spaces between some of the teeth, try using a toothbrush with a single pointed bristle so that all the tooth and gum surfaces can be reached. Toothpicks should be used cautiously because of the risk of damaging the gums.

Around one quarter of adults in the UK have lost their teeth, usually because of gum disease that was not treated soon enough. It is also important to take good care of dentures, cleaning them regularly to reduce the risk of a mouth or gum infection.

For older people who still have some or all of their natural teeth, a dental check-up is recommended at least once a year. Dentures should be checked every three years, and sooner if they are no longer fitting properly or causing soreness in the mouth. Because the gums shrink after the natural teeth are lost and the shape of the mouth may also change, it is often necessary to adjust the structure of the denture or make a new one.

Before having any dental treatment, check that the dentist will provide this under the NHS. Your local Family Health Services Authority can supply a list of NHS dentists in the area. Even under the NHS, you still have to pay a proportion of the charges, so ask the dentist to provide an estimate of the likely bill.

Depression

Although older people are more prone to depression, sometimes as a response to treatment or a chronic illness, symptoms of depression should not be accepted as an inevitable part of getting older. Also, it is important not to allow a serious bout of depression to continue without seeking help from the doctor. Depression will not usually disappear on its own and in severe cases there may be a risk of suicide. Treatment with antidepressants is usually very effective.

Warning symptoms of a depression that should be treated if they persist include waking in the early hours of the morning, generalised aches and pain, a sense of despair, being unable to concentrate, and not feeling like eating anything. Confusion, agitation, extreme apathy and drinking more alcohol than usual can each be the result of depression. Often a friend or relative may have to persuade the depressed person to go to the doctor. Any threat of ending it all should be taken seriously and the doctor called out if necessary.

To ward off depression, it is important to avoid becoming isolated. After retirement, build new social contacts, for example by taking a daytime or evening class, joining a club or getting involved in voluntary work. You might like to contact the Fellowship of Depressives Anonymous* for further information.

Diabetes (maturity onset)

Maturity onset diabetes is the form of diabetes that typically only comes on after the age of 40 and usually does not require insulin injections to keep the condition under control. Unlike the juvenile type of diabetes, where the pancreas stops producing insulin altogether, in the maturity onset or type 2 form the pancreas does release some insulin into the bloodstream, but not enough to prevent a build-up of sugar in the circulation.

Many elderly people with maturity onset diabetes become aware of it only as the result of a routine blood or urine test, which reveals abnormally high blood levels of sugar, or the presence of sugar in the urine.

WARNING SYMPTOMS OF DIABETES

- Excessive thirst; frequent urination.
- Fatigue and weakness.
- Numbness or tingling in the feet and hands.
- Blurred vision.
- Impotence in men.

Symptoms to watch out for are listed in the box. In some sufferers, all that may be needed is a diet with fewer refined carbohydrate (sugary) foods and more high-fibre, unrefined carbohydrate (starchy) foods to help slow down the absorption of sugar into the bloodstream, along with cutting down on fatty foods, particularly saturated fats, to help lose any excess weight.

If these measures are not enough, the doctor can prescribe tablets to keep blood sugar levels normal. In rare cases, insulin injections may be required. Regular check-ups either by the GP or hospital diabetic clinic are advisable to detect the onset of any complications such as eye, nerve or skin damage. Most diabetics monitor the sugar level in their blood or urine using a simple testing kit at home in order to ensure that their condition is not going out of control.

The British Diabetic Association★ can offer further information.

Emphysema

Emphysema is a serious lung disease which involves extensive damage to some of the millions of tiny air sacs (alveoli) that make up the lung tissues. As a result of the walls of these alveoli ballooning and bursting, with clusters of alveoli merging to form fewer, larger air sacs, the surface area of the lungs (through which gases pass to and from the bloodstream) is reduced. The lungs also become less elastic, making it more difficult to breathe, particularly to breathe out.

Symptoms of emphysema include a wheezy cough and breathlessness. Because less oxygen reaches the bloodstream, the skin may develop a bluish tinge. There may also be signs of heart failure, with swelling of the ankles, if the heart is unable to cope with the additional workload resulting from blood no longer flowing freely through the lung circulation.

Emphysema is most commonly caused by heavy smoking, as chemicals inhaled within the tobacco smoke having a toxic effect on the alveoli. Another contributory factor may be air pollution, and a few people develop emphysema because of an inherited defect in a lung enzyme.

Drugs to widen the airways, usually in the form of an inhaler, and steroids to reduce lung inflammation, may be helpful for some sufferers. In severe cases, oxygen may have to be provided in the home.

In addition to giving up smoking and avoiding smoky or polluted atmospheres, which will only make the lung damage worse, an annual flu jab is essential to reduce the risk of a flu-related chest infection. Prompt antibiotic therapy for any chest infection is also essential before it makes the breathing difficulties far worse.

Eye problems

A normal change in the eyes that occurs due to ageing is a gradual loss of elasticity in the internal lens. This condition, known as presbyopia, causes difficulty with near vision. As a result, small print may appear blurred when held at normal reading distance, but can be brought into focus by reading the page at arm's length or, if you are normally short-sighted, by taking your glasses off.

Presbyopia is easily corrected with a pair of reading glasses; it is best to have your eyes checked by an optician to establish the appropriate lens prescription for each eye. Although reading glasses can now be bought over the counter using a do-it-yourself eye chart, the advantage of seeing an optician is to have other more serious eye problems picked up before they cause any permanent damage and loss of vision. If you are short-sighted you may need two sets of lenses – one for reading and one for distance.

A routine eye test is recommended every two years, and sooner if any loss or disturbance of normal vision occurs. Reading glasses usually have to be changed several times, as the lenses become increasingly rigid, until all the focusing has to be done by the spectacle lenses.

There may be a charge for the eye test unless the person is receiving income support or belongs to one of the priority groups, which include anyone over the age of 60, people with glaucoma themselves (or whose close relative has this condition), diabetics and anyone registered blind or partially sighted.

Apart from presbyopia, the three most common eye problems in elderly people are cataracts, glaucoma and macular degeneration. A cataract is usually easily remedied by surgery; glaucoma can be treated successfully with eye drops, tablets or surgery, but any damage that has already been caused by the excessive pressure inside the eye ball cannot be corrected.

Although macular degeneration, a condition where the central part of the retina wears out, is not treatable, much can be done to reduce the handicap resulting from the progressive loss of vision it causes (see Blindness).

Falls

About one third of elderly people are thought to suffer one or more falls each year, half of which are due to an accident such as tripping, while many of the remainder occur with no obvious cause. Because older people, particularly women, are vulnerable to osteoporosis – a condition which weakens the bones (see below) – these falls may cause a fracture, usually of the femur, wrist or spine.

To prevent accidental falls, there are a number of preventive measures (see box). If falls happen out of the blue, or are preceded by dizziness, weakness or some other warning symptom, a check-up from the doctor is essential.

Many of the medical conditions which can cause recurrent falls may be successfully treated, for example anaemia, heart irregularity or vertigo. The doctor can give advice on the easiest way to get up off the floor after a fall. For anyone who lives alone and does not have frequent visitors, it is a good idea to wear a portable alarm trigger so that help can be summoned if the fall has immobilised them (see page 361).

PREVENTIVE MEASURES AGAINST FALLS

- Do not wear loose slippers or long trailing clothing.
- Electric leads should run under the carpet, or around the edge of the room.
- Keep the living areas free from obstacles.
- Remove loose mats or rugs.
- Make sure that floors are not slippery or highly polished.
- Stairs and corridors should be properly lit. Fit two-way switching on stairs.
- Secure loose stair carpets.
- Fit a handrail at each side of the stairs, and add grab-rails in the bathroom.

Foot problems

Older people are more likely than younger ones to develop calluses and corns on their feet. A callus is a thickening of the outer layers of skin due to pressure or irritation; a corn is a callus found on or between the toes. The reason for the greater susceptibility to these skin changes among elderly people is the higher incidence of foot deformities such as bunions, hammer toes and arthritic joints in this age group. As a result, they often find it difficult to buy shoes that fit comfortably without creating areas of friction when they stand or walk.

All corns or calluses should be covered with tape or a non-medicated corn pad for protection. Try to eliminate the cause of the pressure, for example by changing to a different pair of shoes. Soak thickened areas of skin in warm water to soften them, and then gently rub them with a pumice stone. Do not use non-prescription medicated corn pads, and never attempt to trim calluses yourself.

See a chiropodist if a corn or callus becomes painful, tender or inflamed. For people who suffer from persistent or recurrent calluses or corns as a result of a foot deformity, which can be structural or postural, the chiropodist may construct a specially moulded insole. Occasionally, an orthopaedic surgeon may have to perform some type of corrective surgery. The chiropodist can also deal with bunions.

Anyone with diabetes or a poor circulation should have chiropody treatment routinely every few months because they are extremely vulnerable to infection of the skin if it becomes irritated or damaged.

Chiropody services are free for people over the age of 60; however, in some parts of the UK there may be a long delay due to a shortage of state registered chiropodists. If you are seeking private treatment, make sure the chiropodist is state registered, shown by the letters SRCh after his or her name. The Society of Chiropodists and Podiatrists* can supply names of state registered chiropodists in your area.

Gout

Gout is a type of arthritis that characteristically attacks one joint at a time, usually the joint at the base of the big toe. It develops as a result of the deposition of uric acid crystals inside the joint, which cause it to become temporarily inflamed, and so extremely painful and swollen with redness of the overlying skin.

Treatment of an attack involves large doses of an anti-inflammatory drug and sometimes colchicine to suppress the inflammation rapidly. If the cause is abnormally high levels of uric acid in the blood and attacks are recurrent, the doctor may prescribe a drug which reduces the production of uric acid in the body or a drug to increase the amount of uric acid passed in the urine.

Occasionally, uric acid crystallises as white deposits under the skin (tophi), which may then ulcerate and have to be removed surgically.

Gout sufferers are advised to reduce their dietary intake of purine, which is converted in the body to uric acid. Foods to avoid because they are high in purine include offal (liver, kidney, heart), game, anchovies, mackerel, herring, scallops, sardines, whitebait and mussels. Foods to eat only in moderation because they contain a fair amount of purine include meat, poultry, fish not mentioned above, peas, green beans, lentils, spinach, mushrooms, asparagus and cauliflower. The Arthritis Research Campaign* produces a free leaflet on the condition.

Haemorrhoids (see Piles)

Hair loss

Gradual, mild thinning of the hair on top of the head is a normal part of ageing; unless the individual has inherited the condition known as male-pattern baldness, some hair should remain covering most of the scalp. Hair loss affects about 50 per cent of men by the age of 50.

In male-pattern baldness, which may also affect a few women after the menopause, hair is lost initially from the temples and crown to be replaced by very fine, downy hair. As the affected area of scalp widens, the normal hair line recedes.

There are many other causes of excessive hair loss which may occur whatever your age. Your doctor should be able to tell whether there is some underlying treatable condition by examining the scalp and skin on other parts of the body.

For hair loss that is causing distress or embarrassment, there are a variety of possible measures including wigs, toupees or a hair transplant. Application of a solution of the drug minoxidil (which was originally introduced to treat high blood pressure) may induce regrowth of fine hair in some people, but the results are not impressive.

Heart attack

A heart attack, also known as a coronary thrombosis or myocardial infarction, is a serious condition in which part of the heart muscle dies after interruption of its normal blood supply. In most cases, a heart attack is caused by the formation of a blood clot in one of the coronary arteries which encircle the heart. The clot develops in a section of the artery that is already narrowed by fatty deposits (see Arteriosclerosis).

Symptoms of a heart attack may include pain across the centre of the chest, pain spreading into the neck, jaw, shoulders or arms, sweating, nausea, vomiting, palpitations and breathlessness. Risk factors for a heart attack are divided into unavoidable ones, such as getting older, a family history of heart attacks, diabetes and high blood pressure, as well as avoidable ones, such as smoking, drinking too much alcohol, eating foods high in saturated fats and cholesterol, and being overweight.

Anyone suspected of having a heart attack should be seen by a doctor as soon as possible. A new type of medication is available which, injected into the circulation, can quickly dissolve the blood clots that cause most heart attacks. These clot-busting drugs can halt a heart attack and minimise the muscle damage as long as they are injected within a few hours of the onset of symptoms.

After a heart attack, assuming there have not been any serious complications, ask the doctor to recommend an appropriate exercise programme. Taking regular exercise after an attack can reduce the chance of a recurrence.

Hernia

An abdominal hernia is the abnormal protrusion of an internal organ, usually part of the intestine, through a gap or weakness in the abdominal muscle wall. This type of hernia is more common in elderly people because the abdominal muscles tend to lose some of their strength and tone, partly because older people tend to be less active and because they tend to put on weight around the abdomen later in life.

If you notice a bulge on the abdominal wall or in the groin see your doctor. The main risk from an abdominal hernia is obstruction of the intestine or its blood supply as a result of the protruding loop becoming compressed, which in turn can lead to potentially fatal complications such as peritonitis or gangrene.

Surgical repair is recommended in most cases to prevent these complications recurring. The operation is usually relatively easy for the surgeon to perform, keeping the patient in hospital for a few days at the most. Before returning to normal activities, particularly doing any carrying or lifting, it is essential to follow a supervised programme of exercises to stretch and strengthen the abdominal muscles – otherwise the risk of recurrence is much greater.

For those people who are not fit enough to have an operation, a surgical truss or corset may be provided to prevent the hernia from bulging through the muscle wall. To be effective, it must be possible to ease the hernia gently back inside the abdomen; the truss should be put on before getting out of bed and then worn all day.

If a hernia suddenly becomes painful, tender, swollen or inflamed, seek medical attention at once, as these are signs that the intestine is under pressure.

High blood pressure

Blood pressure is the force that pushes blood around the circulation; it is generated by the pumping action of the heart and the natural elasticity of the artery walls. It is when this pressure is too high, a condition known as hypertension, that problems can arise.

Blood pressure tends to increase steadily with age because the arteries in older people are less elastic and often narrowed by fatty deposits (see Arteriosclerosis). An excessively high blood pressure at any age usually occurs without any obvious cause, although in a few cases there is an underlying medical reason, for example kidney damage, a blood vessel disease or a hormone disorder.

Most people with dangerously high blood pressure experience no warning symptoms, which is why doctors like to check everyone's blood pressure regularly. The measurement of blood pressure comes as two figures: the higher one is the reading at the moment the heart beats, the lower one is when the heart is relaxed. For people over the age of 60, the ideal blood pressure is 140/90 or less.

If the upper reading is much higher than 140, or the lower reading is 100 or more, your GP will encourage you to take such steps as losing excess weight, taking regular gentle exercise, cutting down on salt and stopping smoking. Relaxation or meditation can also help.

If despite all this the blood pressure remains high, medication is usually recommended. This is because untreated hypertension causes damage to arteries, particularly in the heart, brain, kidneys and eyes, resulting in a greater risk of heart attack, stroke, kidney failure and blindness.

Hypothermia

Hypothermia is a potentially fatal condition in which the body's internal temperature falls to below 35°C/95°F. Elderly people are more vulnerable to hypothermia because as the body ages it becomes less sensitive to the cold. Not only are older people less likely to feel cold when their body temperature drops, but they are also less efficient at generating body heat, for example through shivering.

A number of medical problems that are more common among older people, such as immobility due to arthritis or an underactive thyroid gland, also increase the risk of hypothermia. Death due to hypothermia may occur as a direct result of a low body temperature, which can interfere with normal breathing and the heartbeat; or it may be an indirect cause, through making a heart or chest complaint worse or reducing resistance to infections such as pneumonia.

All elderly people should take steps to protect themselves against the cold, for example by living in one warm room if it is too difficult or expensive to heat the whole house, eating and drinking properly, wrapping up in several thin layers of clothing, doing regular arm and leg exercises, if possible, and getting the windows and doors properly insulated.

Help the Aged* runs the National Winter Warmth Campaign, which gives more advice on how to avoid hypothermia.

It is also essential for anyone who cares for an elderly person to be aware of the warning symptoms of hypothermia, which include pale cold skin, puffiness of the face, increasing drowsiness and confusion, slurring of the speech and shallow breathing. First aid measures while waiting for medical help are to wrap the person in a warm blanket and if he or she is conscious to give a warm drink. However, it is dangerous to give alcohol, rub the skin, apply a hot water bottle or put the person into a hot bath.

Incontinence

Incontinence of either urine or faeces is not a normal part of growing old. Although it is an embarrassing problem that most elderly people would rather not talk about, incontinence is often curable and so it is important to visit your doctor for advice and treatment.

In older men, incontinence of urine is usually the result of an enlarged prostate gland (see Prostate enlargement) and takes the form of dribbling after passing urine, or not being able to get to a toilet in time. Treatment involves a surgical operation, but drugs are being developed that may help by shrinking the prostate, thereby taking pressure off the bladder and urethra.

In older women, incontinence of urine may be due to urinary infection, which should respond to antibiotics; or to a weakness of the pelvic muscles, usually as a result of stretching during childbirth. Pelvic muscle weakness typically causes 'stress incontinence', where a small amount of urine leaks out during coughing, sneezing or laughing.

If the pelvic muscles do not respond to an exercise programme, or if in addition to the muscle weakness there is a prolapse of the uterus which is stretching the neck of the bladder, surgical repair will usually be recommended. For anyone not well enough to have this operation, a plastic ring pessary inserted inside the vagina to hold the uterus in place may be sufficient to relieve the urinary symptoms.

Incontinence of faeces in elderly people is often due to prolonged constipation, the faeces having become compacted inside the rectum and lower colon and the resulting irritation of the bowel wall leading to the formation of a small amount of diarrhoea, which leaks out without warning. Treatment of the constipation, which may in such extreme cases require an enema, should relieve the problem.

In many parts of the UK, there are continence advisers – specially trained nurses – who can explain the practical measures, and give advice on the best aids available, to make it easier to cope with incontinence that cannot be cured. Ask your doctor, health visitor or district nurse whether there is a local continence adviser; if not, one of them should be able to offer support and provide information.

There is also the Continence Foundation* where you can get advice from health professionals with a special interest and expertise in bladder and bowel control.

Indigestion

When someone complains of indigestion he or she may be suffering from any of a wide variety of symptoms including heartburn, belching, a bloating discomfort, wind, abdominal pain or nausea. The most common reasons for all these digestive symptoms are bad eating habits, such as eating or drinking too much, eating too quickly, not relaxing for long enough after a meal, or eating too soon before going to bed.

If you develop abdominal discomfort or heartburn, you may subconsciously swallow air to try to relieve it, resulting in belching and bloating – flatulence – which makes your symptoms feel much worse.

For an acute attack of indigestion in whatever form, take a dose of antacid. Your pharmacist will be able to recommend one from the dozens of different brands on the market. The antacid should relieve indigestion within an hour or so; however, if the symptoms persist or suddenly get worse, for example an abdominal pain lasting more than four hours, see your doctor.

Recurrent attacks of indigestion should also be investigated by the GP; they may be caused by a peptic ulcer, acid reflux due to a hiatus hernia, irritable bowel syndrome or, rarely, stomach cancer. A physical examination and a few tests can exclude any serious condition; your doctor can then prescribe appropriate medication.

Insomnia

People often seem to need less sleep as they get older. This should not be regarded as a problem as long as the reduced amount of sleep is not causing tiredness, anxiety or distress. Insomnia is not just being unable to sleep for as long as you want, but sleep may be very fitful, causing the person to wake feeling tired and out of sorts; he or she may take a long time to fall asleep, or wake up in the early hours of the morning and be unable to fall asleep again.

If you are having trouble sleeping in one of the above ways, adopt the following measures to try to alleviate the problem:

- Take some exercise during the day, preferably outdoors.
- Stay up until you feel sleepy.
- Have a milky bedtime drink, but avoid tea and coffee which contain stimulants.
- Don't eat a large meal late in the evening.
- Make sure your bedroom is not too cold or hot.
- Get up at the same time each morning, regardless of how well you have slept.

It is also worth noting that many older people sleep better having had a short nap during the day.

See your doctor if insomnia persists despite these measures. Sometimes the underlying cause is depression, in which case anti-depressants will usually help stop the early morning waking that is a characteristic of depression. Sleeping pills which contain a sedative may be prescribed as a short-term measure, but regular use can lead to addiction and unpleasant withdrawal symptoms if you stop taking them suddenly.

Leg ulcers

Leg ulcers are a common problem in elderly people, especially women. Most of them occur in association with varicose veins, because the pooling of blood that occurs in the leg veins in this condition causes the surrounding skin tissues to become unhealthy and vulnerable to relatively minor trauma.

A few leg ulcers are due to disease of the arteries, which interferes with the normal supply of oxygen and nutrients to the skin tissues, again making them unhealthy and at risk of gangrene as well as ulceration. Diabetics are particularly susceptible to leg ulcers, not only because they are more likely to develop arterial disease but also because this disease can damage the nerves in the legs so that minor injuries to the skin may not be noticed.

Ulcers as a result of varicose veins are usually treated with compression bandages and elevation of the ulcerated leg to help reduce blood pooling and allow the skin to heal naturally. Arterial ulcers are cleaned and dressed, antibiotics are prescribed to treat any infection, and drugs may be given to try to improve the circulation, but compression bandages must not be applied because they will make the problem worse by causing further constriction of the arteries.

To reduce the risk of developing a leg ulcer, take regular exercise, don't smoke, eat a healthy balanced diet, lose excess weight if you can, take good care of your skin, protect your legs from accidental knocks and if you suffer from varicose veins consider wearing compression hosiery.

Medication problems

The main problem for elderly people with regard to their medication is that they may be taking several drugs at the same time. This can be confusing, particularly if doses are being taken at different times of the day and some of the drugs are taken more frequently than others.

Make a chart with each of the drugs and the times of the doses written on it, leaving a space to tick off each time a dose is taken. It is helpful to write what the drug has been prescribed for on the container, for example 'pain', 'dizziness', 'blood pressure'.

Do not put all the drugs for one day in the same bottle, as this can lead to dangerous mistakes over which drug is for which condition.

If you are taking several medications, make sure you tell the doctor about all of them before any new drug is prescribed. Some drugs can be dangerous when taken in combination. For the same reason, check with the pharmacist before starting any new over-the-counter medication.

When a condition such as arthritis makes it difficult to take the childproof tops off the bottles, ask the pharmacist to provide alternative containers; but this makes it even more important to keep all medications out of the reach of children.

Any unexpected symptoms that you think might be a side effect of a drug should be reported at once to the doctor, but do not stop the drug abruptly without checking that it is safe to do so. If a drug does not seem to be working, make another appointment with the doctor.

Anyone on long-term medication should ideally have a check-up every three months, and certainly at least every six months, to make sure the treatment is still necessary and not causing any hidden complications.

Menopause

The menopause is a normal stage in a woman's life that occurs around the age of 50. While the menopause can be said to be complete once the menstrual periods have stopped, the processes leading up to this point begin several years earlier and the symptoms associated with the menopause may continue for several years afterwards.

Hormonal changes are the cause of the various processes and symptoms that occur with the menopause. As the amount of oestrogen being made in the ovaries gradually decreases, ovulation (egg release) may cease completely and the menstrual cycle becomes irregular.

A wide variety of symptoms, both physical and emotional, may be experienced including hot flushes, night sweats, palpitations, vaginal dryness, mood swings, depression and forgetfulness. The reduction in oestrogen levels also accelerates the process of osteoporosis, which makes a woman more susceptible to angina and heart attacks and makes the bones become more fragile. There is also a tendency to put on weight, particularly around the abdomen.

Hormone replacement therapy (HRT) can help relieve most of the menopausal symptoms, as well as providing additional protection against osteoporosis and coronary heart disease. A woman may wish to discuss with her GP or at the well-women clinic whether HRT might be suitable for her.

In addition to HRT, other measures that can help minimise some of the unwanted effects of the menopause include regular exercise to tone up the muscles, a sensible diet to avoid gaining weight, using moisturising cream or an emollient to counteract dry skin and stopping smoking, which is a major risk factor for both osteoporosis and coronary heart disease.

Finally, if menstrual bleeding occurs after the menopause, it is essential to have this checked by a doctor, as post-menopausal bleeding can be a warning symptom of cancer.

Obesity

Energy requirements, in the form of calories provided by our food, gradually decrease with age, partly because the body requires less energy for cell processes at rest, partly because older people tend to take less physical exercise during the day and therefore burn up fewer calories overall.

However, most elderly people do not adjust their calorie intake to match these changes. As a result the excess calories are laid down as fatty tissue, causing a steady increase in weight that can progress to obesity. In addition to the undesirable effect of being overweight from the point of view of appearance, obesity is bad for long-term health because it increases the risk of developing high blood pressure, diabetes, osteoarthritis and even cancer.

To avoid obesity, you should follow a diet which restricts high-calorie foods such as biscuits, cakes, chocolate, sweets and cuts down on fatty foods like butter, full-fat cheese and fried meals, while continuing to eat foods high in vitamins, minerals and fibre.

The ideal daily diet should include fresh fruit and vegetables, wholegrain bread and cereals and lean meats such as poultry. To ensure you get sufficient calcium without too many calories, choose low-fat milk, cheeses and yoghurts. For more on healthy eating, see Chapter 28.

Osteoarthritis

Wear and tear of the cartilage surfaces inside a joint, resulting in pain, stiffness and swelling, is the cause of the most common form of arthritis, known as osteoarthritis. This wearing out of the joint tends to occur gradually with advancing years, so that most people in their sixties have osteoarthritis in at least some of their joints.

The joints most commonly affected are those that have taken the most punishment over the years, like the hips, the knees and the joints at the base of the neck and lower back. Factors which increase the risk of osteoarthritis include being overweight, overuse of a joint playing a particular sport, or a serious or recurrent injury to a joint when younger.

There is no cure for osteoarthritis but symptoms can usually be controlled with painkillers or anti-inflammatory drugs taken by mouth or applied to the affected joints as a gel. Exercises to strengthen the muscles around an arthritic joint, under the guidance of a doctor or physiotherapist, can also help by protecting the joint against further damage. The Arthritis Research Campaign* produces a leaflet on the subject.

In severe cases, where the arthritic joint has become very painful or stiff, it may be necessary to be referred to the hospital for a joint replacement operation.

Osteoporosis

In osteoporosis, the bones become brittle and fragile as the result of a gradual loss of minerals, including calcium, from their internal structure. Affected bones are more likely to break as a consequence of relatively minor trauma, such as falling over in the street.

As part of the normal ageing process, almost everyone experiences a reduction in their bone density. After the age of 35, the amount of new bone being formed to replace the continuous degeneration of old bone is reduced and the body also becomes less efficient at absorbing calcium from digested food and storing it in the bones.

The gradual decline in bone mass speeds up in women after the menopause because of the loss of the protective effect of oestrogen. Other factors that may accelerate the onset of osteoporosis include inactivity such as prolonged bed rest, smoking and drinking too much alcohol.

To avoid osteoporosis, it is important to build up strong bones earlier in life by taking regular exercise, particularly activities that put stress on the bones; by eating adequate amounts of calcium, especially during pregnancy and breastfeeding, when calcium requirements go up, by not smoking, and drinking alcohol only in moderation. Hormone replacement therapy taken for at least 12–18 months during the menopause can also protect against osteoporosis.

Even when osteoporosis is already established, it is still worth increasing calcium and vitamin D intake and following a gentle exercise programme. Particular care must be taken to avoid any accidental falls by making the home extra safe (see under Falls earlier in the chapter) and not going outdoors in icy weather, if possible.

In severe cases, a drug may be prescribed to try to halt the continuing loss of minerals from the bones. However, as yet, no medication is available that can restore the bone strength to normal, which is why prevention of this disease is so important.

More information can be obtained from the National Osteoporosis Society.*

Parkinson's disease

Parkinson's disease affects the part of the brain which controls all body movements. The exact cause is unknown, but the symptoms occur as a result of depletion of one of the brain chemicals – dopamine – in this area, which in turn interferes with the transmission of nerve impulses involved in the co-ordination of muscle action.

The incidence of Parkinson's disease increases significantly in elderly people, rising to 1 in 100 over the age of 65, and 1 in 50 over the age of 80. Symptoms tend to come on gradually and typically include a coarse tremor in the hands, muscle stiffness, difficulty starting and stopping movements such as walking, and a fixed facial expression with staring eyes. Sufferers tend to stoop forward and walk with a shuffling gait.

Several different drugs may be tried before the symptoms are brought under reasonable control. The amount of drug and the timing of each dose have to be adjusted carefully to suit the individual's response. A great deal of research is under way to develop more effective treatments and one day to find a cure.

Physiotherapy and occupational therapy can help improve mobility and maintain independence to a limited extent but, unfortunately, the condition tends to become more severe with time. For details of a self-help group in your part of the country, write to the Parkinson's Disease Society.*

Peptic ulcer

In older people, a common reason for developing an ulcer in the stomach or duodenum – popularly referred to as a peptic ulcer – is long-term treatment with an anti-inflammatory drug to relieve the symptoms of a painful condition such as arthritis. Another medication that can also cause peptic ulceration when taken on a regular basis is a corticosteroid such as prednisolone, taken to suppress inflammatory and allergic disorders.

Warning symptoms of a peptic ulcer include recurrent attacks of abdominal pain, nausea and vomiting, belching and feeling bloated. Vomiting material that looks like coffee grounds or passing black tarry stools are signs that a peptic ulcer is bleeding.

To reduce the risk of developing a peptic ulcer, try to take an ordinary painkiller such as paracetamol or codeine rather than anti-inflammatory drugs which include aspirin and ibuprofen. Doctors now sometimes prescribe a drug to protect the lining of the stomach and duodenum at the same time as prescribing an anti-inflammatory.

Because a peptic ulcer can cause serious complications, such as profuse bleeding or perforation leading to peritonitis, it is essential to visit the doctor if you develop any of the warning symptoms described above.

Piles (haemorrhoids)

Piles are swollen blood vessels in the lower part of the rectum and anal canal, similar to the varicose veins that many people develop in their legs. As many as 40 per cent of men will suffer from piles at some time in their lives, although many of them will never go for treatment because they are too embarrassed or shy.

The most common cause of piles is thought to be straining while passing stools. The risk is increased if the person is constipated, with hard bowel movements that take more time and effort to pass. Symptoms include:

- bleeding during a bowel movement, which causes spots of blood to appear on the toilet bowl and toilet paper
- irritation around the anus
- slight mucous discharge.

Any bleeding from the anus should be checked out by a doctor. Although it is not usually due to any serious bowel disorder, it could be an early warning sign of bowel cancer, particularly if the blood is mixed in with the stools.

The diagnosis of piles may be obvious if they are visible around the opening to the anus. However, the doctor may insert a small instrument known as a proctoscope just inside the rectum to separate the bowel walls – a simple and painless procedure – to look for internal piles.

To relieve anal irritation due to piles, have daily warm salt baths and ask your pharmacist for a soothing emollient to apply. You may also need to use a course of suppositories (which contain an astringent to shrink the swollen inflamed tissue and a corticosteroid to reduce the inflammation) night and morning and after any bowel movement. It is also important to increase your intake of fluids and high-fibre foods, which, by helping to soften the stools, should reduce the need to strain or sit for long periods on the toilet.

Pneumonia

Pneumonia is a condition where the lungs become inflamed; it is usually as a result of an infection from bacteria or viruses, although there are other causes, such as accidental inhalation of a piece of food or a poisonous gas. Symptoms of pneumonia include a productive cough, discoloured or blood-stained sputum, fever and chills, chest pains and breathlessness.

In elderly people, pneumonia can be extremely serious, either because the immune system which defends the body against infections does not work as efficiently later on in life, or because the pneumonia aggravates an underlying chronic disorder such as heart failure or chronic bronchitis.

Antibiotics will be prescribed for a bacterial pneumonia and also in many cases of viral pneumonia to prevent a secondary bacterial infection of the inflamed lung tissues. Hospital admission may be necessary so that oxygen can be given and, in extreme cases, mechanical ventilation initiated until the infection is brought under control.

Because pneumonia is a fairly common complication of flu in elderly people, an annual flu jab is recommended for everyone over the age of 65, especially anyone with a chronic heart or lung condition.

Prostate enlargement

An enlarged prostate gland is a very common problem among older men, although why it should affect some men more than others is not known. The prostate sits at the base of the bladder and surrounds the urethra, which is the narrow tube that carries urine and, in men, semen to the tip of the penis. The function of the prostate is to produce most of the seminal fluid, secretions which transport and nourish the sperm after ejaculation.

Enlargement of the prostate closes off the upper part of the urethra and, as a result, may cause a variety of urinary symptoms such as difficulty starting the flow, a poor stream, dribbling after urination, having to get up to pass urine during the night and rushing to the toilet frequently during the day. Symptoms should always be investigated as they may indicate more serious problems, such as prostate cancer.

Embarrassment causes many men to delay seeing their doctor until these symptoms become intolerable. However, treatment is usually successful at restoring near-normal urinary function. The usual procedure is a surgical rebore, where a narrow instrument with viewing and cutting devices is passed up the urethra and the obstructing tissue pared away.

New forms of treatment under investigation include the inflation of a tiny balloon inside the urethra to relieve the constriction, the use of a microwave beam to heat up the prostate gland and a drug which, by preventing hormonal stimulation of the prostate, shrinks the gland and improves the flow of urine as a result.

Rheumatoid arthritis

Rheumatoid arthritis (RA) affects roughly one million people in the UK. It is a severe form of arthritis and, although the exact cause is unknown, is believed to be an autoimmune disease where the body's immune system starts to attack the joints. The resulting inflammation causes pain, tenderness, swelling, redness and warmth in many joints, usually in a symmetrical pattern on either side of the body.

Other symptoms of RA include severe joint stiffness which is typically worse in the early morning, loss of grip strength and sometimes fever, generalised weakness and malaise.

Although RA is popularly thought to be a disease of old age, it usually strikes people first in their thirties. The condition then commonly flares up intermittently, with periods of remission which may last several months, even years. Also, many sufferers develop only a mild disability and are able to remain mobile and independent.

In the past, RA used to cause severe joint deformities in those people who were seriously affected by the disease. By the time they reached their sixties and beyond, even though the arthritis often seemed to burn itself out, they would be left housebound and possibly in a wheelchair. However, with the development of powerful drugs, which can slow down the disease and limit the amount of damage to the joints, the risk of permanent handicap in these more severe cases has been reduced considerably.

Various aids are available to help the arthritic cope with everyday tasks. Artificial joints can now be used to replace knees, fingers and shoulders as well as the hips, if they have been left very stiff or uncomfortable. The Arthritis Research Campaign* can supply more information; and see also Chapter 29 on exercise.

Sexual problems

A common myth about growing older is that an active sex life should end at 60. However, for many couples, love-making actually improves once they become free from the pressures of work and the menopause has removed the worry of an unwanted pregnancy. Some couples may prefer to cease their love-making, while others would like to continue demonstrating their mutual love in a physical way, but encounter some difficulty such as discomfort or impotence.

For any sexual problem, the first step is to talk openly with your partner. The family doctor is usually the best person to consult next. There may be an underlying medical reason which can be corrected, for example a change in medication if a particular drug is thought to be the cause of impotence; or application of a vaginal lubricant or oestrogen cream, if discomfort is due to post-menopausal inflammation of the vaginal lining.

If a medical disorder such as heart failure or osteoarthritis is causing love-making to be uncomfortable because of breathlessness or joint pain respectively, the doctor may be able to recommend alternative positions for sexual intercourse which are less stressful. Referral to a professional counsellor, usually through the organisation Relate,* can help a couple learn to communicate better and resolve any sexual fears or anxieties.

Skin problems

All older people can expect to see some changes to their skin as a result of the ageing process. Older people who have been regularly exposed to the ultraviolet radiation of strong sunlight earlier in life without taking appropriate precautions, such as wearing a broad-brimmed sun-hat, putting on a sunscreen and keeping out of the midday sun, are much more likely to develop the three characteristic changes that occur in the skins of older people: severe wrinkling, thickened and roughened skin and large numbers of brown spots (also known as age spots) that typically appear on the face and the backs of the hands.

To treat skin-ageing, there is now an effective cream which contains retinoic acid (a derivative of vitamin A). Retinoic acid, which is available on prescription, can reduce wrinkling and roughening of the skin, as well as causing the age spots to fade. A new form of laser therapy has also been developed to remove unsightly age spots from exposed areas of skin.

WARNING

See your doctor if you develop any new blemish on your skin; or if a mole or blemish changes size, colour or shape, itches, bleeds, crusts over or becomes painful. This may signify a skin cancer and the earlier it is treated, the greater the chance of a successful cure.

Stroke

A stroke is caused by the interruption of the normal blood supply to part of the brain, resulting in damage to those brain cells deprived of oxygen for more than a few minutes. The three main types of stroke are a cerebral thrombosis, where a blood clot (thrombus) obstructs one of the main arteries in the brain; a cerebral embolism, where a fragment of blood clot that has broken off from a thrombus elsewhere in the circulation blocks a brain artery; and a cerebral haemorrhage, where a blood vessel in the brain ruptures.

Symptoms from a stroke depend primarily on which part of the brain has been damaged, as each brain area controls specific functions related to particular parts of the body. Typical symptoms may include sudden onset of numbness or weakness (usually on one side of the body), loss of speech or slurring of words, a sudden severe headache, unexplained dizziness, a sudden fall, or blurred vision.

Measures to reduce the risk of a stroke include not smoking, drinking alcohol only in moderation, cutting down on foods high in cholesterol and saturated fats and taking regular exercise. Also, have your blood pressure checked regularly as a high level that goes untreated may cause a stroke without any warning symptoms.

If a stroke has occurred, the main part of therapy is a rehabilitation programme that may need to include speech therapy, as well as physiotherapy and occupational therapy. Recovery is unpredictable, but progress may continue to be made for over a year or even longer. For information and practical advice, contact the Stroke Association.*

Transient ischaemic attacks

A transient ischaemic attack (TIA) is a mini-stroke which causes similar symptoms to a normal stroke, but, because there is no permanent damage to the brain, these symptoms resolve completely within 24 hours, leaving no additional disability.

Even if the TIA symptoms disappear within minutes, it is still essential to see your doctor for a full check-up as a TIA is a warning signal that a major stroke could be on the way. Around 10 per cent of strokes are preceded by one or more TIAs, with perhaps a few days or even several months between them.

For some people who have had a TIA, the doctor may recommend aspirin or anticoagulant therapy, or surgery to remove fatty deposits from one of the brain arteries, as a way of reducing the chance of a future stroke.

Varicose veins

Around 20 per cent of the population suffer from varicose veins – bulging, twisted swollen veins usually confined to the lower legs. For most sufferers, the symptoms they cause are only mild and can be eased by wearing elastic support hosiery and not standing still for long periods. The typical symptoms are aching legs, swelling of the feet and ankles and a few visible swollen veins on the calves and thighs.

Varicose veins are generally caused by damaged valves inside the veins, which allow a backflow of blood down the leg and from the deep veins out into the superficial veins that run just under the skin. This pooling of blood in the veins causes them to swell under pressure.

Anyone with mild varicose veins should take various precautions to try to avoid making them worse, such as wearing elastic support stockings or socks, not crossing the legs or ankles, not standing for a long time, and never putting on a garter or elastic stocking top that presses into the thigh and obstructs the circulation. In addition to keeping weight within normal limits, you should ask your GP to recommend a programme of leg exercises to help the circulation through the veins.

Complications from more severe varicose veins include thrombophlebitis (painful tender swelling along a vein) as well as leg ulceration, both of which should be treated as soon as possible by your doctor.

Part 7

Sorting out your affairs

Chapter 32

Making your will

Four out of ten adults in Britain do not bother to make a will. Often people do not want to think about it, and even if they do, they do not know where to start. However, it may be very important to make one if you are likely to be affected by the inheritance tax limits or by the 'intestacy' rules (see below).

Throughout this chapter, leaving somebody 'money' includes leaving them particular possessions or property, unless specified otherwise. Similarly, where giving someone 'property' or 'possessions' is mentioned, this includes gifts of money. Note that this chapter covers the rules in England and Wales; see pages 467–9 for the main differences in Scotland.

Why should you make a will?

The first purpose of writing a will is to ensure that your possessions go to the people you want. If you do not write a will this may not happen. Instead, your property will be divided among relatives according to the 'intestacy' rules – see Chart 1. The spouse of the deceased always gets his or her personal effects, such as furniture or the car, as well as any money they are entitled to. For how joint property is treated, see page 460.

Chart 1 shows that if you do not make a will your property will not necessarily go to the people you want. For example, if you are married you may well want to leave everything to your spouse. But under current rules, if you personally owned more than £125,000 and you have children this would not happen. Instead, your property would be divided between your spouse and your children. And if you live with someone but are not married, your partner might not get anything at all.

Chart 1: Who your money would go to if you died without making a will (in England and Wales)

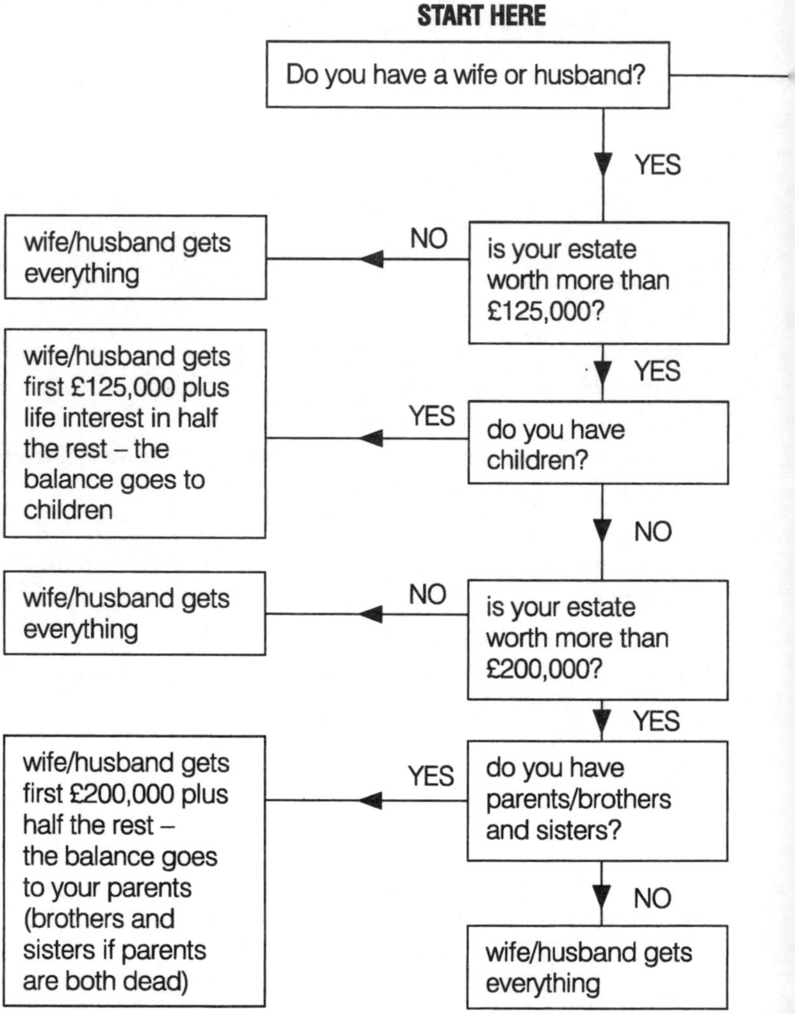

START HERE

Do you have a wife or husband? ──

↓ YES

wife/husband gets everything ◀── NO — is your estate worth more than £125,000?

↓ YES

wife/husband gets first £125,000 plus life interest in half the rest – the balance goes to children ◀── YES — do you have children?

↓ NO

wife/husband gets everything ◀── NO — is your estate worth more than £200,000?

↓ YES

wife/husband gets first £200,000 plus half the rest – the balance goes to your parents (brothers and sisters if parents are both dead) ◀── YES — do you have parents/brothers and sisters?

↓ NO

wife/husband gets everything

Notes:

1. Adopted and illegitimate children count as legitimate. Relatives who are descended from the same pair of ancestors as the deceased will inherit before any relative who only shared one common ancestor, e.g. half-brothers and sisters.

2. As a general rule, if a relative who would have inherited dies before you, his or her share is divided equally between his or her children, e.g. if you have had a son and a daughter and the son predeceased you, his children – your grandchildren – would inherit his share.

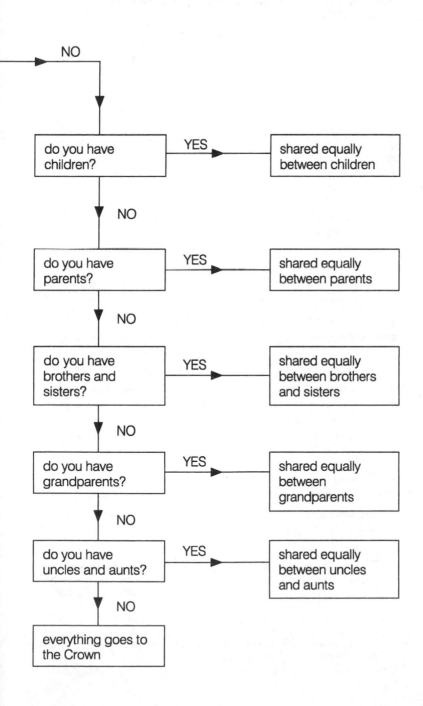

NO

do you have children? — YES → shared equally between children

NO

do you have parents? — YES → shared equally between parents

NO

do you have brothers and sisters? — YES → shared equally between brothers and sisters

NO

do you have grandparents? — YES → shared equally between grandparents

NO

do you have uncles and aunts? — YES → shared equally between uncles and aunts

NO

everything goes to the Crown

A second reason for making a will is that it allows you to specify who you would like to sort out your affairs after your death. This is especially important if you might leave money or property to children under 18, in which case it must be held in trust. This means that someone named in the will is given the responsibility of looking after the money or property until the children are old enough to inherit. Money held in trust must usually be invested in a limited range of secure investments, such as British Government stocks, but in your will you can give the trustees freedom to invest in whatever way they choose.

EXAMPLE 1

Bridget's husband Tom died aged 62: their two sons were grown-up. Bridget and Tom owned their home in Suffolk as joint tenants so it passed directly to Bridget, as did their joint bank account. Tom also left around £175,000 in shares and other investments.

There was no will so Bridget, with the help of a solicitor, valued the assets in the estate and applied for a grant of administration from the court of probate. With this legal authority she contacted Tom's stockbroker (who held his shares) and the life insurance company and had the assets transferred to her as administrator.

Under the intestacy rules, the first £125,000 of Tom's investments went to Bridget. The remaining £50,000 was divided in two: half was split between the children (£12,500 each), and under the intestacy rules the remaining £25,000 had to be held in trust for Bridget. She has a 'life interest' in this, which means that she can spend the income, but must leave the capital for the children. The inconvenience of setting up a trust and paying money to the children could have been avoided if Tom had written a will.

A will provides a suitable opportunity to express wishes about who you would like to act as guardians for your children. You can also say how you would like to be buried, whether you would like to be cremated or whether you would like to donate your body to medicine. These wishes are not legally binding, even if expressed in a will. However, a will is probably the best place to state your views on such matters.

One further reason to make a will is that it may help you to avoid paying more inheritance tax than you need. If you leave behind property worth more than £231,000 (in the 1999–2000 tax year), the

Inland Revenue can take up to 40 per cent of anything over the £231,000 limit. However, certain gifts (including those to your husband or wife) are tax-free. A will can help you make the best of these tax exemptions. Inheritance tax is explained in Chapter 33.

Who should make your will?

You can have a will written by a solicitor, by a will-writing company, or through a bank. Alternatively, you may be able to do it yourself, if your financial and family affairs are not too complicated.

Writing your own will

You should not write your own will if any of the following apply:

- you have been married more than once
- you want to do more than simply divide your property among your relatives or friends
- you will be providing for someone with a physical or mental disability
- you own a business or a farm
- you want to pass on your home intact to someone other than your spouse
- you were born abroad or are likely to be considered 'domiciled' abroad (i.e. if your permanent home is overseas and you are likely to end your days there)
- you are involved with family trusts.

If you are likely to be liable for inheritance tax, you might also benefit from professional advice.

If none of these applies to you, it is a fairly straightforward matter to write your own will. However, you will need some help and advice to do it correctly. Do not just write out your will on a sheet of paper or one of the will forms available from legal stationers. There are a number of technical phrases you will need to know to make sure that your will makes proper legal sense. Which? Books★ publishes *Make Your Own Will*, an action pack that explains what you should do and provides you with the necessary forms, if you live in England or Wales. There are also a number of books available on the subject.

The lowest charge for a simple will is in the region of £30, including VAT. For most people a will costs around £50 but if your circumstances require a particularly complicated will, it can cost as much as £200.

Solicitors

There is no sure-fire way of picking a good solicitor. Ask your friends if they can recommend one. Alternatively, try contacting a few local solicitors from your phone book. Many are willing to give an introductory interview for free, or a rough estimate of how much they expect it will cost to draw up your will.

Will-writing companies

There are a number of companies which specialise in making wills. Many specialist will writers have formal legal training and can provide a service as good as that of a solicitor. However, some do not have sufficient legal training. They may know enough to make simple wills, but not enough to recognise when they are out of their depth. In general, if you are not sure where to go, you will be safer going to a solicitor than to a specialist will-writing company.

Banks, building societies and life insurance companies

Some banks, building societies and insurance companies offer a will-writing service, though a few will insist that they are named as executors of the will – a course best avoided, as they are often costly and sometimes very slow to sort out an estate.

Witnessing and storing your will

When your will is written it must be witnessed. This means that at least two people must see you sign the will, and then must sign it themselves, attesting to the fact that they saw you sign it. They do not have to read the will.

If you leave anything to the people who witness your will or to their spouses, they will not be allowed to accept your bequest, so make sure you do not ask anyone to witness your will to whom you might want to leave something. If you have your will written by a solicitor, the solicitor and a colleague will usually volunteer to witness the will.

Keep your will in an obvious place where people can find it, or tell someone where it is. There are many stories of wills only coming to light months after the estate has been divided up on the assumption that no will existed.

You should review your will regularly. If your circumstances change you may need to write a new one. For example, if you get married your will is automatically revoked and you will need to make a new one.

Revoking and changing your will

Never write anything on your will. Any amendments to a will are assumed to have been made after the will was signed and will therefore be ignored. If you make too many changes to a will it may not be possible to tell what your original intention was, in which case the entire will may be considered invalid.

There are two ways to change a will. You can draft a codicil, which must be witnessed and signed in the same way as a will (though not necessarily using the same witnesses) and then kept with the will. Alternatively, you can start from scratch and write a new will.

A will is usually entirely revoked if:

- you write a new will which includes the standard phrase stating that you revoke all other wills
- you get married
- you destroy the will, with the intention of revoking it, or if someone else destroys it at your instruction and in your presence.

Divorce does not invalidate the entire will; however, all gifts to your ex-spouse, and the appointment of your ex-spouse as executor, will be automatically revoked.

Dividing up your property

When deciding who to leave your possessions to, the first thing to work out is how much you own – known legally as your 'estate'. Things to think about are:

- the market value of your home, less outstanding mortgages, and of any other homes or land

- any money, including interest earned, from all sources (the bank, National Savings, building society accounts, other deposits)
- any investments (stocks, shares, unit trusts etc.)
- any amounts to be paid out on your life insurance policy, including any bonuses (unless they are written in trust)
- the value of any antiques, jewellery, furniture and other effects
- the value of your car and other possessions, e.g. caravan, dinghy etc.
- the amounts of any loans you are owed
- the value of any business or farm that you own
- any interests you may have in trusts or settlements (i.e. rights you have to income, capital or property held in trust).

You need to deduct from the total of your money and effects any outstanding loans that you owe (apart from mortgages, which you took into account when assessing the value of your home); also deduct an amount for your funeral expenses. You will then be left with the current value of your estate.

Jointly held assets can be held in two different ways – either by 'joint tenants', or by 'tenants in common'. In England and Wales it is assumed, in the absence of any other arrangement, that jointly owned property is owned by 'joint tenants'. This means that both owners have an equal interest in the whole property. In the event of one joint owner dying the entire property automatically belongs to the other joint tenant, regardless of any will, and regardless of the intestacy rules. It does not form part of the deceased person's estate for the intestacy rules. (This is particularly confusing as it does form part of the estate when calculating inheritance tax.)

Alternatively, it is possible to own property as 'tenants in common'. This means that each owner owns a share of the property absolutely. They are free to do with this share as they see fit. So, if you and your spouse owned your home as tenants in common, you would each be free to leave your portion of the house to whoever you chose. This can prove useful for reducing your liability to inheritance tax (see pages 480–81). In Scotland, it is assumed that property is owned by tenants in common, rather than joint tenants, in the absence of any other arrangement.

If you wish to switch from owning property as joint tenants to owning property as tenants in common, the procedure is very straightforward. All the owners simply need to sign a declaration to the effect that they own the property as tenants in common, and specifying the shares held by each. It is more complicated to switch from being tenants in common to joint tenants. Consult a solicitor if you need to do this.

Who to leave things to?

You can leave property to people and organisations such as companies, charities, hospitals, schools, universities or political parties. You can leave property to children but it must then be held in trust for them, usually until they reach 18. You can also leave money to be held in trust for adults or unborn descendants – for example, you could leave money to be held in trust and paid, say, to your great grandchildren or the first woman to land on the moon. You can even leave money to be held in trust and used for certain purposes – for example, to pay for a party once a year on your birthday. You cannot leave money to pets or other animals, however, and if it is unclear whom you mean the gift to go to, it will be treated according to the rules of Chart 1.

You are free to leave your money and property to whoever you like, but under the Inheritance (Provision for Family and Dependants) Act 1975 certain people have the right to challenge your will. Your spouse, your children, any ex-spouses and anyone who was financially dependent on you at the time of your death are entitled to 'reasonable financial provision' from your will and can go to court if they do not get it. If you do not want to leave anything to the people listed above you should seek advice from a solicitor.

What sorts of gifts can you give?

Legacies/bequests
When specifying a particular possession to be given to someone make sure you use entirely unambiguous phrases. For example, do not leave someone your 'favourite' clock, as it will be impossible to confirm unequivocally which was your favourite. You can make gifts which are unspecific so long as your intention is clear. For example, you could say in your will that certain friends are allowed

to come and select items of your jewellery, or choose their favourite picture. But if it is not clear what you intended, the gift will 'fail'. This means that the relevant money or property will go to the residuary beneficiary (see below). If the residuary legacy fails it will be treated as if no will had been written (see above). Also make sure that all your legacies and bequests come to less than your estate.

It is normal to make legacies 'free of tax'. This means that all the inheritance tax to be paid will fall on the residuary legacy (see below). If the residuary legacy was not large enough to cover the tax bill, then recipients of any gifts would still have to pay some tax. If you do not make legacies free of tax then, providing your estate is large enough for you to pay inheritance tax, the recipient of the gift will have to pay the necessary tax.

Residuary legacy

You will not be able to know for certain how much your estate will be worth when you die, so you will have to name a beneficiary who is to receive the 'residue' – i.e. everything which is left after all the other legacies have been made. Normally, the residuary legacy is the largest part of the estate. For example, if you are married, it is common to leave a few gifts to relatives and friends, but the residue – your home and most of your wealth – to your spouse (but see page 482 for the inheritance tax implications of this).

Gifts for life

Normally, if you leave somebody something in your will, it is an 'absolute' gift. This means they are free to do with the gift as they please. However, it is possible to give somebody a sum of money, or a possession, for them to have only as long as they live, after which the property must go to someone else – known as the 'ultimate beneficiary'. This might happen if, for example, you had children from a first marriage, remarried but had no further children. Your will might leave all your property to your second spouse for his or her lifetime, after which your children would inherit.

If you leave someone money or property for life, trustees (see opposite) will control the property until the ultimate beneficiary or beneficiaries inherit. If you have left someone a particular possession or your house for life, they will be able to use it until they die. If you have left someone a sum of money for life, the trustees will invest the money, and the lifetime beneficiary will receive the income earned by the investments, but the capital will be passed on to the ultimate beneficiary.

Executors and trustees

Executors

In your will you must specify who is to take charge after your death and make sure that all the wishes expressed in your will are carried out properly. This person is your 'executor' and has the power and the duty to pay off any debts, pay any inheritance tax you owe, and then distribute the remaining property according to your will. If you do not write a will, or if your will does not name an executor, your next of kin will usually take on the role, although they are then called your 'administrator' rather than 'executor'.

You can appoint up to four executors. It is sensible to appoint at least two, in case one cannot act. Someone who is named as executor in a will is free to refuse to take on the responsibility, so make sure that whoever you name is willing to do the job. If more than one person acts as executor they must act together, and none can act without the agreement of the others.

You can appoint either friends and relatives or professionals, such as solicitors, as your executors. The safest course of action, wherever possible, is to appoint lay executors, such as friends and relatives. They will be free to hire professional help and can charge the costs to the estate. They can also charge their own expenses to the estate. If you appoint professionals as executors, they will insist on a clause being added to the will allowing them to charge their fees to the estate. (This is because the law does not allow any executor to profit from being an executor, unless the will specifies otherwise.)

If possible, you should appoint the people who will inherit most under your will as your executors. They can then make sure that the cost of sorting out your will is kept to a minimum. However, you should not appoint as executors people who are likely to argue, or who live very far apart and would not be able to work together conveniently.

Trustees

If a trust might arise from your will, you will need to appoint trustees. The most common reason for a trust arising is that one of your beneficiaries is under 18, in which case the inheritance must be held by trustees until the beneficiary is old enough to inherit. You will also need trustees if you make a gift for life (see pages 462–3), or if you set up a discretionary trust (see Chapter 33). It is usual to name your executors as trustees.

Powers of executors and trustees

The law sets strict limits on what trustees and executors can do but you can extend these powers in your will if you wish. The most common reasons for extending the powers of executors and trustees are as follows.

Appropriation

Normally, where property is being divided between people, executors have the power to give specific items instead of money only with the beneficiary's consent. However, you can alter your will to allow your executors to do this without the beneficiary's consent.

Investment

The law limits trustees to investing only in very safe – but possibly poorly performing – investments. It is common to alter this and allow trustees to invest in a wider range of investments.

Advancement

If money is held in trust for children, the trustees are allowed to use up to all the income and half the capital to pay for the maintenance and education of the child. You can extend this so that all the money can be used for the child's benefit. If money is held in trust for adults you can also give the trustees extra powers.

Problems with wills

At the moment, after someone dies it is not possible to dismiss their professional executors such as solicitors and banks. If you are dissatisfied with the way you are treated by the professional executors or trustees of a friend's or relative's will – for example, you feel they are not giving you enough information – there is little you can do except complain. However, if you feel there has been maladministration, fraud or negligence, you can take certain steps – although they may well not solve your problems.

If you are dissatisfied because of the maladministration of a will, complain to the Banking Ombudsman★ (if the executor is a bank), or the Office for the Supervision of Solicitors★ (if the executor is a solicitor).

If an executor or trustee fails to carry out the terms of the will, or loses money through neglect or fraud, consult a solicitor. Although it is expensive, you can go to court to get compensation and ask the court to oversee the estate's administration. However, it is hard to prove that someone has been negligent, rather than simply doing a bad job.

If you are unhappy with a bank's charges as executor, you can do nothing practical unless the executor has broken the terms of the will. If you are unhappy with a solicitor's fees, you can apply to have the bill checked by the Law Society;★ if they refuse, contact the Office for the Supervision of Solicitors.★ Solicitors' clients can ask the Law Society to make a solicitor reduce unreasonable bills. Residuary beneficiaries of wills can apply where the solicitors are the only executors.

Enduring power of attorney

Your will determines who is to sort out your affairs after you have died. So long as you are of 'sound mind' at the time you make a will, it will be valid. However, you may wish to appoint someone to look after your affairs in the event of your becoming unable to do so through mental incapacity. In England or Wales you can do this by appointing an 'enduring power of attorney' (which the government plans to replace, in due course, by a 'continuing' power of attorney). In Scotland such a move is not currently possible, but legislation is planned.

Note that an enduring power of attorney is quite different from a normal power of attorney. A normal power of attorney is used to allow someone to sort out your affairs while, say, you are abroad. It would lapse if you became mentally incapable and unable to appreciate the significance of it. An enduring power of attorney does not lapse in these circumstances. Moreover, it can be drafted so that it comes into effect only in the event of your becoming mentally unable to conduct your own affairs.

Under normal circumstances, if you become mentally ill and unable to manage your own affairs, the Court of Protection★ at the

Public Trust Office will either manage your affairs itself or else will appoint someone who volunteers, such as a relative or close friend, to do this. By giving someone an enduring power of attorney you effectively specify whom you want to look after your affairs.

Setting up an enduring power of attorney

You need to complete a legal document, not unlike a will, to give someone an enduring power of attorney. There is a standard wording for doing this – a form is available from legal stationers and most solicitors. The form must be signed by both the 'donor' – the person giving someone power of attorney – and the attorney. The signing of the document must be witnessed by at least one person, who must then also sign the document. Anyone can act as witness, though it is best to avoid your, or your attorney's, spouse.

The person you name as your attorney must be over 18 when they agree to act and must not be a bankrupt. As with executors of wills, you can name a friend, relative or solicitor to act as your attorney. If you appoint a solicitor he or she will charge for his or her services. If you appoint a friend or relative, he or she will be able to charge for all reasonable expenses – including the cost of hiring professional help from, say, a solicitor – incurred in administering your affairs.

When the attorney believes that the donor is becoming mentally ill and incapable of looking after his or her own affairs, the 'enduring power' must be registered with the Court of Protection.* There is a small fee to pay. The Court of Protection will notify certain relatives of the attorney's application. They can then object if necessary. The attorney does not have to produce any medical evidence, but it is often a good idea to get a doctor's report just in case there are any objections.

When the Court of Protection receives the application for enduring power of attorney, it will first wait to see if any objection is made. If so, the court will consider the objection and can refuse the application if it considers that the donor is not becoming mentally ill, or if it considers that force or undue pressure were used to make the donor give the power in the first place. The Court can also refuse an application on the grounds that the attorney is unsuitable or because the Court has already appointed someone else to look after the donor's affairs.

If the Court accepts the application, the power of attorney is registered. From then on the attorney has the authority to act on the donor's behalf in relation to business and financial affairs. Although the attorney has this power, there is no duty to take any actions at all. However, if the attorney does act for the donor, it must be with adequate skill and care. If the standard wording of an enduring power of attorney is used, the powers are very wide, but the donor might have restricted them – for example, by insisting that a third party agrees to certain actions or that certain property (e.g. the home) cannot be disposed of.

The law does not allow the attorney's powers to be extended beyond those set out in the standard wording (which follows the Enduring Power of Attorney Act 1985). In particular, the attorney has no powers to take decisions about the welfare or medical treatment of the donor.

If you have strong feelings about the medical treatment or social care that you would want to receive if you were no longer mentally capable of making your own decisions, you can set out your wishes in writing – sometimes called a 'living will' or 'advance statement'. It is likely that this document would be legally binding, though any medical practitioner who objected to your wishes is entitled to refuse to treat you. The Patients Association* publishes a booklet about living wills.

The law in Scotland

In Scotland, the law on wills varies in many important respects from the law in England. Below are the main differences.

Joint property

This is almost always held as a tenancy in common rather than as a joint tenancy, so a husband would not automatically inherit the wife's share of jointly owned property. In practice, though, the title deeds usually state that the spouse should inherit the entire home. Similarly, with joint bank accounts, the money is assumed to remain the property of whoever deposited it.

Intestacy

If you die without leaving a will, your estate is divided into three categories: 'prior rights', 'legal rights' and 'free estate'. If you are married, your spouse will automatically inherit a proportion of your 'prior rights' estate. These are:

- your share of any joint home, up to £110,000 – the remainder is distributed as part of the 'legal rights'. If you have a mortgage on your property your spouse's share of the home will only be the net value of the home – i.e. after deduction of debts. This is the case even if you have a life insurance policy designed to pay off the mortgage on your death
- furnishings, up to £20,000 (this does not include cars)
- a cash sum of £30,000, if there are surviving children, or £50,000 if there are none.

Legal rights

The 'legal rights' are divided between your spouse and any children you have. If there are no children your spouse will get at least half the moveable estate (roughly everything except lands and buildings), and if there are children, your spouse will get at least one third of the moveable estate and another third will be divided among the children. If you leave children but no spouse, the children get half the moveable estate.

Free estate

This is what is left after any debts, prior rights and legal rights have been satisfied (so if you have no spouse and no children it consists of your whole estate). The free estate is distributed in broadly the following order, using up each category of relatives before moving on to the next:

- children
- parents, brothers and sisters (or nephews and nieces if no surviving parents or siblings)
- spouse
- uncles and aunts
- grandparents
- great uncles and aunts.

Witnessing your will

Wills made before 1 August 1995 were valid if simply signed by the person making the will if it was in his or her own handwriting (a holograph will) or if the person had written by hand above the signature at the end of the typed will: 'adopted as holograph'.

Since then, to be valid a will must be signed by the testator at the foot of each page and must be witnessed by one witness, preferably (but not necessarily) someone who does not stand to benefit from the will. The witness signs at the foot of the last page and his or her address must be given. For more information about the differences that apply to wills made in Scotland, see *Wills and Probate*, published by Which? Books.*

Provision for family and dependants

The Inheritance (Provision for Family and Dependants) Act 1975 does not apply in Scotland. However, the system of 'legal rights' for spouses and children ensures that your spouse has a right to at least one third of your moveable estate, as have your children.

Note that you can still effectively disinherit your children if your estate is small enough to fall completely within the limits for the 'prior rights'. If you do not write a will in these circumstances, your spouse will be entitled to all 'prior' rights before distribution of legal rights.

Revocation of wills

In Scotland, marriage does not revoke your will, and divorce does not automatically invalidate gifts to your ex-spouse. If you have a child after you have made your will, it is assumed that you would have wanted to write a will including the child. The child (and only the child) can therefore apply to have the will set aside, in which case the estate will be divided according to the rules of intestacy. In Scotland, a will destroyed at your instruction but not in your presence will be revoked.

Chapter 33

Inheritance tax

Inheritance tax is a tax on what you leave when you die – your estate – and on certain gifts you make while you are still alive. The tax is complicated, and avoiding it can be complicated. This chapter sets out to explain the bare essentials. If, as a result of reading this, you think you need to take action, you may be best advised to get professional advice and help, especially where large sums of money are involved. Accountants and solicitors often specialise in estate planning.

Three rules to remember

Anyone who has money, property or other assets to pass on should remember three important rules. The first rule is that you do not have to be a duke to worry about 'death duties' – or inheritance tax, as the modern equivalent is called. The seriously rich usually have accountants and other advisers to make sure they keep their tax bills to a minimum. It is often relatively modest estates which are stung most heavily by inheritance tax. However, there are some straight-forward ways of reducing the tax.

Rule number two: using tax-free methods to pass on your wealth will not, in most cases, save you a penny in tax. With a few exceptions, any inheritance tax due is paid after you have died. Estate planning – i.e. finding ways to avoid inheritance tax – is a way of saving your heirs tax. It is of no real benefit to you. On the contrary, you actually incur a risk. Estate planning may mean you lose control over your own assets.

The third rule is that the regulations on inheritance tax can be changed – usually in the annual Budget. Some Budgets make few or no changes, but a wholesale reform of the tax cannot be ruled out, especially when there is a change of government. This is a hazard which can make any estate planning ineffective. The rules described in this chapter apply to the 1999–2000 tax year.

WARNING

In trying to avoid one tax, you may be confronted by another. Capital gains tax is a tax on the increase in value of things during the time you have owned them (less an allowance to reflect length of ownership). You can be taxed on an increase in value when you dispose of an asset – and disposal includes giving something away.

For example, you may have a holiday cottage which you would like to give to your grandchildren to help keep down the value of your estate when you die. Before doing so, check what capital gains tax you might incur. You might still decide that a small capital gains tax bill now is preferable to a potentially larger inheritance tax bill. Capital gains tax is covered in Chapter 17.

How inheritance tax is levied

There are a few types of gift – mainly gifts to companies and some types of trust – on which inheritance tax may be due immediately, though this is payable at only half the rate on death. But inheritance tax is most likely to be due only after you have died, on:

- your estate – what you leave when you die
- some gifts you make in the seven years before you die.

These may be gifts which are taxable only if you die within seven years of making them (known as 'potentially exempt transfers' or PETs), or gifts which were taxable at the time you made them, on which further tax may be due.

The rate of tax

Some gifts, plus part of what you leave on death, may become chargeable to inheritance tax when you die. This applies to gifts both of cash and of non-cash assets, such as a house. Whether tax is payable depends on the 'running total' of chargeable gifts you have made in the seven years before each gift, or before you die as far as your estate on death is concerned.

There is no tax on the first £231,000 (known as the 'nil-rate band') of the running total. Above £231,000, the tax rate on death is 40 per cent. However, tax on gifts you make in the last seven years of your life may be reduced on a sliding scale – see Table 1 on page 475.

The key word here is chargeable. A distinction needs to be made between what is chargeable but on which no tax need be paid because it falls within the £231,000 band, and what is exempt (tax-free). A range of gifts – or transfers, as the Inland Revenue calls them – which you make while you are alive, and part or all of what you leave on your death could be exempt. Transfers which are exempt do not count towards the £231,000 nil-rate band.

Chargeable – or tax-free?

Gifts you make while you are alive
These may fall into one of three categories:

- transfers which are exempt whenever they are made during your lifetime
- transfers which are chargeable to tax at the time you make the gift
- transfers which will be exempt if you live at least seven years after making them, but otherwise become chargeable – known as 'potentially exempt transfers' (PETs).

Tax-free lifetime gifts
Small gifts
In each tax year, you can make any number of gifts with a value of £250 or less to different people. But you cannot claim this exemption for gifts which exceed £250, not even for the first £250's worth.

Gifts out of expenditure
Gifts that form part of your regular expenditure and come out of your income are tax-free so long as they really do come out of your income, not your capital, and do not affect your ability to maintain your normal standard of living. For example, you might pay the regular contributions on a savings plan taken out for your grandchildren. Note that 'income' means net income after tax and does not include the capital element of an annuity you have bought with your savings (see page 144) or the tax-free lump sum of a pension plan (see page 69).

Wedding gifts

Wedding gifts are tax-free within limits. Each parent of the bride and groom can make gifts worth up to £5,000; grandparents can each make gifts worth up to £2,500; others can make gifts worth up to £1,000.

Gifts within the family

Gifts to your husband or wife are tax-free, unless the spouse receiving the gift is 'domiciled' outside the UK, in which case only the first £55,000 given is tax-free. Your country of domicile is not necessarily where you currently live, but depends on where you have your permanent home and where you are likely to end your days.

Gifts for the maintenance of your ex-spouse are tax-free, as are transfers of property to an ex-spouse under a divorce settlement. Also tax-free are gifts for the maintenance of your or your spouse's children if they are under 18 or still in full-time education or training, and gifts to meet the regular needs of old or infirm relatives who cannot support themselves.

Yearly exemption

In each tax year you can make other gifts worth up to £3,000 which are not covered by any of the above exemptions. Any unused part of this tax-free £3,000 can be carried forward just one year, but can be used only if the following year's £3,000 exemption is used up first.

Public bodies

A number of gifts to public bodies are tax-free, including: gifts to charity; gifts to many museums, art galleries and universities; gifts to national and local government; gifts to the National Trust and a number of other bodies; gifts of property and possessions of outstanding national interest made to approved non-profit-making bodies; gifts to political parties; gifts of land to a registered housing association; and gifts of shares or securities to a trust which holds them for the benefit of employees, if the trustees hold more than half the ordinary shares of the company and have voting control.

Gifts which are partly tax-free

Where tax-free gifts have limits – such as wedding gifts – gifts in excess of the limit do not incur an immediate tax bill if they count as PETs. But they will become chargeable if you do not live at least seven years after making them.

Lifetime gifts immediately chargeable to tax

A small number of gifts are immediately chargeable to tax. These are mainly gifts to companies and to discretionary trusts (see page 479).

Where gifts are immediately chargeable, any inheritance tax due depends on what other chargeable gifts you have made in the previous seven years. The first £231,000 worth of chargeable gifts in any seven-year period falls within the nil-rate band, and there is no tax. Tax on gifts in excess of the £231,000 nil-rate band is due at only half the rate on death, i.e. at 20 per cent. But if you die within seven years of making a chargeable gift, extra tax may be due – see below. The recipient is normally liable to pay any tax on these gifts. But if you agree to pay any tax due – i.e. make a 'net chargeable transfer' – then the tax itself counts as part of the gift and is added to the running total. The example below shows how this affects the tax bill.

EXAMPLE

Henry has already made chargeable transfers of £231,000 within the last seven years, so any further chargeable transfers will be taxed. He makes another chargeable transfer of £50,000 and agrees to pay the tax due. In this case, he does not pay tax of 20 per cent on £50,000. Instead he needs to work out what figure, after deducting tax at 20 per cent, would leave a net (after-tax) gift of £50,000.

To do this, Henry 'grosses up' the £50,000 gift, i.e. divides it by 0.8. He comes up with an answer of £62,500. £62,500 minus £50,000 is £12,500. So the total gift is worth £62,500, tax of 20 per cent on £62,500 is £12,500 and the net gift is £50,000. When it comes to working out Henry's running total for any future chargeable gifts, this gift is worth £62,500.

Lifetime gifts which might become taxable

Any lifetime gift which is not tax-free or immediately chargeable will be exempt if you live for more than seven years. If you die less than seven years after making the gift, it is reassessed as if it had been a chargeable transfer all along. Tax is payable on the reassessed PET only if the total of chargeable gifts in the seven years up to the time you made the PET comes to more than the nil-rate band in force at the time of your death – i.e. £231,000 in 1999–2000. And, if tax is due, it might be reduced according to the sliding scale in Table 1 if you had survived more than three years after making the gift.

Table 1: The sliding scale of tax

Years between gift and death	Tax rate
Up to 3 years	40 per cent
More than 3 years, up to 4 years	32 per cent
More than 4 years, up to 5 years	24 per cent
More than 5 years, up to 6 years	16 per cent
More than 6 years, up to 7 years	8 per cent
More than 7 years	Tax-free

Inheritance tax on death

There is no tax on some transfers when you die, including:

- transfers to your husband or wife (up to £55,000 only, if your husband or wife is not domiciled in the UK – see 'Gifts within the family' on page 473)
- transfers to public bodies and charities (see 'Public bodies' on page 473)
- the estate of someone whose death was caused by active military service
- lump sums paid at their discretion by trustees of your employer's pension scheme or a personal pension plan if you die before reaching retirement age.

On death, two things happen. First, the tax position of individual PETs and chargeable transfers made in the seven years before your death is reassessed:

- PETs may become taxable (see above).
- Tax on chargeable gifts is recalculated using the nil-rate band and death tax rate applicable at the time of death. If this comes to more than the tax paid at the time the gift was first made, there is extra tax to pay, although it may be reduced according to the same sliding scale which applies to tax on PETs – see Table 1. If it comes to less, there is no more tax to pay, but unfortunately you are not allowed to claim a refund either.

The second thing to happen is that the reassessed PETs become part of your total of gifts over the seven years up to death, along with any chargeable transfers. Your nil-rate band of £231,000 is used up against the earliest gifts first, so later gifts, including your estate (which is treated as the final gift you make), may become taxable or suffer more tax than at first anticipated. The reducing scale of tax shown in Table 1 does not apply to tax on your estate. If tax is due, your estate bears tax at the full death rate of 40 per cent in 1999–2000.

Planning to avoid the tax

If you want to save your heirs a tax bill, how do you go about it?

Make lifetime gifts

Make tax-free gifts, or gifts which are potentially tax-free as soon as you can, if you can afford to do so. If you die between three and seven years after making a potentially tax-free gift, the tax rate will be reduced (see Table 1), and after seven years no tax will be due at all. Even if you die within seven years, there may be no tax on some or all of the potentially tax-free gifts if they fall within the £231,000 nil-rate band.

WARNING

If you do not properly give something away, but continue to benefit from it in some way, you may be making a 'gift with reservation'. This is as good as making no gift at all, as far as inheritance tax goes. Such a gift will still count as being part of your estate when it comes to totting up the value of your estate. For example, if you gave your house away but continued to live in it you would probably be making a gift with reservation – though the Inland Revenue might be persuaded that the gift was without strings attached if you paid a full market rent for it.

Use your will

If you are married, there will be no tax if you leave everything to your husband or wife – but when your husband or wife dies, there might be tax on his or her estate. Rather than leave everything to your husband or wife, you can use your will to make gifts to other members of your family (assuming that leaves enough for the surviving spouse to live on). There will still be no tax to pay if the gifts fall within the £231,000 nil-rate band, and there will be less tax when your husband or wife dies.

Share your wealth with your husband or wife

If one of you has fewer assets than the other, you could try to 'equalise' your wealth. This just means the richer partner giving assets to the poorer. Gifts between husband and wife are normally tax-free, but you can then both 'use your will' as described above. Do not forget that there may be income tax implications, too – see pages 233–7.

Look for gifts which will rise in value

Give away first those assets which are likely to grow fastest in value – that way, any increase in value will be outside your estate and the inheritance tax net. One way to put assets outside the inheritance tax net is to put investments 'in trust' for children or grandchildren – see below.

Make use of trusts

Planning to avoid inheritance tax may mean considering the use of trusts – although there are other reasons to use trusts. A trust (which you may also come across as a form of 'settlement') is a legal arrangement which allows you to give away assets to one or more 'beneficiaries' but restrict or direct how and when they can be used.

Trusts come in various forms. Here is an outline of the sorts of trust people mainly use. Anyone who thinks they might benefit from setting up a trust ought to get professional advice on whether a trust makes sense, what the income tax, capital gains tax and inheritance tax implications are, and how to set one up.

Interest in possession trusts

With this type of trust, one or more people has a right to the income from the trust's assets, or a right to use the assets, such as a house. One or more people will eventually become the owner of the assets at, say, a specified date, or when a specified event has taken place.

Sometimes, the person with the 'interest in possession', who is entitled to the income from or use of the asset, may be the same as the person with the 'reversionary interest', who is entitled to eventual ownership. For example, you might put a portfolio of shares in trust for each of your grandchildren, allowing them outright ownership when they reach a certain age.

Equally, the different types of beneficiary may be different people. For example, you may put assets in trust, for your spouse to benefit from the income, but for your children to acquire the assets when your spouse dies.

This sort of trust allows you to reduce the value of your estate without passing (immediate) control of the capital to the people who will benefit from the income. A trust like this can also be set up in your will not to avoid inheritance tax but, for example, to allow your husband or wife to be provided for during his or her life while ensuring that your wealth is eventually passed on to your children and grandchildren.

If you make a gift to this type of trust while you are alive, it will be exempt from inheritance tax if you live for seven years after making it, although the trust may have to pay some income and capital gains tax. The person with the interest in possession is treated for inheritance tax purposes as if they own the trust assets outright. This has two implications:

- When their interest ceases, the person with the interest in possession is deemed to have made a gift to whoever holds the reversionary interest. If the interest in possession comes to an end during their lifetime, the gift will usually count as a PET.

- The reversionary interest itself has no value for inheritance tax purposes, so you can give it away without any effect on your inheritance tax position at all. This opens up a useful planning opportunity. For example, if you are left a reversionary interest by a parent but you have no need of the trust assets yourself, you could give your reversionary interest away to your children, so that they, not you, become the owners of the assets when the interest in possession ends. This is an example of 'generation skipping'.

Discretionary trusts

Unlike interest in possession trusts, discretionary trusts allow the trustees to decide who, amongst a number of named or defined beneficiaries, will benefit from the assets in the trust. Discretionary trusts let you transfer assets while you are alive in order to lower the value of your estate, while maintaining flexibility over who will benefit. The potential beneficiaries could be wide, for example your spouse, your children, grandchildren, and great-grandchildren.

It is gifts to this sort of trust which are chargeable while you are still alive (see page 474) – except for some special types of discretionary trust, and for gifts which fall within one of the tax-free exemptions listed on pages 472–4 or within the £231,000 nil-rate band (see page 472). Discretionary trusts are liable to a 'periodic tax charge' every ten years. This tax is worked out according to a formula which produces a maximum tax rate of six per cent every ten years. For some people, this is a price worth paying for the benefits of using this type of trust.

Accumulation and maintenance trusts

These are a version of discretionary trust often used to benefit children and grandchildren, while lowering the value of your estate. The trustees can use their discretion to pay out for the maintenance, education or benefit of children who are the beneficiaries. Transfers into this sort of trust are not immediately chargeable to inheritance tax, and will be exempt from the tax once you have lived for seven years after making the gift.

But these trusts are subject to a number of rules:

- At least one of the beneficiaries must be alive when the trust is made. So if you set up the trust in favour of your grandchildren, you must have at least one grandchild living when you make the trust (it does not affect the trust if he or she then dies). You can, of course, name specific beneficiaries rather than a class (e.g. 'my grandchildren') of beneficiaries.
- At least one of the beneficiaries must have a right to at least part of the trust's property by the age of 25.
- The trust must not last more than 25 years, unless all the beneficiaries have at least one grandparent in common.

Trusts through life insurance

The proceeds of a policy 'written in trust' do not form part of your estate, so there will be no inheritance tax to pay. And because the proceeds do not form part of your estate, they can be paid speedily to the beneficiaries of the trusts without the need to get probate. Insurance companies can usually arrange for a policy to be written in trust fairly easily.

You can also use a life insurance policy written in trust to pay for an inheritance tax bill. For instance, you could take out a policy written in trust, with the proceeds going to people to whom you have made gifts, so that they will be able to afford a tax bill if you die within seven years of making the gift. Or you could take out a 'whole life' policy (explained on pages 111–12) to pay any inheritance tax bill on what you leave when you die.

Premiums paid into a life policy written in trust will not count as chargeable gifts if they fall within one of the tax-free gifts on pages 472–4 – they may well be classed as coming out of your normal expenditure.

What to do with your home

Some people have few assets in the way of stocks and shares or cash in the bank, but they own a valuable property which would land their estate with an inheritance tax bill. Simply giving your home away to your children while you continue to live in it may not save inheritance tax – see 'Warning' on page 476. However, there is another option.

It might make sense for a married couple or other joint owners of a home to become 'tenants in common' rather than 'joint tenants'. Property which is held as a joint tenancy automatically becomes the property of the remaining joint tenant(s) when one joint tenant dies. Tenants in common, however, can choose who inherits their share of a property.

As tenants in common, a husband and wife could each leave their share of a property to a child or grandchild. Half the house would be passed on when one of you dies, half when the remaining partner dies. In this way, both husband and wife could make use of the £231,000 nil-rate band. Without this sort of arrangement, the whole house might pass to the surviving husband or wife. There would be no inheritance tax on the first death, because transfers between husband

and wife are exempt. But on the second death, there could be tax if the house were worth more than the £231,000 nil-rate band.

For more on different types of ownership see pages 460–1. Be warned that anyone thinking of entering this sort of arrangement should think very carefully about who will inherit half the house when the first partner dies. Things can go wrong even in the most amicable of families.

Business and agricultural property

Provided you have owned business assets for at least two years before they are transferred (or, possibly, if you owned the assets for less than two years but they replaced other property acquired more than two years before), you will get 100 per cent relief on gifts of:

- unincorporated businesses (i.e. if you are a sole trader or a partner in a partnership)
- unquoted shares

You pay only half the tax on:

- land, buildings, machinery or plant you own used mainly or wholly by a business controlled by you or a partnership to which you belong
- quoted shares with a controlling interest.

The relief is not usually available in respect of businesses dealing in shares or other securities, land or buildings or businesses which make or hold investments. Shares on the Alternative Investment Market (AIM) count as unquoted.

A similar relief is available for agricultural land or buildings if certain conditions are met. You get 100 per cent relief if you have vacant possession or can get it within 24 months; and, since 1 September 1995, you also get 100 per cent relief where the land is tenanted. You must have owned the land for seven years if someone else farmed it, or you must have farmed it yourself for two years.

The point to bear in mind about business property relief and agricultural property relief is that although you may pay less or no tax when you pass on business or agricultural property, this may affect the planning you may need to do for the rest of what you own. But the detailed rules on how these types of relief work can be complicated. Get professional advice if you think they apply to you.

Who pays the tax?

Any tax due on what you leave when you die comes out of your estate. The estate will also pay the tax due (if any) on gifts you make in the seven years before you die if the recipient does not pay it within 12 months. Note that the tax is normally due from the person who received the gift. The timing of your gifts can affect the tax bill.

For example, suppose you give £60,000 to each of your four children when they reach their 30th birthdays, an age they all reach in the seven years before you die. For the sake of this example, the only other transfers you make while you are alive are tax-free (such as wedding gifts to your children). The first three children will have no need to worry about a tax bill, because their gift falls within the £231,000 nil-rate band. But the youngest child, who received £60,000 one year before your death, faces a tax bill on the £9,000 of the gift which exceeds the nil-rate band. Tax of 40 per cent of £9,000 comes to £3,600.

To avoid this problem, you could take out life insurance policies, written in trust for the benefit of any of your children who risk a tax bill. Alternatively, you could state in your will that any tax should be paid by your estate, though that will mean less for whoever receives the 'residue' of your estate – what is left after tax and all other gifts.

The pitfalls of estate planning

It is important to reiterate that estate planning will benefit your heirs, not you, and it could lead you into difficulty.

Complicated schemes

Some tax-saving schemes on offer are complicated. They can be too clever for their own good and could be nullified by Inland Revenue rules and rulings. Some may become pointless as a result of subsequent unforeseeable changes in tax legislation. It is usually sensible to get professional help on estate planning, especially where large sums of money are involved.

Off-the-peg schemes

Insurance companies and other providers of financial services often sell off-the-peg schemes to save inheritance tax – often involving complicated gift and loan arrangements. Before entering one of these arrangements, it is sensible to get a second opinion from someone outside the company selling the scheme. Is it right for you? What are the administrative charges involved? Will it do the trick of saving inheritance tax? The fact that a scheme is on sale from an insurance company does not mean that the Inland Revenue will accept that it saves inheritance tax.

Leaving yourself short

One school of thought predicts that the coming decades will see a generation of inheritors, as people inherit homes (if nothing else) from home-owning parents and grandparents. But others reject this scenario. Medical science, they say, is allowing people to live longer lives, but people will need all their wealth to pay for nursing and other services (see Chapter 9) – as well as general living costs. So do not be too hasty to give away assets you may need to finance extra expenses as you grow older.

Changing family circumstances

There is a danger in devising schemes which rely on the goodwill of children or grandchildren. Even the closest family can fall apart. And even if you remain on good terms with your heirs, there are other pitfalls. If they were to die before you, or to get divorced, you could find that your erstwhile wealth is in the hands of people who do not have your interests at heart.

Saving tax, but incurring other costs

Efforts to avoid inheritance tax may save less money than you would expect if, for instance, you incur a capital gains tax bill instead, or if you are sacrificing investment performance.

Postponing your planning

It is possible for your heirs to do some estate planning after you have died. So, for example, if you were to leave everything to your husband or wife there would be no inheritance tax to pay – and you would not risk giving too much away to other people and leaving your spouse short. But this could result in a much larger tax bill when your surviving partner dies. He or she could choose, however, to make transfers of wealth after you have died as if you had made them in your will, in order to make use of the £231,000 nil-rate band. Rearranging an estate has to be done within two years of death and must have the approval of everyone who is affected.

Addresses

AA Road Safety Unit
Norfolk House, Priestly Road,
Basingstoke, Hants RG24 9NY
Tel: (0990) 448866

AA Used Car Data Check
Tel: (0800) 2324999

Abbeyfield Society
Abbeyfield House, 53 Victoria
Street, St Albans, Herts AL1 3UW
Tel: (01727) 857536
Fax: (01727) 846168
Email: *abbeyf@geo2.poptel.org.uk*
Web site: *www.vois.org.uk/abbeyfield*

ABTA (Association of British Travel Agents
68–71 Newman Street,
London W1P 4AH
Tel: (0901) 201 5050
Web site: *www.abtanet.com*

ACAS (Advisory, Conciliation and Arbitration Service)
Brandon House, 180 Borough
High Street, London SE1 1LW
Tel: 020-7210 3000
Email: *library@libraryacas.demon.co.uk*
Web site: *www.acas.org.uk*

Age Concern England
Astral House, 1268 London Road,
London SW16 4ER
Tel: 020-8679 8000
Fax: 020-8765 7211
Web site: *www.ace.org.uk*

Age Concern Northern Ireland
3 Lower Crescent,
Belfast BT7 1NR
Tel: (028) 9024 5729
Fax: (028) 9023 5497
Email: *ageconcern.ni@btinternet.com*

Age Concern Scotland
113 Rose Street,
Edinburgh EH2 3DT
Tel: 0131-220 3345
Fax: 0131-220 2779
Email: *acs@ccis.org.uk*

Age Concern Wales
4th Floor, 1 Cathedral Road,
Cardiff CF1 9SD
Tel: (029) 2037 1566
Fax: (029) 2039 9562
Email: *enquiries@accymru.org.uk*
Web site: *www.accymru.org.uk*

Age Concern Information Line
Tel: (0800) 009966

Agency Standards Office
Tel: (0645) 555105 *(helpline)*

Alzheimer's Disease Society
Gordon House, 10 Greencoat Place,
London SW1P 1PH
Tel: 020-7306 0606
Fax: 020-7306 0808
Email: *info@alzheimers.org.uk*
Web site: *www.alzheimers.org.uk*

Anchor Trust
Fountain Court,
Oxford Spires Business Park,
Kidlington, Oxon OX5 1NZ
Tel: (01865) 854000
Fax: (01865) 854001
Web site: *www.anchor.org.uk*

Arthritis Research Campaign
PO Box 177,
Chesterfield, Derbys S41 7TQ
Tel: (01246) 558033
Fax: (01246) 558007
Email: *info@arc.org.uk*
Web site: *www.arc.org.uk*

Association of British Insurers
51 Gresham Street,
London EC2V 7HQ
Tel: 020-7600 3333
Fax 020-7696 8999
Email: *info@abi.org.uk*
Web site: *www.abi.org.uk*

Association of Chartered Certified Accountants
29 Lincoln's Inn Fields,
London WC2 A3B
Tel: 020-7242 6855
Fax: 020-7831 8054
Web site: *www.acca.org.uk*

Association of Consulting Actuaries
1 Wardrobe Place,
London EC4V 5AG
Tel: 020-7248 3163
Fax: 020-7236 1889
Email: *acahelp@aca.org.uk*
Web site: *www.aca.org.uk*

Association of Independent Tour Operators (AITO)
133A St Margaret's Road,
Twickenham TW1 1RG
Tel: 020-8744 9280
Fax: 020-8744 3187
Email: *aito@martex.co.uk*
Web site: *www.aito.co.uk*

Association of Investment Trust Companies
Durrant House, 8-13 Chiswell
Street, London EC1Y 4YY
Tel: 020-7282 5555
Fax: 020-7282 5556
Email: *info@aitc.co.uk*
Web site: *www.aitc.co.uk*

Association of Private Client Investment Managers and Stockbrokers (APCIMS)
112 Middlesex Street,
London E1 7HY
Tel: 020-7247 7080
Fax: 020-7377 0939
Email: *info@apcims.co.uk*
Web site: *www.apcims.co.uk*

Association of Relocation Agents
PO Box 189
Diss, Norfolk IP22 1PE
Tel: (08700) 737475
Fax: (01359) 251508
Email: *info@relocationagents.com*
Web site: *www.relocationagents.com*

Association of Temporary and
Interim Executive Services
(Federation of Recruitment and
Employment Services)
36-38 Mortimer Street,
London W1N 7RB
• Tel: (0800) 320 588 *(jobseekers line)*
Fax: 020-7255 2878
Email: *info@fres.co.uk*
Web site: *www.fres.co.uk*
(no callers to the office)

Back Care Association
16 Elmtree Road,
Teddington TW11 8ST
Tel: 020-8977 5474
Fax: 020-8943 5318
Email: *back/pain@compuserve.com*
Web site: *www.backpain.org*

BACUP (British Association of
Cancer United Patients)
3 Bath Place, Rivington Street,
London EC2A 3DR
Tel: (0808) 8001234 *(freephone)*
Tel: 020-7696 9000 *(general enquiries)*
Tel: 020-7613 2121 *(careline)*
Fax: 020-7696 9002
Email: *info@cancerbacup.org*
Web site: *www.cancerbacup.org.uk*

Bank of England Brokerage Service
Bank of England Registrars
PO Box 333, Gloucester GL1 1ZY
Tel: (01452) 398333
Fax: (01452) 398027
Email: *admin@registrarsdept.demon.co.uk*
Web site: *www.bankofengland.co.uk*

Banking Ombudsman
70 Grays Inn Road,
London WC1X 8NB
Tel: 020-7404 9944
Fax: 020-7405 5052
Email: *bankingombudsman@obo.org.uk*
Web site: *www.obo.org.uk*

Benefits Enquiry Line
(0800) 882200

BREAK
20 Hooks Hill Road, Sheringham,
Norfolk NR26 8NL
Tel: (01263) 823170

British Airways Travel Clinic
Tel: (01276) 685040

British Association for Counselling
1 Regent Place, Rugby,
Warks CV21 2PJ
Tel: (01788) 550899
Tel: (01788) 578328 *(information*
line only)
Fax: (01788) 562189
Email: *bac@bac.co.uk*
Web site: *www.counselling.co.uk*

British Association of Removers (BAR)
3 Churchill Court, 58 Station Road,
North Harrow HA2 7SA
Tel: 020-8861 3331
Fax: 020-8861 3332
Email: *movers@bar.co.uk*
Web site: *www.barmovers.com*

British Deaf Association
1 Worship Street,
London EC2A 2AB
Tel: 020-7588 3520
Fax: 020-7588 3527
Email: *info@bda.org.uk*

British Diabetic Association
10 Queen Anne Street,
London W1M 0BD
Tel: 020-7323 1531
Tel: 020-7636 6112 *(care service)*
Fax: 020-7637 3644
Email: *bda@diabetes.org.uk*
Web site: *www.diabetes.org.uk*

British Executive Service Overseas
164 Vauxhall Bridge Road,
London SW1V 2RB
Tel: 020-7630 0644
Fax: 020-7630 0624
Email: *bso@bso.org*

British Franchise Association
Thames View,
Newtown Road, Henley-on-Thames,
Oxon RG9 1HG
Tel: (01491) 578049
Fax: (01491) 573517
Email: *mailroom:@british-franchise.
org.uk*
Web site: *www.british-franchise.org.uk*

**British Insurance and Investment
Brokers' Association**
14 Bevis Marks, London EC3A 7NT
Tel: 020-7623 9043
Fax: 020-7626 9676
Web site: *www.biba.org.uk*

British Medical Association
Tavistock Square,
London WC1H 9JP
Tel: 020-7387 4499
Web site: *www.bma.org.uk*

British Red Cross
National Headquarters,
9 Grosvenor Crescent,
London SW1X 7EJ
Tel: 020-7235 5454
fax: 020-7245 6315
Email: *info@redcross.org.uk*
Web site: *www.redcross.org.uk*

British Telecom (BT)
Complaints Review Service
Tel: (0800) 545458
Customer Services 150
Directory Enquiries 192
Line Faults 151
Sales (0800) 800150
Security (0800) 455455

**British Venture Capital Association
(BVCA)**
Essex House, 12-13 Essex Street,
London WC2R 3AA
Tel: 020-7240 3846
Fax: 020-7240 3849
Email: *bvca@bbca.co.uk*
Web site: *www.bvca.co.uk*

Building Societies Ombudsman
Office of the Building Societies
Ombudsman, Millbank Tower,
Millbank, London SW1P 4XS
Tel: 020-7931 0044
Fax: 020-7931 8485/7233 9836
Email: *bldgsocombudsman@easynet.co.uk*
(*Written complaints to be marked
'Complaints Bureau'*)

Business in the Community
2nd Floor, 12 Pilcher Gate,
The Lace Market, Nottingham NG1
1QE
Tel: 0115-911 6666
Fax: 0115-911 6667
Email: *bitc@bitcen.nettonect.co.uk*
Web site: *www.bitc.org.uk*

Business Connect (Wales)
Tel: (0345) 969798

Business Link (England)
Tel: (0345) 567765

Business Shop (Scotland)
Tel: (0800) 787878

Cable Communications Association (CCA)
5th floor, Artillery House,
Artillery Row, London SW1P 1RT
Tel: 020-7222 2900
Fax: 020-7799 1471
Web site: *www.cable.co.uk*

Cable Hotline
Tel: (0990) 111777

Camping and Caravanning Club
Greenfields House, Westwood
Way, Coventry CV4 8JH
Tel: (024) 7669 4995
Fax: (024) 7669 4886
Web site: *www.campingand
caravanningclub.co.uk*

Care & Repair (England)
Castle House, Kirtley Drive,
Nottingham NG7 1LD
Tel: 0115-979 9091
Fax: 0115-985 9457
Web site: *www.care-repair.eng.
demon.co.uk*

Care & Repair Cymru
Norbury House, Norbury Road,
Cardiff CF5 3AS
Tel: (029) 2057 6286
Fax: (029) 2057 6283

Care & Repair Northern Ireland
Fold Housing Association,
3-6 Redburn Square, Holywood,
Co. Down BT18 9HZ
Tel: (028) 9042 8314
Fax: (028) 90428167
Email: *fold@dprecruit.co.uk*

Carers National Association
Ruth Pitter House, 20-25 Glasshouse
Yard, London EC1A 4JT
Tel: 020-7490 8818
Fax: 020-7490 8824
Email: *internet@ukcarers.org*
Web site: *www.carersuk.demon.co.uk*

Chartered Institute of Arbitrators
24 Angel Gate, City Road,
London EC1V 2RS
Tel: 020-7837 4483
Fax: 020-7837 4185
Email: *info@arbitrators.org*
Web site: *www.arbitrators.org*

Chartered Insurance Institute (CII)
31 Hillcrest Road,
London E18 2JP
Tel: 020-7606 3835
Fax: 020-8530 3052
Email: *cii@cii-customerservs.demon.co.uk*
Web site: *www.cii.co.uk*

Chartered Society of Physiotherapy
14 Bedford Row,
London WC1R 4ED
Tel: 020-7242 1941
Fax: 020-7306 6611
Web site: *www.csp.org.uk*

Commission for Racial Equality
Elliot House, 10-12 Allington
Street, London SW1E 5EH
Tel: 020-7828 7022
Fax: 020 7630 7605
Email: *info@cre.gov.uk*
Web site: *www.cre.gov.uk*

Companies House
(England and Wales)
Crown Way, Cardiff CF14 3UZ
Tel: (029) 2038 0801
Fax: (029) 2038 0517
Web site: *www.companieshouse.gov.uk*

Companies Registry
(Northern Ireland)
Registry of Companies, Credit
Unions and Industrial and Provident
Societies,
IBD House, 64 Chichester Street,
Belfast BT1 4JX
Tel: (028) 9023 4488
Fax: (028) 9054 4888
Web site: *www.dedni.gov.uk/
registry/index.htm*

Companies House
(Scotland)
Argyle House, 37 Castle Terrace,
Edinburgh EH1 2EB
Tel: 0131-535 5800
Fax: 0131-535 5820
Web site: *www.companieshouse.gov.uk*

Confederation of Passenger Transport
Imperial House, 15–19 Kingsway,
London WC2B 6UN
Tel: 020-7240 3131
Fax: 020-7240 6565
Email: *admin@cpt-uk.org*
Web site: *www.cpt-uk.org/cpt*

Consumers' Association
2 Marylebone Road,
London NW1 4DF
Tel: 020-7770 7000
Fax: 020-7770 7600
Email: *which@which.net*
Web site: *www.which.net*

Continence Foundation
307 Haton Square, 16 Baldwins
Gardens, London EC1N 7RJ
Tel: 020-7831 9831
Fax: 020-7468 6876
Email: *continence.foundation@
dial.pipex.com£*
Web site: *www.vois.org.uk/cf*

**Council for the Advancement of
Communication for Deaf People**
Durham University Science Park,
Block 4, Stockton Road, Durham
DH1 3UZ
Tel: 0191-383 1155
Fax: 0191-383 7914
Email: *durham@cacdp.demon.co.uk*
Web site: *www.cacdp.demon.co.uk*

**Council for Registered Gas
Installers (CORGI)**
1 Elmwood, Chineham Business
Park, Crockford Lane,
Basingstoke, Hants RG24 8WG
Tel: (01256) 372200
Fax: (01256) 708144
Email: *enquiries@corgi-gas.co.uk*

Court of Protection
Public Trust Office,
Stewart House, 24 Kingsway,
London WC2B 6JX
Tel: 020-7664 7000
Fax: 020-7664 7705
Web site: *www.publictrust.gov.uk*

Countryside Agency
John Dower House,
Crescent Place,
Cheltenham GL50 3RA
Tel: (01242) 521381
Fax: (01242) 584270
Web site: *www.countryside.gov.uk*

CRUSE Bereavement Care
Cruse House, 126 Sheen Road,
Richmond, Surrey TW9 1UR
Tel: 020-8940 4818
Fax: 020-8940 7638

Data Protection Registrar
Wycliffe House, Water Lane,
Wilmslow,
Cheshire SK9 5AF
Tel: (01625) 545745
Fax: (01625) 524510
Email: *data@wycliffe.demon.co.uk*
Web site: *www.dataprotection.gov.uk*

**Department of the Environment,
Transport and the Regions**
Eland House, Bressenden Place,
London SW1E 5DU
Tel: 020-7890 3333
Tel: (0870) 1226 236 *(brochure line)*
Fax: 020-7890 6589
Web site: *www.detr.gov.uk*

Department of Health Publications
Tel: (0800) 555777
Fax: (01623) 724524
Web site: *www.doh.gov.uk*

Department of Social Security (DSS)
Overseas Branch,
Longbenton,
Newcastle upon Tyne NE98 1YX
Tel: 0191-213 5000
Tel: 020-7712 2171
Web site: *www.dss.gov.uk*

**Department of Trade and Industry
(DTI)**
1 Victoria Street,
London SW1H 0ET
Tel: 020-7215 5000
Fax: 020-7222 0612
Timeshare Guide enquiries:
Tel: 020-7215 0387/0344

**Department of the Environment,
Transport and the Regions**
Mobility Unit, Great Minster
House, 76 Marsham Street,
London SW1P 4DR
Tel: 020-7271 5252
Tel: (0870) 226236 *(publications)*
Web site: *www.DETR.gov.uk*

DFEE Publications
Tel: (0845) 6022260

DIAL UK
National Association of
Disablement Information and
Advice Lines, Park Lodge, St
Catherine's Hospital, Tickhill Road,
Doncaster DN4 8QN
Tel: (01302) 310123
Fax: (01302) 310404
Email: *dialuk@aol.com*
Web site: *www.members.aol.com/dialuk*

Disability Alliance ERA
Universal House,
88-94 Wentworth Street,
London E1 7SA
Tel: 020-7247 8776
Fax: 020-7247 8765

Disability Discrimination Act
leaflets
Tel: (0345) 622633
Tel: (0345) 622644 *(textphone)*
Web site: *www.disability.gov.uk*

Disability Information Trust
Mary Marlborough Centre,
Nuffield Orthopaedic Centre,
Headington, Oxford OX3 7LD
Tel: (01865) 227592
Fax: (01865) 227596
Email: *ditrust@btconnect.com*
Web site: *www.home/btconnect.com/
ditrust/home.htm*

Disabled Living Centres Council
Redbank House, 4 St Chad Street,
Manchester M8 8QA
Tel: 0161-834 1044
Fax: 0161-835 3591
Email: *dlcc@dlcc.demon.co.uk*
Web site: *www.dlcc.demon.co.uk*

Disabled Living Foundation
380–384 Harrow Road,
London W9 2HU
Tel: 020-7289 6111
Fax: 020-7266 2922
Email: *dlfinfo@dlf.org.uk*
Web site: *www.dlf.org.uk*

DoE Water Service
Northland House,
3 Frederick Street,
Belfast BT1 2NR
Tel: (0345) 440088 *(helpline)*
Tel (0345) 023206 *(textphone)*

Driver and Vehicle Licensing Agency (DVLA)
Swansea SA1 1AA
Tel: (01792) 772151
Fax: (01792) 772151
Web site: *www.open.gov.uk/dvla*

DTI Publications Orderline
Admail 528, London SW1W 8YT
Tel: (0870) 1502500
Fax: (0870) 1502333
Email: *dtipubs@echristian.co.uk*
Web site: *www.dti.gov.uk*

EAGA Ltd (Energy Action Grants Agency)
2nd Floor, Eldon Court,
Eldon Square, Newcastle upon Tyne
NE1 7HA
Tel: (0800) 181667
Fax: 0191-230 1823
Web site: *www.eaga.co.uk*

Elderly Accommodation Counsel
46A Chiswick High Road,
London W4 1SZ
Tel: 020-8742 1182
Fax: 020-8995 7714
Email: *enquiries@e-a-c.demon.co.uk*

Employment Agency Standards
Department of Trade and Industry,
Bay 135, 1 Victoria Street,
London SW1H 0ET
Tel: (0645) 555105
Fax: 020-7215 2636
Email: *mailbox.ir2@irdv.dti.gov.uk*

Energy Savings Trust
21 Dartmouth Street,
London SW1H 9BP
Tel: 020-7222 0101
Fax: 020-7654 2444
Web site: *www.est.org.uk*

Employment Opportunities
Tel: 020-7726 4961

Employment Service Direct Jobline
Tel: (0845) 6060234

English Tourism Council
1 Regent Street,
Piccadilly Circus, London SW1 4XT
Tel: 020-7846 9000
Fax: 020-7808 3801
Web site: *www.englishtourism.org.uk*

Energy Environmental and Waste Directorate
c/o Dept. of the Environment,
Transport and the Regions
Eland House, London
SW1E 5DU
Tel: 020-7890 6655
Fax: 020-7890 6659
Web site: *www.detr.gov.uk*

Equal Opportunities Commission
Overseas House, Quay Street,
Manchester M3 3HN
Tel: 0161-833 9244
Fax: 0161-835 1657
Email: *info@aoc.org.uk*
Web site: *www.aoc.org.uk*

Farm Holiday Bureau UK Ltd
National Agricultural Centre,
Stoneleigh Park, Warks CV8 2LZ
Tel: (024) 7669 6909
Fax: (024) 7669 6630
Email: *admin@fhbaccom.demon.co.uk*
Web site: *www.webscape.co.uk/
formaccom/*

**Federation of Recruitment and
Employment Services**
36–38 Mortimer Street,
London W1N 7RB
Tel: 020-7323 4300
Fax: 020-7255 2878
Web site: *www.fres.co.uk*

**Fellowship of Depressives
Anonymous**
Box FDA, Wormiston House,
32–36 Pelham Street,
Nottingham NG1 2EG
Tel: (01702) 433838
Fax: (01702) 433843

**FIDI (Fédération Internationale des
Déménageurs Internationaux)**
60 rue Picard, Bte 5,
1210 Brussels, Belgium
Tel: (0032 2) 426 5160
Web site: *www.fidi.com*

Financial Services Authority (FSA)
25 The North Colonnade, Canary
Wharf, London
E14 5HS
Tel: 020-7676 1000
Tel: (0800) 9173311 *(leaflets line)*
Tel: (0845) 6061234 *(public enquiries
helpline)*
Fax 020-7676 1099
Email: *enquiries@fsa.co.uk*
Web site: *www.fsa.gov.uk*

Gas Consumers Council
Abford House, 15 Wilton Road,
London SW1V 1LT
Tel: 020-7931 0977
Fax: 020-7630 9934
Email: *gcc@gascc.org.uk*

Health Education Authority (HEA)
Trevelyan House, 30 Great Peter
Street, London
SW1P 2HW
Tel: 020-7222 5300
Tel: 020-7413 1990 *('Active for Life'
hotline)*
Web site: *www.hea.org.uk*

**Health and Safety Executive Gas
Safety Line**
Tel: (0800) 300363

Help the Aged
16–18 St James's Walk,
London EC1R 0BE
Tel: 020-7253 0253 *(general enquiries
and Housing Division)*
Fax: 020-7251 0747

**Help the Aged Care Fees Advisory
Service**
Tel: (0500) 767476

Help the Aged Insurance Services
Tel: (0800) 413180

Help the Aged Seniorline
Tel: (0808) 800565 *(Mon-Fri,*
9am-4pm)

HMSO
Stationery Office Books,
PO Box 276, Battersea,
London SW8 5DT
Tel: (0870) 6005522 *(enquiries)*
Fax: 020-7873 8200 *(orders)*
Web site: *www.tso-online.co.uk*
Email: *book.enquiries@theso.co.uk*
Email: *book.orders@theso.co.uk*
('Door to Door' costs £5.99 plus
VAT plus £2.50 postage and packing.
Please quote ref: 0115517472)

Holiday Care Service
2nd Floor, Imperial Building,
Victoria Road, Horley,
Surrey RH6 7PZ
Tel: (01293) 774535
Fax: (01293) 784647
Email: *holiday.care@virgin.net*

Home Improvement Trust
7 Mansfield Road,
Nottingham
NG1 3FB
Tel: 0115-934 9511
Fax: 0115-934 9501

HOMES *(Housing Organisations*
Mobility and Exchange Services)
242 Vauxhall Bridge Road,
London SW1V 1AU
Tel: 020-7963 0200
Fax: 020-7963 0249

HPI Register
Tel: (01722) 422422
Fax: (01722) 412164
Web site: *www.hpicheck.com*

IFA Promotion
28 Greville Street, London EC1N 8S4
Tel: 020-7831 4027
Tel: 0117-971 1177 *(consumer hotline)*
Fax: 020-7831 4920
Email: *contact@ifap.org.uk*
Web site: *www.ifap.org.uk*

Incorporated Society of Valuers
and Auctioneers (ISVA)
3 Cadogan Gate,
London SW1X 0AS
Tel: 020-7235 2282
Fax: 020-7235 4390
Email: *hq@isva.co.uk*
Web site: *www.isva.co.uk*

Independent Housing Ombudsman
Scheme
Norman House, 105–109 Strand,
London WC2R 0AA
Tel: 020-7836 3630
Tel: (0345) 125973 (lo-call)

Inland Revenue
Look in the phone book for
the number of your local office
Inland Revenue
(Publications Section)
Tel: 020-7438 6420
Tel: (0645) *000404 (for helpsheet*
IR284)

Institute of Actuaries
Tel: 020-77632 2100
Fax: 020-7632 2111
Web site: *www.actuaries.org.uk*

Institute of Advanced Motorists
IAM House, 359 Chiswick
High Road, London W4 4HS
Tel: 020-8994 4403
Fax: 020-8994 9249
Web site: *www.iam.org.uk*

Institute of Chartered Accountants in England and Wales
PO Box 433, Chartered
Accountants Hall, Moorgate Place,
London EC2P 2BJ
Tel: 020-7920 8100
Fax: 020-7920 0547
Web site: *www.icaew.co.uk*

Institute of Chartered Accountants in Scotland
27 Queen Street,
Edinburgh EH2 1LA
Tel: 0131-225 5673
Fax: 0131-225 3813
Email: *icas@icas.org.uk*
Web site: *www.icas.org.uk*

Institute of Personnel and Development (IPD)
IPD House, 35 Camp Road,
London SW19 4UX
Tel: 020-8971 9000
Fax: 020-8263 3333
Web site: *www.ipd.co.uk*

Institute of Public Loss Assessors
14 Red Lion Street, Chesham,
Bucks HP5 1HB
Tel: (01494) 782342
Fax: (01494) 774928

Insurance Brokers' Registration Council
Higham Business Centre, Midland
Road, Higham Ferrers, Northants
NN10 8DW
Tel: (01933) 359083)
Fax: (01933) 359077

Insurance Ombudsman Bureau
City Gate One, 135 Park Street,
London SE1 9EA
Tel: (0845) 6006666

Interval International Ltd
Coombe Hill House, Beverley
Way, London SW20 0AR
Tel: 020-8336 9300
Fax: 020-8336 9399
Web site: *www.interval-intl.com*

Investment Management Regulatory Organisation (IMRO)
see 'Financial Services Authority"

Investment Ombudsman
6 Frederick's Place, London
EC2R 8BT
Tel: 020-7796 3065
Fax: 020-7726 0574

Investors' Compensation Scheme
The Cotton Centre, Cottons Lane,
London SE1 2QB
Tel: 020-7367 6000
Fax: 020-7367 6001
Web site: *www.fsa.gov.uk*

Jobcentre
*Look in the phone book
under 'Employment Service'*

Law Society
113 Chancery Lane,
London WC2A 1PL
Tel: 020-7242 1222
Accident Line: (0500) 192939

Law Society of Northern Ireland
Law Society House,
98 Victoria Street, Belfast BT1 3JZ
Tel: (028) 9023 1614
Fax: (028) 9023 2606

Law Society of Scotland
Law Society Hall,
26 Drumsheugh Gardens,
Edinburgh EH3 7YR
Tel: 0131-226 7411
Fax: 0131-225 2934
Email: *lawscot@lawscot.org.uk*
Web site: *www.lawscot.org.uk*

Leasehold Advisory Service
8 Maddox Street,
London W1R 9PN
Tel: 020-7493 3116
Fax: 020-7493 4318
Email: *info@lease-advice.org*
Web site: *www.lease-advice.org*

Legal Services Ombudsman
22 Oxford Court, Oxford Street,
Manchester M2 3WQ
Tel: 0161-236 9532
Fax: 0161-236 2651
Email: *enquiries.olso@gtrut.gov.uk*

Life Insurance Association
LIA House, Station Approach,
Chorleywood, Rickmansworth,
Herts WD3 5PF
Tel: (01923) 285333
Fax: (01923) 285395
Web site: *www.lia.co.uk*

Local Enterprise Development Unit
LEDU House, Upper Galwally,
Belfast BT8 6TB
Tel: (028) 9049 1031
Fax: (028) 9069 1432
Email: *ledu@ledu-northernireland.ni.gov.uk*

London Mobility Unit
New Zealand Unit,
80 Haymarket,
London SW1Y 4TZ
Tel: 020-7321 2480

Mail Order Traders Association
40 Waterloo Raod, Birkdale,
Southport PR8 2NG
Tel: (01704) 563787
Fax: (01704) 551247
Email: *malcomlandau@compuserve.com*

Mediation UK
Alexander House, Telephone
Avenue, Bristol BS1 4BS
Tel: 0117-904 6661
Fax: 0117-904 3331
Email: *mediationuk@mediationuk.org.uk*

Medical Advisory Service for Travellers Abroad (MASTA)
Keppel Street, London WC1 6HJ
Tel: (09068) 224100 *(premium-rate healthline)*
Tel: 0113-238 7575 *(mail order)*

Mobility Advice and Vehicle Information Service (MAVIS)
'O' Wing, MacAdam Avenue,
Old Wokingham Road,
Crowthorne, Berks RG45 6XD
Tel: (01344) 661000
Fax: (01344) 661066
Email: *mavis@detr.gov.uk*
Web site: *www.mobility-unit.detr.gov.uk/mavis.htm*

Money Management magazine
Maple House, 149 Tottenham
Court Road,
London W1P 9LL
Tel: 020-7896 2575
Fax: 020-7896 2592
Email: *amanda.nottage@ft.com*
Web site: *www.ft.com*

**Money Management Register of
Fee-based Advisors**
c/o Matrix Data Ltd, FREEPOST 22
(SW1565),
London W1E 7E2
Tel: (0870) 0131925

Motability
Goodman House, Station
Approach, Harlow, Essex
CM20 2ET
Tel: (01279) 635666
Fax: (01279) 632000
Web site: *www.motability.co.uk*

**National Association of Estate
Agents (NAEA)**
Arbon House, 21 Jury Street,
Warwick, Warks CV34 4EH
Tel: (01926) 496800
Fax: (01926) 400953
Email: *info@naea.co.uk*
Web site: *www.naea.co.uk*

**National Association of
Goldsmiths**
78A Luke Street,
London EC2A 4XG
Tel: 020-7613 4445
Fax: 020-7613 4990
Email: *paul@jewellersuk.com*
Web site: *www.jewellers.org*

**National Association for Mental
Health (MIND)**
Granta House, 15–19 Broadway,
London E15 4BQ
Tel: 020-8519 2122
Fax: 020-8522 1725
Email: *contact.@mind.org.uk*
Web site: *www.mind.org.uk*

**National Association of Volunteer
Bureaux**
New Oxford House, 16 Waterloo
Street, Birmingham B2 5UG
Tel: 0121-633 4555
Fax: 0121-633 4043
Email: *navbteam@waverider.co.uk*
Web site: *www.navb.org.uk*

National Association of Widows
54–57 Allison Street, Digbeth,
Birmingham B5 5TH
Tel: 0121-643 8348

National Breakdown
Green Flag Ltd, Green Flag House,
Cote Lane, Leeds LS28 5GF
Tel: 0113-239 3666
Fax: 0113-257 3111
Web site: *www.greenflag.co.uk*

**National Business Angels Network
(NBAN)**
3rd Floor, 40–42 Cannon Street,
London EC4N 6JJ
Tel: 020-7329 2929
Fax: 020-7329 2626
Email: *info@nationalbusangels.co.uk*
Web site: *www.nationalbusangels.co.uk*

National Debtline
Tel: 0121-359 8501 *(Mon, Thurs
10am-4pm;*
Tues, Weds 10am-7pm;
Fri 10am-12pm)
(0645) 500511 *(lo-call)*

National Extension College
18 Brooklands Avenue,
Cambridge CB2 2HN
Tel: (01223) 316644
Fax: (01223) 313586
Web site: *www.nec.ac.uk*

National Federation of Shopmobility
85 High Street, Worcester WR1 2ET
Tel/fax: (01905) 617761
Email: *shopmob@dircon.co.uk*

National House Building Council
Buildmark House, Chiltern Avenue,
Amersham,
Bucks HP6 5AP
Tel: (01494) 434477
Fax: (01494) 728521

*National Institute for Adult
Continuing Education*
21 De Montfort Street,
Leicester LE1 7GE
Tel: 0116-255 1451
Fax: 0116-285 4514
Email: *enquiries@niace.org.uk*
Web site: *www.niace.org.uk*

National Minimum Wage Helpline
Tel: (0845) 6000678

National Osteoporosis Society
PO Box 10, Radstock,
Bath BA3 3YB
Tel: (01761) 471771
Fax: (01761) 471104
Web site: *www.nos.org.uk*

National Retreat Association
Central Hall, 256 Bermondsey
Street, London SE1 3UJ
Tel: 020-7357 7736
Fax: 020-7357 7724
Email: *nra@retreats.org.uk*
Web site: *www.restreats.org.uk*

National Savings
Helpline: (0645) 645000
Fax: (01253) 832025
Email: *customerenquiries@
nationalsavings.co.uk*
Web site: *www.nationalsavings.co.uk*

New Homes Marketing Board
82 New Cavendish Street,
London W1M 8AD
Tel: 020-7608 5100
Fax: 020-7608 5101
Email: *hbf@hbf.co.uk*
Web site: *www.hbf.co.uk*

Northern Ireland Tourist Board
St Anne's Court, 59 North Street,
Belfast BT1 1NB
Tel: (028) 90231221
Fax: (028) 90312424
Web site: *www.ni-tourism.com*

*Occupational Pensions Advisory
Service (OPAS)*
11 Belgrave Road,
London SW1V 1RB
Tel: 020-7233 8080
Fax: 020-7233 8016
Email: *opas@iclweb.com*
Web site: *www.opas.org.uk*
(Written enquiries preferred)

*Occupational Pensions Regulatory
Authority (OPRA)*
Invicta House, Trafalgar Place,
Brighton BN1 4DW
Tel: (01273) 627600
Fax: (01273) 627688
Email: *helpdesk@opra.gov.uk*
Web site: *www.opra.gov.uk*

Office of Fair Trading and Consumer Information Line
Field House, 15–25 Bream's
Buildings, London EC4A 1PR
Tel: (0345) 224499
Tel: 020-7211 8800 *(general*
• *switchboard)*
Fax: 020-7211 8800
Email: *enquiries@oft.gov.uk*
Web site: *www.oft.gov.uk*

Office of Fair Trading (OFT)
15–25 Bream's Buildings,
London EC4A 1PR
Tel: (0345) 224499
Web site: *www.ft.gov.uk/html/consume*

Office for the Supervision of Solicitors
Victoria Court, 8 Dormer Place,
Leamington Spa,
Warks CV32 5AE
Tel: (01926) 820082
Fax: (01926) 431435
Web site: *www.lawsociety.org.uk*

OFGEM (Office of Gas and Electricity Markets)
3 Tiger's Road,
Wigston,
Leicester LE18 4UX
Tel: 0116-278 5354
Fax: 0116-278 0027

OFGEM (Scotland)
48 St Vincent Street, Glasgow G2 5TS
Tel: 0141-331 2200
(see above also)

OFREG (Office for the Regulation of Electricity and Gas)
Brookmount Buildings, 42 Fountain
Street, Belfast BT1 5EA
Tel: (028) 9031 1588
Fax: (028) 9031 1740
Email: *ofreg@nicf.gov.uk*
Web site: *www.ofreg.nicf.gov.uk/*

OFTEL (Office of Telecommunications)
50 Ludgate Hill,
London EC4M 7JJ
Tel: 020-7634 8888
Tel: 020-7634 8700 *(complaints)*
Fax: 020-7634 8943
Web site: *www.oftel.gov.uk*

OFWAT (Office of Water Services)
Centre City Tower, 7 Hill
Street, Birmingham B5 4UA
Tel: 0121-625 1300
Fax: 0121-625 1400
Web site: *www.open.gov.uk/ofwat/*

Ombudsman for Estate Agents (OEA)
Beckett House, 4 Bridge Street,
Salisbury, Wilts SP1 2LX
Tel: (01722) 333306
Fax: (01722) 332296
Email: *post@oea.co.uk*
Web site: *www.oea.com*

Open College of the Arts
Houndhill, Worsbrough, Barnsley,
S. Yorks. S70 6TU
Tel: (01226) 730495
Fax: (01226) 730838
Email: *open.arts@ukonline.co.uk*
Web site: *www.oca-uk.com*

Open and Distance Learning Quality Council
Westminster Hall, Storey's Gate,
London SW14 9NH
Tel: 020-7233 3466
Fax: 020-7233 3469
Email: *odlqc@dial.pipex.com*
Web site: *www.odlqc.org.uk/odlqc*

Open University (OU)
Walton Hall, Milton Keynes
MK7 6AA
Tel: (01908) 274066
Fax: (01908) 653744
Web site: *www.open.ac.uk*

Organisation for Timeshare in Europe
15–19 Great Titchfield Street,
London W1P 7SB
Tel: 020-7291 0901
Fax: 020-7291 0910

Parkinson's Disease Society
215 Vauxhall Bridge Road,
London SW1 1EJ
Tel: 020-7931 8080
Tel: (0808) 880303 *(helpline Mon-Fri, 9.30 am-5.30 pm)*
Fax: 020-7233 9908
Email: *mailbox@pdsuk.demon.co.uk*

Patients' Association
PO Box 935, Harrow, Middlesex
HA1 3YT
Tel: 020-8423 8999 *(advice line)*
Tel: 020-8423 9111 *(administration)*
Fax: 020-8423 1115
Web site: *www.patientsassociation.com*

Pension Schemes Registry
PO Box 1NN,
Newcastle upon Tyne NE99 1NN
Tel: 0191-225 6393/4
Fax: 0191-225 6390 *(surnames A-Je)*
Fax: 0191-225 6391 *(surnames Jf -K)*
Web site: *www.opra.co.uk*

Personal Insurance Arbitration Service
Chartered Institute of Arbitrators,
24 Angel Gate, City Road,
London EC1V 2RS
Tel: 020-7837 4483
Fax: 020-7837 4185
Email: *71411.2735@compuserve.com*
Web site: *www.arbitrators.org*

Personal Investment Authority (PIA)
see 'Financial Services Authority'

Personal Investment Authority Ombudsman Bureau
see 'Financial Services Authority'

Premier Retirement Services
1 Loweridge Mews,
London NW6 2DP
Tel: 020-7328 9898
Fax: 020-7328 0010

Pre-Retirement Association
9 Chesham Road, Guildford,
Surrey GU1 3LF
Tel: (01483) 301170
Fax: (01483) 300981
Email: *info@pra.uk.com*
Web site: *www.pra.uk.com*

PRIME
Walkden House, 3–10 Melton
Street, London
NW1 2EJ
Tel: 020-8765 7852
Fax: 020-8765 7879
Email: *prime@ace.org.uk*

Proshare UK Ltd
Library Chambers, 13–14 Basinghall
Street, London
EC2 5HU
Tel: 020-7600 0984
Fax: 020-7600 0947
Web site: *www.proshare.org.uk*

**Public Trust Office, Protection
Division**
(England and Wales)
Stewart House, 24 Kingsway,
London WC2B 6JX
Tel: 020-7664 7000
Fax: 020-7664 7705

**Public Trust Office, Protection
Division**
(Northern Ireland)
Office of Care and Protection,
Royal Courts of Justice,
Chichester Street,
Belfast BT1 3JF
Tel: (028) 9023 5111 (ext. 2348)
Fax: (028) 9031 3793

RAC Response
PO Box 306, Bristol BS99 5RY
Tel: (0990) 722722
Fax: (01454) 208277
Web site: *www.rac.co.uk*

RCI Europe Ltd
Kettering Parkway, Kettering,
Northants. NN15 6EY
Tel: (01536) 310101
Fax: (01536) 411037
Web site: *www.rci.com*

Rail Europe
French Railways House, 179
Piccadilly, London
W1V 0BA
Tel: (0870) 5848848
Web site: *raileurope.co.uk*

REACH
Bear Wharf, 27 Bankside,
London SE1 9ET
Tel: 020-7928 0452
Fax: 020-7928 0798
Email: *volework@btinternet.com*
Web site: *www.volework.org.uk*

Redundancy Payments Helpline
Tel: (0500) 848489
Fax: 0121-454 7881

Relate
National Headquarters, Herbert Gray
College, Little Church Street,
Rugby, Warks CV21 3AP
Tel: (01788) 573241
Fax: (01788) 535007
Web site: *www.relate.org.uk*

**Retired and Senior Volunteer
Programme**
237 Pentonville Road,
London N1 9NJ
Tel: 020-7278 6601
Fax: 020-7833 8434
Email: *csv_rsvp@compuserve.com*

Retirement Pension Forecast and Advice Service (RPFA)
Pensions and Overseas Benefits Directorate,
Newcastle upon Tyne NE98 1BA
Tel: 0191-218 7585
Fax: 0191-218 7006
Web site: *www.dss.gov.uk/ ba/htgarpf.htm*

Retirement Homes Specialists
1 Loveridge Mews,
London NW6 2DP
Tel: 020-7328 9898

Revenue Adjudicator's Office
8 Haymarket, London SW1Y 4SP
Tel: 020-7930 2292
Fax: 020-7930 2298
Email: *adjudicators@gtnet.gov.uk*
Web site: *www.open.gov.uk/ adjoss/aodemo1.htm*

Riba Publications Ltd
56–64 Leonard Street,
London EC2A 4LT
Tel: 020-7251 0791
Fax: 020-7608 2375

RICA (Research Institute for Consumer Affairs)
24 Highbury Crescent,
London N5 1RX
Tel: 020-7704 5200
Fax: 020-7704 5208
Email: *mail@ricability.org.uk*

Royal Association for Disability and Rehabilitation (RADAR)
Unit 12, City Forum, 250 City Road,
London EC1V 8AF
Tel: 020-7250 3222
Fax: 020-7250 0212
Email: *radar@radar.org.uk*
Web site: *www.radar.org.uk*

Royal Institution of Chartered Surveyors (RICS)
12 Great George Street, Parliament Square, London
SW1P 3AD
Tel: 020-7222 7000
Fax: 020-7695 1505
Email: *info@rics.org.uk*
Web site: *www.rics.org.uk*

Royal National Institute for the Blind (RNIB)
224–228 Great Portland Street,
London W1N 6AA
Tel: 020-7388 1266
Fax: 020-7388 2034
Web site: *www.rnib.org.uk*

Royal National Institute for Deaf People (RNID)
19–23 Featherstone Street,
London EC1Y 8SL
Tel: 020-7296 8000
Fax: 020-7296 8199
Web site: *www.rnid.org.uk*

Royal Society for the Prevention of Accidents
Rospa House, Edgbaston Park,
353 Bristol Road, Birmingham
B5 7ST
Tel: 0121-248 2000
Fax: 0121-248 2001
Web site: *www.rospa.com*

RPI (current figures)
Tel: 020-7533 5874

Saga
Saga Holidays Ltd, Saga Building, Middelburg Square, Folkestone, Kent CT20 1AZ
Tel: (0800) 300500
Fax: (01303) 221638
Web site: *www.saga.co.uk*

Scottish Homes
1403–7 Gallowgate, Glasgow
G31 4EU
Tel: 0141-554 3733
Fax: 0141-556 2302

Scottish Tourist Board
23 Ravelston Terrace,
Edinburgh EH4 3TP
Tel: 0131-332 2433
Fax: 0131-343 1513
Email: *info@stb.gov.uk*
Web site: *www.holiday.scotland.net*

**Securities and Futures Authority
(SFA)**
Cottons Centre, Cottons Lane,
London SE1 2QB
Tel: 020-7378 9000
Fax: 020-7403 7569
Web site: *www.sfa.org.uk*

Self-assessment helpline
Tel: (0645) 000444

Society of Chiropodists and Podiatrists
53 Welbeck Street,
London W1M 7HE
Tel: 020-7486 3381
Fax: 020-7935 6359
Email: *enq@scpod.org.uk*
Web site: *www.feetforlife.org.uk*

Society of Pension Consultants (SPC)
St Bartholemew House,
92 Fleet Street,
London EC4Y 1DG
Tel: 020-7353 1688
Fax: 020-7353 9296
Email: *john.mortimer@spc.uk.com*
Web site: *www.spc.uk.com*

Sport England
16 Upper Woburn Place,
London WC1H 0QP
Tel: 020-7273 1500
Fax: 020-7583 5740
Email: *info@english.sports.gov.uk*
Web site: *www.english.sports.gov.uk*

Stroke Association
Stroke House, 123–127 Whitecross
Street, London
EC1Y 8JJ
Tel: 020-7566 0300
Fax: 020-7490 2686
Email: *stroke@stroke.org.uk*
Web site: *www.stroke.org.uk*

Summer Academy
Keynes College, The University,
Canterbury CT2 7NP
Tel: (01227) 470402
Fax: (01227) 784338
Email: *summeracademy@ukc.ac.uk*
Web site: *www.ukc.ac.uk/sa/index.html*

Supreme Court
(Scotland)
Parliament Square,
Edinburgh EH1 1RF
Tel: 0131-225 2595
Fax: 0131-240 6711
Email: *enquiries@supreme.courts.gov.uk*
Web site: *www.scotcourts.gov.uk*

Tax Credit Helpline
Tel: (0845) 605 5858
Tel: (0845) 609 7000
(Northern Ireland)

Third Age Employment Network
St James's Walk, Clerkenwell Green,
London EC1R 0BE
Tel: 020-7242 6273
Fax: 020-7421 3425
Email: *taen@helptheaged.org.uk*
Web site: *www.taen.co.uk*

Third Age Network
Friary Mews, 28 Commercial
Road, Guildford, Surrey GU1 4SX
Tel: (01483) 440582

Third Age Trust
University of the Third Age (U3A),
26 Harrison Street,
London WC1H 8JG
Tel: 020-7837 8838
Fax: 020-7837 8845
Email: *e-mail.nationaloffice@u3a.org.uk*
Web site: *www.u3a.org.uk*

TransCo
Tel: (0800) 371782 *(helpline)*
Tel: (0800) 111999 *(emergency service)*

Tripscope
The Courtyard, Evelyn Road,
London W4 5JL
Tel: 020-8994 9294
Fax: 020-8994 3618
Email: *tripscope@cableinet.co.uk*

Victim Support
Cranmer House, 39 Brixton
Road, London SW9 6DZ
Tel: 020-7735 9166
Fax: 020-7582 5712

Wales Tourist Board
Brunel House, 2 Fitzalan Road,
Cardiff CF24 0UY
Tel: 029) 2049 9909
Fax: (029) 2048 3031
Web site: *www.visitwales.com*

Water Industry Commissioner
Ochil House, Springkerse
Business Park, Stirling FK7 7XE
Tel: (01786) 430200
Fax: (01786) 462018
Email: *swscc@scottishwater.co.uk*
Web site: *www.scottishwater.co.uk*

Which? Books
Castlemead, Gascoyne Way,
Hertford X, SG14 1LH
Tel: (0800) 252100
Web site: *www.which.net*

Which? Personal Service
Tel: (0800) 252100
Fax: (0800) 533053
Web site: *www.which.net*

**Workers' Educational Association
(WEA)**
17 Victoria Park Square,
London E2 9PB
Tel: 020-8983 1515
Fax: 020-8983 4840
Email: *info@wea.org.uk*
Web site: *www.wea.org.uk*

Workright Information Line
Tel: (0845) 6000925

Index

WHICH? BOOKS

The following titles were available as this book went to press.

General reference (legal, financial, practical, etc.)

Be Your Own Financial Adviser
401 Legal Problems Solved
150 Letters that Get Results
The Which? Guide to an Active Retirement
The Which? Guide to Changing Careers
The Which? Guide to Choosing a Career
The Which? Guide to Computers
The Which? Guide to Computers for Small Businesses
The Which? Guide to Divorce
The Which? Guide to Domestic Help
The Which? Guide to Employment
The Which? Guide to Gambling
The Which? Guide to Getting Married
The Which? Guide to Giving and Inheriting
The Which? Guide to Home Safety and Security
The Which? Guide to Insurance
The Which? Guide to the Internet
The Which? Guide to Money
The Which? Guide to Pensions
The Which? Guide to Renting and Letting
The Which? Guide to Shares
The Which? Guide to Starting Your Own Business
The Which? Guide to Working from Home
Which? Way to Beat the System
Which? Way to Clean It
Which? Way to Buy, Sell and Move House
Which? Way to Buy, Own and Sell a Flat
Which? Way to Save and Invest
Which? Way to Save Tax
What to Do When Someone Dies
Wills and Probate

Action Pack (A5 wallet with forms and 28-page book inside)

Make Your Own Will

Health

Understanding HRT and the Menopause
The Which? Guide to Complementary Medicine
The Which? Guide to Children's Health
The Which? Guide to Managing Asthma
The Which? Guide to Managing Stress
The Which? Guide to Men's Health
The Which? Guide to Women's Health
Which? Medicine

Gardening

The Gardening Which? Guide to Patio and Container
  Plants
The Gardening Which? Guide to Small Gardens
The Gardening Which? Guide to Successful Perennials
The Gardening Which? Guide to Successful Propagation
The Gardening Which? Guide to Successful Pruning
The Gardening Which? Guide to Successful Shrubs

Do-it-yourself

The Which? Book of Do-It-Yourself
The Which? Book of Home Improvements
The Which? Book of Plumbing and Central Heating
The Which? Book of Wiring and Lighting
The Which? Guide to Painting and Decorating
The Which? HomePlanner
Which? Way to Fix It

Which? Way to Save and Invest

Whether you've got £50 or £5,000 to play with, it pays to pick the right investment. Many more people are shareholders as a result of privatisations and building society conversions. But deciding what to do with your spare cash can be a daunting task. You want to make sure that your dependants are protected and that you are prepared for the future, for retirement and for any emergency.

This book helps you to work out an overall investment strategy to suit your financial circumstances and ensure that you make the most of your savings. Written in straightforward language, it covers all the important areas of saving and investing from the traditional choices such as National Savings and banks, to unit trusts, investment trusts and commodities. Tax-efficient savings and investments are highlighted in a separate chapter.

Paperback   210 x 120mm   416 pages   £14.99

Available from bookshops, and by post from
Which?, Dept TAZM, Castlemead,
Gascoyne Way, Hertford X, SG14 1LH

You can also order using your credit card
by phoning FREE on (0800) 252100
(quoting Dept TAZM)

The Which? Guide to Giving and Inheriting

Giving is easy, but it takes planning to make sure that those to whom you're giving receive as much as possible. Gifts are often wrapped in an unnecessary tax bill or miss out on available tax relief. Even if your means are fairly modest, you may be unwittingly – and needlessly – storing up a tax bill for your heirs.

With the use of handy calculators and over 40 examples of typical situations, *The Which? Guide to Giving and Inheriting* shows you how a knowledge of the tax rules, and taking simple steps such as making a will, can help you to:

- use the tax system to increase the value of your giving
- exercise some control over the way your gifts may be used
- ensure that you pass on your home and possessions intact
- make tax-efficient donations to charities.

Paperback   216 x 135mm   240 pages   £9.99

Available from bookshops, and by post from
Which?, Dept TAZM, Castlemead,
Gascoyne Way, Hertford X, SG14 1LH

You can also order using your credit card
by phoning FREE on (0800) 252100
(quoting Dept TAZM)

Wills and Probate

If you die without making a will your wealth could go to
the very person you least want to have it and your loved
ones could lose out, perhaps to the Inland Revenue.

The practical, easy-to-follow advice contained in *Wills
and Probate* has already helped thousands of people to
make their wills. Whether you are single, married, divorced
or co-habiting, it will show you how to write your will in
such a way that your wishes can be carried out without
any complications. The book not only provides sample
text, but demonstrates how to change it at a later date.

The second part of the book covers probate: the
administration of the estate of someone who has died. The
book will enable you to decide whether you can execute
the will confidently by yourself or whether you should call
on professional help. A detailed case history runs through
this section, including draft letters to exemplify the various
points made.

Covering the law and procedure in England and Wales,
and outlining the main differences which apply in
Scotland and Northern Ireland, this revised edition
highlights changes in government policy towards
inheritance and describes what happens if there is no will.

Paperback   216 x 135mm   240 pages   £10.99

Available from bookshops, and by post from
Which?, Dept TAZM, Castlemead,
Gascoyne Way, Hertford X, SG14 1LH

You can also order using your credit card
by phoning FREE on (0800) 252100
(quoting Dept TAZM)

The Which? Guide to Women's Health

'*An excellent guide ... presents facts clearly, in a balanced and unpatronising manner ... manages to be fully comprehensive.*' British Medical Association

The key to a good life is good health, both physical and mental. Knowing how to achieve and maintain this is central to your well-being. Men and women share many health troubles – cancer, heart attacks, strokes and a huge array of minor but distressing ailments. However, many of these conditions, like acne and arthritis, manifest themselves differently in women because of the effect of female hormones, which makes different treatment necessary.

Unlike other health guides, *The Which? Guide to Women's Health* looks at every part of the body (such as skin, eyes and reproductive organs) from a woman's point of view. The importance of emotional and mental stability in supporting all-over physical health is emphasised, and self-help and complementary therapies are covered where relevant.

This revised and updated edition includes a new chapter on cosmetic surgery covering the pros and cons of procedures such as liposuction and breast reduction, plus new information on recent developments in contraception and antenatal tests. Whether you are 17 or 70, this guide's practical advice on how to care for your body, how to recognise your symptoms and when to seek medical advice can help you take an active role in staying healthy.

Paperback   216 x 135mm   448 pages   £9.99

Available from bookshops, and by post from
Which?, Dept TAZM, Castlemead,
Gascoyne Way, Hertford X, SG14 1LH

You can also order using your credit card
by phoning FREE on (0800) 252100
(quoting Dept TAZM)